poligamist

11/24
STRAND PRICE
$5.00

THE MODERN
STUDENT'S LIBRARY

EACH VOLUME EDITED BY A LEADING
AMERICAN AUTHORITY

This series is composed of such works as
are conspicuous in the province of literature
for their enduring influence. Every volume
is recognized as essential to a liberal education and will tend to infuse a love for true
literature and an appreciation of the qualities which cause it to endure.

*A descriptive list of the volumes published in
this series appears in the last pages
of this volume*

CHARLES SCRIBNER'S SONS

THE MODERN STUDENT'S LIBRARY

POEMS

By

WILLIAM WORDSWORTH

THE MODERN STUDENT'S LIBRARY

POEMS

BY

WILLIAM WORDSWORTH

SELECTED AND EDITED
WITH AN INTRODUCTION

BY

GEORGE McLEAN HARPER

PROFESSOR OF ENGLISH, PRINCETON UNIVERSITY
AUTHOR OF "WILLIAM WORDSWORTH, HIS LIFE,
WORKS, AND INFLUENCE."

CHARLES SCRIBNER'S SONS

NEW YORK   CHICAGO   BOSTON

Copyright, 1923, by
CHARLES SCRIBNER'S SONS

Printed in the United States of America

CONTENTS

CONTENTS

CONTENTS

INTRODUCTION

Appreciation of Wordsworth's poetry depends in an unusual degree upon knowing when and for what purposes it was written. He was a man of keen sensibility and strong impulses, who felt bound to express in verse the opinions which he held on great subjects; and as these opinions changed, his utterance varied. Not only figuratively but literally "the fashion of his countenance was altered" in accordance with his views on human progress, character, and destiny. Compare his portrait by Shuter, showing him as he was at about twenty-eight, with any of those painted after he had passed the age of forty-five, and you will find it hard to believe that they represent the same man. Of the alert, enthusiastic radical, dressed like a French Republican, wearing his long hair unpowdered as a protest against the war-tax, scarce a trace remains in the resigned yet somewhat apprehensive saint portrayed by Pickersgill. The difference is not due entirely to age, but rather to a change in the passions that ruled the man. Curiosity has given place to meditation; confidence in himself and human beings generally has faded away, and if in its stead there has descended faith in some higher power, this faith has been dearly purchased.

Wordsworth was endowed with fine senses; seeing and hearing were to him a perpetual feast. He was much affected also by the persons who surrounded him, quickly caught and powerfully drawn by the currents of thought that swirled about him; and if he often appeared to stand too long anchored here or there, it was not because he felt no inward impulse to move, but because loyalty and native obstinacy caused him to hold on with all his might to old objects of enthusiasm. Some men have been substantially the same at all periods of their lives; what their youth promised their maturity has fulfilled. With Wordsworth this was not the case, so far at least as his opinions and

xiii

motives are concerned. Certain physical and moral traits no doubt remained unaltered, such, for example, as his rich perceptions and his love of honesty and simplicity; but at various points in the course of his development he faced towards different directions, and his works cannot be understood by one who does not know the varied purposes which determined from time to time their subjects and their forms. Wordsworth himself is described in his own words when he declares that the Poet is a man "endowed with more lively sensibility, more enthusiasm and tenderness, who has a greater knowledge of human nature, and a more comprehensive soul, than are supposed to be common among mankind." Furthermore, with all his attention to the external world and the unequalled accuracy of his account of what he saw and heard, the report that he really makes is about himself, the effect upon his own mind. In giving us primarily a record of his mental states, rather than pretending to tell what really happened outside, he was treating his subjects in a truly scientific as well as poetical way and with uncommon fairness to his readers.

These, then, are the reasons why we must have considerable knowledge of his life, the circumstances and persons that influenced his life, the changing ideals and purposes of his life, if we are to understand his poetry. Everyone, therefore, who desires really to know the meaning of Wordsworth's poems should, while reading them, bear in mind the dates of their composition. Wordsworth himself arranged them in a most unsatisfactory grouping, according to a psychological system of his own invention. It is the one defect of the Oxford edition, which has been employed for the text of the present volume of selections, that its learned editor, Thomas Hutchinson, felt constrained to adopt the poet's classification. The chronological order, which we have unhesitatingly used, is better, even though it involves giving a prominent place to several immature juvenile poems, important for critical and biographical reasons rather than for artistic excellence.

The following outline may serve to show the main points at which Wordsworth's life, and consequently his poetry, underwent change. He was born at Cockermouth in the county of Cumberland, in 1770; spent the best part of his

boyhood as a boarder in the village of Hawkshead, among
the mountains, attending a remarkably simple and pleasant
classical school; entered St. John's College, Cambridge, in
1787; made a long journey on foot through France, Switzerland, and Northern Italy, with a fellow-student, in the
summer of 1790; graduated in 1791; lived obscurely in
London for some months; went to France again for about
a year, coming back to London just before the execution
of Louis XVI and the outbreak of war between England and
the French Republic early in 1793; left at Orleans or Blois
a French lady, Annette Vallon, who had borne him a child
and to whom he apparently intended to return for the purpose of marrying her; published *An Evening Walk* and
Descriptive Sketches in 1793; was closely associated with
a group of British revolutionists, and led a wandering life
until he settled with his sister, in September, 1795, at a
farmhouse called Racedown, in Dorset; met Samuel Taylor
Coleridge in that year; went to live near him in Somerset-
shire, in 1797; published jointly with him a little book of
their poems, called *Lyrical Ballads*, in 1798.

Here it seems wise to pause and take breath. Let us look
back over these twenty-eight years and see what they
meant for poetry. In the present volume the period before
Wordsworth went to France and became a convert to
the Revolutionary doctrine of human equality is represented
chiefly by the long descriptive poem, *An Evening Walk*.
It was begun at Hawkshead, in 1787, and was written in
the style (later called by Wordsworth and Coleridge
"Gaudyverse," in contempt) which had prevailed in English
poetry since the death of Milton; and yet it contains prom-
ising indications of naturalness and bold simplicity. *Descriptive Sketches*, which, like *An Evening Walk*, is reprinted
here from the first edition and not as it was afterwards
softened down by the poet, was written while he was in the
full fervor of Revolutionary enthusiasm, and so was *Guilt
and Sorrow*. They abound in democratic and pacifistic
doctrine. It should be noted that while *Descriptive Sketches*
contains many of those poetic licenses and bookish substi-
tutes for plain speech which may well be called "Gaudyverse," the diction and sentence-structure of *Guilt and Sorrow* are free from conventionality, being carefully simple.

The subjects and characters treated in this latter poem are also such as a propagandist of democracy would be likely to choose. With hardly any exceptions all the poems Wordsworth composed between 1791 and 1802 were made with the same intention. The young poet was a man of principle; his principles were those of Revolutionary France; he was convinced that the distinctions between rich and poor, high and low, were false and cruel; he deliberately preferred to write about events that might happen every day and people who could be encountered everywhere; and furthermore he believed that a poet should avoid the use of expressions which could be understood only by readers of a particular class. Thus from his political principles he derived a literary theory which was destined to affect the whole course of English poetry for at least one hundred and thirty years.

A considerable number of the poems dating from the decade that began in 1795 were devoted to the joys and sorrows of the poor. The poet makes note of their peculiar relation to the world, studying the way in which want has crippled them; but, what is even more unusual, he treats them as if their poverty were the least significant thing about them, for he portrays them as in no essential respect different from other people. He does not make them speak in dialect, nor does he attribute to them a peculiar cast of mind or suppose them incapable of the same feelings that animate men and women to whom wealth has brought leisure and education. Such poems are *The Reverie of Poor Susan, Alice Fell, Simon Lee, The Old Cumberland Beggar, The Pet Lamb,* and *The Sailor's Mother. Alice Fell,* because of its stark simplicity, has been generally misunderstood. Some have declared that its purpose is to prove the importance of private property as a support for morality and happiness, by way of recantation of the writer's previous utterances in favor of more or less communistic views. Others see in it no purpose and are disappointed. The full title which Wordsworth himself gave it ought to settle the question: *Alice Fell, or Poverty.* It is plainly a sympathetic illustration of the pathos of extreme penury, drawn with realism so complete as to baffle the still-existing admirers of "Gaudyverse."

In *Resolution and Independence*, which is more widely known by the more attractive though less explanatory title of *The Leech Gatherer*, Wordsworth turns upon himself and asks whether it is safe and really good that he should continue trying to carry out in practice his theory that a simple and economically unproductive life is the best. He had been acting almost literally upon that command which so few Christians even pretend to obey: "Take no thought for your life, what ye shall eat, or what ye shall drink; nor yet for your body, what ye shall put on;" and the possible consequences alarmed him. The poem tells how he threw off his depression and recovered "faith in the whispers of the lonely Muse." We learn from the triumphant conclusion that William Wordsworth, the defiant foe of conventionality, the resolutely independent and unworldly man, the trusting child of Nature, was still holding his own.

There were, besides Coleridge, two human influences which have left deep traces in Wordsworth's poetry written during this great decade: that of his sister, Dorothy, whose presence is not only seen in several pieces like the lines *To My Sister*, *The Sparrow's Nest*, and *Tintern Abbey*, where she is mentioned, but is felt in many others; and the unknown child Lucy whom he once loved and lost.

Coleridge, with characteristic hospitality of mind, gave a genial welcome to Wordsworth's views, which, it should be remembered, were little less than seditious in a country that was after all governed by a form of monarchy, a country, moreover, engaged in war with France. To Wordsworth's interest in political and social reform, was now added an interest in psychology, and we find that most of the poems he composed before 1799 are illustrations of a particular theory about the constitution and operation of the human mind. He and Coleridge, accepting the teaching of Locke, Hartley, and Hume, believed that all human knowledge originated in the perceptions made by the five senses; that these perceptions grouped themselves together into ideas and principles, hopes, fears, and beliefs, by some process of association; and that there were no innate ideas. *We Are Seven* was written to prove that a child, contrary to what had been taught for centuries by orthodox philosophers, possessed no inborn light on so important a subject as death:

> "A simple child,
> That lightly draws its breath,
> And feels its life in every limb,
> What can it know of death?"

The *Anecdote for Fathers* has a similar psychological import: until the sense-perceptions of a child have risen by "association" above the level of mere first knowledge, to the level of ideas and generalizations, it is absurd to urge it to express an opinion which should involve processes of abstraction and comparison. It was his interest in psychology that caused Wordsworth so often to choose children and old people and defectives as the subjects of his poems at this time. In these persons, who have not acquired or who have lost the power of self-protection, whose motives lie open to scrutiny, he found it relatively easy to study the mind of man.

Wordsworth was much more audacious as a philosopher than Coleridge, and terribly consistent, in the years of his freedom. He pushed, much farther than Coleridge dared to go, into the consequences of his theory of knowledge. If we know nothing except what was originally revealed to us through our senses, then, he assumed, we have no use for a supernaturally revealed religion; and so he said: "I am

> Well pleased to recognize
> In nature and the language of the sense,
> The anchor of my purest thoughts, the nurse,
> The guide, the guardian of my heart, and soul
> Of all my moral being."

Coleridge, shocked and alarmed, gave notice, with regret, that his friend was "a semi-atheist." And there can be no reasonable doubt that Wordsworth's poetry prior to 1805 is consistently that of a man who has renounced orthodox Christianity with all its special dogmas and symbols. One cannot but be struck by the fact that this manifestly very religious man, in a broad sense of the word, seldom, before the year 1805, uses any of the names expressive of Divine Personality, except as mere exclamations. He has made for

himself a natural religion, and is quite serious, and consistent with what he wrote in many other poems, when he
declares, in *The Tables Turned:*

> "One impulse from a vernal wood
> May teach you more of man,
> Of moral evil and of good,
> Than all the sages can."

There is no use trying to blink the fact: Wordsworth, in the
period when he wrote his most original and most beautiful
poetry, held such views as would keep a man from being
received into most of our churches, or allowed to testify
in some of our courts, or permitted to teach in many of our
schools, or even, perhaps, passed by our immigration author-
ities. He was in fact treated as an "undesirable" by some
of the elder generation in his family, being forbidden to
visit his sister in the parsonage of their uncle, with whom
she lived; he and Coleridge were regarded as dangerous
characters by some of their neighbors in Somerset; and a
government spy was sent down from London to watch their
movements. Not long after his second visit to France,
Wordsworth wrote the letter to the Bishop of Llandaff,
which, for some reason, possibly prudential, he appears not
to have sent to its address. It was found among the poet's
papers and printed for the first time in 1876, twenty-six
years after his death, and is reproduced in this volume
partly because it is almost inaccessible elsewhere and partly
because it contains an explicit declaration of his political
and social principles and shows what a complete radical he
was.

The inquiring and renovating spirit of Rousseau had no
doubt roused Wordsworth even at the university and in
London, before he made his long sojourn abroad. In France
he read, as he tells us, "the master pamphlets of the day,"
which surely included Rousseau's *Social Contract* and his
Discourses written to prove that civilization was a failure
and that the sources of political and social inequality among
men were not in Nature but in the oppressive institutions
which the strong few had invented and the many weak had
stupidly accepted. The State, the Church, and the School
had become corrupt and must be reformed, simplified, hu-

manized. These ideas were further inculcated in the young poet by a Republican officer named Beaupuy, who became his friend in 1792, when they were both living at Blois and attending nightly the sessions of a Revolutionary club in that town. Upon Wordsworth's return to England he became a disciple of William Godwin and a reader of his *Enquiry Concerning Political Justice*, which was published in 1793. Godwin carried the Revolutionary principles to logical but not always practical conclusions. He was absolute in argument, pushing everywhere to extremes, subordinating all other considerations to what he called reason, but what was often only a method of formal proof insufficiently related to experience. That he should have captivated the intellect of an idealist like Wordsworth is not surprising; and indeed the man who refuses to see anything exalted in Godwin's philosophy must be singularly lacking in that passion for truth irrespective of consequences which is a fine attribute of "noble mind."

But Wordsworth was a realist, too. He had good eyes in his head and could see for himself that Godwin's dream of a perfect world was not likely to be fulfilled before mankind had undergone centuries of preparation, and that even then there would be losses as well as gains. As a follower of Godwin he was called upon to dislike and denounce almost all the relationships which hold society together; as a lover of life as it is, in village and farm, he could not feel consistently bitter against the organs of public order and religion. He was like Dr. Johnson's old college mate who tried hard to become a philosopher, but could not, because "cheerfulness was always breaking in."

The source of Wordsworth's cheerfulness was Nature herself. He found "joy in widest commonalty spread." The open air, the irrepressible vitality of vegetation, the happiness of living creatures, the spontaneous gayety of children, the self-satisfying activities of busy people, the many natural consolations of old age, the glorious expansions of genius in such souls as those of his friend and his sister, made it impossible for him to remain forever under a cloud of negations. Life was positive, real, and good. He felt pulsing through his veins the vital throbs that thrill the world, and

" 'Tis my faith," he declared, "that every flower enjoys the air it breathes."

We chatter glibly about "love of Nature" and "worship of Nature," and it is said with feeble iteration that Wordsworth is "the poet of Nature." Let us ask ourselves what these phrases really signify. It is safe to say that they meant to him something immeasurably more precise than what they mean to those who think they can catalogue him thus. He actually did worship Nature, because he worshipped nothing else. He uses, with regard to Nature, some of the sublime and solemn expressions which theists reserve for a Personal God. He is the poet of Nature, not just because he wrote about the green linnet and the lesser celandine and the daisy and the skylark, but because he undertook to proclaim and celebrate, in his hieratic office, the identity of Nature and God. These remarks, be it remembered, refer to him only as he was before the turning-point in his spiritual life, which, so far as can be determined from his poetry, was in the year 1805.

The most important poetical publication in the English language since the appearance of *Paradise Lost* has been *Lyrical Ballads*. Yet what an insignificant-looking volume that first edition of *Lyrical Ballads* was! Contemptible, some said; regrettable, said others; and the 500 copies had a "heavy sale." Nearly all the poems in it are included among our selections, viz.: *Lines Left Upon a Seat in a Yew Tree, Goody Blake and Harry Gill, To My Sister, Simon Lee, Anecdote for Fathers, We Are Seven, Lines Written in Early Spring, The Thorn, The Last of the Flock, Expostulation and Reply, The Tables Turned, Animal Tranquillity and Decay,* and *Lines Written a Few Miles above Tintern Abbey. Guilt and Sorrow* is an expansion of a poem called *The Female Vagrant,* which appeared in *Lyrical Ballads.* Only five of Wordsworth's contributions, and of course the four that were written by Coleridge, have been omitted.

In the autumn of 1798, a few days after the publication of their little book, Wordsworth and Coleridge, with Dorothy, departed for Germany, where they separated, the brother and sister going to spend several months at the little town of Goslar, and Coleridge settling down to the study of metaphysics at the University of Göttingen. During this winter Wordsworth's excitement over politics appears to have subsided, and he fell back upon wistful memories of English scenes and incidents of humble life in the North Country where he was born and reared. On their return, in the spring of 1799, he and Dorothy walked into the region of lakes and mountains, as he has related in the lines beginning "Bleak season was it, turbulent and wild," and there, at Grasmere, they rented for a small sum a plain little stone cottage, which was to be their home until the summer of 1808, living with extreme frugality, mindless of wordly advancement and the pursuit of wealth, but rich in the happiness which Nature confers and busy with poetry. Coleridge was their frequent and welcome guest. Here he and Wordsworth thought out, and the latter composed, the famous Preface to the second (1800) edition of *Lyrical Ballads*. It is an explicit statement of the principles that underlie the new poetry, and there will be few to dispute the statement that it is the most effective as well as the most eloquent piece of literary criticism in the English language after Sidney's *Defense of Poesy*. The early years at Grasmere, particularly 1800 and 1802, were very productive. The poem that reflects most fully the kind of life that interested Wordsworth at this time, his views of society, and his method of composition, is probably *Michael*. His purpose seemed now to be less dogmatic than it was two years before. He was content to portray Nature and human beings as they are and let his readers draw their own inferences. He had escaped from the obsession of Godwin's rigorous logic. He was blessed with the companionship of an exquisite sister, one of the most adorable and delightful of women. He was frequently visited by Coleridge, a man of infinite charm and the loftiest intellect. He had a few plain, respectable neighbors. Nature in some of her most endearing aspects was at his door, tamed to the use of man and seemingly a part of man's domesticity; while he had but to walk a few steps to be among the lonely tarns and threatening peaks.

Nevertheless, his heart was not altogether at Grasmere. Public affairs still troubled him, and he read with painful excitement the news of battles and campaigns on the Continent. He had entirely disapproved of the war against France, from its beginning in 1793 to about 1797; but when Napoleon emerged in 1798 as the conqueror of Switzerland and Italy, with vast imperialistic designs upon the Orient, and the evident purpose of making himself master of the world, Wordsworth began to see that English liberty, imperfect though he deemed it, was to be preferred before this travesty of Republicanism. But he was too stubborn to admit that he had changed his mind, and, moreover, he was restrained by the thought that Annette Vallon and the child, Caroline, were French. During the brief period of peace, in 1802, he and Dorothy hastened to France, met the mother and daughter at Calais, and arrived at some arrangement with Annette. It must have been an agreement to part completely, for at once Wordsworth began writing, and publishing in the newspapers, those patriotic sonnets in which he gloried in the fact that England was the implacable foe of Napoleon; and furthermore, within two months he had married Mary Hutchinson, a girl friend of his sister. The poem called *A Farewell* was written shortly before leaving Grasmere on this prolonged excursion, so full of painful possibilities and happy hopes.

The next year was enlivened by a journey through the west and south of Scotland, made by William, Dorothy, and Coleridge, with a horse and cart. It furnished material for most of the lovely poems composed in 1803.

Repentance and anxiety in connection with his grievous ill-doing, the responsibilities of family life, the awful events of the war, which was raging anew, the disappointment of his hopes for a blessed revolution, and finally the death of his sailor brother, John, wrought in Wordsworth a profound change of heart, not sudden, hardly even admitted by himself to himself. To estimate its extent, one should read carefully the *Lines Written a Few Miles above Tintern Abbey*, in which he proclaims his confidence in the sufficiency of Nature—a proclamation repeated in *Peter Bell*— and then, immediately, turn to two poems composed in that crucial year 1805, the *Ode to Duty* and *Elegiac Stanzas Suggested by a Picture of Peele Castle in a Storm*. Here we find him honestly confessing that he needs something more than Nature's guidance, even while he holds fast with lingering attachment to the thought that, perhaps, for some souls, purer and more childlike than his, Nature may indeed be an all-sufficient light. He that comprehends these two poems and perceives that they stand at the very centre and turning-point of the man's moral history and of his poetic career, containing in line after line the essence of many of his other poems, may truly say that he knows the secret of Wordsworth. Everything that is unique or characteristic in his work radiates from this focus. That it is a double focus, and that even here we find no certainty, but only a question, are significant facts. Wordsworth was, in truth, not sure what he should profess. He was outspoken enough on both sides of the sharp divide which broke his life into two incompatible sections, frank in his naturalism before 1805, and vehement in the statement of supernaturalism throughout the long years that came after that. And to his immense credit, be it said, he was clear-eyed when he stood at the apex and looked before and after. Henceforth he is most careful to avoid even the appearance of naturalism; the names and attributes of God are mentioned with increasing frequency in his verse; he labors to be orthodox; he even alters some of his early poems so as to give them a less pagan as well as a less politically radical effect; but all in vain for any reader with eyes in his head, since doubt and a sense of loss perplex the thread of discourse and darken the colors that were once so bright.

Another poem of this crucial period is the *Intimations of Immortality from Recollections of Early Childhood*. Its real subject, a recurring one with Wordsworth, is the superiority of natural perceptions, the fresh, direct perceptions of a child, over those that are made when experience and tradition have dulled our faculties. We have here, and in the *Anecdote for Fathers* and *We Are Seven*, variations upon the theme propounded by Rousseau, that the progress of the arts and sciences has tended to corrupt the morals of mankind. The child is father of the man, and if we would live well and preserve our original innocence and insight we must look back with respect, or natural piety, to the fountain-light of all our day, the master-light of all our seeing. This, at least, seems to have been the thought with which the poet began the ode and wrote the first nine stanzas. But in the last two he is overcome by the same mood which dominated the composition of *Elegiac Stanzas* and the *Ode to Duty*, and he adds that we must find strength

> "In the soothing thoughts that spring
>   Out of human suffering;
> In the faith that looks through death,
> In years that bring the philosophic mind."

Interpretation of Wordsworth's poetry has been rendered extremely difficult and interesting by his habit of altering lines and whole passages long after they were originally composed. *The Prelude*, which has high autobiographical value, high historical value as a first-hand report of the French Revolution by a man of genius who witnessed an important part of it, and high philosophical value as a comment on the theories about nature and social life that inspired the leaders of that movement, was composed, for the most part, in 1800, 1804, and 1805, though some sections of it date from earlier years; but it was not published until 1850, after Wordsworth's death. He kept retouching it at intervals during that time, endeavoring, no doubt, to tone down the religious naturalism of the first three books and the political radicalism of the ninth, tenth, and eleventh, and to bring the whole into conformity with his later views. This process has deprived it of much of the authority it would otherwise have had as a source of knowledge of his early adventures and opinions. Yet even as we possess it now, it is easy to see that the mood of 1805, the mood of recantation, expressing itself in the twelfth, thirteenth, and fourteenth books, which date, on the whole, from that year, contrasts sharply with the mood or moods of the preceding eleven.

The Prelude was intended to serve as the introduction to an enormous philosophical poem in three parts. A fragment of the first of these was written, and is represented in this volume, by three selections which contain the best lines. A second part, *The Excursion*, containing matter composed at various periods between 1795 and 1814, but chiefly after 1808, was published in 1814. The third part seems not to have been undertaken at all.

The first selection from *The Excursion* is a narrative and descriptive piece begun in 1795 and known at first to Wordsworth and his friends as "Margaret, or the Ruined Cottage." He incorporated it rather violently into *The Excursion*, where it stands out from its surroundings as a beautiful example of his second manner, the plain, realistic manner which he used after abandoning his first, conventional and artificial style, as seen in *An Evening Walk* and *Descriptive Sketches*. The selection from the Fourth Book shows him working in a much later manner, on an extremely abstruse subject. In its kind, what one might call "the philosophical sublime," it is surpassed by Milton, but by few if any other of our poets.

Whatever may have been the effect of Wordsworth's religious change upon his character and everyday behavior, it is plain that his poetical powers, his boldness and originality, began to depart from him after 1805. The uncommon intensity of his interest in Nature had been due, in a considerable degree, to his theoretical veneration of Nature as a divine power, and when he gave up his theory he lost much of his peculiar insight. Similarly, his enthusiasm for the doctrine of human equality had enabled him to see fine points in the conduct of quite ordinary persons, and when he lost this enthusiasm he turned his gaze away from men, women, and children in humble circumstances and began to write about legendary and historical characters, as hundreds of other poets had done.

Naturally enough, and perhaps without his being conscious of the fact, his style suffered a corresponding alteration, and by 1812 he had fallen back, on several occasions, into the use of words which he would have scornfully rejected a few years before as belonging to the artificial vocabulary of "Gaudyverse." He could write of wild ducks, for example, as "the feathered tenants of the flood," which is as remote from the language of real life as anything in Pope or Collins.

In the *Song at the Feast of Brougham Castle* we find the last great poem which he composed under his old impulses, belief in the essential equality of men, trust in the moralizing power of Nature, and reverence for the ideals of childhood. The meaning and force of the whole poem are revealed in the last four stanzas.

It is a commonplace to say that *Laodamia,* written in 1814, is a wonderful example of true classical poetry, classical in every sense of the word,—as being founded on a Greek legend, composed with Greek clearness and restraint, and written with Virgilian elevation and regard for the exact meaning of words, in language which the best English writers of the seventeenth and eighteenth centuries might have used in their happiest moments. No one has remarked, publicly at least, that it is also, probably, an apologia for Wordsworth's final separation from Annette, a highly idealized and imaginatively transformed account of the meeting and parting at Calais in the summer of 1802. In like manner, and even more obviously, *Dion* is the most condensed expression of his reason for giving up and finally condemning the French Revolution. He lost faith, not in the cause itself, but in the instruments. This is all summed up in the last three lines of the poem:

> "Him only pleasure leads, and peace attends,
> Him, only him, the shield of Jove defends,
> Whose means are fair and spotless as his ends."

The Warning and the lines which immediately precede it have been included in the present volume to show how alarmed Wordsworth was in his old age by the democratic movement which resulted in Catholic emancipation, the abolition of penalties on combination of workmen, the repeal of the Test and Corporation Acts, the extension of the franchise, Free Trade, and other measures, which were among the reforms for which he pleaded in his letter to the Bishop of Llandaff. Truly we have here a different man, a trembling conservative in place of a hopeful radical, and so he remained until his death, in 1850.

Throughout the long years when his poetical inspiration was declining, Wordsworth's artistic skill, his technique, continued to develop, and occasionally the deeper power returned and he produced noble sonnets and other pieces, such as *Mutability,* the farewell to Sir Walter Scott, *The Pillar of Trajan,* and the touching lines entitled *Memory,* which may be read as a reiteration, by the aged poet, of the prophecy uttered by the boy of sixteen in the first of all our selections, *Dear native regions, I foretell*. It is pleasant to remark that the last poem, perhaps, which Wordsworth wrote, the lines upon the Old Man and the Redbreast, with which the selections end, returns to those subjects that roused the noble ardor of his youth,—the essential worth of poor men and the loveliness of living things.

GEORGE McLEAN HARPER.

POEMS

By

WILLIAM WORDSWORTH

EXTRACT

From the conclusion of a poem, composed in anticipation of leaving school.

[Composed 1786.—Published 1815.]

Dear native regions, I foretell,
From what I feel at this farewell,
That, wheresoe'er my steps may tend,
And whensoe'er my course shall end,
If in that hour a single tie
Survive of local sympathy,
My soul will cast the backward view,
The longing look alone on you.

Thus, while the Sun sinks down to rest
Far in the regions of the west,
Though to the vale no parting beam
Be given, not one memorial gleam,
A lingering light he fondly throws
On the dear hills where first he rose.

WRITTEN IN VERY EARLY YOUTH

[Composed 1786 (?).—Published *Morning Post* February 13, 1802; ed. 1807.]

Calm is all nature as a resting wheel.
The kine are couched upon the dewy grass;
The horse alone, seen dimly as I pass,
Is cropping audibly his later meal:
Dark is the ground; a slumber seems to steal
O'er vale, and mountain, and the starless sky.

Now, in this blank of things, a harmony,
Home-felt, and home-created, comes to heal
That grief for which the senses still supply
Fresh food; for only then, when memory
Is hushed, am I at rest. My Friends! restrain
Those busy cares that would allay my pain;
Oh! leave me to myself, nor let me feel
The officious touch that makes me droop again.

1

AN EVENING WALK

[As originally published, 1793.]

Far from my dearest friend, 'tis mine to rove
Thro' bare grey dell, high wood, and pastoral cove;
His wizard course where hoary Derwent takes
Thro' craggs, and forest glooms, and opening lakes,
Staying his silent waves, to hear the roar
That stuns the tremulous cliffs of high Lodore:
Where silver rocks the savage prospect chear
Of giant yews that frown on Rydale's mere;
Where peace to Grasmere's lonely island leads,
To willowy hedgerows, and to emerald meads;
Leads to her bridge, rude church, and cottag'd grounds,
Her rocky sheepwalks, and her woodland bounds;
Where, bosom'd deep, the shy Winander peeps
'Mid clust'ring isles, and holly-sprinkl'd steeps;
Where twilight glens endear my Esthwaite's shore,
And memory of departed pleasures, more.

Fair scenes! with other eyes, than once, I gaze
The ever-varying charm your round displays,
Than when, erewhile, I taught, "a happy child,"
The echoes of your rocks my carols wild:
Then did no ebb of chearfulness demand
Sad tides of joy from Melancholy's hand;
In youth's wild eye the livelong day was bright,
The sun at morning, and the stars of night,
Alike, when first the vales the bittern fills,
Or the first woodcocks roam'd the moonlight hills.

Return Delights! with whom my road begun,
Where Life rear'd laughing up her morning sun;
When Transport kiss'd away my april tear,
"Rocking as in a dream the tedious year;"
When link'd with thoughtless Mirth I cours'd the plain,
And hope itself was all I knew of pain.
For then, ev'n then, the little heart would beat
At times, while young Content forsook her seat,
And wild Impatience, panting upward, show'd
Where tipp'd with gold the mountain-summits glow'd.

Alas! the idle tale of man is found
Depicted in the dial's moral round;
With Hope Reflexion blends her social rays
To gild the total tablet of his days;
Yet still, the sport of some malignant Pow'r,
He knows but from its shade the present hour.

While, Memory at my side, I wander here,
Starts at the simplest sight th' unbidden tear,
A form discover'd at the well-known seat,
A spot, that angles at the riv'let's feet,
The ray the cot of morning trav'ling nigh,
And sail that glides the well-known alders by.
But why, ungrateful, dwell on idle pain?
To shew her yet some joys to me remain,
Say, will my friend, with soft affection's ear,
The history of a poet's ev'ning hear?

When, in the south, the wan noon brooding still,
Breath'd a pale steam around the glaring hill,
And shades of deep embattl'd clouds were seen
Spotting the northern cliffs with lights between;
Gazing the tempting shades to them deny'd,
When stood the shorten'd herds amid the tide,
Where, from the barren wall's unshelter'd end,
Long rails into the shallow lakes extend;
When schoolboys stretch'd their length upon the green
And round the humming elms, a glimmering scene!
In the brown park, in flocks, the troubl'd deer
Shook the still twinkling tail and glancing ear;
When horses in the wall-girt intake stood,
Unshaded, eying far below, the flood,
Crouded behind the swain, in mute distress,
With forward neck the closing gate to press;
And long, with wistful gaze, his walk survey'd
Till dipp'd his pathway in the river shade;

—Then Quiet led me up the huddling rill,
Bright'ning with water-breaks the sombrous gill;
To where, while thick above the branches close,
In dark-brown bason its wild waves repose,

Inverted shrubs, and moss of darkest green,
Cling from the rocks, with pale wood-weeds between;
Save that, atop, the subtle sunbeams shine,
On wither'd briars that o'er the craggs recline;
Sole light admitted here, a small cascade,
Illumes with sparkling foam the twilight shade.
Beyond, along the vista of the brook,
Where antique roots its bustling path o'erlook,
The eye reposes on a secret bridge
Half grey, half shagg'd with ivy to its ridge.

—Sweet rill, farewell! To-morrow's noon again,
Shall hide me wooing long thy wildwood strain;
But now the sun has gain'd his western road,
And eve's mild hour invites my steps abroad.

While, near the midway cliff, the silver'd kite
In many a whistling circle wheels her flight;
Slant wat'ry lights, from parting clouds a-pace,
Travel along the precipice's base;
Chearing its naked waste of scatter'd stone
By lychens grey, and scanty moss o'er-grown,
Where scarce the foxglove peeps, and thistle's beard,
And desert stone-chat, all day long, is heard.

How pleasant, as the yellowing sun declines,
And with long rays and shades the landscape shines;
To mark the birches' stems all golden light,
That lit the dark slant woods with silvery white;
The willows weeping trees, that twinkling hoar,
Glanc'd oft upturn'd along the breezy shore,
Low bending o'er the colour'd water, fold
Their moveless boughs and leaves like threads of gold;
The skiffs with naked masts at anchor laid,
Before the boat-house peeping thro' the shade;
Th' unwearied glance of woodman's echo'd stroke;
And curling from the trees the cottage smoke.

Their pannier'd train a groupe of potters goad,
Winding from side to side up the steep road;
The peasant from yon cliff of fearful edge

Shot, down the headlong pathway darts his sledge;
Bright beams the lonely mountain horse illume,
Feeding 'mid purple heath, "green rings," and broom;
While the sharp slope the slacken'd team confounds,
Downward the pond'rous timber-wain resounds;
Beside their sheltering cross of wall, the flock
Feeds on in light, nor thinks of winter's shock;
In foamy breaks the rill, with merry song,
Dash'd down the rough rock, lightly leaps along;
From lonesor . chapel at the mountain's feet,
Three humble bells their rustic chime repeat;
Sounds from the water-side the hammer'd boat;
And blasted quarry thunders heard remote.

Ev'n here, amid the sweep of endless woods,
Blue pomp of lakes, high cliffs, and falling floods,
Not undelightful are the simplest charms
Found by the verdant door of mountain farms.

Sweetly ferocious round his native walks,
Gaz'd by his sister-wives, the monarch stalks;
Spur clad his nervous feet, and firm his tread,
A crest of purple tops his warrior head.
Bright sparks his black and haggard eyeball hurls
Afar, his tail he closes and unfurls;
Whose state, like pine-trees, waving to and fro,
Droops, and o'er canopies his regal brow,
On tiptoe rear'd he blows his clarion throat,
Threaten'd by faintly answering farms remote.

Bright'ning the cliffs between where sombrous pine,
And yew-trees o'er the silver rocks recline,
I love to mark the quarry's moving trains,
Dwarf pannier'd steeds, and men, and numerous wains;
How busy the enormous hive within,
While Echo dallies with the various din!
Some, hardly heard their chisel's clinking sound,
Toil, small as pigmies, in the gulph profound;
Some, dim between th' aereal cliffs descry'd,
O'erwalk the viewless plank from side to side;
These by the pale-blue rocks that ceaseless ring
Glad from their airy baskets hang and sing.

Hung o'er a cloud, above the steep that rears
It's edge all flame, the broad'ning sun appears;
A long blue bar it's ægis orb divides,
And breaks the spreading of it's golden tides;
And now it touches on the purple steep
That flings his shadow on the pictur'd deep.
Cross the calm lakes blue shades the cliffs aspire,
With tow'rs and woods a "prospect all on fire;"
The coves and secret hollows thro' a ray
Of fainter gold a purple gleam betray;
The gilded turf arrays in richer green
Each speck of lawn the broken rocks between;
Deep yellow beams the scatter'd boles illume,
Far in the level forest's central gloom;
Waving his hat, the shepherd in the vale
Directs his winding dog the cliffs to scale,
That, barking busy 'mid the glittering rocks,
Hunts, where he points, the intercepted flocks;
Where oaks o'erhang the road the radiance shoots
On tawny earth, wild weeds, and twisted roots;
The Druid stones their lighted fane unfold,
And all the babbling brooks are liquid gold;
Sunk to a curve the day-star lessens still,
Gives one bright glance, and sinks behind the hill.

In these lone vales, if aught of faith may claim,
Thin silver hairs, and ancient hamlet fame;
When up the hills, as now, retreats the light,
Strange apparitions mock the village sight.

A desperate form appears, that spurs his steed,
Along the midway cliffs with violent speed;
Unhurt pursues his lengthen'd flight, while all
Attend, at every stretch, his headlong fall.
Anon, in order mounts a gorgeous show
Of horsemen shadows winding to and fro;
And now the van is gilt with evening's beam,
The rear thro' iron brown betrays a sullen gleam;
Lost gradual o'er the heights in pomp they go,
While silent stands th' admiring vale below;

Till, but the lonely beacon all is fled,
That tips with eve's last gleam his spiry head.
Now while the solemn evening Shadows sail,
On red slow-waving pinions down the vale,
And, fronting the bright west in stronger lines,
The oak its dark'ning boughs and foliage twines,
I love beside the flowing lake to stray,
Where winds the road along the secret bay;
By rills that tumble down the woody steeps,
And run in transport to the dimpling deeps;
Along the "wild meand'ring" shores to view,
Obsequious Grace the winding swan pursue.
He swells his lifted chest, and backward flings
His bridling neck between his tow'ring wings;
Stately, and burning in his pride, divides
And glorying looks around, the silent tides:
On as he floats, the silver'd waters glow,
Proud of the varying arch and moveless form of snow.
While tender Cares and mild domestic Loves,
With furtive watch pursue her as she moves;
The female with a meeker charm succeeds,
And her brown little ones around her leads,
Nibbling the water lilies as they pass,
Or playing wanton with the floating grass:
She in a mother's care, her beauty's pride
Forgets, unweary'd watching every side,
She calls them near, and with affection sweet
Alternately relieves their weary feet;
Alternately they mount her back, and rest
Close by her mantling wings' embraces prest.

Long may ye roam these hermit waves that sleep,
In birch besprinkl'd cliffs embosom'd deep;
These fairy holms untrodden, still, and green,
Whose shades protect the hidden wave serene;
Whence fragrance scents the water's desart gale,
The violet, and the lily of the vale;
Where, tho' her far-off twilight ditty steal,
They not the trip of harmless milkmaid feel.

Yon tuft conceals your home, your cottage bow'r,
Fresh water rushes strew the verdant floor;
Long grass and willows form the woven wall,
And swings above the roof the poplar tall.
Thence issuing oft, unwieldly as ye stalk,
Ye crush with broad black feet your flow'ry walk;
Safe from your door ye hear at breezy morn,
The hound, the horse's tread, and mellow horn;
At peace inverted your lithe necks ye lave,
With the green bottom strewing o'er the wave;
No ruder sound your desart haunts invades,
Than waters dashing wild, or rocking shades.
Ye ne'er, like hapless human wanderers, throw
Your young on winter's winding sheet of snow.

Fair swan! by all a mother's joys caress'd,
Haply some wretch has ey'd, and call'd thee bless'd;
Who faint, and beat by summer's breathless ray,
Hath dragg'd her babes along this weary way;
While arrowy fire extorting feverish groans,
Shot stinging through her stark o'er-labour'd bones.
—With backward gaze, lock'd joints, and step of pain,
Her seat scarce left, she strives, alas! in vain,
To teach their limbs along the burning road
A few short steps to totter with their load,
Shakes her numb arm that slumbers with its weight,
And eyes through tears the mountain's shadeless height;
And bids her soldier come her woes to share,
Asleep on Bunker's charnel hill afar;
For hope's deserted well why wistful look?
Chok'd is the pathway, and the pitcher broke.

I see her now, deny'd to lay her head,
On cold blue nights, in hut or straw-built shed;
Turn to a silent smile their sleepy cry,
By pointing to a shooting star on high:
I hear, while in the forest depth he sees,
The Moon's fix'd gaze between the opening trees,
In broken sounds her elder grief demand,
And skyward lift, like one that prays, his hand,
If, in that country, where he dwells afar,

His father views that good, that kindly star;
—Ah me! all light is mute amid the gloom,
The interlunar cavern of the tomb.
—When low-hung clouds each star of summer hide,
And fireless are the valleys far and wide,
Where the brook brawls along the painful road,
Dark with bat haunted ashes stretching broad,
The distant clock forgot, and chilling dew,
Pleas'd thro' the dusk their breaking smiles to view,
Oft has she taught them on her lap to play
Delighted, with the glow-worm's harmless ray
Toss'd light from hand to hand; while on the ground
Small circles of green radiance gleam around.

Oh! when the bitter showers her path assail,
And roars between the hills the torrent gale,
—No more her breath can thaw their fingers cold,
Their frozen arms her neck no more can fold;
Scarce heard, their chattering lips her shoulder chill,
And her cold back their colder bosoms thrill;
All blind she wilders o'er the lightless heath,
Led by Fear's cold wet hand, and dogg'd by Death;
Death, as she turns her neck the kiss to seek,
Breaks off the dreadful kiss with angry shriek.
Snatch'd from her shoulder with despairing moan,
She clasps them at that dim-seen roofless stone.—
"Now ruthless Tempest launch thy deadliest dart!
Fall fires—but let us perish heart to heart."
Weak roof a cow'ring form two babes to shield,
And faint the fire a dying heart can yield;
Press the sad kiss, fond mother! vainly fears
Thy flooded cheek to wet them with its tears;
Soon shall the Light'ning hold before thy head
His torch, and shew them slumbering in their bed,
No tears can chill them, and no bosom warms,
Thy breast their death-bed, coffin'd in thine arms.
  Sweet are the sounds that mingle from afar,
Heard by calm lakes, as peeps the folding star,
Where the duck dabbles 'mid the rustling sedge,
And feeding pike starts from the water's edge,
Or the swan stirs the reeds, his neck and bill

Wetting, that drip upon the water still;
And heron, as resounds the trodden shore,
Shoots upward, darting his long neck before.
While, by the scene compos'd, the breast subsides,
Nought wakens or disturbs its tranquil tides;
Nought but the char that for the may-fly leaps,
And breaks the mirror of the circling deeps;
Or clock, that blind against the wanderer born,
Drops at his feet, and stills his droning horn.
—The whistling swain that plods his ringing way
Where the slow waggon winds along the bay;
The sugh of swallow flocks that twittering sweep,
The solemn curfew swinging long and deep;
The talking boat that moves with pensive sound,
Or drops his anchor down with plunge profound;
Of boys that bathe remote the faint uproar,
And restless piper wearying out the shore;
These all to swell the village murmurs blend,
That soften'd from the water-head descend.
While in sweet cadence rising small and still
The far-off minstrels of the haunted hill,
As the last bleating of the fold expires,
Tune in the mountain dells their water lyres.

Now with religious awe the farewell light
Blends with the solemn colouring of the night;
'Mid groves of clouds that crest the mountain's brow,
And round the West's proud lodge their shadows throw,
Like Una shining on her gloomy way,
The half seen form of Twilight roams astray;
Thence, from three paly loopholes mild and small,
Slow lights upon the lake's still bosom fall,
Beyond the mountain's giant reach that hides
In deep determin'd gloom his subject tides.
—'Mid the dark steeps repose the shadowy streams,
As touch'd with dawning moonlight's hoary gleams,
Long streaks of fairy light the wave illume
With bordering lines of intervening gloom,
Soft o'er the surface creep the lustres pale
Tracking with silvering path the changeful gale.
—'Tis restless magic all; at once the bright

Breaks on the shade, the shade upon the light,
Fair Spirits are abroad; in sportive chase
Brushing with lucid wands the water's face,
While music stealing round the glimmering deeps
Charms the tall circle of th' enchanted steeps.
—As thro' th' astonish'd woods the notes ascend,
The mountain streams their rising song suspend;
Below Eve's listening Star the sheep walk stills
It's drowsy tinklings on th' attentive hills;
The milkmaid stops her ballad, and her pail
Stays its low murmur in th' unbreathing vale;
No night-duck clamours for his wilder'd mate,
Aw'd, while below the Genii hold their state.
—The pomp is fled, and mute the wondrous strains,
No wrack of all the pageant scene remains,
So vanish those fair Shadows, human joys,
But Death alone their vain regret destroys.
Unheeded Night has overcome the vales,
On the dark earth the baffl'd vision fails,
If peep between the clouds a star on high,
There turns for glad repose the weary eye;
The latest lingerer of the forest train,
The lone black fir, forsakes the faded plain;
Last evening sight, the cottage smoke no more,
Lost in the deepen'd darkness, glimmers hoar;
High towering from the sullen dark-brown mere,
Like a black wall, the mountain steeps appear,
Thence red from different heights with restless gleam
Small cottage lights across the water stream,
Nought else of man or life remains behind
To call from other worlds the wilder'd mind,
Till pours the wakeful bird her solemn strains
Heard by the night-calm of the wat'ry plains.
—No purple prospects now the mind employ
Glowing in golden sunset tints of joy,
But o'er the sooth'd accordant heart we feel
A sympathetic twilight slowly steal,
And ever, as we fondly muse, we find
The soft gloom deep'ning on the tranquil mind.
Stay! pensive, sadly-pleasing visions, stay!
Ah no! as fades the vale, they fade away.

Yet still the tender, vacant gloom remains,
Still the cold cheek its shuddering tear retains.

The bird, with fading light who ceas'd to thread
Silent the hedge or steaming rivulet's bed,
From his grey re-appearing tower shall soon
Salute with boding note the rising moon,
Frosting with hoary light the pearly ground,
And pouring deeper blue to Aether's bound;
Rejoic'd her solemn pomp of clouds to fold
In robes of azure, fleecy white, and gold,
While rose and poppy, as the glow-worm fades,
Checquer with paler red the thicket shades.
  Now o'er the eastern hill, where Darkness broods
O'er all its vanish'd dells, and lawns, and woods
Where but a mass of shade the sight can trace,
She lifts in silence up her lovely face;
Above the gloomy valley flings her light,
Far to the western slopes with hamlets white;
And gives, where woods the checquer'd upland strew,
To the green corn of summer autumn's hue.
  Thus Hope, first pouring from her blessed horn
Her dawn, far lovelier than the Moon's own morn;
'Till higher mounted, strives in vain to chear
The weary hills, impervious, black'ning near;
—Yet does she still, undaunted, throw the while
On darling spots remote her tempting smile.
—Ev'n now she decks for me a distant scene,
(For dark and broad the gulph of time between)
Gilding that cottage with her fondest ray,
(Sole bourn, sole wish, sole object of my way;
How fair its lawn and silvery woods appear!
How sweet its streamlet murmurs in mine ear!)
Where we, my friend, to golden days shall rise,
'Till our small share of hardly-paining sighs
(For sighs will ever trouble human breath)
Creep hush'd into the tranquil breast of Death.
  But now the clear-bright Moon her zenith gains,
And rimy without speck extend the plains;
The deepest dell the mountain's breast displays,
Scarce hides a shadow from her searching rays;

From the dark-blue "faint silvery threads" divide
The hills, while gleams below the azure tide;
The scene is waken'd, yet its peace unbroke,
By silver'd wreaths of quiet charcoal smoke,
That, o'er the ruins of the fallen wood,
Steal down the hills, and spread along the flood.
The song of mountain streams unheard by day,
Now hardly heard, beguiles my homeward way.
All air is, as the sleeping water, still,
List'ning th' aëreal music of the hill,
Broke only by the slow clock tolling deep,
Or shout that wakes the ferry-man from sleep,
Soon follow'd by his hollow-parting oar,
And echo'd hoof approaching the far shore;
Sound of clos'd gate, across the water borne,
Hurrying the feeding hare thro' rustling corn;
The tremulous sob of the complaining owl;
And at long intervals the mill-dog's howl;
The distant forge's swinging thump profound;
Or yell in the deep woods of lonely hound.

DESCRIPTIVE SKETCHES

[As originally published, 1793.]

Were there, below, a spot of holy ground,
By Pain and her sad family unfound,
Sure, Nature's GOD that spot to man had giv'n,
Where murmuring rivers join the song of ev'n;
Where falls the purple morning far and wide
In flakes of light upon the mountain-side;
Where summer Suns in ocean sink to rest,
Or moonlight Upland lifts her hoary breast;
Where Silence, on her night of wing, o'er-broods
Unfathom'd dells and undiscover'd woods;
Where rocks and groves the power of water shakes
In cataracts, or sleeps in quiet lakes.
But doubly pitying Nature loves to show'r
Soft on his wounded heart her healing pow'r,
Who plods o'er hills and vales his road forlorn,
Wooing her varying charms from eve to morn.

No sad vacuities his heart annoy,
Blows not a Zephyr but it whispers joy;
For him lost flowers their idle sweets exhale;
He tastes the meanest note that swells the gale;
For him sod-seats the cottage-door adorn,
And peeps the far-off spire, his evening bourn!
Dear is the forest frowning o'er his head,
And dear the green-sward to his velvet tread;
Moves there a cloud o'er mid-day's flaming eye?
Upward he looks—and calls it luxury;
Kind Nature's charities his steps attend,
In every babbling brook he finds a friend,
While chast'ning thoughts of sweetest use, bestow'd
By Wisdom, moralize his pensive road.
Host of his welcome inn, the noon-tide bow'r,
To his spare meal he calls the passing poor;
He views the Sun uprear his golden fire,
Or sink, with heart alive like Memnon's lyre;
Blesses the Moon that comes with kindest ray
To light him shaken by his viewless way.
With bashful fear no cottage children steal
From him, a brother at the cottage meal,
His humble looks no shy restraint impart,
Around him plays at will the virgin heart.
While unsuspended wheels the village dance,
The maidens eye him with inquiring glance,
Much wondering what sad stroke of crazing Care
Or desperate Love could lead a wanderer there.
   Me, lur'd by hope her sorrows to remove,
A heart, that could not much itself approve,
O'er Gallia's wastes of corn dejected led,
Her road elms rustling thin above my head,
Or through her truant pathway's native charms,
By secret villages and lonely farms,
To where the Alps, ascending white in air,
Toy with the Sun, and glitter from afar.
   Ev'n now I sigh at hoary Chartreuse' doom
Weeping beneath his chill of mountain gloom.
Where now is fled that Power whose frown severe
Tam'd "sober Reason" till she crouch'd in fear?
That breath'd a death-like peace these woods around,

Broke only by th' unvaried torrent's sound,
Or prayer-bell by the dull cicada drown'd.
The cloister startles at the gleam of arms,
And Blasphemy the shuddering fane alarms;
Nod the cloud-piercing pines their troubl'd heads,
Spires, rocks, and lawns, a browner night o'erspreads.
Strong terror checks the female peasant's sighs,
And start th' astonish'd shades at female eyes.
The thundering tube the aged angler hears,
And swells the groaning torrent with his tears.
From Bruno's forest screams the frighted jay,
And slow th' insulted eagle wheels away.
The cross with hideous laughter Demons mock,
By angels planted on the aereal rock.
The "parting Genius" sighs with hollow breath
Along the mystic streams of Life and Death,
Swelling the outcry dull, that long resounds
Portentous, thro' her old woods' trackless bounds,
Deepening her echoing torrents' awful peal
And bidding paler shades her form conceal,
Vallombre, 'mid her falling fanes, deplores,
For ever broke, the sabbath of her bow'rs.
   More pleas'd, my foot the hidden margin roves
Of Como bosom'd deep in chestnut groves.
No meadows thrown between, the giddy steeps
Tower, bare or silvan, from the narrow deeps.
To towns, whose shades of no rude sound complain,
To ringing team unknown and grating wain,
To flat-roof'd towns, that touch the water's bound,
Or lurk in woody sunless glens profound,
Or from the bending rocks obtrusive cling,
And o'er the whiten'd wave their shadows fling;
Wild round the steeps the little pathway twines,
And Silence loves its purple roof of vines.
The viewless lingerer hence, at evening, sees
From rock-hewn steps the sail between the trees;
Or marks, mid opening cliffs, fair dark-ey'd maids
Tend the small harvest of their garden glades,
Or, led by distant warbling notes, surveys,
With hollow ringing ears and darkening gaze,
Binding the charmed soul in powerless trance,

Lip-dewing Song and ringlet-tossing Dance,
Where sparkling eyes and breaking smiles illume
The bosom'd cabin's lyre-enliven'd gloom;
Or stops the solemn mountain-shades to view
Stretch, o'er their pictur'd mirror, broad and blue,
Tracking the yellow sun from steep to steep,
As up th' opposing hills, with tortoise foot, they creep.
Here half a village shines, in gold array'd,
Bright as the moon, half hides itself in shade.
From the dark sylvan roofs the restless spire,
Inconstant glancing, mounts like springing fire,
There, all unshaded, blazing forests throw
Rich golden verdure on the waves below.
Slow glides the sail along th' illumined shore,
And steals into the shade the lazy oar,
Soft bosoms breathe around contagious sighs,
And amourous music on the water dies.
Heedless how Pliny, musing here, survey'd
Old Roman boats and figures thro' the shade,
Pale Passion, overpower'd, retires and woos
The thicket, where th' unlisten'd stock-dove coos.
    How bless'd, delicious Scene! the eye that greets
Thy open beauties, or thy lone retreats;
Th' unwearied sweep of wood thy cliffs that scales,
The never-ending waters of thy vales;
The cots, those dim religious groves embow'r,
Or, under rocks that from the water tow'r
Insinuated, sprinkling all the shore,
Each with his household boat beside the door,
Whose flaccid sails in forms fantastic droop,
Bright'ning the gloom where thick the forests stoop;
—Thy torrents shooting from the clear-blue sky,
Thy towns, like swallows' nests that cleave on high;
That glimmer hoar in eve's last light, descry'd
Dim from the twilight water's shaggy side,
Whence lutes and voices down th' enchanted woods
Steal, and compose the oar-forgotten floods,
While Evening's solemn bird melodious weeps,
Heard, by star-spotted bays, beneath the steeps;
—Thy lake, mid smoking woods, that blue and grey
Gleams, streak'd or dappled, hid from morning's ray

Slow-travelling down the western hills, to fold
It's green-ting'd margin in a blaze of gold;
From thickly-glittering spires the matin-bell
Calling the woodman from his desert-cell,
A summons to the sound of oars, that pass,
Spotting the steaming deeps, to early mass;
Slow swells the service o'er the water born,
While fill each pause the ringing woods of morn.
　　Farewell! those forms that, in thy noon-tide shade,
Rest, near their little plots of wheaten glade;
Those steadfast eyes, that beating breasts inspire
To throw the "sultry ray" of young Desire;
Those lips, whose tides of fragrance come, and go,
Accordant to the cheek's unquiet glow;
Those shadowy breasts in love's soft light array'd,
And rising, by the moon of passion sway'd.
—Thy fragrant gales and lute-resounding streams,
Breathe o'er the failing soul voluptuous dreams;
While Slavery, forcing the sunk mind to dwell
On joys that might disgrace the captive's cell,
Her shameless timbrel shakes along thy marge,
And winds between thine isles the vocal barge.
　　Yet, arts are thine that rock th' unsleeping heart,
And smiles to Solitude and Want impart.
I lov'd, mid thy most desert woods astray,
With pensive step to measure my slow way,
By lonely, silent cottage-doors to roam,
The far-off peasant's day-deserted home;
Once did I pierce to where a cabin stood,
The redbreast peace had bury'd it in wood,
There, by the door a hoary-headed sire
Touch'd with his wither'd hand an aged lyre;
Beneath an old-grey oak as violets lie,
Stretch'd at his feet with steadfast, upward eye,
His children's children join'd the holy sound,
A hermit—with his family around.
Hence shall we seek where fair Locarno smiles
Embower'd in walnut slopes and citron isles,
Or charms that smile on Tusa's evening stream,
While mid dim towers and woods her waters gleam:
From the bright wave, in solemn gloom, retire

The dull-red steeps, and darkening still, aspire,
To where afar rich orange lustres glow
Round undistinguish'd clouds, and rocks, and snow;
Or, led where Viamala's chasms confine
Th' indignant waters of the infant Rhine,
Bend o'er th' abyss?—the else impervious gloom
His burning eyes with fearful light illume.
The Grison gypsey here her tent has plac'd,
Sole human tenant of the piny waste;
Her tawny skin, dark eyes, and glossy locks,
Bend o'er the smoke that curls beneath the rocks.

—The mind condemn'd, without reprieve, to go
O'er life's long deserts with it's charge of woe,
With sad congratulation joins the train,
Where beasts and men together o'er the plain
Move on,—a mighty caravan of pain;
Hope, strength, and courage, social suffering brings,
Freshening the waste of sand with shades and springs.
—She solitary through the desert drear
Spontaneous wanders, hand in hand with Fear.
A giant moan along the forest swells
Protracted, and the twilight storm foretells,
And, ruining from the cliffs their deafening load
Tumbles, the wildering Thunder slips abroad;
On the high summits Darkness comes and goes,
Hiding their fiery clouds, their rocks, and snows;
The torrent, travers'd by the lustre broad,
Starts like a horse beside the flashing road;
In the roof'd bridge, at that despairing hour,
She seeks a shelter from the battering show'r.
—Fierce comes the river down; the crashing wood
Gives way, and half its pines torment the flood;
Fearful, beneath, the Water-spirits call,
And the bridge vibrates, tottering to its fall.
—Heavy, and dull, and cloudy is the night,
No star supplies the comfort of its light,
Glimmer the dim-lit Alps, dilated, round,
And one sole light shifts in the vale profound;
While, opposite, the waning moon hangs still,
And red, above her melancholy hill.

By the deep quiet gloom appall'd, she sighs,
Stoops her sick head, and shuts her weary eyes.
—Breaking th' ascending roar of desert floods,
And insect buzz, that stuns the sultry woods,
She hears, upon the mountain forest's brow,
The death-dog, howling loud and long, below;
On viewless fingers counts the valley-clock,
Followed by drowsy crow of midnight cock.
—Bursts from the troubl'd Larch's giant boughs
The pie, and chattering breaks the night's repose.
Low barks the fox: by Havoc rouz'd the bear,
Quits, growling, the white bones that strew his lair;
The dry leaves stir as with the serpent's walk,
And, far beneath, Banditti voices talk;
Behind her hill the Moon, all crimson, rides,
And his red eyes the slinking water hides;
Then all is hushed; the bushes rustle near,
And with strange tinglings sings her fainting ear.
—Vex'd by the darkness, from the piny gulf
Ascending, nearer howls the famish'd wolf,
While thro' the stillness scatters wild dismay,
Her babe's small cry, that leads him to his prey.

   Now, passing Urseren's open vale serene,
Her quiet streams, and hills of downy green,
Plunge with the Russ embrown'd by Terror's breath,
Where danger roofs the narrow walks of death;
By floods, that, thundering from their dizzy height,
Swell more gigantic on the steadfast sight;
Black drizzling craggs, that beaten by the din,
Vibrate, as if a voice complain'd within;
Bare steeps, where Desolation stalks, afraid,
Unsteadfast, by a blasted yew upstay'd;
By cells whose image, trembling as he prays,
Awe struck, the kneeling peasant scarce surveys;
Loose-hanging rocks the Day's bless'd eye that hide,
And crosses rear'd to Death on every side,
Which with cold kiss Devotion planted near,
And, bending, water'd with the human tear,
Soon fading "silent" from her upward eye,
Unmov'd with each rude form of Danger nigh,
Fix'd on the anchor left by him who saves

Alike in whelming snows and roaring waves.
On as we move, a softer prospect opes,
Calm huts, and lawns between, and sylvan slopes.
While mists, suspended on th' expiring gale,
Moveless o'er-hang the deep secluded vale,
The beams of evening, slipping soft between,
Light up of tranquil joy a sober scene;
Winding its dark-green wood and emerald glade,
The still vale lengthens underneath the shade;
While in soft gloom the scattering bowers recede,
Green dewy lights adorn the freshen'd mead,
Where solitary forms illumin'd stray
Turning with quiet touch the valley's hay,
On the low brown wood-huts delighted sleep
Along the brighten'd gloom reposing deep.
While pastoral pipes and streams the landscape lull,
And bells of passing mules that tinkle dull,
In solemn shapes before th' admiring eye
Dilated hang the misty pines on high,
Huge convent domes with pinnacles and tow'rs,
And antique castles seen thro' drizzling show'rs.
From such romantic dreams my soul awake,
Lo! Fear looks silent down on Uri's lake,
By whose unpathway'd margin still and dread
Was never heard the plodding peasant's tread.
Tower like a wall the naked rocks, or reach
Far o'er the secret water dark with beach,
More high, to where creation seems to end,
Shade above shade the desert pines ascend,
And still, below, where mid the savage scene
Peeps out a little speck of smiling green,
There with his infants man undaunted creeps
And hangs his small wood-hut upon the steeps.
A garden-plot the desert air perfumes,
'Mid the dark pines a little orchard blooms,
A zig-zag path from the domestic skiff
Threading the painful cragg surmounts the cliff.
—Before those hermit doors, that never know
The face of traveller passing to and fro,
No peasant leans upon his pole, to tell
For whom at morning toll'd the funeral bell,

Their watch-dog ne'er his angry bark forgoes,
Touch'd by the beggar's moan of human woes,
The grassy seat beneath their casement shade
The pilgrim's wistful eye hath never stay'd.
—There, did the iron Genius not disdain
The gentle Power that haunts the myrtle plain,
There might the love-sick maiden sit, and chide
Th' insuperable rocks and severing tide,
There watch at eve her lover's sun-gilt sail
Approaching, and upbraid the tardy gale,
There list at midnight till is heard no more,
Below, the echo of his parting oar,
There hang in fear, when growls the frozen stream,
To guide his dangerous tread the taper's gleam.
  'Mid stormy vapours ever driving by,
Where ospreys, cormorants, and herons cry,
Where hardly giv'n the hopeless waste to chear
Deny'd the bread of life the foodful ear,
Dwindles the pear on autumn's latest spray,
And apple sickens pale in summer's ray,
Ev'n here Content has fix'd her smiling reign
With Independence child of high Disdain.
Exulting mid the winter of the skies,
Shy as the jealous chamois, Freedom flies,
And often grasps her sword, and often eyes,
Her crest a bough of Winter's bleakest pine,
Strange "weeds" and alpine plants her helm entwine,
And wildly-pausing oft she hangs aghast,
While thrills the "Spartan fife" between the blast.
  'Tis storm; and hid in mist from hour to hour
All day the floods a deeper murmur pour,
And mournful sounds, as of a Spirit lost,
Pipe wild along the hollow-blustering coast,
'Till the Sun walking on his western field
Shakes from behind the clouds his flashing shield.
Triumphant on the bosom of the storm,
Glances the fire-clad eagle's wheeling form;
Eastward, in long perspective glittering, shine
The wood-crown'd cliffs that o'er the lake recline;
Wide o'er the Alps a hundred streams unfold,
At once to pillars turn'd that flame with gold;

Behind his sail the peasant strives to shun
The west that burns like one dilated sun,
Where in a mighty crucible expire
The mountains, glowing hot, like coals of fire,
But lo! the boatman, over-aw'd, before
The pictur'd fane of Tell suspends his oar;
Confused the Marathonian tale appears,
While burn in his full eyes the glorious tears.
And who but feels a power of strong controul,
Felt only there, oppress his labouring soul,
Who walks, where honour'd men of ancient days
Have wrought with god-like arm the deeds of praise?
Say, who, by thinking on Canadian hills,
Or wild Aosta lull'd by Alpine rills,
On Zutphen's plain; or where with soften'd gaze
The old grey stones the plaided chief surveys,
Can guess the high resolve, the cherish'd pain
Of him whom passion rivets to the plain,
Where breath'd the gale that caught Wolfe's happiest sigh,
And the last sun-beam fell on Bayard's eye,
Where bleeding Sydney from the cup retir'd,
And glad Dundee in "faint huzzas" expir'd.
  But now with other soul I stand alone
Sublime upon this far-surveying cone,
And watch from pike to pike amid the sky
Small as a bird the chamois-chaser fly.
'Tis his with fearless step at large to roam
Thro' wastes, of Spirits wing'd the solemn home,
Thro' vacant worlds where Nature never gave
A brook to murmur or a bough to wave,
Which unsubstantial Phantoms sacred keep;
Thro' worlds where Life and Sound, and Motion sleep,
Where Silence still her death-like reign extends,
Save when the startling cliff unfrequent rends:
In the deep snow the mighty ruin drown'd,
Mocks the dull ear of Time with deaf abortive sound;
—To mark a planet's pomp and steady light
In the least star of scarce-appearing night,
And neighbouring moon, that coasts the vast profound,
Wheel pale and silent her diminish'd round,
While far and wide the icy summits blaze

Rejoicing in the glory of her rays;
The star of noon that glitters small and bright,
Shorn of his beams, insufferably white,
And flying fleet behind his orb to view
Th' interminable sea of sable blue.
—Of cloudless suns no more ye frost-built spires
Refract in rainbow hues the restless fires!
Ye dewy mists the arid rocks o'er-spread
Whose slippery face derides his deathful tread!
—To wet the peak's impracticable sides
He opens of his feet the sanguine tides,
Weak and more weak the issuing current eyes
Lapp'd by the panting tongue of thirsty skies.
—At once bewildering mists around him close,
And cold and hunger are his least of woes;
The Demon of the snow with angry roar
Descending, shuts for aye his prison door.
Craz'd by the strength of hope at morn he eyes
As sent from heav'n the raven of the skies,
Then with despair's whole weight his spirits sink,
No bread to feed him, and the snow his drink,
While ere his eyes can close upon the day,
The eagle of the Alps o'ershades his prey.
—Meanwhile his wife and child with cruel hope
All night the door at every moment ope;
Haply that child in fearful doubt may gaze,
Passing his father's bones in future days,
Start at the reliques of that very thigh,
On which so oft he prattled when a boy.
    Hence shall we turn where, heard with fear afar,
Thunders thro' echoing pines the headlong Aar?
Or rather stay to taste the mild delights
Of pensive Underwalden's pastoral heights?
—Is there who mid these awful wilds has seen
The native Genii walk the mountain green?
Or heard, while other worlds their charms reveal,
Soft music from th' aereal summit steal?
While o'er the desert, answering every close,
Rich steam of sweetest perfume comes and goes.
—And sure there is a secret Power that reigns
Here, where no trace of man the spot profanes,

Nought but the herds that pasturing upward creep,
Hung dim-discover'd from the dangerous steep,
Or summer hamlet, flat and bare, on high
Suspended, mid the quiet of the sky.
How still! no irreligious sound or sight
Rouzes the soul from her severe delight.
No idle voice the sabbath region fills
Of Deep that calls to Deep across the hills,
Broke only by the melancholy sound
Of drowsy bells for ever tinkling round;
Faint wail of eagle melting into blue
Beneath the cliffs, and pine-woods steady sugh;
The solitary heifer's deepen'd low;
Or rumbling heard remote of falling snow.
Save that, the stranger seen below, the boy
Shouts from the echoing hills with savage joy.
  When warm from myrtle bays and tranquil seas,
Comes on, to whisper hope, the vernal breeze,
When hums the mountain bee in May's glad ear,
And emerald isles to spot the heights appear,
When shouts and lowing herds the valley fill,
And louder torrents stun the noon-tide hill,
When fragrant scents beneath th' enchanted tread
Spring up, his little all around him spread,
The pastoral Swiss begins the cliffs to scale,
To silence leaving the deserted vale,
Up the green mountain tracking Summer's feet,
Each twilight earlier call'd the Sun to meet,
With earlier smile the ray of morn to view
Fall on his shifting hut that gleams mid smoking dew;
Bless'd with his herds, as in the patriarch's age,
The summer long to feed from stage to stage;
O'er azure pikes serene and still, they go,
And hear the rattling thunder far below;
Or lost at eve in sudden mist the day
Attend, or dare with minute-steps their way;
Hand from the rocks that tremble o'er the steep,
And tempt the icy valley yawning deep,
O'er-walk the chasmy torrent's foam-lit bed,
Rock'd on the dizzy larch's narrow tread,
Whence Danger leans, and pointing ghastly, joys

To mock the mind with "desperation's toys";
Or steal beneath loose mountains, half-deterr'd,
That sigh and shudder to the lowing herd.
—I see him, up the midway cliff he creeps
To where a scanty knot of verdure peeps,
Thence down the steep a pile of grass he throws
The fodder of his herds in winter snows.
Far different life to what tradition hoar
Transmits of days more bless'd in times of yore.
Then Summer lengthen'd out his season bland,
And with rock-honey flow'd the happy land.
Continual fountains welling chear'd the waste,
And plants were wholesome, now of deadly taste.
Nor Winter yet his frozen stores had pil'd
Usurping where the fairest herbage smil'd;
Nor Hunger forc'd the herds from pastures bare
For scanty food the treacherous cliffs to dare.
Then the milk-thistle bad those herds demand
Three times a day the pail and welcome hand.
But human vices have provok'd the rod
Of angry Nature to avenge her God,
Thus does the father to his sons relate,
On the lone mountain top, their chang'd estate.
Still, Nature, ever just, to him imparts
Joys only given to uncorrupted hearts.
—'Tis morn: with gold the verdant mountain glows,
More high, the snowy peaks with hues of rose.
Far stretch'd beneath the many-tinted hills,
A mighty waste of mist the valley fills,
A solemn sea! whose vales and mountains round
Stand motionless, to awful silence bound.
A gulf of gloomy blue, that opens wide
And bottomless, divides the midway tide.
Like leaning masts of stranded ships appear
The pines that near the coast their summits rear
Of cabins, woods, and lawns a pleasant shore
Bounds calm and clear the chaos still and hoar;
Loud thro' that midway gulf ascending, sound
Unnumber'd streams with hollow roar profound.
Mounts thro' the nearer mist the chaunt of birds,
And talking voices, and the low of herds,

The bark of dogs, the drowsy tinkling bell,
And wild-wood mountain lutes of saddest swell.
Think not, suspended from the cliff on high
He looks below with undelighted eye.
—No vulgar joy is his, at even tide
Stretch'd on the scented mountain's purple side.
For as the pleasures of his simple day
Beyond his native valley hardly stray,
Nought round its darling precincts can he find
But brings some past enjoyment to his mind,
While Hope that ceaseless leans on Pleasure's urn
Binds her wild wreathes, and whispers his return.

Once Man entirely free, alone and wild,
Was bless'd as free—for he was Nature's child.
He, all superior but his God disdain'd,
Walk'd none restraining, and by none restrain'd,
Confess'd no law but what his reason taught,
Did all he wish'd, and wish'd but what he ought.
As Man in his primæval dower array'd
The image of his glorious sire display'd,
Ev'n so, by vestal Nature guarded, here
The traces of primæval Man appear.
The native dignity no forms debase,
The eye sublime, and surly lion-grace.
The slave of none, of beasts alone the lord,
He marches with his flute, his book, and sword,
Well taught by that to feel his rights, prepar'd
With this "the blessings he enjoys to guard."

And as on glorious ground he draws his breath,
Where Freedom oft, with Victory and Death,
Hath seen in grim array amid their Storms
Mixed with auxiliar Rocks, three hundred Forms;
While twice ten thousand corselets at the view
Dropp'd loud at once, Oppression shriek'd, and flew.
Oft as those sainted Rocks before him spread,
An unknown power connects him with the dead.
For images of other worlds are there,
Awful the light, and holy is the air,
Uncertain thro' his fierce uncultur'd soul
Like lighted tempests troubled transports roll;
To viewless realms his Spirit towers amain,

Beyond the senses and their little reign.
And oft, when pass'd that solemn vision by,
He holds with God himself communion high,
When the dread peal of swelling torrents fills
The sky-roof'd temple of the eternal hills,
And savage Nature humbly joins the rite,
While flash her upward eyes severe delight.
Or gazing from the mountain's silent brow,
Bright stars of ice and azure worlds of snow,
Where needle peaks of granite shooting bare
Tremble in ever-varying tints of air,
Great joy by horror tam'd dilates his heart,
And the near heav'ns their own delights impart.
—When the Sun bids the gorgeous scene farewell,
Alps overlooking Alps their state upswell;
Huge Pikes of Darkness named, of Fear and Storms,
Lift, all serene, their still, illumin'd forms,
In sea-like reach of prospect round him spread,
Ting'd like an angel's smile all rosy red.

When downward to his winter hut he goes,
Dear and more dear the lessening circle grows,
The hut which from the hills his eyes employs
So oft, the central point of all his joys.
And as a swift by tender cares oppress'd
Peeps often ere she dart into her nest,
So to th' untrodden floor, where round him looks
His father helpless as the babe he rocks,
Oft he descends to nurse the brother pair,
Till storm and driving ice blockade him there;
There hears, protected by the woods behind,
Secure, the chiding of the baffled wind,
Hears Winter, calling all his Terrors round,
Rush down the living rocks with whirlwind sound.
Thro' Nature's vale his homely pleasures glide
Unstain'd by envy, discontent, and pride,
The bound of all his vanity to deck
With one bright bell a favourite heifer's neck;
Content upon some simple annual feast,
Remember'd half the year, and hop'd the rest,
If dairy produce, from his inner hoard,
Of thrice ten summers consecrate the board.

—Alas! in every clime a flying ray
Is all we have to chear our wintry way,
Condemn'd, in mists and tempests ever rife,
To pant slow up the endless Alp of life.
"Here," cried a swain, whose venerable head
Bloom'd with the snow-drops of Man's narrow bed,
Last night, while by his dying fire, as clos'd
The day, in luxury my limbs respos'd,
"Here Penury oft from misery's mount will guide
Ev'n to the summer door his icy tide,
And here the avalanche of Death destroy
The little cottage of domestic Joy.
But, ah! th' unwillling mind may more than trace
The general sorrows of the human race:
The churlish gales, that unremitting blow
Cold from necessity's continual snow,
To us the gentle groups of bliss deny
That on the noon-day bank of leisure lie.
Yet more; the tyrant Genius, still at strife
With all the tender Charities of life,
When close and closer they begin to strain,
No fond hand left to staunch th' unclosing vein,
Tearing their bleeding ties leaves Age to groan
On his wet bed, abandon'd and alone.
For ever, fast as they of strength become
To pay the filial debt, for food to roam,
The father forc'd by Powers that only deign
That solitary Man disturb their reign,
From his bare nest amid the storms of heaven
Drives, eagle-like, his sons as he was driven,
His last dread pleasure! watches to the plain—
And never, eagle-like, beholds again."
     When the poor heart has all its joys resign'd,
Why does their sad remembrance cleave behind?
Lo! by the lazy Seine the exile roves,
Or where thick sails illume Batavia's groves;
Soft o'er the waters mournful measures swell,
Unlocking bleeding Thought's "memorial cell;"
At once upon his heart Despair has set
Her seal, the mortal tear his cheek has wet;
Strong poison not a form of steel can brave

Bows his young hairs with sorrow to the grave.
  Gay lark of hope thy silent song resume!
Fair smiling lights the purpled hills illume!
Soft gales and dews of life's delicious morn.
And thou! lost fragrance of the heart return!
Soon flies the little joy to man allow'd,
And tears before him travel like a cloud.
For come Diseases on, and Penury's rage,
Labour, and Pain, and Grief, and joyless Age,
And Conscience dogging close his bleeding way
Cries out, and leads her Spectres to their prey,
'Till Hope-deserted, long in vain his breath
Implores the dreadful untried sleep of Death.
—Mid savage rocks and seas of snow that shine
Between interminable tracts of pine,
Round a lone fane the human Genii mourn,
Where fierce the rays of woe collected burn.
—From viewless lamps a ghastly dimness falls,
And ebbs uncertain on the troubled walls,
Dim dreadful faces thro' the gloom appear,
Abortive Joy, and Hope that works in fear,
While strives a secret Power to hush the croud,
Pain's wild rebellious burst proclaims her rights aloud.
  Oh give not me that eye of hard disdain
That views undimm'd Einsiedlen's wretched fane.
Mid muttering prayers all sounds of torment meet,
Dire clap of hands, distracted chase of feet,
While loud and dull ascends the weeping cry,
Surely in other thoughts contempt may die.
If the sad grave of human ignorance bear
One flower of hope—Oh pass and leave it there.
—The tall Sun, tip-toe on an Alpine spire,
Flings o'er the desert blood-red streams of fire.
At such an hour there are who love to stray,
And meet the gladdening pilgrims on their way.
—Now with joy's tearful kiss each other greet,
Nor longer naked be your way-worn feet,
For ye have reach'd at last the happy shore,
Where the charm'd worm of pain shall gnaw no more.
How gayly murmur and how sweetly taste
The fountains rear'd for you amid the waste!

Yes I will see you when ye first behold
Those turrets tipp'd by hope with morning gold,
And watch, while on your brows the cross ye make,
Round your pale eyes a wintry lustre wake.
—Without one hope her written griefs to blot,
Save in the land where all things are forgot,
My heart, alive to transports long unknown,
Half wishes your delusion were it's own.
Last let us turn to where Chamouny shields,
Bosom'd in gloomy woods, her golden fields,
Five streams of ice amid her cots descend,
And with wild flowers and blooming orchards blend,
A scene more fair than what the Grecian feigns
Of purple lights and even vernal plains.
Here lawns and shades by breezy rivulets fann'd,
Here all the Seasons revel hand in hand.
—Red stream the cottage lights; the landscape fades,
Erroneous wavering mid the twilight shades.
Alone ascends that mountain nam'd of white
That dallies with the Sun the summer night.
Six thousand years amid his lonely bounds
The voice of Ruin, day and night, resounds.
Where Horror-led his sea of ice assails,
Havoc and Chaos blast a thousand vales,
In waves, like two enormous serpents, wind
And drag their length of deluge train behind.
Between the pine's enormous boughs descry'd
Serene he towers, in deepest purple dy'd;
Glad Day-light laughs upon his top of snow,
Glitter the stars above, and all is black below.
    At such an hour I heav'd the human sigh,
When roar'd the sullen Arve in anger by,
That not for thee, delicious vale! unfold
Thy reddening orchards, and thy fields of gold;
That thou, the slave of slaves art doom'd to pine,
While no Italian arts their charms combine
To teach the skirt of thy dark cloud to shine;
For thy poor babes that, hurrying from the door,
With pale-blue hands, and eyes that fix'd implore,
Dead muttering lips, and hair of hungry white,
Besiege the traveller whom they half affright.

—Yes, were it mine, the cottage meal to share
Forc'd from my native mountains bleak and bare;
O'er Anet's hopeless seas of marsh to stray,
Her shrill winds roaring round my lonely way;
To scent the sweets of Piedmont's breathing rose,
And orange gale that o'er Lugano blows;
In the wide range of many a weary round,
Still have my pilgrim feet unfailing found,
As despot courts their blaze of gems display,
Ev'n by the secret cottage far away
The lily of domestic joy decay;
While Freedom's farthest hamlets blessings share,
Found still beneath her smile, and only there.
The casement shade more luscious woodbine binds,
And to the door a neater pathway winds,
At early morn the careful housewife, led
To cull her dinner from its garden bed,
Of weedless herbs a healthier prospect sees,
While hum with busier joy her happy bees;
In brighter rows her table wealth aspires,
And laugh with merrier blaze her evening fires;
Her infant's cheeks with fresher roses glow,
And wilder graces sport around their brow;
By clearer taper lit a cleanlier board
Receives at supper hour her tempting hoard;
The chamber hearth with fresher boughs is spread,
And whiter is the hospitable bed.
—And thou! fair favoured region! which my soul
Shall love, 'till Life has broken her golden bowl,
Till Death's cold touch her cistern-wheel assail,
And vain regret and vain desire shall fail;
Tho' now, where erst the grey-clad peasant stray'd,
To break the quiet of the village shade
Gleam war's discordant habits thro' the trees,
And the red banner mock the sullen breeze;
'Tho, now no more thy maids their voices suit
To the low-warbled breath of twilight lute,
And heard, the pausing village hum between,
No solemn songstress lull the fading green,
Scared by the fife, and rumbling drum's alarms,
And the short thunder, and the flash of arms;

While, as Night bids the startling uproar die,
Sole sound, the sourd renews his mournful cry:
—Yet, hast thou found that Freedom spreads her pow'r
Beyond the cottage hearth, the cottage door:
All nature smiles; and owns beneath her eyes
Her fields peculiar, and peculiar skies.
Yes, as I roam'd where Loiret's waters glide
Thro' rustling aspins heard from side to side,
When from October clouds a milder light
Fell, where the blue flood rippled into white,
Methought from every cot the watchful bird
Crowed with ear-piercing power 'till then unheard;
Each clacking mill, that broke the murmuring streams,
Rock'd the charm'd thought in more delightful dreams
Chasing those long long dreams the falling leaf
Awoke a fainter pang of moral grief;
The measured echo of the distant flail
Winded in sweeter cadence down the vale;
A more majestic tide the water roll'd
And glowed the sun-gilt groves in richer gold:
—Tho' Liberty shall soon, indignant, raise
Red on his hills his beacon's comet blaze;
Bid from on high his lonely cannon sound,
And on ten thousand hearths his shout rebound;
His larum-bell from village-tow'r to tow'r
Swing on th' astounded ear it's dull undying roar:
Yet, yet rejoice, tho' Pride's perverted ire
Rouze Hell's own aid, and wrap thy hills in fire.
Lo! from th' innocuous flames, a lovely birth!
With it's own Virtues springs another earth;
Nature, as in her prime, her virgin reign
Begins, and Love and Truth compose her train;
With pulseless hand, and fix'd unwearied gaze,
Unbreathing Justice her still beam surveys:
No more, along thy vales and viny groves,
Whole hamlets disappearing as he moves,
With cheeks o'erspread by smiles of baleful glow,
On his pale horse shall fell Consumption go.
   Oh give, great God, to Freedom's waves to ride
Sublime o'er Conquest, Avarice, and Pride,
To break, the vales where Death with Famine scow'rs,

And dark Oppression builds her thick-ribb'd tow'rs;
Where Machination her fell soul resigns,
Fled panting to the centre of her mines;
Where Persecution decks with ghastly smiles
Her bed, his mountains mad Ambition piles;
Where Discord stalks dilating, every hour,
And crouching fearful at the feet of Pow'r,
Like Lightnings eager for th' almighty word,
Look up for sign of havoc, Fire and Sword,
—Give them, beneath their breast while Gladness springs,
To brood the nations o'er with Nile-like wings;
And grant that every sceptred child of clay,
Who cries, presumptuous, "here their tides shall stay,"
Swept in their anger from th' affrighted shore,
With all his creatures sink—to rise no more.
  To-night, my friend, within this humble cot
Be the dead load of mortal ills forgot,
Renewing, when the rosy summits glow
At morn, our various journey, sad and slow.

GUILT AND SORROW;

OR

INCIDENTS UPON SALISBURY PLAIN.

[Begun 1791-92.—Completed 1793-94. Published 1842.]

I

A Traveller on the skirt of Sarum's Plain
Pursued his vagrant way, with feet half bare;
Stooping his gait, but not as if to gain
Help from the staff he bore; for mien and air
Were hardy, though his cheek seemed worn with care
Both of the time to come, and time long fled;
Down fell in straggling locks his thin grey hair;
A coat he wore of military red
But faded, and stuck o'er with many a patch and shred.

II

While thus he journeyed, step by step led on,
He saw and passed a stately inn, full sure
That welcome in such house for him was none.
No board inscribed the needy to allure
Hung there, no bush proclaimed to old and poor
And desolate, "Here you will find a friend!"
The pendent grapes glittered above the door;—
On he must pace, perchance till night descend,
Where'er the dreary roads their bare white lines extend.

III

The gathering clouds grew red with stormy fire,
In streaks diverging wide and mounting high;
That inn he long had passed; the distant spire,
Which oft as he looked back had fixed his eye,
Was lost, though still he looked, in the blank sky.
Perplexed and comfortless he gazed around,
And scarce could any trace of man descry,
Save cornfields stretched and stretching without bound;
But where the sower dwelt was nowhere to be found.

IV

No tree was there, no meadow's pleasant green,
No brook to wet his lip or soothe his ear;
Long files of corn-stacks here and there were seen,
But not one dwelling-place his heart to cheer.
Some labourer, thought he, may perchance be near;
And so he sent a feeble shout—in vain;
No voice made answer, he could only hear
Winds rustling over plots of unripe grain,
Or whistling thro' thin grass along the unfurrowed plain.

V

Long had he fancied each successive slope
Concealed some cottage, whither he might turn
And rest; but now along heaven's darkening cope
The crows rushed by in eddies, homeward borne.
Thus warned he sought some shepherd's spreading thorn

Or hovel from the storm to shield his head,
But sought in vain; for now, all wild, forlorn,
And vacant, a huge waste around him spread;
The wet cold ground, he feared, must be his only bed.

VI

And be it so—for to the chill night shower
And the sharp wind his head he oft hath bared ;
A Sailor he, who many a wretched hour
Hath told; for, landing after labour hard,
Full long endured in hope of just reward,
He to an armed fleet was forced away
By seamen, who perhaps themselves had shared
Like fate; was hurried off, a helpless prey,
'Gainst all that in *his* heart, or theirs perhaps, said nay.

VII

For years the work of carnage did not cease,
And death's dire aspect daily he surveyed,
Death's minister; then came his glad release,
And hope returned, and pleasure fondly made
Her dwelling in his dreams. By Fancy's aid
The happy husband flies, his arms to throw
Round his wife's neck; the prize of victory laid
In her full lap, he sees such sweet tears flow
As if thenceforth nor pain nor trouble she could know.

VIII

Vain hope! for fraud took all that he had earned.
The lion roars and gluts his tawny brood
Even in the desert's heart; but he, returned,
Bears not to those he loves their needful food.
His home approaching, but in such a mood
That from his sight his children might have run,
He met a traveller, robbed him, shed his blood;
And when the miserable work was done
He fled, a vagrant since, the murderer's fate to shun.

IX

From that day forth no place to him could be
So lonely, but that thence might come a pang
Brought from without to inward misery.
Now, as he plodded on, with sullen clang
A sound of chains along the desert rang;
He looked, and saw upon a gibbet high
A human body that in irons swang,
Uplifted by the tempest whirling by;
And, hovering, round it often did a raven fly.

X

It was a spectacle which none might view,
In spot so savage, but with shuddering pain;
Nor only did for him at once renew
All he had feared from man, but roused a train
Of the mind's phantoms, horrible as vain.
The stones, as if to cover him from day,
Rolled at his back along the living plain;
He fell, and without sense or motion lay;
But, when the trance was gone, feebly pursued his way.

XI

As one whose brain habitual frenzy fires
Owes to the fit in which his soul hath tossed
Profounder quiet, when the fit retires,
Even so the dire phantasma which had crossed
His sense, in sudden vacancy quite lost,
Left his mind still as a deep evening stream.
Nor, if accosted now, in thought engrossed,
Moody, or inly troubled, would he seem
To traveller who might talk of any casual theme.

XII

Hurtle the clouds in deeper darkness piled,
Gone is the raven timely rest to seek;
He seemed the only creature in the wild
On whom the elements their rage might wreak;
Save that the bustard, of those regions bleak

Shy tenant, seeing by the uncertain light
A man there wandering, gave a mournful shriek,
And half upon the ground, with strange affright,
Forced hard against the wind a thick unwieldy flight.

XIII

All, all was cheerless to the horizon's bound;
The weary eye—which, wheresoe'er it strays,
Marks nothing but the red sun's setting round,
Or on the earth strange lines, in former days
Left by gigantic arms—at length surveys
What seems an antique castle spreading wide;
Hoary and naked are its walls, and raise
Their brow sublime: in shelter there to bide
He turned, while rain poured down smoking on every side.

XIV

Pile of Stone-henge! so proud to hint yet keep
Thy secrets, thou that lov'st to stand and hear
The Plain resounding to the whirlwind's sweep,
Inmate of lonesome Nature's endless year;
Even if thou saw'st the giant wicker rear
For sacrifice its throngs of living men,
Before thy face did ever wretch appear,
Who in his heart had groaned with deadlier pain
Than he who, tempest-driven, thy shelter now would gain?

XV

Within that fabric of mysterious form
Winds met in conflict, each by turns supreme;
And, from the perilous ground dislodged, through storm
And rain he wildered on, no moon to stream
From gulf of parting clouds one friendly beam,
Nor any friendly sound his footsteps led;
Once did the lightning's faint disastrous gleam
Disclose a naked guide-post's double head,
Sight which, tho' lost at once, a gleam of pleasure shed.

XVI

No swinging sign-board creaked from cottage elm
To stay his steps with faintness overcome;
'Twas dark and void as ocean's watery realm
Roaring with storms beneath night's starless gloom;
No gipsy cower'd o'er fire of furze or broom;
No labourer watched his red kiln glaring bright,
Nor taper glimmered dim from sick man's room;
Along the waste no line of mournful light
From lamp of lonely toll-gate streamed athwart the night.

XVII

At length, though hid in clouds, the moon arose;
The downs were visible—and now revealed
A structure stands, which two bare slopes enclose.
It was a spot where, ancient vows fulfilled,
Kind pious hands did to the Virgin build
A lonely Spital, the belated swain
From the night terrors of that waste to shield:
But there no human being could remain,
And now the walls are named the "Dead House" of the plain.

XVIII

Though he had little cause to love the abode
Of man, or covet sight of mortal face,
Yet when faint beams of light that ruin showed
How glad he was at length to find some trace
Of human shelter in that dreary place.
Till to his flock the early shepherd goes,
Here shall much-needed sleep his frame embrace.
In a dry nook where fern the floor bestrows
He lays his stiffened limbs,—his eyes begin to close;

XIX

When hearing a deep sigh, that seemed to come
From one who mourned in sleep, he raised his head,
And saw a woman in the naked room
Outstretched, and turning on a restless bed:
The moon a wan dead light around her shed.

He waked her—spake in tone that would not fail,
He hoped, to calm her mind; but ill he sped,
For of that ruin she had heard a tale
Which now with freezing thoughts did all her powers assail;

XX

Had heard of one who, forced from storms to shroud,
Felt the loose walls of this decayed Retreat
Rock to incessant neighings shrill and loud,
While his horse pawed the floor with furious heat;
Till on a stone, that sparkled to his feet,
Struck, and still struck again, the troubled horse:
The man half raised the stone with pain and sweat,
Half raised, for well his arm might lose its force
Disclosing the grim head of a late murdered corse.

XXI

Such tale of this lone mansion she had learned,
And when that shape, with eyes in sleep half-drowned,
By the moon's sullen lamp she first discerned,
Cold stony horror all her senses bound.
Her he addressed in words of cheering sound;
Recovering heart, like answer did she make;
And well it was that of the corse there found
In converse that ensued she nothing spake;
She knew not what dire pangs in him such tale could wake.

XXII

But soon his voice and words of kind intent
Banished that dismal thought; and now the wind
In fainter howlings told its *rage* was spent:
Meanwhile discourse ensued of various kind,
Which by degrees a confidence of mind
And mutual interest failed not to create.
And, to a natural sympathy resigned,
In that forsaken building where they sate
The Woman thus retraced her own untoward fate.

XXIII

"By Derwent's side my father dwelt—a man
Of virtuous life, by pious parents bred;
And I believe that, soon as I began
To lisp, he made me kneel beside my bed,
And in his hearing there my prayers I said:
And afterwards, by my good father taught,
I read, and loved the books in which I read;
For books in every neighbouring house I sought,
And nothing to my mind a sweeter pleasure brought.

XXIV

"A little croft we owned—a plot of corn,
A garden stored with peas, and mint, and thyme,
And flowers for posies, oft on Sunday morn
Plucked while the church bells rang their earliest chime.
Can I forget our freaks at shearing time!
My hen's rich nest through long grass scarce espied;
The cowslip-gathering in June's dewy prime;
The swans that with white chests upreared in pride
Rushing and racing came to meet me at the waterside!

XXV

"The staff I well remember which upbore
The bending body of my active sire;
His seat beneath the honied sycamore
Where the bees hummed, and chair by winter fire;
When market-morning came, the neat attire
With which, though bent on haste, myself I decked;
Our watchful house-dog, that would tease and tire
The stranger till its barking-fit I checked;
The red-breast, known for years, which at my casement
    pecked.

XXVI

"The suns of twenty summers danced along,—
Too little marked how fast they rolled away:
But, through severe mischance and cruel wrong,
My father's substance fell into decay:

We toiled and struggled, hoping for a day
When Fortune might put on a kinder look;
But vain were wishes, efforts vain as they;
He from his old hereditary nook
Must part; the summons came;—our final leave we took.

XXVII

"It was indeed a miserable hour
When, from the last hill-top, my sire surveyed,
Peering above the trees, the steeple tower
That on his marriage day sweet music made!
Till then he hoped his bones might there be laid
Close by my mother in their native bowers:
Bidding me trust in God, he stood and prayed;—
I could not pray:—through tears that fell in showers
Glimmered our dear-loved home, alas! no longer ours!

XXVIII

"There was a Youth whom I had loved so long,
That when I loved him not I cannot say:
'Mid the green mountains many a thoughtless song
We two had sung, like gladsome birds in May;
When we began to tire of childish play,
We seemed still more and more to prize each other;
We talked of marriage and our marriage day;
And I in truth did love him like a brother,
For never could I hope to meet with such another.

XXIX

"Two years were passed since to a distant town
He had repaired to ply a gainful trade:
What tears of bitter grief, till then unknown,
What tender vows our last sad kiss delayed!
To him we turned:—we had no other aid:
Like one revived, upon his neck I wept;
And her whom he had loved in joy, he said,
He well could love in grief; his faith he kept;
And in a quiet home once more my father slept.

XXX

"We lived in peace and comfort; and were blest
With daily bread, by constant toil supplied.
Three lovely babes had lain upon my breast;
And often, viewing their sweet smiles, I sighed,
And knew not why. My happy father died,
When threatened war reduced the children's meal:
Thrice happy! that for him the grave could hide
The empty loom, cold hearth, and silent wheel,
And tears which flowed for ills which patience might not
      heal.

XXXI

" 'Twas a hard change; an evil time was come;
We had no hope, and no relief could gain:
But soon, with proud parade, the noisy drum
Beat round to clear the streets of want and pain.
My husband's arms now only served to strain
Me and his children hungering in his view;
In such dismay my prayers and tears were vain:
To join those miserable men he flew,
And now to the sea-coast, with numbers more, we drew.

XXXII

"There were we long neglected, and we bore
Much sorrow ere the fleet its anchor weighed;
Green fields before us, and our native shore,
We breathed a pestilential air, that made
Ravage for which no knell was heard. We prayed
For our departure; wished and wished—nor knew,
'Mid that long sickness and those hopes delayed,
That happier days we never more must view.
The parting signal streamed—at last the land withdrew.

XXXIII

"But the calm summer season now was past.
On as we drove, the equinoctial deep
Ran mountains high before the howling blast,
And many perished in the whirlwind's sweep.

We gazed with terror on their gloomy sleep,
Untaught that soon such anguish must ensue,
Our hopes such harvest of affliction reap,
That we the mercy of the waves should rue:
We reached the western world, a poor devoted crew.

XXXIV

"The pains and plagues that on our heads came down,
Disease and famine, agony and fear,
In wood or wilderness, in camp or town,
It would unman the firmest heart to hear.
All perished—all in one remorseless year,
Husband and children! one by one, by sword
And ravenous plague, all perished: every tear
Dried up, despairing, desolate, on board
A British ship I waked, as from a trance restored."

XXXV

Here paused she, of all present thought forlorn,
Nor voice, nor sound, that moment's pain expressed,
Yet Nature, with excess of grief o'er-borne,
From her full eyes their watery load released.
He too was mute: and, ere her weeping ceased,
He rose, and to the ruin's portal went,
And saw the dawn opening the silvery east
With rays of promise, north and southward sent;
And soon with crimson fire kindled the firmament.

XXXVI

"O come," he cried, "come, after weary night
Of such rough storm, this happy change to view."
So forth she came, and eastward looked; the sight
Over her brow like dawn of gladness threw;
Upon her cheek, to which its youthful hue
Seemed to return, dried the last lingering tear,
And from her grateful heart a fresh one drew;
The whilst her comrade to her pensive cheer
Tempered fit words of hope; and the lark warbled near.

XXXVII

They looked and saw a lengthening road, and wain
That rang down a bare slope not far remote:
The barrows glistered bright with drops of rain,
Whistled the waggoner with merry note,
The cock far off sounded his clarion throat;
But town, or farm, or hamlet, none they viewed,
Only were told there stood a lonely cot
A long mile thence. While thither they pursued
Their way, the Woman thus her mournful tale renewed.

XXXVIII

"Peaceful as this immeasurable plain
Is now, by beams of dawning light imprest,
In the calm sunshine slept the glittering main;
The very ocean hath its hour of rest.
I too forgot the heavings of my breast.
How quiet 'round me ship and ocean were!
As quiet all within me. I was blest,
And looked, and fed upon the silent air
Until it seemed to bring a joy to my despair.

XXXIX

"Ah! how unlike those late terrific sleeps,
And groans that rage of racking famine spoke;
The unburied dead that lay in festering heaps,
The breathing pestilence that rose like smoke,
The shriek that from the distant battle broke,
The mine's dire earthquake, and the pallid host
Driven by the bomb's incessant thunderstroke
To loathsome vaults, where heart-sick anguish tossed,
Hope died, and fear itself in agony was lost!

XL

"Some mighty gulf of separation passed,
I seemed transported to another world;
A thought resigned with pain, when from the mast
The impatient mariner the sail unfurled,
And, whistling, called the wind that hardly curled

The silent sea. From the sweet thoughts of home
And from all hope I was for ever hurled.
For me—farthest from earthly port to roam
Was best, could I but shun the spot where man might come.

XLI

"And oft I thought (my fancy was so strong)
That I, at last, a resting-place had found;
'Here will I dwell,' said I, 'my whole life long,
Roaming the illimitable waters round;
Here will I live, of all but heaven disowned,
And end my days upon the peaceful flood.'—
To break my dream the vessel reached its bound;
And homeless near a thousand homes I stood,
And near a thousand tables pined and wanted food.

XLII

"No help I sought; in sorrow turned adrift,
Was hopeless, as if cast on some bare rock;
Nor morsel to my mouth that day did lift,
Nor raised my hand at any door to knock.
I lay where, with his drowsy mates, the cock
From the cross-timber of an outhouse hung:
Dismally tolled, that night, the city clock!
At morn my sick heart hunger scarcely stung,
Nor to the beggar's language could I fit my tongue.

XLIII

"So passed a second day; and, when the third
Was come, I tried in vain the crowd's resort.
—In deep despair, by frightful wishes stirred,
Near the sea-side I reached a ruined fort;
There, pains which nature could no more support,
With blindness linked, did on my vitals fall;
And, after many interruptions short
Of hideous sense, I sank, nor step could crawl:
Unsought for was the help that did my life recall.

XLIV

"Borne to a hospital, I lay with brain
Drowsy and weak, and shattered memory;

I heard my neighbours in their beds complain
Of many things which never troubled me—
Of feet still bustling round with busy glee,
Of looks where common kindness had no part,
Of service done with cold formality,
Fretting the fever round the languid heart,
And groans which, as they said, might make a dead man
    start.

XLV

"These things just served to stir the slumbering sense,
Nor pain nor pity in my bosom raised.
With strength did memory return; and, thence
Dismissed, again on open day I gazed,
At houses, men, and common light, amazed.
The lanes I sought, and, as the sun retired,
Came where beneath the trees a faggot blazed;
The travellers saw me weep, my fate inquired,
And gave me food—and rest, more welcome, more desired.

XLVI

"Rough potters seemed they, trading soberly
With panniered asses driven from door to door;
But life of happier sort set forth to me,
And other joys my fancy to allure—
The bag-pipe dinning on the midnight moor
In barn unlighted; and companions boon,
Well met from far with revelry secure
Among the forest glades, while jocund June
Rolled fast along the sky his warm and genial moon.

XLVII

"But ill they suited me—those journeys dark
O'er moor and mountain, midnight theft to hatch!
To charm the surly house-dog's faithful bark,
Or hang on tip-toe at the lifted latch.
The gloomy lantern, and the dim blue match,
The black disguise, the warning whistle shrill,
And ear still busy on its nightly watch,
Were not for me, brought up in nothing ill:
Besides, on griefs so fresh my thoughts were brooding still.

XLVIII

"What could I do, unaided and unblest?
My father! gone was every friend of thine:
And kindred of dead husband are at best
Small help; and, after marriage such as mine,
With little kindness would to me incline.
Nor was I then for toil or service fit;
My deep-drawn sighs no effort could confine;
In open air forgetful would I sit
Whole hours, with idle arms in moping sorrow knit.

XLIX

"The roads I paced, I loitered through the fields;
Contentedly, yet sometimes self-accused,
Trusted my life to what chance bounty yields,
Now coldly given, now utterly refused.
The ground I for my bed have often used:
But what afflicts my peace with keenest ruth,
Is that I have my inner self abused,
Forgone the home delight of constant truth,
And clear and open soul, so prized in fearless youth.

L

"Through tears the rising sun I oft have viewed,
Through tears have seen him towards that world descend
Where my poor heart lost all its fortitude:
Three years a wanderer now my course I bend—
Oh! tell me whither—for no earthly friend
Have I."—She ceased, and weeping turned away;
As if because her tale was at an end,
She wept; because she had no more to say
Of that perpetual weight which on her spirit lay.

LI

True sympathy the Sailor's looks expressed,
His looks—for pondering he was mute the while.
Of social Order's care for wretchedness,
Of Time's sure help to calm and reconcile,
Joy's second spring and Hope's long-treasured smile,

'Twas not for *him* to speak—a man so tried.
Yet, to relieve her heart, in friendly style
Proverbial words of comfort he applied,
And not in vain, while they went pacing side by side.

LII

Ere long, from heaps of turf, before their sight,
Together smoking in the sun's slant beam,
Rise various wreaths that into one unite
Which high and higher mounts with silver gleam:
Fair spectacle,—but instantly a scream
Thence bursting shrill did all remark prevent;
They paused, and heard a hoarser voice blaspheme,
And female cries. Their course they thither bent,
And met a man who foamed with anger vehement.

LIII

A woman stood with quivering lips and pale,
And, pointing to a little child that lay
Stretched on the ground, began a piteous tale;
How in a simple freak of thoughtless play
He had provoked his father, who straightway,
As if each blow were deadlier than the last,
Struck the poor innocent. Pallid with dismay
The Soldier's Widow heard and stood aghast;
And stern looks on the man her grey-haired Comrade cast.

LIV

His voice with indignation rising high
Such further deed in manhood's name forbade;
The peasant, wild in passion, made reply
With bitter insult and revilings sad;
Asked him in scorn what business there he had;
What kind of plunder he was hunting now;
The gallows would one day of him be glad;—
Though inward anguish damped the Sailor's brow,
Yet calm he seemed as thoughts so poignant would allow.

LV

Softly he stroked the child, who lay outstretched
With face to earth; and, as the boy turned round
His battered head, a groan the Sailor fetched
As if he saw—there and upon that ground—
Strange repetition of the deadly wound
He had himself inflicted. Through his brain
At once the griding iron passage found;
Deluge of tender thoughts then rushed amain,
Nor could his sunken eyes the starting tear restrain.

LVI

Within himself he said—What hearts have we!
The blessing this a father gives his child!
Yet happy thou, poor boy! compared with me,
Suffering not doing ill—fate far more mild.
The stranger's looks and tears of wrath beguiled
The father, and relenting thoughts awoke;
He kissed his son—so all was reconciled.
Then, with a voice which inward trouble broke
Ere to his lips it came, the Sailor them bespoke.

LVII

"Bad is the world, and hard is the world's law
Even for the man who wears the warmest fleece;
Much need have ye that time more closely draw
The bond of nature, all unkindness cease,
And that among so few there still be peace;
Else can ye hope but with such numerous foes
Your pains shall ever with your years increase?"—
While from his heart the appropriate lesson flows,
A correspondent calm stole gently o'er his woes.

LVIII

Forthwith the pair passed on; and down they look
Into a narrow valley's pleasant scene
Where wreaths of vapour tracked a winding brook,
That babbled on through groves and meadows green;
A low-roofed house peeped out the trees between;

The dripping groves resound with cheerful lays,
And melancholy lowings intervene
Of scattered herds, that in the meadow graze,
Some amid lingering shade, some touched by the sun's rays.

LIX

They saw and heard, and, winding with the road
Down a thick wood, they dropt into the vale;
Comfort by prouder mansions unbestowed
Their wearied frames, she hoped, would soon regale.
Ere long they reached that cottage in the dale;
It was a rustic inn;—the board was spread,
The milk-maid followed with her brimming pail,
And lustily the master carved the bread,
Kindly the housewife pressed, and they in comfort fed.

LX

Their breakfast done, the pair, though loth, must part;
Wanderers whose course no longer now agrees.
She rose and bade farewell! and, while her heart
Struggled with tears nor could its sorrow ease,
She left him there; for, clustering round his knees,
With his oak-staff the cottage children played;
And soon she reached a spot o'erhung with trees
And banks of ragged earth; beneath the shade
Across the pebbly road a little runnel strayed.

LXI

A cart and horse beside the rivulet stood;
Chequering the canvas roof the sunbeams shone.
She saw the carman bend to scoop the flood
As the wain fronted her,—wherein lay one,
A pale-faced Woman, in disease far gone.
The carman wet her lips as well behoved;
Bed under her lean body there was none,
Though even to die near one she most had loved
She could not of herself those wasted limbs have moved.

LXII

The Soldier's Widow learned with honest pain
And homefelt force of sympathy sincere,
Why thus that worn-out wretch must there sustain
The jolting road and morning air severe.
The wain pursued its way; and following near
In pure compassion she her steps retraced
Far as the cottage. "A sad sight is here,"
She cried aloud; and forth ran out in haste
The friends whom she had left but a few minutes past.

LXIII

While to the door with eager speed they ran,
From her bare straw the Woman half upraised
Her bony visage—gaunt and deadly wan;
No pity asking, on the group she gazed
With a dim eye, distracted and amazed;
Then sank upon her straw with feeble moan.
Fervently cried the housewife—"God be praised,
I have a house that I can call my own;
Nor shall she perish there, untended and alone!"

LXIV

So in they bear her to the chimney seat,
And busily, though yet with fear, untie
Her garments, and, to warm her icy feet
And chafe her temples, careful hands apply.
Nature reviving, with a deep-drawn sigh
She strove, and not in vain, her head to rear;
Then said—"I thank you all; if I must die,
The God in heaven my prayers for you will hear;
Till now I did not think my end had been so near.

LXV

"Barred every comfort labour could procure,
Suffering what no endurance could assuage,
I was compelled to seek my father's door,
Though loth to be a burthen on his age.
But sickness stopped me in an early stage

Of my sad journey; and within the wain
They placed me—there to end life's pilgrimage,
Unless beneath your roof I may remain:
For I shall never see my father's door again.

LXVI

"My life, Heaven knows, hath long been burthensome;
But, if I have not meekly suffered, meek
May my end be! Soon will this voice be dumb:
Should child of mine e'er wander hither, speak
Of me, say that the worm is on my cheek.—
Torn from our hut, that stood beside the sea
Near Portland lighthouse in a lonesome creek,
My husband served in sad captivity
On shipboard, bound till peace or death should set him free.

LXVII

"A sailor's wife I knew a widow's cares,
Yet two sweet little ones partook my bed;
Hope cheered my dreams, and to my daily prayers
Our heavenly Father granted each day's bread;
Till one was found by stroke of violence dead,
Whose body near our cottage chanced to lie;
A dire suspicion drove us from our shed;
In vain to find a friendly face we try,
Nor could we live together those poor boys and I;

LXVIII

"For evil tongues made oath how on that day
My husband lurked about the neighbourhood;
Now he had fled, and whither none could say,
And *he* had done the deed in the dark wood—
Near his own home!—but he was mild and good;
Never on earth was gentler creature seen;
He'd not have robbed the raven of its food.
My husband's loving kindness stood between
Me and all worldly harms and wrongs however keen."

LXIX

Alas! the thing she told with labouring breath
The Sailor knew too well. That wickedness
His hand had wrought; and when, in the hour of death,
He saw his Wife's lips move his name to bless
With her last words, unable to suppress
His anguish, with his heart he ceased to strive;
And, weeping loud in this extreme distress,
He cried—"Do pity me! That thou shouldst live
I neither ask nor wish—forgive me, but forgive!"

LXX

To tell the change that voice within her wrought
Nature by sign or sound made no essay;
A sudden joy surprised expiring thought,
And every mortal pang dissolved away.
Borne gently to a bed, in death she lay;
Yet still, while over her the husband bent,
A look was in her face which seemed to say,
"Be blest: by sight of thee from heaven was sent
Peace to my parting soul, the fulness of content."

LXXI

She slept in peace,—his pulses throbbed and stopped,
Breathless he gazed upon her face,—then took
Her hand in his, and raised it, but both dropped,
When on his own he cast a rueful look.
His ears were never silent; sleep forsook
His burning eyelids stretched and stiff as lead;
All night from time to time under him shook
The floor as he lay shuddering on his bed;
And oft he groaned aloud, "O God, that I were dead!"

LXXII

The Soldier's Widow lingered in the cot;
And, when he rose, he thanked her pious care
Through which his Wife, to that kind shelter brought,
Died in his arms; and with those thanks a prayer
He breathed for her, and for that merciful pair.

The corse interred, not one hour he remained
Beneath their roof, but to the open air
A burthen, now with fortitude sustained,
He bore within a breast where dreadful quiet reigned.

LXXIII

Confirmed of purpose, fearlessly prepared
For act and suffering, to the city straight
He journeyed, and forthwith his crime declared:
"And from your doom," he added, "now I wait,
Nor let it linger long, the murderer's fate."
Not ineffectual was that piteous claim:
"O welcome sentence which will end though late,"
He said, "the pangs that to my conscience came
Out of that deed. My trust, Saviour! is in thy name!"

LXXIV

His fate was pitied. Him in iron case
(Reader, forgive the intolerable thought)
They hung not:—no one on *his* form or face
Could gaze, as on a show by idlers sought;
No kindred sufferer, to his death-place brought
By lawless curiosity or chance,
When into storm the evening sky is wrought,
Upon his swinging corse an eye can glance,
And drop, as he once dropped, in miserable trance.

LINES

Left upon a Seat in a Yew-tree, which stands near the lake of Esthwaite,
on a desolate part of the shore, commanding a beautiful prospect.

[Begun 1787.—Completed 1795.—Published 1798.]

Nay, Traveller! rest. This lonely Yew-tree stands
Far from all human dwelling: what if here
No sparkling rivulet spread the verdant herb?
What if the bee love not these barren boughs?
Yet, if the wind breathe soft, the curling waves,
That break against the shore, shall lull thy mind
By one soft impulse saved from vacancy.

——————————————————————Who he was
That piled these stones and with the mossy sod
First covered, and here taught this aged Tree
With its dark arms to form a circling bower,
I well remember.—He was one who owned
No common soul. In youth by science nursed,
And led by nature into a wild scene
Of lofty hopes, he to the world went forth
A favoured Being, knowing no desire
Which genius did not hallow; 'gainst the taint
Of dissolute tongues, and jealousy, and hate,
And scorn,—against all enemies prepared,
All but neglect. The world, for so it thought,
Owed him no service; wherefore he at once
With indignation turned himself away,
And with the food of pride sustained his soul
In solitude.—Stranger! these gloomy boughs
Had charms for him; and here he loved to sit,
His only visitants a straggling sheep,
The stone-chat, or the glancing sandpiper:
And on these barren rocks, with fern and heath,
And juniper and thistle, sprinkled o'er,
Fixing his downcast eye, he many an hour
A morbid pleasure nourished, tracing here
An emblem of his own unfruitful life:
And, lifting up his head, he then would gaze
On the more distant scene,—how lovely 'tis
Thou seest,—and he would gaze till it became
Far lovelier, and his heart could not sustain
The beauty, still more beauteous! Nor, that time,
When nature had subdued him to herself,
Would he forget those Beings to whose minds
Warm from the labours of benevolence
The world, and human life, appeared a scene
Of kindred loveliness; then he would sigh,
Inly disturbed, to think that others felt
What he must never feel: and so, lost Man!
On visionary views would fancy feed,
Till his eye streamed with tears. In this deep vale
He died,—this seat his only monument.

If Thou be one whose heart the holy forms
Of young imagination have kept pure,
Stranger! henceforth be warned; and know that pride,
Howe'er disguised in its own majesty,
Is littleness; that he who feels contempt
For any living thing, hath faculties
Which he has never used; that thought with him
Is in its infancy. The man whose eye
Is ever on himself doth look on one,
The least of Nature's works, one who might move
The wise man to that scorn which wisdom holds
Unlawful, ever. O be wiser, Thou!
Instructed that true knowledge leads to love;
True dignity abides with him alone
Who, in the silent hour of inward thought,
Can still suspect, and still revere himself,
In lowliness of heart.

THE OLD CUMBERLAND BEGGAR.

[Composed 1797.—Published 1800.]

I saw an aged Beggar in my walk;
And he was seated, by the highway side,
On a low structure of rude masonry
Built at the foot of a huge hill, that they
Who lead their horses down the steep rough road
May thence remount at ease. The aged Man
Had placed his staff across the broad smooth stone
That overlays the pile; and, from a bag
All white with flour, the dole of village dames,
He drew his scraps and fragments, one by one;
And scanned them with a fixed and serious look
Of idle computation. In the sun,
Upon the second step of that small pile,
Surrounded by those wild unpeopled hills,
He sat, and ate his food in solitude:
And ever, scattered from his palsied hand,
That, still attempting to prevent the waste,
Was baffled still, the crumbs in little showers

Fell on the ground; and the small mountain birds,
Not venturing yet to peck their destined meal,
Approached within the length of half his staff.

Him from my childhood have I known; and then
He was so old, he seems not older now;
He travels on, a solitary Man,
So helpless in appearance, that for him
The sauntering Horseman throws not with a slack
And careless hand his alms upon the ground,
But stops,—that he may safely lodge the coin
Within the old Man's hat; nor quits him so,
But still, when he has given his horse the rein,
Watches the aged Beggar with a look
Sidelong, and half-reverted. She who tends
The toll-gate, when in summer at her door
She turns her wheel, if on the road she sees
The aged Beggar coming, quits her work,
And lifts the latch for him that he may pass.
The post-boy, when his rattling wheels o'ertake
The aged Beggar in the woody lane,
Shouts to him from behind; and, if thus warned
The old man does not change his course, the boy
Turns with less noisy wheels to the roadside,
And passes gently by, without a curse
Upon his lips or anger at his heart.

He travels on, a solitary Man;
His age has no companion. On the ground
His eyes are turned, and, as he moves along,
They move along the ground; and, evermore,
Instead of common and habitual sight
Of fields with rural works, of hill and dale,
And the blue sky, one little span of earth
Is all his prospect. Thus, from day to day,
Bow-bent, his eyes for ever on the ground,
He plies his weary journey; seeing still,
And seldom knowing that he sees, some straw,
Some scattered leaf, or marks which, in one track,
The nails of cart or chariot-wheel have left
Impressed on the white road,—in the same line,

At distance still the same. Poor Traveller!
His staff trails with him; scarcely do his feet
Disturb the summer dust; he is so still
In look and motion, that the cottage curs,
Ere he has passed the door, will turn away,
Weary of barking at him. Boys and girls,
The vacant and the busy, maids and youths,
And urchins newly breeched—all pass him by:
Him even the slow-paced waggon leaves behind.

But deem not this Man useless.—Statesmen! ye
Who are so restless in your wisdom, ye
Who have a broom still ready in your hands
To rid the world of nuisances; ye proud,
Heart-swoln, while in your pride ye contemplate
Your talents, power, or wisdom, deem him not
A burthen of the earth! 'Tis Nature's law
That none, the meanest of created things,
Of forms created the most vile and brute,
The dullest or most noxious, should exist
Divorced from good—a spirit and pulse of good,
A life and soul, to every mode of being
Inseparably linked. Then be assured
That least of all can aught—that ever owned
The heaven-regarding eye and front sublime
Which man is born to—sink, howe'er depressed,
So low as to be scorned without a sin;
Without offence to God cast out of view;
Like the dry remnant of a garden-flower
Whose seeds are shed, or as an implement
Worn out and worthless. While from door to door,
This old Man creeps, the villagers in him
Behold a record which together binds
Past deeds and offices of charity,
Else unremembered, and so keeps alive
The kindly mood in hearts which lapse of years,
And that half-wisdom half-experience gives,
Make slow to feel, and by sure steps resign
To selfishness and cold oblivious cares.
Among the farms and solitary huts,
Hamlets and thinly-scattered villages,

Where'er the aged Beggar takes his rounds,
The mild necessity of use compels
To acts of love; and habit does the work
Of reason; yet prepares that after-joy
Which reason cherishes. And thus the soul,
By that sweet taste of pleasure unpursued,
Doth find herself insensibly disposed
To virtue and true goodness.
      Some there are,
By their good works exalted, lofty minds,
And meditative, authors of delight
And happiness, which to the end of time
Will live, and spread, and kindle: even such minds
In childhood, from this solitary Being,
Or from like wanderer, haply have received
(A thing more precious far than all that books
Or the solicitudes of love can do!)
That first mild touch of sympathy and thought,
In which they found their kindred with a world
Where want and sorrow were. The easy man
Who sits at his own door,—and, like the pear
That overhangs his head from the green wall,
Feeds in the sunshine; the robust and young,
The prosperous and unthinking, they who live
Sheltered, and flourish in a little grove
Of their own kindred;—all behold in him
A silent monitor, which on their minds
Must needs impress a transitory thought
Of self-congratulation, to the heart
Of each recalling his peculiar boons,
His charters and exemptions; and, perchance,
Though he to no one give the fortitude
And circumspection needful to preserve
His present blessings, and to husband up
The respite of the season, he, at least,
And 'tis no vulgar service, makes them felt.

Yet further.————Many, I believe, there are
Who live a life of virtuous decency,
Men who can hear the Decalogue and feel
No self-reproach; who of the moral law

Established in the land where they abide
Are strict observers; and not negligent
In acts of love to those with whom they dwell,
Their kindred, and the children of their blood.
Praise be to such, and to their slumbers peace!
—But of the poor man ask, the abject poor;
Go, and demand of him, if there be here
In this cold abstinence from evil deeds,
And these inevitable charities,
Wherewith to satisfy the human soul?
No—man is dear to man; the poorest poor
Long for some moments in a weary life
When they can know and feel that they have been,
Themselves, the fathers and the dealers-out
Of some small blessings; have been kind to such
As needed kindness, for this single cause,
That we have all of us one human heart.
—Such pleasure is to one kind Being known,
My neighbour, when with punctual care, each week,
Duly as Friday comes, though pressed
By her own wants, she from her store of meal
Takes one unsparing handful for the scrip
Of this old Mendicant, and, from her door
Returning with exhilarated heart,
Sits by her fire, and builds her hope in heaven.

Then let him pass, a blessing on his head!
And while in that vast solitude to which
The tide of things has borne him, he appears
To breathe and live but for himself alone,
Unblamed, uninjured, let him bear about
The good which the benignant law of Heaven
Has hung around him: and, while life is his,
Still let him prompt the unlettered villagers
To tender offices and pensive thoughts.
—Then let him pass, a blessing on his head!
And, long as he can wander, let him breathe
The freshness of the valleys; let his blood
Struggle with frosty air and winter snows;
And let the chartered wind that sweeps the heath
Beat his grey locks against his withered face.

Reverence the hope whose vital anxiousness
Gives the last human interest to his heart.
May never House, misnamed of Industry,
Make him a captive!—for that pent-up din,
Those life-consuming sounds that clog the air,
Be his the natural silence of old age!
Let him be free of mountain solitudes;
And have around him, whether heard or not,
The pleasant melody of woodland birds.
Few are his pleasures: if his eyes have now
Been doomed so long to settle upon earth
That not without some effort they behold
The countenance of the horizontal sun,
Rising or setting, let the light at least
Find a free entrance to their languid orbs,
And let him, *where* and *when* he will, sit down
Beneath the trees, or on a grassy bank
Of highway side, and with the little birds
Share his chance-gathered meal; and, finally,
As in the eye of Nature he has lived,
So in the eye of Nature let him die!

ANIMAL TRANQUILLITY AND DECAY

[Composed 1798 (? 1797).—Published 1798.]

The little hedgerow birds,
That peck along the road, regard him not.
He travels on, and in his face, his step,
His gait, is one expression: every limb,
His look and bending figure, all bespeak
A man who does not move with pain, but moves
With thought.—He is insensibly subdued
To settled quiet: he is one by whom
All effort seems forgotten; one to whom
Long patience hath such mild composure given,
That patience now doth seem a thing of which
He hath no need. He is by nature led
To peace so perfect that the young behold
With envy, what the Old Man hardly feels.

THE REVERIE OF POOR SUSAN

[Composed 1797.—Published 1800.]

At the corner of Wood Street, when daylight appears,
Hangs a Thrush that sings loud, it has sung for three years:
Poor Susan has passed by the spot, and has heard
In the silence of morning the song of the Bird.

'Tis a note of enchantment; what ails her? She sees
A mountain ascending, a vision of trees;
Bright volumes of vapour through Lothbury glide,
And a river flows on through the vale of Cheapside.

Green pastures she views in the midst of the dale,
Down which she so often has tripped with her pail;
And a single small cottage, a nest like a dove's,
The one only dwelling on earth that she loves.

She looks, and her heart is in heaven; but they fade,
The mist and the river, the hill and the shade;
The stream will not flow, and the hill will not rise,
And the colours have all passed away from her eyes!

A NIGHT-PIECE

[Composed January 25, 1798.—Published 1815.]

————The sky is overcast
With a continuous cloud of texture close,
Heavy and wan, all whitened by the Moon,
Which through that veil is indistinctly seen,
A dull, contracted circle, yielding light
So feebly spread that not a shadow falls,
Chequering the ground—from rock, plant, tree, or tower.
At length a pleasant instantaneous gleam
Startles the pensive traveller while he treads
His lonesome path, with unobserving eye
Bent earthwards; he looks up—the clouds are split
Asunder,—and above his head he sees
The clear Moon, and the glory of the heavens.
There in a black-blue vault she sails along,

Followed by multitudes of stars, that, small
And sharp, and bright, along the dark abyss
Drive as she drives: how fast they wheel away,
Yet vanish not!—the wind is in the tree,
But they are silent;—still they roll along
Immeasurably distant; and the vault,
Built round by those white clouds, enormous clouds,
Still deepens its unfathomable depth.
At length the Vision closes; and the mind,
Not undisturbed by the delight it feels,
Which slowly settles into peaceful calm,
Is left to muse upon the solemn scene.

WE ARE SEVEN

[Composed 1798.—Published 1800.]

——A simple Child,
That lightly draws its breath,
And feels its life in every limb,
What should it know of death?

I met a little cottage Girl:
She was eight years old, she said;
Her hair was thick with many a curl
That clustered round her head.

She had a rustic, woodland air,
And she was wildly clad:
Her eyes were fair, and very fair;
—Her beauty made me glad.

"Sisters and brothers, little maid,
How many may you be?"
"How many? Seven in all," she said,
And wondering looked at me.

"And where are they? I pray you tell."
She answered, "Seven are we;
And two of us at Conway dwell,
And two are gone to sea.

"Two of us in the church-yard lie,
My sister and my brother;
And, in the church-yard cottage, I
Dwell near them with my mother."

"You say that two at Conway dwell,
And two are gone to sea,
Yet ye are seven! I pray you tell,
Sweet Maid, how this may be."

Then did the little Maid reply,
"Seven boys and girls are we;
Two of us in the church-yard lie,
Beneath the church-yard tree."

"You run about, my little Maid,
Your limbs they are alive;
If two are in the church-yard laid,
Then ye are only five."

"Their graves are green, they may be seen,"
The little Maid replied,
"Twelve steps or more from my mother's door,
And they are side by side.

"My stockings there I often knit,
My kerchief there I hem;
And there upon the ground I sit,
And sing a song to them.

"And often after sun-set, Sir,
When it is light and fair,
I take my little porringer,
And eat my supper there.

"The first that died was sister Jane;
In bed she moaning lay,
Till God released her of her pain;
And then she went away.

"So in the church-yard she was laid;
And, when the grass was dry,
Together round her grave we played,
My brother John and I.

"And when the ground was white with snow,
And I could run and slide,
My brother John was forced to go,
And he lies by her side."

"How many are you, then," said I,
"If they two are in heaven?"
Quick was the little Maid's reply,
"O Master! we are seven."

"But they are dead; those two are dead!
Their spirits are in heaven!"
'Twas throwing words away; for still
The little Maid would have her will,
And said, "Nay, we are seven!"

ANECDOTE FOR FATHERS

"Retine vim istam, falsa enim dicam, si coges."—EUSEBIUS.

[Composed 1798.—Published 1798.]

I have a boy of five years old;
His face is fair and fresh to see;
His limbs are cast in beauty's mould,
And dearly he loves me.

One morn we strolled on our dry walk,
Our quiet home all full in view,
And held such intermitted talk
As we are wont to do.

My thoughts on former pleasures ran;
I thought of Kilve's delightful shore,
Our pleasant home when spring began,
A long, long year before.

A day it was when I could bear
Some fond regrets to entertain;
With so much happiness to spare,
I could not feel a pain.

The green earth echoed to the feet
Of lambs that bounded through the glade,
From shade to sunshine, and as fleet
From sunshine back to shade.

Birds warbled round me—and each trace
Of inward sadness had its charm;
Kilve, thought I, was a favoured place,
And so is Liswyn farm.

My boy beside me tripped, so slim
And graceful in his rustic dress!
And, as we talked, I questioned him,
In very idleness.

"Now tell me, had you rather be,"
I said, and took him by the arm,
"On Kilve's smooth shore, by the green sea,
Or here at Liswyn farm?"

In careless mood he looked at me,
While, still I held him by the arm,
And said, "At Kilve I'd rather be
Than here at Liswyn farm."

"Now, little Edward, say why so:
My little Edward, tell me why."—
"I cannot tell, I do not know."—
"Why, this is strange," said I;

"For here are woods, hills smooth and warm:
There surely must some reason be
Why you would change sweet Liswyn farm
For Kilve by the green sea."

At this my boy hung down his head,
He blushed with shame, nor made reply;
And three times to the child I said,
"Why, Edward, tell me why?"

His head he raised—there was in sight,
It caught his eye, he saw it plain—
Upon the house-top, glittering bright,
A broad and gilded vane.

Then did the boy his tongue unlock,
And eased his mind with this reply:
"At Kilve there was no weather-cock;
And that's the reason why."

O dearest, dearest boy! my heart
For better lore would seldom yearn,
Could I but teach the hundredth part
Of what from thee I learn.

THE THORN

[Composed 1798.—Published 1798.]

I

"There is a Thorn—it looks so old,
In truth, you'd find it hard to say
How it could ever have been young,
It looks so old and grey.
Not higher than a two years' child
It stands erect, this aged Thorn;
No leaves it has, no prickly points;
It is a mass of knotted joints,
A wretched thing forlorn.
It stands erect, and like a stone
With lichens is it overgrown.

II

"Like rock or stone, it is o'ergrown,
With lichens to the very top,
And hung with heavy tufts of moss,
A melancholy crop:
Up from the earth these mosses creep,
And this poor Thorn they clasp it round
So close, you'd say that they are bent
With plain and manifest intent
To drag it to the ground;
And all have joined in one endeavour
To bury this poor Thorn for ever.

III

"High on a mountain's highest ridge,
Where oft the stormy winter gale
Cuts like a scythe, while through the clouds
It sweeps from vale to vale;
Not five yards from the mountain path,
This Thorn you on your left espy;
And to the left, three yards beyond,
You see a little muddy pond
Of water—never dry,
Though but of compass small, and bare
To thirsty suns and parching air.

IV

"And, close beside this aged Thorn,
There is a fresh and lovely sight,
A beauteous heap, a hill of moss,
Just half a foot in height.
All lovely colours there you see,
All colours that were ever seen;
And mossy network too is there,
As if by hand of lady fair
The work had woven been;
And cups, the darlings of the eye,
So deep is their vermilion dye.

V

"Ah me! what lovely tints are there
Of olive green and scarlet bright,
In spikes, in branches, and in stars,
Green, red and pearly white!
This heap of earth o'ergrown with moss,
Which close beside the Thorn you see,
So fresh in all its beauteous dyes,
Is like an infant's grave in size,
As like as like can be:
But never, never any where,
An infant's grave was half so fair.

VI

"Now would you see this aged Thorn,
This pond, and beauteous hill of moss,
You must take care and choose your time
The mountain when to cross.
For oft there sits between the heap,
So like an infant's grave in size,
And that same pond of which I spoke,
A Woman in a scarlet cloak,
And to herself she cries,
'O misery! oh misery!
Oh woe is me! oh misery!'

VII

"At all times of the day and night
This wretched Woman thither goes;
And she is known to every star,
And every wind that blows;
And there, beside the Thorn, she sits
When the blue daylight's in the skies,
And when the whirlwind's on the hill,
Or frosty air is keen and still,
And to herself she cries,
'Oh misery! oh misery!
Oh woe is me! oh misery!'"

VIII

"Now wherefore, thus, by day and night,
In rain, in tempest, and in snow,
Thus to the dreary mountain-top
Does this poor Woman go?
And why sits she beside the Thorn
When the blue daylight's in the sky
Or when the whirlwind's on the hill,
Or frosty air is keen and still,
And wherefore does she cry?—
O wherefore? wherefore? tell me why
Does she repeat that doleful cry?"

IX

"I cannot tell; I wish I could;
For the true reason no one knows:
But would you gladly view the spot,
The spot to which she goes;
The hillock like an infant's grave,
The pond—and Thorn, so old and grey;
Pass by her door—'tis seldom shut—
And if you see her in her hut—
Then to the spot away!
I never heard of such as dare
Approach the spot when she is there."

X

"But wherefore to the mountain-top
Can this unhappy Woman go,
Whatever star is in the skies,
Whatever wind may blow?"
"Full twenty years are past and gone
Since she (her name is Martha Ray)
Gave with a maiden's true good-will
Her company to Stephen Hill;
And she was blithe and gay,
While friends and kindred all approved
Of him whom tenderly she loved.

XI

"And they had fixed the wedding day,
The morning that must wed them both;
But Stephen to another Maid
Had sworn another oath;
And, with this other Maid, to church
Unthinking Stephen went—
Poor Martha! on that woeful day
A pang of pitiless dismay
Into her soul was sent;
A fire was kindled in her breast,
Which might not burn itself to rest.

XII

"They say, full six months after this,
While yet the summer leaves were green,
She to the mountain-top would go,
And there was often seen.
What could she seek?—or wish to hide?
Her state to any eye was plain;
She was with child, and she was mad;
Yet often was she sober sad
From her exceeding pain.
O guilty Father—would that death
Had saved him from that breach of faith!

XIII

"Sad case for such a brain to hold
Communion with a stirring child!
Sad case, as you may think, for one
Who had a brain so wild!
Last Christmas-eve we talked of this,
And grey-haired Wilfred of the glen
Held that the unborn infant wrought
About its mother's heart, and brought
Her senses back again:
And, when at last her time drew near,
Her looks were calm, her senses clear.

XIV

"More know I not, I wish I did,
And it should all be told to you;
For what became of this poor child
No mortal ever knew;
Nay—if a child to her was born
No earthly tongue could ever tell;
And if 'twas born alive or dead,
Far less could this with proof be said;
But some remember well
That Martha Ray about this time
Would up the mountain often climb.

XV

"And all that winter, when at night
The wind blew from the mountain-peak,
'Twas worth your while, though in the dark,
The churchyard path to seek:
For many a time and oft were heard
Cries coming from the mountain head:
Some plainly living voices were;
And others, I've heard many swear,
Were voices of the dead:
I cannot think, whate'er they say,
They had to do with Martha Ray.

XVI

"But that she goes to this old Thorn,
The Thorn which I described to you,
And there sits in a scarlet cloak,
I will be sworn is true.
For one day with my telescope,
To view the ocean wide and bright,
When to this country first I came,
Ere I had heard of Martha's name,
I climbed the mountain's height:—
A storm came on, and I could see
No object higher than my knee.

XVII

" 'Twas mist and rain, and storm and rain:
No screen, no fence could I discover;
And then the wind! in sooth, it was
A wind full ten times over.
I looked around, I thought I saw
A jutting crag,—and off I ran,
Head-foremost, through the driving rain,
The shelter of the crag to gain;
And, as I am a man,
Instead of jutting crag I found
A Woman seated on the ground.

XVIII

"I did not speak—I saw her face;
Her face!—it was enough for me;
I turned about and heard her cry,
'Oh misery! oh misery!'
And there she sits, until the moon
Through half the clear blue sky will go;
And when the little breezes make
The waters of the pond to shake,
As all the country know,
She shudders, and you hear her cry,
'Oh misery! oh misery!'"

XIX

"But what's the Thorn? and what the pond?
And what the hill of moss to her?
And what the creeping breeze that comes
The little pond to stir?"
"I cannot tell; but some will say
She hanged her baby on the tree;
Some say she drowned it in the pond,
Which is a little step beyond:
But all and each agree,
The little Babe was buried there,
Beneath that hill of moss so fair.

XX

"I've heard, the moss is spotted red
With drops of that poor infant's blood;
But kill a new-born infant thus,
I do not think she could!
Some say if to the pond you go,
And fix on it a steady view,
The shadow of a babe you trace,
A baby and a baby's face,
And that it looks at you;
Whene'er you look on it, 'tis plain
The baby looks at you again.

XXI

"And some had sworn an oath that she
Should be to public justice brought;
And for the little infant's bones
With spades they would have sought.
But instantly the hill of moss
Before their eyes began to stir!
And, for full fifty yards around,
The grass—it shook upon the ground!
Yet all do still aver
The little Babe lies buried there,
Beneath that hill of moss so fair.

XXII

"I cannot tell how this may be,
But plain it is the Thorn is bound
With heavy tufts of moss that strive
To drag it to the ground;
And this I know, full many a time,
When she was on the mountain high,
By day, and in the silent night,
When all the stars shone clear and bright,
That I have heard her cry,
'Oh misery! oh misery!
Oh woe is me! oh misery!'"

GOODY BLAKE AND HARRY GILL

A TRUE STORY

[Composed 1798.—Published 1798.]

Oh! what's the matter? what's the matter?
What is't that ails young Harry Gill?
That evermore his teeth they chatter,
Chatter, chatter, chatter still!
Of waistcoats Harry has no lack,
Good duffle grey, and flannel fine;
He has a blanket on his back,
And coats enough to smother nine.

In March, December, and in July,
'Tis all the same with Harry Gill;
The neighbours tell, and tell you truly,
His teeth they chatter, chatter still.
At night, at morning, and at noon,
'Tis all the same with Harry Gill;
Beneath the sun, beneath the moon,
His teeth they chatter, chatter still!

Young Harry was a lusty drover,
And who so stout of limb as he?
His cheeks were red as ruddy clover;
His voice was like the voice of three.
Old Goody Blake was old and poor;
Ill fed she was, and thinly clad;
And any man who passed her door
Might see how poor a hut she had.

All day she spun in her poor dwelling:
And then her three hours' work at night,
Alas! 'twas hardly worth the telling,
It would not pay for candle-light.
Remote from sheltered village-green,
On a hill's northern side she dwelt,
Where from sea-blasts the hawthorns lean,
And hoary dews are slow to melt.

By the same fire to boil their pottage,
Two poor old Dames, as I have known,
Will often live in one small cottage;
But she, poor Woman! housed alone.
'Twas well enough, when summer came,
The long, warm, lightsome summer-day,
Then at her door the *canty* Dame
Would sit, as any linnet, gay.

But when the ice our streams did fetter,
Oh then how her old bones would shake!
You would have said, if you had met her,
'Twas a hard time for Goody Blake.
Her evenings then were dull and dead:
Sad case it was, as you may think,
For very cold to go to bed;
And then for cold not sleep a wink.

O joy for her! whene'er in winter
The winds at night had made a rout;
And scattered many a lusty splinter
And many a rotten bough about.
Yet never had she, well or sick,
As every man who knew her says,
A pile beforehand, turf or stick,
Enough to warm her for three days.

Now, when the frost was past enduring,
And made her poor old bones to ache,
Could any thing be more alluring
Than an old hedge to Goody Blake?
And, now and then, it must be said,
When her old bones were cold and chill,
She left her fire, or left her bed,
To seek the hedge of Harry Gill.

Now Harry he had long suspected
This trespass of old Goody Blake;
And vowed that she should be detected—
That he on her would vengeance take,
And oft from his warm fire he'd go,

And to the fields his road would take;
And there, at night, in frost and snow,
He watched to seize old Goody Blake.

And once, behind a rick of barley,
Thus looking out did Harry stand:
The moon was full and shining clearly,
And crisp with frost the stubble land.
—He hears a noise—he's all awake—
Again?—on tip-toe down the hill
He softly creeps—'tis Goody Blake;
She's at the hedge of Harry Gill!

Right glad was he when he beheld her:
Stick after stick did Goody pull:
He stood behind a bush of elder,
Till she had filled her apron full.
When with her load she turned about,
The by-way back again to take;
He started forward, with a shout,
And sprang upon poor Goody Blake.

And fiercely by the arm he took her,
And by the arm he held her fast,
And fiercely by the arm he shook her,
And cried, "I've caught you then at last!"
Then Goody, who had nothing said,
Her bundle from her lap let fall;
And, kneeling on the sticks, she prayed
To God that is the judge of all.

She prayed, her withered hand uprearing,
While Harry held her by the arm—
"God! who art never out of hearing,
O may he never more be warm!"
The cold, cold moon above her head,
Thus on her knees did Goody pray;
Young Harry heard what she had said:
And icy cold he turned away.

He went complaining all the morrow
That he was cold and very chill:
His face was gloom, his heart was sorrow,
Alas! that day for Harry Gill!
That day he wore a riding-coat,
But not a whit the warmer he:
Another was on Thursday brought,
And ere the Sabbath he had three.

'Twas all in vain, a useless matter,
And blankets were about him pinned;
Yet still his jaws and teeth they clatter,
Like a loose casement in the wind.
And Harry's flesh it fell away;
And all who see him say, 'tis plain,
That, live as long as live he may,
He never will be warm again.

No word to any man he utters,
A-bed or up, to young or old;
But ever to himself he mutters,
"Poor Harry Gill is very cold."
A-bed or up, by night or day;
His teeth they chatter, chatter still.
Now think, ye farmers all, I pray,
Of Goody Blake and Harry Gill!

SIMON LEE

THE OLD HUNTSMAN

With an incident in which he was concerned.

[Composed 1798.—Published 1798.]

In the sweet shire of Cardigan,
Not far from pleasant Ivor-hall,
An old Man dwells, a little man,—
'Tis said he once was tall.
Full five-and-thirty years he lived
A running huntsman merry;
And still the centre of his cheek
Is red as a ripe cherry.

No man like him the horn could sound,
And hill and valley rang with glee
When Echo bandied, round and round,
The halloo of Simon Lee.
In those proud days, he little cared
For husbandry or tillage;
To blither tasks did Simon rouse
The sleepers of the village.

He all the country could outrun,
Could leave both man and horse behind;
And often, ere the chase was done,
He reeled, and was stone-blind.
And still there's something in the world
At which his heart rejoices;
For when the chiming hounds are out,
He dearly loves their voices!

But, oh the heavy change!—bereft
Of health, strength, friends, and kindred, see!
Old Simon to the world is left
In liveried poverty.
His Master's dead,—and no one now
Dwells in the Hall of Ivor;
Men, dogs, and horses, all are dead;
He is the sole survivor.

And he is lean and he is sick;
His body, dwindled and awry,
Rests upon ankles swoln and thick;
His legs are thin and dry.
One prop he has, and only one,
His wife, an aged woman,
Lives with him, near the waterfall,
Upon the village Common.

Beside their moss-grown hut of clay,
Not twenty paces from the door,
A scrap of land they have, but they
Are poorest of the poor.
This scrap of land he from the heath

Enclosed when he was stronger;
But what to them avails the land
Which he can till no longer?

Oft, working by her Husband's side,
Ruth does what Simon cannot do;
For she, with scanty cause for pride,
Is stouter of the two.
And, though you with your utmost skill
From labour could not wean them,
'Tis little, very little—all
That they can do between them.

Few months of life has he in store
As he to you will tell,
For still, the more he works, the more
Do his weak ankles swell.
My gentle Reader, I perceive
How patiently you've waited,
And now I fear that you expect
Some tale will be related.

O Reader! had you in your mind
Such stores as silent thought can bring,
O gentle Reader! you would find
A tale in every thing.
What more I have to say is short,
And you must kindly take it:
It is no tale; but, should you think,
Perhaps a tale you'll make it.

One summer-day I chanced to see
This old Man doing all he could
To unearth the root of an old tree,
A stump of rotten wood.
The mattock tottered in his hand;
So vain was his endeavour,
That at the root of the old tree
He might have worked for ever.

"You're overtasked, good Simon Lee,
Give me your tool," to him I said;
And at the word right gladly he
Received my proffered aid.
I struck, and with a single blow
The tangled root I severed,
At which the poor old Man so long
And vainly had endeavoured.

The tears into his eyes were brought.
And thanks and praises seemed to run
So fast out of his heart, I thought
They never would have done.
—I've heard of hearts unkind, kind deeds
With coldness still returning;
Alas! the gratitude of men
Hath oftener left me mourning.

LINES WRITTEN IN EARLY SPRING

[Composed 1798.—Published 1798.]

I heard a thousand blended notes,
While in a grove I sate reclined,
In that sweet mood when pleasant thoughts
Bring sad thoughts to the mind.

To her fair works did Nature link
The human soul that through me ran;
And much it grieved my heart to think
What man has made of man.

Through primrose tufts, in that green bower,
The periwinkle trailed its wreaths;
And 'tis my faith that every flower
Enjoys the air it breathes.

The birds around me hopped and played,
Their thoughts I cannot measure:—
But the least motion which they made,
It seemed a thrill of pleasure.

The budding twigs spread out their fan,
To catch the breezy air;
And I must think, do all I can,
That there was pleasure there.

If this belief from heaven be sent,
If such be Nature's holy plan,
Have I not reason to lament
What man has made of man?

TO MY SISTER

[Composed 1798.—Published 1798.]

It is the first mild day of March:
Each minute sweeter than before,
The redbreast sings from the tall larch
That stands beside our door.

There is a blessing in the air,
Which seems a sense of joy to yield
To the bare trees, and mountains bare,
And grass in the green field.

My sister! ('tis a wish of mine)
Now that our morning meal is done,
Make haste, your morning task resign;
Come forth and feel the sun.

Edward will come with you;—and, pray,
Put on with speed your woodland dress;
And bring no book: for this one day
We'll give to idleness.

No joyless forms shall regulate
Our living calendar:
We from to-day, my Friend, will date
The opening of the year.

Love, now a universal birth,
From heart to heart is stealing,
From earth to man, from man to earth:
—It is the hour of feeling.

One moment now may give us more
Than years of toiling reason:
Our minds shall drink at every pore
The spirit of the season.

Some silent laws our hearts will make,
Which they shall long obey:
We for the year to come may take
Our temper from to-day.

And from the blessed power that rolls
About, below, above,
We'll frame the measure of our souls:
They shall be tuned to love.

Then come, my Sister! come, I pray,
With speed put on your woodland dress;
And bring no book: for this one day
We'll give to idleness.

EXPOSTULATION AND REPLY

[Composed 1798.—Published 1798.]

"Why, William, on that old grey stone,
Thus for the length of half a day,
Why, William, sit you thus alone,
And dream your time away?

"Where are your books?—that light bequeathed
To Beings else forlorn and blind!
Up! up! and drink the spirit breathed
From dead men to their kind.

"You look round on your Mother Earth,
As if she for no purpose bore you;
As if you were her first-born birth,
And none had lived before you!"

One morning thus, by Esthwaite lake,
When life was sweet, I knew not why,
To me my good friend Matthew spake,
And thus I made reply:

"The eye—it cannot choose but see;
We cannot bid the ear be still;
Our bodies feel, where'er they be,
Against or with our will.

"Nor less I deem that there are Powers
Which of themselves our minds impress;
That we can feed this mind of ours
In a wise passiveness.

"Think you, 'mid all this mighty sum
Of things for ever speaking,
That nothing of itself will come,
But we must still be seeking?

"—Then ask not wherefore, here, alone,
Conversing as I may,
I sit upon this old grey stone,
And dream my time away."

THE TABLES TURNED

AN EVENING SCENE ON THE SAME SUBJECT

[Composed 1798.—Published 1798.]

Up! up! my Friend, and quit your books;
Or surely you'll grow double:
Up! up! my Friend, and clear your looks;
Why all this toil and trouble?

The sun, above the mountain's head,
A freshening lustre mellow
Through all the long green fields has spread,
His first sweet evening yellow.

Books! 'tis a dull and endless strife:
Come, hear the woodland linnet,
How sweet his music! on my life,
There's more of wisdom in it.

And hark! how blithe the throstle sings!
He, too, is no mean preacher:
Come forth into the light of things,
Let Nature be your Teacher.

She has a world of ready wealth,
Our minds and hearts to bless—
Spontaneous wisdom breathed by health,
Truth breathed by cheerfulness.

One impulse from a vernal wood
May teach you more of man,
Of moral evil and of good,
Than all the sages can.

Sweet is the lore which Nature brings;
Our meddling intellect
Mis-shapes the beauteous forms of things:—
We murder to dissect.

Enough of Science and of Art;
Close up those barren leaves;
Come forth, and bring with you a heart
That watches and receives.

✓ *Responds to Nature*

LINES

Composed a few miles above Tintern Abbey, on revisiting the banks of
the Wye during a tour. July 13, 1798.

[Composed July 13, 1798.—Published 1798.]

Five years have past; five summers, with the length
Of five long winters! and again I hear
These waters, rolling from their mountain-springs
With a soft inland murmur.—Once again
Do I behold these steep and lofty cliffs,
That on a wild secluded scene impress
Thoughts of more deep seclusion; and connect
The landscape with the quiet of the sky.

The day is come when I again repose
Here, under this dark sycamore, and view
These plots of cottage-ground, these orchard-tufts,
Which at this season, with their unripe fruits,
Are clad in one green hue, and lose themselves
'Mid groves and copses. Once again I see
These hedge-rows, hardy hedge-rows, little lines
Of sportive wood run wild: these pastoral farms,
Green to the very door; and wreaths of smoke
Sent up, in silence, from among the trees!
With some uncertain notice, as might seem
Of vagrant dwellers in the houseless woods,
Or of some Hermit's cave, where by his fire
The Hermit sits alone.

                      These beauteous forms,
Through a long absence, have not been to me
As is a landscape to a blind man's eye:
But oft, in lonely rooms, and 'mid the din
Of towns and cities, I have owed to them,
In hours of weariness, sensations sweet,
Felt in the blood, and felt along the heart;
And passing even into my purer mind,
With tranquil restoration:—feelings too
Of unremembered pleasure: such, perhaps,
As have no slight or trivial influence
On that best portion of a good man's life,
His little, nameless, unremembered, acts
Of kindness and of love. Nor less, I trust,
To them I may have owed another gift,
Of aspect more sublime; that blessed mood,
In which the burthen of the mystery,
In which the heavy and the weary weight
Of all this unintelligible world,
Is lightened:—that serene and blessed mood,
In which the affections gently lead us on,—
Until, the breath of this corporeal frame
And even the motion of our human blood
Almost suspended, we are laid asleep
In body, and become a living soul:

spiritual clairvoyant *business*

While with an eye made quiet by the power
Of harmony, and the deep power of joy,
We see into the life of things.

                                        If this
Be but in vain belief, yet, oh! how oft—
In darkness and amid the many shapes
Of joyless daylight; when the fretful stir
Unprofitable, and the fever of the world,
Have hung upon the beatings of my heart—
How oft, in spirit, have I turned to thee,
O sylvan Wye! thou wanderer thro' the woods,
How often has my spirit turned to thee!

    And now, with gleams of half-extinguished thought,
With many recognitions dim and faint,
And somewhat of a sad perplexity,
The picture of the mind revives again:
While here I stand, not only with the sense
Of present pleasure, but with pleasing thoughts
That in this moment there is life and food
For future years. And so I dare to hope,
Though changed, no doubt, from what I was when first
I came among these hills; when like a roe
I bounded o'er the mountains, by the sides
Of the deep rivers, and the lonely streams,
Wherever nature led: more like a man
Flying from something that he dreads than one
Who sought the thing he loved. For nature then
(The coarser pleasures of my boyish days,
And their glad animal movements all gone by)
To me was all in all.—I cannot paint
What then I was. The sounding cataract
Haunted me like a passion: the tall rock,
The mountain, and the deep and gloomy wood,
Their colours and their forms, were then to me
An apppetite; a feeling and a love,
That had no need of a remoter charm,
By thought supplied, nor any interest

Unborrowed from the eye.—That time is past,
And all its aching joys are now no more,
And all its dizzy raptures. Not for this
Faint I, nor mourn nor murmur; other gifts
Have followed; for such loss, I would believe,
Abundant recompense. For I have learned
To look on nature, not as in the hour
Of thoughtless youth; but hearing often-times
The still, sad music of humanity,
Nor harsh nor grating, though of ample power
To chasten and subdue. And I have felt
A presence that disturbs me with the joy
Of elevated thoughts; a sense sublime
Of something far more deeply interfused,
Whose dwelling is the light of setting suns,
And the round ocean and the living air,
And the blue sky, and in the mind of man:—
A motion and a spirit, that impels
All thinking things, all objects of all thought,
And rolls through all things. Therefore am I still
A lover of the meadows and the woods,
And mountains; and of all that we behold
From this green earth; of all the mighty world
Of eye, and ear,—both what they half create,
And what perceive; well pleased to recognise
In nature and the language of the sense
The anchor of my purest thoughts, the nurse,
The guide, the guardian of my heart, and soul
Of all my moral being.

                              Nor perchance,
If I were not thus taught, should I the more
Suffer my genial spirits to decay:
For thou art with me here upon the banks
Of this fair river; thou my dearest Friend,
My dear, dear Friend; and in thy voice I catch
The language of my former heart, and read
My former pleasures in the shooting lights
Of thy wild eyes. Oh! yet a little while

May I behold in thee what I was once,
My dear, dear Sister! and this prayer I make,
Knowing that Nature never did betray
The heart that loved her; 'tis her privilege,
Through all the years of this our life, to lead
From joy to joy: for she can so inform
The mind that is within us, so impress
With quietness and beauty, and so feed
With lofty thoughts, that neither evil tongues,
Rash judgments, nor the sneers of selfish men,
Nor greetings where no kindness is, nor all
The dreary intercourse of daily life,
Shall e'er prevail against us, or disturb
Our cheerful faith, that all which we behold
Is full of blessings. Therefore let the moon
Shine on thee in thy solitary walk;
And let the misty mountain-winds be free
To blow against thee: and, in after years,
When these wild ecstasies shall be matured
Into a sober pleasure; when thy mind
Shall be a mansion for all lovely forms,
Thy memory be as a dwelling-place
For all sweet sounds and harmonies; oh! then,
If solitude, or fear, or pain, or grief,
Should be thy portion, with what healing thoughts
Of tender joy wilt thou remember me,
And these my exhortations! Nor, perchance—
If I should be where I no more can hear
Thy voice, nor catch from thy wild eyes these gleams
Of past existence—wilt thou then forget
That on the banks of this delightful stream
We stood together; and that I, so long
A worshipper of Nature, hither came
Unwearied in that service: rather say
With warmer love—oh! with far deeper zeal
Of holier love. Nor wilt thou then forget
That after many wanderings, many years
Of absence, these steep woods and lofty cliffs,
And this green pastoral landscape, were to me
More dear, both for themselves and for thy sake!

THE AFFLICTION OF MARGARET——

[Probably composed 1798.—Published 1807.]

I

Where art thou, my beloved Son,
Where art thou, worse to me than dead?
Oh find me, prosperous or undone!
Or, if the grave be now thy bed,
Why am I ignorant of the same
That I may rest; and neither blame
Nor sorrow may attend thy name?

II

Seven years, alas! to have received
No tidings of an only child;
To have despaired, have hoped, believed,
And been for evermore beguiled;
Sometimes with thoughts of very bliss!
I catch at them, and then I miss;
Was ever darkness like to this?

III

He was among the prime in worth,
An object beauteous to behold;
Well born, well bred; I sent him forth
Ingenuous, innocent, and bold:
If things ensued that wanted grace,
As hath been said, they were not base;
And never blush was on my face.

IV

Ah! little doth the young-one dream,
When full of play and childish cares,
What power is in his wildest scream,
Heard by his mother unawares!
He knows it not, he cannot guess:
Years to a mother bring distress;
But do not make her love the less.

V

Neglect me! no, I suffered long
From that ill thought; and, being blind,
Said, "Pride shall help me in my wrong:
Kind mother have I been, as kind
As ever breathed:" and that is true;
I've wet my path with tears like dew,
Weeping for him when no one knew.

VI

My Son, if thou be humbled, poor,
Hopeless of honour and of gain,
Oh! do not dread thy mother's door;
Think not of me with grief and pain:
I now can see with better eyes;
And worldly grandeur I despise,
And fortune with her gifts and lies.

VII

Alas! the fowls of heaven have wings,
And blasts of heaven will aid their flight;
They mount—how short a voyage brings
The wanderers back to their delight!
Chains tie us down by land and sea;
And wishes, vain as mine, may be
All that is left to comfort thee.

VIII

Perhaps some dungeon hears thee groan,
Maimed, mangled by inhuman men;
Or thou upon a desert thrown
Inheritest the lion's den;
Or hast been summoned to the deep,
Thou, thou and all thy mates, to keep
An incommunicable sleep.

IX

I look for ghosts; but none will force
Their way to me: 'tis falsely said

That there was ever intercourse
Between the living and the dead;
For, surely, then I should have sight
Of him I wait for day and night,
With love and longings infinite.

X

My apprehensions come in crowds;
I dread the rustling of the grass;
The very shadows of the clouds
Have power to shake me as they pass:
I question things and do not find
One that will answer to my mind;
And all the world appears unkind.

XI

Beyond participation lie
My troubles, and beyond relief:
If any chance to heave a sigh,
They pity me, and not my grief.
Then come to me, my Son, or send
Some tidings that my woes may end;
I have no other earthly friend!

THE FORSAKEN

[Probably composed 1798.—Published 1842.]

The peace which others seek they find;
The heaviest storms not longest last;
Heaven grants even to the guiltiest mind
An amnesty for what is past;
When will my sentence be reversed?
I only pray to know the worst;
And wish, as if my heart would burst.

O weary struggle! silent years
Tell seemingly no doubtful tale;
And yet they leave it short, and fears
And hopes are strong and will prevail.

My calmest faith escapes not pain;
And, feeling that the hope is vain,
I think that he will come again.

EXTRACT FROM THE PROLOGUE TO PETER BELL

[Composed 1802.—Published 1819.]

"Long have I loved what I behold,
The night that calms, the day that cheers;
The common growth of mother-earth
Suffices me—her tears, her mirth,
Her humblest mirth and tears.

"The dragon's wing, the magic ring,
I shall not covet for my dower,
If I along that lowly way
With sympathetic heart may stray,
And with a soul of power.

"These given, what more need I desire
To stir, to soothe, or elevate?
What nobler marvels than the mind
May in life's daily prospect find,
May find or there create?"

EXTRACT FROM PETER BELL.

[Composed 1798.—Published 1819.]

"He, two-and-thirty years or more,
Had been a wild and woodland rover;
Had heard the Atlantic surges roar
On farthest Cornwall's rocky shore,
And trod the cliffs of Dover.

"And he had seen Caernarvon's towers,
And well he knew the spire of Sarum;
And he had been where Lincoln bell
Flings o'er the fen that ponderous knell—
A far-renowned alarum!

"At Doncaster, at York, and Leeds,
And merry Carlisle had he been;
And all along the Lowlands fair,
All through the bonny shire of Ayr;
And far as Aberdeen.

"And he had been at Inverness;
And Peter, by the mountain-rills,
Had danced his round with Highland lasses;
And he had lain beside his asses
On lofty Cheviot Hills:

"And he had trudged through Yorkshire dales,
Among the rocks and winding *scars;*
Where deep and low the hamlets lie
Beneath their little patch of sky
And little lot of stars:

"And all along the indented coast,
Bespattered with the salt-sea foam;
Where'er a knot of houses lay
On headland, or in hollow bay;—
Sure never man like him did roam!

"As well might Peter in the Fleet
Have been fast bound, a begging debtor;—
He travelled here, he travelled there;—
But not the value of a hair
Was heart or head the better.

"He roved among the vales and streams,
In the green wood and hollow dell;
They were his dwellings night and day,—
But nature ne'er could find the way
Into the heart of Peter Bell.

"In vain, through every changeful year,
Did Nature lead him as before;
A primrose by a river's brim
A yellow primrose was to him,
And it was nothing more.

"Small change it made in Peter's heart
To see his gentle panniered train
With more than vernal pleasure feeding,
Where'er the tender grass was leading
Its earliest green along the lane.

"In vain, through water, earth, and air,
The soul of happy sound was spread,
When Peter on some April morn,
Beneath the broom or budding thorn,
Made the warm earth his lazy bed.

"At noon, when, by the forest's edge
He lay beneath the branches high,
The soft blue sky did never melt
Into his heart; he never felt
The witchery of the soft blue sky!"

NUTTING

[Composed 1799.—Published 1800.]

————————————It seems a day
(I speak of one from many singled out)
One of those heavenly days that cannot die;
When, in the eagerness of boyish hope,
I left our cottage threshold, sallying forth
With a huge wallet o'er my shoulders slung,
A nutting-crook in hand; and turned my steps
Tow'rd some far-distant wood, a Figure quaint,
Tricked out in proud disguise of cast-off weeds
Which for that service had been husbanded,
By exhortation of my frugal Dame—
Motley accoutrement, of power to smile
At thorns, and brakes, and brambles,—and in truth
More ragged than need was! O'er pathless rocks,
Through beds of matted fern, and tangled thickets,
Forcing my way, I came to one dear nook

Unvisited, where not a broken bough
Drooped with its withered leaves, ungracious sign
Of devastation; but the hazels rose
Tall and erect, with tempting clusters hung,
A virgin scene!—A little while I stood,
Breathing with such suppression of the heart
As joy delights in; and with wise restraint
Voluptuous, fearless of a rival, eyed
The banquet;—or beneath the trees I sate
Among the flowers, and with the flowers I played;
A temper known to those who, after long
And weary expectation, have been blest
With sudden happiness beyond all hope.
Perhaps it was a bower beneath whose leaves
The violets of five seasons re-appear
And fade, unseen by any human eye;
Where fairy water-breaks do murmur on
For ever; and I saw the sparkling foam,
And—with my cheek on one of those green stones
That, fleeced with moss, under the shady trees,
Lay round me, scattered like a flock of sheep—
I heard the murmur and the murmuring sound,
In that sweet mood when pleasure loves to pay
Tribute to ease; and, of its joy secure,
The heart luxuriates with indifferent things,
Wasting its kindliness on stocks and stones,
And on the vacant air. Then up I rose,
And dragged to earth both branch and bough, with crash
And merciless ravage: and the shady nook
Of hazels, and the green and mossy bower,
Deformed and sullied, patiently gave up
Their quiet being: and unless I now
Confound my present feelings with the past,
Ere from the mutilated bower I turned
Exulting, rich beyond the wealth of kings,
I felt a sense of pain when I beheld
The silent trees, and saw the intruding sky.—
Then, dearest Maiden, move along these shades
In gentleness of heart; with gentle hand
Touch—for there is a spirit in the woods.

[Composed 1799.—Published 1800.]

Strange fits of passion have I known:
    And I will dare to tell,
But in the Lover's ear alone,
    What once to me befell.

When she I loved looked every day
    Fresh as a rose in June,
I to her cottage bent my way,
    Beneath an evening-moon.

Upon the moon I fixed my eye,
    All over the wide lea;
With quickening pace my horse drew nigh
    Those paths so dear to me.

And now we reached the orchard-plot;
    And, as we climbed the hill,
The sinking moon to Lucy's cot
    Came near, and nearer still.

In one of those sweet dreams I slept,
    Kind Nature's gentlest boon!
And all the while my eyes I kept
    On the descending moon.

My horse moved on; hoof after hoof
    He raised, and never stopped:
When down behind the cottage roof,
    At once, the bright moon dropped.

What fond and wayward thoughts will slide
    Into a Lover's head!
"O mercy!" to myself I cried,
    "If Lucy should be dead!"

[Composed 1799.—Published 1800.]

She dwelt among the untrodden ways
    Beside the springs of Dove,
A Maid whom there were none to praise
    And very few to love:

A violet by a mossy stone
  Half hidden from the eye!
—Fair as a star, when only one
  Is shining in the sky.

She lived unknown, and few could know
  When Lucy ceased to be;
But she is in her grave, and, oh,
  The difference to me!

[Composed 1799.—Published 1800.]

I travelled among unknown men,
  In lands beyond the sea;
Nor, England! did I know till then
  What love I bore to thee.

'Tis past, that melancholy dream!
  Nor will I quit thy shore
A second time; for still I seem
  To love thee more and more.

Among thy mountains did I feel
  The joy of my desire;
And she I cherished turned her wheel
  Beside an English fire.

Thy mornings showed, thy nights concealed,
  The bowers where Lucy played;
And thine too is the last green field
  That Lucy's eyes surveyed.

[Composed 1799.—Published 1800.]

Three years she grew in sun and shower,
Then Nature said, "A lovelier flower
  On earth was never sown;
This Child I to myself will take;
She shall be mine, and I will make
  A Lady of my own.

"Myself will to my darling be
Both law and impulse: and with me
The Girl, in rock and plain,
In earth and heaven, in glade and bower,
Shall feel an overseeing power
To kindle or restrain.

"She shall be sportive as the fawn
That wild with glee across the lawn
Or up the mountain springs;
And hers shall be the breathing balm,
And hers the silence and the calm
Of mute insensate things.

"The floating clouds their state shall lend
To her; for her the willow bend;
Nor shall she fail to see
Even in the motions of the Storm
Grace that shall mould the Maiden's form
By silent sympathy.

"The stars of midnight shall be dear
To her; and she shall lean her ear
In many a secret place
Where rivulets dance their wayward round,
And beauty born of murmuring sound
Shall pass into her face.

"And vital feelings of delight
Shall rear her form to stately height,
Her virgin bosom swell;
Such thoughts to Lucy I will give
While she and I together live
Here in this happy dell."

Thus Nature spake—The work was done—
How soon my Lucy's race was run!
She died, and left to me
This heath, this calm, and quiet scene;
The memory of what has been,
And never more will be.

[Composed 1799.—Published 1800.]

A slumber did my spirit seal;
　I had no human fears:
She seemed a thing that could not feel
　The touch of earthly years.

No motion has she now, no force;
　She neither hears nor sees;
Rolled round in earth's diurnal course,
　With rocks, and stones, and trees.

A POET'S EPITAPH

[Composed 1799.—Published 1800.]

Art thou a Statist in the van
　Of public conflicts trained and bred?
—First learn to love one living man;
　Then may'st thou think upon the dead.

A Lawyer art thou?—draw not nigh!
　Go, carry to some fitter place
The keenness of that practised eye,
　The hardness of that sallow face.

Art thou a Man of purple cheer?
　A rosy Man, right plump to see?
Approach; yet, Doctor, not too near,
　This grave no cushion is for thee.

Or art thou one of gallant pride,
　A Soldier and no man of chaff?
Welcome!—but lay thy sword aside,
　And lean upon a peasant's staff.

Physician art thou?—one, all eyes,
　Philosopher!—a fingering slave,
One that would peep and botanize
　Upon his mother's grave?

Wrapt closely in thy sensual fleece,
   O turn aside,—and take, I pray,
That he below may rest in peace,
   Thy ever-dwindling soul, away!

A Moralist perchance appears;
   Led, Heaven knows how! to this poor sod:
And he has neither eyes nor ears;
   Himself his world, and his own God;

One to whose smooth-rubbed soul can cling
   Nor form, nor feeling, great or small;
A reasoning, self-sufficing thing,
   An intellectual All-in-all!

Shut close the door; press down the latch;
   Sleep in thy intellectual crust;
Nor lose ten tickings of thy watch
   Near this unprofitable dust

But who is He, with modest looks,
   And clad in homely russet brown?
He murmurs near the running brooks
   A music sweeter than their own.

He is retired as noontide dew,
   Or fountain in a noon-day grove;
And you must love him, ere to you
   He will seem worthy of your love.

The outward shows of sky and earth,
   Of hill and valley, he has viewed;
And impulses of deeper birth
   Have come to him in solitude.

In common things that round us lie
   Some random truths he can impart,—
The harvest of a quiet eye
   That broods and sleeps on his own heart.

But he is weak; both Man and Boy,
    Hath been an idler in the land;
Contented if he might enjoy
    The things which others understand.

—Come hither in thy hour of strength;
    Come, weak as is a breaking wave!
Here stretch thy body at full length;
    Or build thy house upon this grave.

MATTHEW

[Composed 1799.—Published 1800.]

In the School of ———— *is a tablet, on which are inscribed, in gilt letters, the Names of the several persons
who have been Schoolmasters there since the foundation
of the School, with the time at which they entered upon
and quitted their office. Opposite to one of those Names
the Author wrote the following lines:*

If Nature, for a favourite child,
    In thee hath tempered so her clay,
That every hour thy heart runs wild,
    Yet never once doth go astray,

Read o'er these lines; and then review
    This tablet, that thus humbly rears
In such diversity of hue
    Its history of two hundred years.

—When through this little wreck of fame,
    Cipher and syllable! thine eye
Has travelled down to Matthew's name,
    Pause with no common sympathy.

And if a sleeping tear should wake,
    Then be it neither checked nor stayed:
For Matthew a request I make
    Which for himself he had not made.

Poor Matthew, all his frolics o'er,
    Is silent as a standing pool;
Far from the chimney's merry roar,
    And murmur of the village school.

The sighs which Matthew heaved were sighs
    Of one tired out with fun and madness;
The tears which came to Matthew's eyes
    Were tears of light, the dew of gladness.

Yet sometimes, when the secret cup
    Of still and serious thought went round,
It seemed as if he drank it up—
    He felt with spirit so profound.

—Thou soul of God's best earthly mould!
    Thou happy Soul! and can it be
That these two words of glittering gold
    Are all that must remain of thee?

THE TWO APRIL MORNINGS

[Composed 1799.—Published 1800.]

We walked along, while bright and red
    Uprose the morning sun;
And Matthew stopped, he looked, and said,
    "The will of God be done!"

A village schoolmaster was he,
    With hair of glittering grey;
As blithe a man as you could see
    On a spring holiday.

And on that morning, through the grass,
    And by the steaming rills,
We travelled merrily, to pass
    A day among the hills.

"Our work," said I, "was well begun,
  Then from thy breast what thought,
Beneath so beautiful a sun,
  So sad a sigh has brought?"

A second time did Matthew stop;
  And fixing still his eye
Upon the eastern mountain-top,
  To me he made reply:

"Yon cloud with that long purple cleft
  Brings fresh into my mind
A day like this which I have left
  Full thirty years behind.

"And just above yon slope of corn
  Such colours, and no other,
Were in the sky, that April morn,
  Of this the very brother.

"With rod and line I sued the sport
  Which that sweet season gave,
And, to the churchyard come, stopped short
  Beside my daughter's grave.

"Nine summers had she scarcely seen,
  The pride of all the vale;
And then she sang;—she would have been
  A very nightingale.

"Six feet in earth my Emma lay;
  And yet I loved her more,
For so it seemed, than till that day
  I e'er had loved before.

"And, turning from her grave, I met,
  Beside the churchyard yew,
A blooming Girl, whose hair was wet
  With points of morning dew.

"A basket on her head she bare;
  Her brow was smooth and white:
To see a child so very fair,
  It was a pure delight!

"No fountain from its rocky cave
  E'er tripped with foot so free;
She seemed as happy as a wave
  That dances on the sea.

"There came from me a sigh of pain
  Which I could ill confine;
I looked at her, and looked again:
  And did not wish her mine!"

Matthew is in his grave, yet now,
  Methinks, I see him stand,
As at that moment, with a bough
  Of wilding in his hand.

THE FOUNTAIN

A CONVERSATION

[Composed 1799.—Published 1800.]

We talked with open heart, and tongue
  Affectionate and true,
A pair of friends, though I was young,
  And Matthew seventy-two.

We lay beneath a spreading oak,
  Beside a mossy seat;
And from the turf a fountain broke,
  And gurgled at our feet.

"Now, Matthew!" said I, "let us match
  This water's pleasant tune
With some old border-song, or catch
  That suits a summer's noon;

"Or of the church-clock and the chimes
  Sing here beneath the shade,
That half-mad thing of witty rhymes
  Which you last April made!"

In silence Matthew lay, and eyed
  The spring beneath the tree;
And thus the dear old Man replied,
  The grey-haired man of glee:

"No check, no stay, this Streamlet fears;
  How merrily it goes!
'Twill murmur on a thousand years,
  And flow as now it flows.

"And here, on this delightful day,
  I cannot choose but think
How oft, a vigorous man, I lay
  Beside this fountain's brink.

"My eyes are dim with childish tears,
  My heart is idly stirred,
For the same sound is in my ears
  Which in those days I heard.

"Thus fares it still in our decay:
  And yet the wiser mind
Mourns less for what age takes away
  Than what it leaves behind.

"The blackbird amid leafy trees,
  The lark above the hill,
Let loose their carols when they please,
  Are quiet when they will.

"With Nature never do *they* wage
  A foolish strife; they see
A happy youth, and their old age
  Is beautiful and free:

"But we are pressed by heavy laws;
 And often, glad no more,
We wear a face of joy, because
 We have been glad of yore.

"If there be one who need bemoan
 His kindred laid in earth,
The household hearts that were his own;
 It is the man of mirth.

"My days, my Friend, are almost gone,
 My life has been approved,
And many love me! but by none
 Am I enough beloved."

"Now both himself and me he wrongs,
 The man who thus complains!
I live and sing my idle songs
 Upon these happy plains;

"And, Matthew, for thy children dead
 I'll be a son to thee!"
At this he grasped my hand, and said,
 "Alas! that cannot be."

We rose up from the fountain-side;
 And down the smooth descent
Of the green sheep-track did we glide;
 And through the wood we went;

And, ere we came to Leonard's rock,
 He sang those witty rhymes
About the crazy old church-clock,
 And the bewildered chimes.

LUCY GRAY

OR, SOLITUDE

[Composed 1799.—Published 1800.]

Oft I had heard of Lucy Gray:
  And, when I crossed the wild,
I chanced to see at break of day
  The solitary child.

No mate, no comrade Lucy knew;
  She dwelt on a wide moor,
—The sweetest thing that ever grew
  Beside a human door!

You yet may spy the fawn at play,
  The hare upon the green;
But the sweet face of Lucy Gray
  Will never more be seen.

"To-night will be a stormy night—
  You to the town must go;
And take a lantern, Child, to light
  Your mother through the snow."

"That, Father! will I gladly do:
  'Tis scarcely afternoon—
The minster-clock has just struck two,
  And yonder is the moon!"

At this the Father raised his hook,
  And snapped a faggot-band;
He plied his work;—and Lucy took
  The lantern in her hand.

Not blither is the mountain roe:
  With many a wanton stroke
Her feet disperse the powdery snow,
  That rises up like smoke.

The storm came on before its time:
  She wandered up and down;
And many a hill did Lucy climb:
  But never reached the town.

The wretched parents all that night
  Went shouting far and wide;
But there was neither sound nor sight
  To serve them for a guide.

At day-break on a hill they stood
  That overlooked the moor;
And thence they saw the bridge of wood,
  A furlong from their door.

They wept—and, turning homeward, cried,
  "In heaven we all shall meet;"
—When in the snow the mother spied
  The print of Lucy's feet.

Then downwards from the steep hill's edge
  They tracked the footmarks small;
And through the broken hawthorn hedge,
  And by the long stone-wall;

And then an open field they crossed:
  The marks were still the same;
They tracked them on, nor ever lost;
  And to the bridge they came.

They followed from the snowy bank
  Those footmarks, one by one,
Into the middle of the plank;
  And further there were none!

—Yet some maintain that to this day
  She is a living child;
That you may see sweet Lucy Gray
  Upon the lonesome wild.

O'er rough and smooth she trips along,
  And never looks behind;
And sings a solitary song
  That whistles in the wind.

RUTH

[Composed 1799.—Published 1800.]

When Ruth was left half desolate,
Her Father took another Mate;
  And Ruth, not seven years old,
A slighted child, at her own will
Went wandering over dale and hill,
  In thoughtless freedom, bold.

And she had made a pipe of straw,
And music from that pipe could draw
  Like sounds of winds and floods;
Had built a bower upon the green,
As if she from her birth had been
  An infant of the woods.

Beneath her father's roof, alone
She seemed to live; her thoughts her own;
  Herself her own delight;
Pleased with herself, nor sad, nor gay;
And, passing thus the live-long day,
  She grew to woman's height.

There came a Youth from Georgia's shore—
A military casque he wore,
  With splendid feathers drest;
He brought them from the Cherokees;
The feathers nodded in the breeze,
  And made a gallant crest.

From Indian blood you deem him sprung:
But no; he spake the English tongue,
  And bore a soldier's name;

And, when America was free
From battle and from jeopardy,
   He 'cross the ocean came.

With hues of genius on his cheek
In finest tones the Youth could speak:
   —While he was yet a boy,
The moon, the glory of the sun,
And streams that murmur as they run,
   Had been his dearest joy.

He was a lovely Youth! I guess
The panther in the wilderness
   Was not so fair as he;
And, when he chose to sport and play,
No dolphin ever was so gay
   Upon the tropic sea.

Among the Indians he had fought,
And with him many tales he brought
   Of pleasure and of fear;
Such tales as told to any maid
By such a Youth, in the green shade,
   Were perilous to hear.

He told of girls—a happy rout!
Who quit their fold with dance and shout,
   Their pleasant Indian town,
To gather strawberries all day long;
Returning with a choral song
   When daylight is gone down.

He spake of plants that hourly change
Their blossoms, through a boundless range
   Of intermingling hues;
With budding, fading, faded flowers
They stand the wonder of the bowers
   From morn to evening dews.

He told of the magnolia, spread
High as a cloud, high over head!
   The cypress and her spire;
—Of flowers that with one scarlet gleam
Cover a hundred leagues, and seem
   To set the hills on fire.

The Youth of green savannahs spake,
And many an endless, endless lake,
   With all its fairy crowds
Of islands, that together lie
As quietly as spots of sky
   Among the evening clouds.

"How pleasant," then he said, "it were
A fisher or a hunter there,
   In sunshine or in shade
To wander with an easy mind;
And build a household fire, and find
   A home in every glade!

"What days and what bright years! Ah me!
Our life were life indeed, with thee
   So passed in quiet bliss,
And all the while," said he, "to know
That we were in a world of woe,
   On such an earth as this!"

And then he sometimes interwove
Fond thoughts about a father's love:
   "For there," said he, "are spun
Around the heart such tender ties,
That our own children to our eyes
   Are dearer than the sun.

"Sweet Ruth! and could you go with me
My helpmate in the woods to be,
   Our shed at night to rear;
Or run, my own adopted bride,
A sylvan huntress at my side,
   And drive the flying deer!

"Beloved Ruth!"—No more he said.
The wakeful Ruth at midnight shed
  A solitary tear:
She thought again—and did agree
With him to sail across the sea,
  And drive the flying deer.

"And now, as fitting is and **right**,
We in the church our faith will **plight,**
  A husband and a wife."
Even so they did; and I may say
That to sweet Ruth that happy day
  Was more than human life.

Through dream and vision did she sink,
Delighted all the while to think
  That on those lonesome floods,
And green savannahs, she should share
His board with lawful joy, and bear
  His name in the wild woods.

But, as you have before been told,
This Stripling, sportive, gay, and bold,
  And, with his dancing crest,
So beautiful, through savage lands
Had roamed about, with vagrant bands
  Of Indians in the West.

The wind, the tempest roaring high,
The tumult of a tropic sky,
  Might well be dangerous food
For him, a Youth to whom was given
So much of earth—so much of heaven,
  And such impetuous blood.

Whatever in those climes he found
Irregular in sight or sound
  Did to his mind impart
A kindred impulse, seemed allied
To his own powers, and justified
  The workings of his heart.

Nor less, to feed voluptuous thought,
The beauteous forms of nature wrought,
 Fair trees and gorgeous flowers;
The breezes their own languor lent;
The stars had feelings, which they sent
 Into those favoured bowers.

Yet, in his worst pursuits I ween
That sometimes there did intervene
 Pure hopes of high intent:
For passions linked to forms so fair
And stately needs must have their share
 Of noble sentiment.

But ill he lived, much evil saw,
With men to whom no better law
 Nor better life was known;
Deliberately, and undeceived,
Those wild men's vices he received,
 And gave them back his own.

His genius and his moral frame
Were thus impaired, and he became
 The slave of low desires:
A Man who without self-control
Would seek what the degraded soul
 Unworthily admires.

And yet he with no feigned delight
Had wooed the Maiden, day and night
 Had loved her, night and morn:
What could he less than love a Maid
Whose heart with so much nature played?
 So kind and so forlorn!

Sometimes, most earnestly, he said,
"O Ruth! I have been worse than dead;
 False thoughts, thoughts bold and vain,
Encompassed me on every side
When I, in confidence and pride,
 Had crossed the Atlantic main.

"Before me shone a glorious world—
Fresh as a banner bright, unfurled
    To music suddenly:
I looked upon those hills and plains,
And seemed as if let loose from chains,
    To live at liberty.

"No more of this; for now, by thee
Dear Ruth! more happily set free
    With nobler zeal I burn;
My soul from darkness is released,
Like the whole sky when to the east
    The morning doth return."

Full soon that better mind was gone:
No hope, no wish remained, not one,—
    They stirred him now no more;
New objects did new pleasure give,
And once again he wished to live
    As lawless as before.

Meanwhile, as thus with him it fared,
They for the voyage were prepared,
    And went to the sea-shore,
But, when they thither came, the Youth
Deserted his poor Bride, and Ruth
    Could never find him more.

God help thee, Ruth!—Such pains she had,
That she in half a year was mad,
    And in a prison housed;
And there, with many a doleful song
Made of wild words, her cup of wrong
    She fearfully caroused.

Yet sometimes milder hours she knew,
Nor wanted sun, nor rain, nor dew,
    Nor pastimes of the May;
—They all were with her in her cell;
And a clear brook with cheerful knell
    Did o'er the pebbles play.

When Ruth three seasons thus had lain,
There came a respite to her pain;
    She from her prison fled;
But of the Vagrant none took thought;
And where it liked her best she sought
    Her shelter and her bread.

Among the fields she breathed again:
The master-current of her brain
    Ran permanent and free;
And, coming to the Banks of Tone,
There did she rest; and dwell alone
    Under the greenwood tree.

The engines of her pain, the tools
That shaped her sorrow, rocks and pools,
    And airs that gently stir
The vernal leaves—she loved them still;
Nor ever taxed them with the ill
    Which had been done to her.

A Barn her *winter* bed supplies;
But, till the warmth of summer skies
    And summer days is gone,
(And all do in this tale agree)
She sleeps beneath the greenwood tree,
    And other home hath none.

An innocent life, yet far astray!
And Ruth will, long before her day,
    Be broken down and old:
Sore aches she needs must have! but less
Of mind than body's wretchedness,
    From damp, and rain, and cold.

If she is prest by want of food,
She from her dwelling in the wood
    Repairs to a road-side;
And there she begs at one steep place
Where up and down with easy pace
    The horsemen-travellers ride.

That oaten pipe of hers is mute,
Or thrown away; but with a flute
   Her loneliness she cheers:
This flute, made of a hemlock stalk,
At evening in his homeward walk
   The Quantock woodman hears.

I, too, have passed her on the hills
Setting her little water-mills
   By spouts and fountains wild—
Such small machinery as she turned
Ere she had wept, ere she had mourned,
   A young and happy Child!

Farewell! and when thy days are told,
Ill-fated Ruth, in hallowed mould
   Thy corpse shall buried be,
For thee a funeral bell shall ring,
And all the congregation sing
   A Christian psalm for thee.

FRAGMENT OF THE RECLUSE

"ON NATURE'S INVITATION DO I COME"

[Composed probably in 1800.—Published 1851.]

On Nature's invitation do I come,
By Reason sanctioned. Can the choice mislead,
That made the calmest, fairest spot on earth,
With all its unappropriated good,
My own; and not mine only, for with me
Entrenched—say rather peacefully embowered—
Under yon orchard, in yon humble cot,
A younger orphan of a Home extinct,
The only daughter of my parents dwells:
Aye, think on that, my heart, and cease to stir;
Pause upon that, and let the breathing frame
No longer breathe, but all be satisfied.
Oh, if such silence be not thanks to God

For what hath been bestowed, then where, where then
Shall gratitude find rest?   Mine eyes did ne'er
Fix on a lovely object, nor my mind
Take pleasure in the midst of happy thoughts,
But either she, whom now I have, who now
Divides with me this loved abode, was there,
Or not far off.   Where'er my footsteps turned,
Her voice was like a hidden Bird that sang;
The thought of her was like a flash of light
Or an unseen companionship, a breath
Or fragrance independent of the wind.
In all my goings, in the new and old
Of all my meditations, and in this
Favourite of all, in this the most of all. . . .
Embrace me then, ye hills, and close me in.
Now in the clear and open day I feel
Your guardianship: I take it to my heart;
'Tis like the solemn shelter of the night.
But I would call thee beautiful: for mild,
And soft, and gay, and beautiful thou art,
Dear valley, having in thy face a smile,
Though peaceful, full of gladness.   Thou art pleased,
Pleased with thy crags, and woody steeps, thy Lake,
Its one green Island, and its winding shores,
The multitude of little rocky hills,
Thy Church, and cottages of mountain-stone
Clustered like stars some few, but single most,
And lurking dimly in their shy retreats,
Or glancing at each other cheerful looks,
Like separated stars with clouds between.

FRAGMENT OF THE RECLUSE

"BLEAK SEASON WAS IT, TURBULENT AND WILD"

[Composed (probably) in 1800.—Published 1851.]

Bleak season was it, turbulent and wild,
When hitherward we journeyed, side by side,
Through bursts of sunshine and through flying showers
Paced the long Vales, how long they were, and yet

How fast that length of way was left behind,
Wensley's rich Vale and Sedbergh's naked heights.
The frosty wind, as if to make amends
For its keen breath, was aiding to our steps,
And drove us onward as two ships at sea;
Or, like two birds, companions in mid-air,
Parted and reunited by the blast.
Stern was the face of nature; we rejoiced
In that stern countenance; for our souls thence drew
A feeling of their strength. The naked trees,
The icy brooks, as on we passed, appeared
To question us, "Whence come ye? To what end?"

FRAGMENT OF THE RECLUSE

[Composed possibly in 1800.—Published in the Preface to the Excursion, 1814.]

"On Man, on Nature, and on Human Life,
Musing in solitude, I oft perceive
Fair trains of imagery before me rise,
Accompanied by feelings of delight
Pure, or with no unpleasing sadness mixed;
And I am conscious of affecting thoughts
And dear remembrances, whose presence soothes
Or elevates the Mind, intent to weigh
The good and evil of our mortal state.
—To these emotions, whencesoe'er they come,
Whether from breath of outward circumstance,
Or from the Soul—an impulse to herself—
I would give utterance in numerous verse.
Of Truth, of Grandeur, Beauty, Love, and Hope,
And melancholy Fear subdued by Faith;
Of blessed consolations in distress;
Of moral strength, and intellectual Power;
Of joy in widest commonalty spread;
Of the individual Mind that keeps her own
Inviolate retirement, subject there
To Conscience only, and the law supreme
Of that Intelligence which governs all—
I sing:—'fit audience let me find though few!'

"So prayed, more gaining than he asked, the Bard—
In holiest mood. Urania, I shall need
Thy guidance, or a greater Muse, if such
Descend to earth or dwell in highest heaven!
For I must tread on shadowy ground, must sink
Deep—and, aloft ascending, breathe in worlds
To which the heaven of heavens is but a veil.
All strength—all terror, single or in bands,
That ever was put forth in personal form—
Jehovah—with his thunder, and the choir
Of shouting Angels, and the empyreal thrones—
I pass them unalarmed. Not Chaos, not
The darkest pit of lowest Erebus,
Nor aught of blinder vacancy, scooped out
By help of dreams—can breed such fear and awe
As fall upon us often when we look
Into our Minds, into the Mind of Man—
My haunt, and the main region of my song.
—Beauty—a living Presence of the earth,
Surpassing the most fair ideal Forms
Which craft of delicate Spirits hath composed
From earth's materials—waits upon my steps;
Pitches her tents before me as I move,
An hourly neighbour. Paradise, and groves
Elysian, Fortunate Fields—like those of old
Sought in the Atlantic Main—why should they be
A history only of departed things,
Or a mere fiction of what never was?
For the discerning intellect of Man,
When wedded to this goodly universe
In love and holy passion, shall find these
A simple produce of the common day.
—I, long before the blissful hour arrives,
Would chant, in lonely peace, the spousal verse
Of this great consummation:—and, by words
Which speak of nothing more than what we are,
Would I arouse the sensual from their sleep
Of Death, and win the vacant and the vain
To noble raptures; while my voice proclaims
How exquisitely the individual Mind

(And the progressive powers perhaps no less
Of the whole species) to the external World
Is fitted:—and how exquisitely, too—
Theme this but little heard of among men—
The external World is fitted to the Mind;
And the creation (by no lower name
Can it be called) which they with blended might
Accomplish:—this is our highest argument.
—Such grateful haunts foregoing, if I oft
Must turn elsewhere—to travel near the tribes
And fellowships of men, and see ill sights
Of madding passions mutually inflamed;
Must hear Humanity in fields and groves
Pipe solitary anguish; or must hang
Brooding above the fierce confederate storm
Of sorrow, barricadoed evermore
Within the walls of cities—may these sounds
Have their authentic comment; that even these
Hearing, I be not downcast or forlorn!—
Descend, prophetic Spirit! that inspir'st
The human Soul of universal earth,
Dreaming on things to come; and dost possess
A metropolitan temple in the hearts
Of mighty Poets: upon me bestow
A gift of genuine insight; that my Song
With star-like virtue in its place may shine,
Shedding benignant influence, and secure,
Itself, from all malevolent effect
Of those mutations that extend their sway
Throughout the nether sphere!—And if with this
I mix more lowly matter; with the thing
Contemplated, describe the Mind and Man
Contemplating; and who, and what he was—
The transitory Being that beheld
This Vision; when and where, and how he lived;—
Be not this labour useless. If such theme
May sort with highest objects, then—dread Power!
Whose gracious favour is the primal source
Of all illumination,—may my Life
Express the image of a better time.

More wise desires, and simpler manners;—nurse
My Heart in genuine freedom:—all pure thoughts
Be with me;—so shall thy unfailing love
Guide, and support, and cheer me to the end!"

THE BROTHERS

[Composed (in or about) February, 1800.—Published 1800.]

"These Tourists, heaven preserve us! needs must live
A profitable life: some glance along,
Rapid and gay, as if the earth were air,
And they were butterflies to wheel about
Long as the summer lasted: some, as wise,
Perched on the forehead of a jutting crag,
Pencil in hand and book upon the knee,
Will look and scribble, scribble on and look,
Until a man might travel twelve stout miles,
Or reap an acre of his neighbour's corn.
But, for that moping son of Idleness,
Why can he tarry *yonder?*—In our churchyard
Is neither epitaph nor monument,
Tombstone nor name—only the turf we tread
And a few natural graves."

                                    To Jane, his wife,
Thus spake the homely Priest of Ennerdale.
It was a July evening; and he sate
Upon the long stone-seat beneath the eaves
Of his old cottage,—as it chanced, that day,
Employed in winter's work. Upon the stone
His wife sate near him, teasing matted wool,
While, from the twin cards toothed with glittering wire,
He fed the spindle of his youngest child,
Who, in the open air, with due accord
Of busy hands and back-and-forward steps,
Her large round wheel was turning. Towards the field
In which the Parish Chapel stood alone,

Girt round with a bare ring of mossy wall,
While half an hour went by, the Priest had sent
Many a long look of wonder: and at last,
Risen from his seat, beside the snow-white ridge
Of carded wool which the old man had piled
He laid his implements with gentle care,
Each in the other locked; and down the path,
That from his cottage to the church-yard led,
He took his way, impatient to accost
The Stranger, whom he saw still lingering there.

'Twas one well known to him in former days,
A Shepherd-lad; who ere his sixteenth year
Had left that calling, tempted to entrust
His expectations to the fickle winds
And perilous waters; with the mariners
A fellow-mariner; and so had fared
Through twenty seasons; but he had been reared
Among the mountains, and he in his heart
Was half a shepherd on the stormy seas.
Oft in the piping shrouds had Leonard heard
The tones of waterfalls, and inland sounds
Of caves and trees:—and when the regular wind
Between the tropics filled the steady sail,
And blew with the same breath through days and
          weeks,
Lengthening invisibly its weary line
Along the cloudless Main, he, in those hours
Of tiresome indolence, would often hang
Over the vessel's side, and gaze and gaze;
And, while the broad blue wave and sparkling foam
Flashed round him images and hues that wrought
In union with the employment of his heart,
He, thus by feverish passion overcome,
Even with the organs of his bodily eye,
Below him, in the bosom of the deep,
Saw mountains; saw the forms of sheep that grazed
On verdant hills—with dwellings among trees,
And shepherds clad in the same country grey
Which he himself had worn.

                And now, at last,
From perils manifold, with some small wealth
Acquired by traffic 'mid the Indian Isles,
To his paternal home he is returned,
With a determined purpose to resume
The life he had lived there; both for the sake
Of many darling pleasures, and the love
Which to an only brother he has borne
In all his hardships, since that happy time
When, whether it blew foul or fair, they two
Were brother-shepherds on their native hills.
—They were the last of all their race: and now,
When Leonard had approached his home, his heart
Failed in him; and, not venturing to enquire
Tidings of one so long and dearly loved,
He to the solitary church-yard turned;
That, as he knew in what particular spot
His family were laid, he thence might learn
If still his Brother lived, or to the file
Another grave was added.—He had found
Another grave,—near which a full half-hour
He had remained; but, as he gazed, there grew
Such a confusion in his memory,
That he began to doubt; and even to hope
That he had seen this heap of turf before,—
That it was not another grave; but one
He had forgotten. He had lost his path,
As up the vale, that afternoon, he walked
Through fields which once had been well known to
       him:
And oh what joy this recollection now
Sent to his heart! he lifted up his eyes,
And, looking round, imagined that he saw
Strange alteration wrought on every side
Among the woods and fields, and that the rocks,
And everlasting hills themselves were changed.

    By this the Priest, who down the field had come,
Unseen by Leonard, at the church-yard gate
Stopped short,—and thence, at leisure, limb by limb
Perused him with a gay complacency.

Ay, thought the Vicar, smiling to himself,
'Tis one of those who needs must leave the path
Of the world's business to go wild alone:
His arms have a perpetual holiday;
The happy man will creep about the fields,
Following his fancies by the hour, to bring
Tears down his cheek, or solitary smiles
Into his face, until the setting sun
Write fool upon his forehead.—Planted thus
Beneath a shed that over-arched the gate
Of this rude church-yard, till the stars appeared
The good Man might have communed with himself,
But that the Stranger, who had left the grave,
Approached; he recognized the Priest at once,
And, after greetings interchanged, and given
By Leonard to the Vicar as to one
Unknown to him, this dialogue ensued.
    Leonard. You live, Sir, in these dales, a quiet life:
Your years make up one peaceful family;
And who would grieve and fret, if, welcome come
And welcome gone, they are so like each other,
They cannot be remembered? Scarce a funeral
Comes to this church-yard once in eighteen months;
And yet, some changes must take place among you:
And you, who dwell here, even among these rocks,
Can trace the finger of mortality,
And see, that with our threescore years and ten
We are not all that perish——I remember,
(For many years ago I passed this road)
There was a foot-way all along the fields
By the brook-side—'tis gone—and that dark cleft!
To me it does not seem to wear the face
Which then it had!
    Priest. Nay Sir, for aught I know,
That chasm is much the same—
    Leonard. But, surely, yonder—
    Priest. Ay, there, indeed, your memory is a friend
That does not play you false.—On that tall pike
(It is the loneliest place of all these hills)
There were two springs which bubbled side by side,
As if they had been made that they might be

Companions for each other: the huge crag
Was rent with lightning—one hath disappeared;
The other, left behind, is flowing still.
For accident and changes such as these,
We want not store of them;—a waterspout
Will bring down half a mountain; what a feast
For folks that wander up and down like you,
To see an acre's breadth of that wide cliff
One roaring cataract! a sharp May-storm
Will come with loads of January snow,
And in one night send twenty score of sheep
To feed the ravens; or a shepherd dies
By some untoward death among the rocks:
The ice breaks up and sweeps away a bridge;
A wood is felled:—and then for our own homes!
A child is born or christened, a field ploughed
A daughter sent to service, a web spun,
The old house-clock is decked with a new face;
And hence, so far from wanting facts or dates
To chronicle the time, we all have here
A pair of diaries,—one serving, Sir,
For the whole dale, and one for each fire-side—
Yours was a stranger's judgment: for historians,
Commend me to these valleys!
  Leonard. Yet your Church-yard
Seems, if such freedom may be used with you,
To say that you are heedless of the past:
An orphan could not find his mother's grave:
Here's neither head nor foot-stone, plate of brass,
Cross-bones nor skull,—type of our earthly state
Nor emblem of our hopes: the dead man's home
Is but a fellow to that pasture-field.
  Priest. Why, there, Sir, is a thought that's new
    to me!
The stone-cutters, 'tis true, might beg their bread
If every English church-yard were like ours;
Yet your conclusion wanders from the truth:
We have no need of names and epitaphs;
We talk about the dead by our fire-sides.
And then, for our immortal part! *we* want
No symbols, Sir, to tell us that plain tale:

The thought of death sits easy on the man
Who has been born and dies among the mountains.
    Leonard. Your Dalesman, then, do in each other's
        thoughts
Possess a kind of second life: no doubt
You, Sir, could help me to the history
Of half these graves?
    Priest. For eight-score winters past,
With what I've witnessed, and with what I've heard,
Perhaps I might; and, on a winter evening,
If you were seated at my chimney's nook,
By turning o'er these hillocks one by one,
We two could travel, Sir, through a strange round;
Yet all in the broad highway of the world.
Now there's a grave—your foot is half upon it,—
It looks just like the rest; and yet that man
Died broken-hearted.
    Leonard. 'Tis a common case.
We'll take another: who is he that lies
Beneath yon ridge, the last of those three graves?
It touches on that piece of native rock
Left in the church-yard wall.
    Priest. That's Walter Ewbank.
He had as white a head and fresh a cheek
As ever were produced by youth and age
Engendering in the blood of hale fourscore.
Through five long generations had the heart
Of Walter's forefathers o'erflowed the bounds
Of their inheritance, that single cottage—
You see it yonder! and those few green fields.
They toiled and wrought, and still, from sire to son,
Each struggled, and each yielded as before
A little—yet a little,—and old Walter.
They left to him the family heart, and land
With other burthens than the crop it bore.
Year after year the old man still kept up
A cheerful mind,—and buffeted with bond,
Interest, and mortgages; at last he sank,
And went into his grave before his time.
Poor Walter! whether it was care that spurred him
God only knows, but to the very last

He had the lightest foot in Ennerdale:
His pace was never that of an old man:
I almost see him tripping down the path
With his two grandsons after him:—but you,
Unless our Landlord be your host tonight,
Have far to travel,—and on these rough paths
Even in the longest day of midsummer—
 Leonard. But those two Orphans!
 Priest. Orphans!—Such they were—
Yet not while Walter lived:—for, though their parents
Lay buried side by side as now they lie,
The old man was a father to the boys,
Two fathers in one father: and if tears,
Shed when he talked of them where they were not,
And hauntings from the infirmity of love,
Are aught of what makes up a mother's heart,
This old Man, in the day of his old age,
Was half a mother to them.—If you weep, Sir,
To hear a stranger talking about strangers,
Heaven bless you when you are among your kindred!
Ay—you may turn that way—it is a grave
Which will bear looking at.
 Leonard.—These boys—I hope
They loved this good old Man?—
 Priest. They did—and truly:
But that was what we almost overlooked,
They were such darlings of each other. Yes,
Though from the cradle they had lived with Walter,
The only kinsman near them, and though he
Inclined to both by reason of his age,
With a more fond, familiar, tenderness;
They, notwithstanding, had much love to spare,
And it all went into each other's hearts.
Leonard, the elder by just eighteen months,
Was two years taller: 'twas a joy to see,
To hear, to meet them!—From their house the school
Is distant three short miles, and in the time
Of storm and thaw, when every watercourse
And unbridged stream, such as you may have noticed
Crossing our roads at every hundred steps,
Was swoln into a noisy rivulet,

Would Leonard then, when elder boys remained
At home, go staggering through the slippery fords,
Bearing his brother on his back. I have seen him,
On windy days, in one of those stray brooks,
Ay, more than once I have seen him, mid-leg deep,
Their two books lying both on a dry stone,
Upon the hither side: and once I said,
As I remember, looking round these rocks
And hills on which we all of us were born,
That God who made the great book of the world
Would bless such piety—
    Leonard. It may be then—
    Priest. Never did worthier lads break English
        bread;
The very brightest Sunday Autumn saw,
With all its mealy clusters of ripe nuts,
Could never keep those boys away from church,
Or tempt them to an hour of sabbath breach.
Leonard and James! I warrant, every corner
Among these rocks, and every hollow place
That venturous foot could reach, to one or both
Was known as well as to the flowers that grow there.
Like roe-bucks they went bounding o'er the hills;
They played like two young ravens on the crags:
Then they could write, ay, and speak too, as well
As many of their betters—and for Leonard!
The very night before he went away,
In my own house I put into his hand
A Bible, and I'd wager house and field
That, if he be alive, he has it yet.
    Leonard. It seems, these Brothers have not lived
        to be
A comfort to each other—
    Priest. That they might
Live to such end is what both old and young
In this our valley all of us have wished,
And what, for my part, I have often prayed:
But Leonard—
    Leonard. Then James still is left among you!
    Priest. 'Tis of the elder brother I am speaking:
They had an uncle;—he was at that time

A thriving man, and trafficked on the seas:
And, but for that same uncle, to this hour
Leonard had never handled rope or shroud:
For the boy loved the life which we lead here;
And though of unripe years, a stripling only,
His soul was knit to this his native soil.
But, as I said, old Walter was too weak
To strive with such a torrent; when he died,
The estate and house were sold; and all their sheep,
A pretty flock, and which, for aught I know,
Had clothed the Ewbanks for a thousand years:—
Well—all was gone, and they were destitute,
And Leonard, chiefly for his Brother's sake,
Resolved to try his fortune on the seas.
Twelve years are past since we had tidings from him.
If there were one among us who had heard
That Leonard Ewbank was come home again,
From the Great Gavel, down by Leeza's banks,
And down the Enna, far as Egremont,
The day would be a joyous festival;
And those two bells of ours, which there you see—
Hanging in the open air—but, O good Sir!
This is sad talk—they'll never sound for him—
Living or dead.—when last we heard of him,
He was in slavery among the Moors
Upon the Barbary coast.—'Twas not a little
That would bring down his spirit; and no doubt,
Before it ended in his death, the Youth
Was sadly crossed.—Poor Leonard! when we parted,
He took me by the hand, and said to me,
If e'er he should grow rich, he would return,
To live in peace upon his father's land,
And lay his bones among us.
        Leonard. If that day
Should come, 'twould needs be a glad day for him;
He would himself, no doubt, be happy then
As any that should meet him—
        Priest. Happy! Sir—
        Leonard.—You said his kindred all were in their
            graves,

And that he had one Brother—
   Priest. That is but
A fellow-tale of sorrow. From his youth
James, though not sickly, yet was delicate;
And Leonard being always by his side
Had done so many offices about him,
That, though he was not of a timid nature,
Yet still the spirit of a mountain-boy
In him was somewhat checked; and, when his Brother
Was gone to sea, and he was left alone,
The little colour that he had was soon
Stolen from his cheek; he drooped, and pined, and
     pined—
   Leonard. But these are all the graves of full-grown
     men!
   Priest. Ay, Sir, that passed away: we took him
     to us;
He was the child of all the dale—he lived
Three months with one, and six months with another;
And wanted neither food, nor clothes, nor love:
And many, many happy days were his.
But, whether blithe or sad, 'tis my belief
His absent Brother still was at his heart.
And, when he dwelt beneath our roof, we found
(A practice till this time unknown to him)
That often, rising from his bed at night,
He in his sleep would walk about, and sleeping,
He sought his brother Leonard.—You are moved!
Forgive me, Sir: before I spoke to you,
I judged you most unkindly.
   Leonard. But this Youth,
How did he die at last?
   Priest. One sweet May-morning,
(It will be twelve years since when Spring returns)
He had gone forth among the new-dropped lambs,
With two or three companions, whom their course
Of occupation led from height to height
Under a cloudless sun—till he, at length,
Through weariness, or, haply, to indulge
The humour of the moment, lagged behind.
You see yon precipice;—it wears the shape

Of a vast building made of many crags;
And in the midst is one particular rock
That rises like a column from the vale,
Whence by our shepherds it is called THE PILLAR.
Upon its aëry summit crowned with heath,
The loiterer, not unnoticed by his comrades,
Lay stretched at ease; but, passing by the place
On their return, they found that he was gone.
No ill was feared; till one of them by chance
Entering, when evening was far spent, the house
Which at that time was James's home, there learned
That nobody had seen him all that day:
The morning came, and still he was unheard of:
The neighbours were alarmed, and to the brook
Some hastened; some ran to the lake: ere noon
They found him at the foot of that same rock
Dead, and with mangled limbs. The third day after
I buried him, poor Youth, and there he lies!

   Leonard. And that then *is* his grave!—Before his
    death
You say that he saw many happy years?
   Priest. Ay, that he did—
   Leonard. And all went well with him?—
   Priest. If he had one, the Youth had twenty
    homes.
   Leonard. And you believe, then, that his mind
    was easy?—
   Priest. Yes, long before he died, he found that
    time
Is a true friend to sorrow; and, unless
His thoughts were turned on Leonard's luckless for-
   tune,
He talked about him with a cheerful love.
   Leonard. He could not come to an unhallowed
    end!
   Priest. Nay, God forbid!—You recollect I men-
    tioned
A habit which disquietude and grief
Had brought upon him; and we all conjectured
That, as the day was warm, he had lain down
On the soft heath,—and, waiting for his comrades,

He there had fallen asleep; that in his sleep
He to the margin of the precipice
Had walked, and from the summit had fallen head-
        long:
And so no doubt he perished. When the Youth
Fell, in his hand he must have grasped, we think,
His shepherd's staff; for on that Pillar of rock
It had been caught mid-way; and there for years
It hung;—and mouldered there.
               The Priest here ended—
The Stranger would have thanked him, but he felt
A gushing from his heart, that took away
The power of speech. Both left the spot in silence;
And Leonard, when they reached the church-yard
        gate,
As the Priest lifted up the latch, turned round,—
And, looking at the grave, he said, "My Brother!"
The Vicar did not hear the words: and now
He pointed towards his dwelling-place, entreating
That Leonard would partake his homely fare:
The other thanked him with an earnest voice;
But added, that the evening being calm,
He would pursue his journey. So they parted.

It was not long ere Leonard reached a grove
That overhung the road: he there stopped short,
And, sitting down beneath the trees, reviewed
All that the Priest had said: his early years
Were with him:—his long absence, cherished hopes,
And thoughts which had been his an hour before,
All pressed on him with such a weight, that now,
This vale, where he had been so happy, seemed
A place in which he could not bear to live:
So he relinquished all his purposes.
He travelled back to Egremont: and thence,
That night, he wrote a letter to the Priest,
Reminding him of what had passed between them;
And adding, with a hope to be forgiven,
That it was from the weakness of his heart
He had not dared to tell him who he was.
This done, he went on shipboard, and is now
A seaman, a grey-headed Mariner.

MICHAEL

A PASTORAL POEM

[Composed October 11–December 9, 1800.—Published 1800.]

If from the public way you turn your steps
Up the tumultuous brook of Green-head Ghyll,
You will suppose that with an upright path
Your feet must struggle; in such bold ascent
The pastoral mountains front you, face to face.
But, courage! for around that boisterous brook
The mountains have all opened out themselves,
And made a hidden valley of their own.
No habitation can be seen; but they
Who journey thither find themselves alone
With a few sheep, with rocks and stones, and kites
That overhead are sailing in the sky.
It is in truth an utter solitude;
Nor should I have made mention of this Dell
But for one object which you might pass by,
Might see and notice not. Beside the brook
Appears a straggling heap of unhewn stones!
And to that simple object appertains
A story—unenriched with strange events,
Yet not unfit, I deem, for the fireside,
Or for the summer shade. It was the first
Of those domestic tales that spake to me
Of Shepherds, dwellers in the valleys, men
Whom I already loved;—not verily
For their own sakes, but for the fields and hills
Where was their occupation and abode.
And hence this Tale, while I was yet a Boy
Careless of books, yet having felt the power
Of Nature, by the gentle agency
Of natural objects, led me on to feel
For passions that were not my own, and think
(At random and imperfectly indeed)
On man, the heart of man, and human life.
Therefore, although it be a history
Homely and rude, I will relate the same
For the delight of a few natural hearts;

And, with yet fonder feelings, for the sake
Of youthful Poets, who among these hills
Will be my second self when I am gone.

Upon the forest-side in Grasmere Vale
There dwelt a Shepherd, Michael was his name;
An old man, stout of heart, and strong of limb.
His bodily frame had been from youth to age
Of an unusual strength: his mind was keen,
Intense, and frugal, apt for all affairs,
And in his shepherd's calling he was prompt
And watchful more than ordinary men.
Hence had he learned the meaning of all winds,
Of blasts of every tone; and oftentimes,
When others heeded not, He heard the South
Make subterraneous music, like the noise
Of bagpipers on distant Highland hills.
The Shepherd, at such warning, of his flock
Bethought him, and he to himself would say,
"The winds are now devising work for me!"
And, truly, at all times, the storm, that drives
The traveller to a shelter, summoned him
Up to the mountains: he had been alone
Amid the heart of many thousand mists,
That came to him, and left him, on the heights.
So lived he till his eightieth year was past.
And grossly that man errs, who should suppose
That the green valleys, and the streams and rocks,
Were things indifferent to the Shepherd's thoughts.
Fields, where with cheerful spirits he had breathed
The common air; hills, which with vigorous step
He had so often climbed; which had impressed
So many incidents upon his mind
Of hardship, skill or courage, joy or fear;
Which, like a book, preserved the memory
Of the dumb animals, whom he had saved,
Had fed or sheltered, linking to such acts
The certainty of honourable gain;
Those fields, those hills—what could they less? had
          laid
Strong hold on his affections, were to him

A pleasurable feeling of blind love,
The pleasure which there is in life itself.

His days had not been passed in singleness.
His Helpmate was a comely matron, old—
Though younger than himself full twenty years.
She was a woman of a stirring life,
Whose heart was in her house: two wheels she had
Of antique form; this large, for spinning wool;
That small, for flax; and, if one wheel had rest,
It was because the other was at work.
The Pair had but one inmate in their house,
An only Child, who had been born to them
When Michael, telling o'er his years, began
To deem that he was old,—in shepherd's phrase,
With one foot in the grave. This only Son,
With two brave sheep-dogs tried in many a storm,
The one of an inestimable worth,
Made all their household. I may truly say,
That they were as a proverb in the vale
For endless industry. When day was gone,
And from their occupations out of doors
The Son and Father were come home, even then,
Their labour did not cease; unless when all
Turned to the cleanly supper-board, and there,
Each with a mess of pottage and skimmed milk,
Sat round the basket piled with oaten cakes,
And their plain home-made cheese. Yet when the
          meal
Was ended, Luke (for so the Son was named)
And his old Father both betook themselves
To such convenient work as might employ
Their hands by the fire-side; perhaps to card
Wool for the Housewife's spindle, or repair
Some injury done to sickle, flail, or scythe,
Or other implement of house or field.

Down from the ceiling, by the chimney's edge,
That in our ancient uncouth country style
With huge and black projection overbrowed
Large space beneath, as duly as the light

Of day grew dim the Housewife hung a lamp;
An aged utensil, which had performed
Service beyond all others of its kind.
Early at evening did it burn—and late,
Surviving comrade of uncounted hours,
Which, going by from year to year, had found,
And left, the couple neither gay perhaps
Nor cheerful, yet with objects and with hopes,
Living a life of eager industry.
And now, when Luke had reached his eighteenth year,
There by the light of this old lamp they sate,
Father and Son, while far into the night
The Housewife plied her own peculiar work,
Making the cottage through the silent hours
Murmur as with the sound of summer flies.
This light was famous in its neighbourhood,
And was a public symbol of the life
That thrifty Pair had lived. For, as it chanced,
Their cottage on a plot of rising ground
Stood single, with large prospect, north and south,
High into Easedale, up to Dunmail-Raise,
And westward to the village near the lake;
And from this constant light, so regular,
And so far seen, the House itself, by all
Who dwelt within the limits of the vale,
Both old and young, was named THE EVENING STAR.

Thus living on through such a length of years,
The Shepherd, if he loved himself, must needs
Have loved his Helpmate; but to Michael's heart
This son of his old age was yet more dear—
Less from instinctive tenderness, the same
Fond spirit that blindly works in the blood of all—
Than that a child, more than all other gifts
That earth can offer to declining man,
Brings hope with it, and forward-looking thoughts,
And stirrings of inquietude, when they
By tendency of nature needs must fail.
Exceeding was the love he bare to him,
His heart and his heart's joy! For oftentimes
Old Michael, while he was a babe in arms,

Had done him female service, not alone
For pastime and delight, as is the use
Of fathers, but with patient mind enforced
To acts of tenderness; and he had rocked
His cradle, as with a woman's gentle hand.

And in a later time, ere yet the Boy
Had put on boy's attire, did Michael love,
Albeit of a stern unbending mind,
To have the Young-one in his sight, when he
Wrought in the field, or on his shepherd's stool
Sate with a fettered sheep before him stretched
Under the large old oak, that near his door
Stood single, and, from matchless depth of shade,
Chosen for the Shearer's covert from the sun,
Thence in our rustic dialect was called
The Clipping Tree, a name which yet it bears.
There, while they two were sitting in the shade,
With others round them, earnest all and blithe,
Would Michael exercise his heart with looks
Of fond correction and reproof bestowed
Upon the Child, if he disturbed the sheep
By catching at their legs, or with his shouts
Scared them, while they lay still beneath the shears.

And when by Heaven's good grace the boy grew up
A healthy Lad, and carried in his cheek
Two steady roses that were five years old;
Then Michael from a winter coppice cut
With his own hand a sapling, which he hooped
With iron, making it throughout in all
Due requisites a perfect shepherd's staff,
And gave it to the Boy; wherewith equipt
He as a watchman oftentimes was placed
At gate or gap, to stem or turn the flock;
And, to his office prematurely called,
There stood the urchin, as you will divine,
Something between a hindrance and a help;
And for this cause not always, I believe,
Receiving from his Father hire of praise;
Though nought was left undone which staff, or voice,
Or looks, or threatening gestures, could perform.

But soon as Luke, full ten years old, could stand
Against the mountain blasts; and to the heights,
Not fearing toil, nor length of weary ways,
He with his Father daily went, and they
Were as companions, why should I relate
That objects which the Shepherd loved before
Were dearer now? that from the Boy there came
Feelings and emanations—things which were
Light to the sun and music to the wind;
And that the old Man's heart seemed born again?

Thus in his Father's sight the Boy grew up:
And now, when he had reached his eighteenth year,
He was his comfort and daily hope.

While in this sort the simple household lived
From day to day, to Michael's ear there came
Distressful tidings. Long before the time
Of which I speak, the Shepherd had been bound
In surety for his brother's son, a man
Of an industrious life, and ample means;
But unforeseen misfortunes suddenly
Had prest upon him; and old Michael now
Was summoned to discharge the forfeiture,
A grievous penalty, but little less
Than half his substance. This unlooked-for claim,
At the first hearing, for a moment took
More hope out of his life than he supposed
That any old man ever could have lost.
As soon as he had armed himself with strength
To look his trouble in the face, it seemed
The Shepherd's sole resource to sell at once
A portion of his patrimonial fields.
Such was his first resolve; he thought again,
And his heart failed him. "Isabel," said he,
Two evenings after he had heard the news,
"I have been toiling more than seventy years,
And in the open sunshine of God's love
Have we all lived; yet, if these fields of ours
Should pass into a stranger's hand, I think
That I could not lie quiet in my grave.

Our lot is a hard lot; the sun himself
Has scarcely been more diligent than I;
And I have lived to be a fool at last
To my own family. An evil man
That was, and made an evil choice, if he
Were false to us; and, if he were not false,
There are ten thousand to whom loss like this
Had been no sorrow. I forgive him;—but
'Twere better to be dumb than to talk thus.

    When I began, my purpose was to speak
Of remedies and of a cheerful hope.
Our Luke shall leave us, Isabel; the land
Shall not go from us, and it shall be free;
He shall possess it, free as is the wind
That passes over it. We have, thou know'st,
Another kinsman—he will be our friend
In this distress. He is a prosperous man,
Thriving in trade—and Luke to him shall go,
And with his kinsman's help and his own thrift
He quickly will repair this loss, and then
He may return to us. If here he stay,
What can be done? Where every one is poor,
What can be gained?"

    At this the old Man paused,
And Isabel sat silent, for her mind
Was busy, looking back into past times.
There's Richard Bateman, thought she to herself,
He was a parish-boy—at the church-door
They made a gathering for him, shillings, pence,
And halfpennies, wherewith the neighbours bought
A basket, which they filled with pedlar's wares;
And, with this basket on his arm, the lad
Went up to London, found a master there,
Who, out of many, chose the trusty boy
To go and overlook his merchandise
Beyond the seas; where he grew wondrous rich,
And left estates and monies to the poor,
And, at his birth-place, built a chapel floored
With marble, which he sent from foreign lands.
These thoughts, and many others of like sort,
Passed quickly through the mind of Isabel,

And her face brightened. The old Man was glad,
And thus resumed:—"Well, Isabel! this scheme
These two days has been meat and drink to me.
Far more than we have lost is left us yet.
We have enough—I wish indeed that I
Were younger;—but this hope is a good hope.
Make ready Luke's best garments, of the best
Buy for him more, and let us send him forth
To-morrow, or the next day, or to-night:
If he *could* go, the Boy should go to-night."

Here Michael ceased, and to the fields went forth
With a light heart. The Housewife for five days
Was restless morn and night, and all day long
Wrought on with her best fingers to prepare
Things needful for the journey of her son.
But Isabel was glad when Sunday came
To stop her in her work: for, when she lay
By Michael's side, she through the last two nights
Heard him, how he was troubled in his sleep:
And when they rose at morning she could see
That all his hopes were gone. That day at noon
She said to Luke, while they two by themselves
Were sitting at the door, "Thou must not go:
We have no other Child but thee to lose,
None to remember—do not go away,
For if thou leave thy Father he will die."
The Youth made answer with a jocund voice;
And Isabel, when she had told her fears,
Recovered heart. That evening her best fare
Did she bring forth, and all together sat
Like happy people round a Christmas fire.

With daylight Isabel resumed her work;
And all the ensuing week the house appeared
As cheerful as a grove in Spring: at length
The expected letter from their kinsman came,
With kind assurances that he would do
His utmost for the welfare of the Boy;
To which, requests were added, that forthwith
He might be sent to him. Ten times or more

The letter was read over; Isabel
Went forth to show it to the neighbours round;
Nor was there at that time on English land
A prouder heart than Luke's. When Isabel
Had to her house returned, the old Man said,
"He shall depart to-morrow." To this word
The Housewife answered, talking much of things
Which, if at such short notice he should go,
Would surely be forgotten. But at length
She gave consent, and Michael was at ease.

Near the tumultuous brook of Greenhead Ghyll,
In that deep valley, Michael had designed
To build a Sheep-fold; and, before he heard
The tidings of his melancholy loss,
For this same purpose he had gathered up
A heap of stones, which by the streamlet's edge
Lay thrown together, ready for the work.
With Luke that evening thitherward he walked:
And soon as they had reached the place he stopped,
And thus the old Man spake to him:—"My son,
To-morrow thou wilt leave me: with full heart
I look upon thee, for thou art the same
That wert a promise to me ere thy birth,
And all thy life hast been my daily joy.
I will relate to thee some little part
Of our two histories; 'twill do thee good
When thou art from me, even if I should touch
On things thou canst not know of.——After thou
First cam'st into the world—as oft befalls
To new-born infants—thou didst sleep away
Two days, and blessings from thy Father's tongue
Then fell upon thee. Day by day passed on,
And still I loved thee with increasing love.
Never to living ear came sweeter sounds
Than when I heard thee by our own fireside
First uttering, without words, a natural tune;
While thou, a feeding babe, didst in thy joy
Sing at thy Mother's breast. Month followed month,
And in the open fields my life was passed
And on the mountains; else I think that thou

Hadst been brought up upon thy Father's knees.
But we were playmates, Luke: among these hills,
As well thou knowest, in us the old and young
Have played together, nor with me didst thou
Lack any pleasure which a boy can know."
Luke had a manly heart; but at these words
He sobbed aloud. The old Man grasped his hand,
And said, "Nay, do not take it so—I see
That these are things of which I need not speak.
—Even to the utmost I have been to thee
A kind and a good Father: and herein
I but repay a gift which I myself
Received at others' hands; for, though now old
Beyond the common life of man, I still
Remember them who loved me in my youth.
Both of them sleep together: here they lived,
As all their Forefathers had done; and, when
At length their time was come, they were not loth
To give their bodies to the family mould.
I wished that thou shouldst live the life they lived,
But 'tis a long time to look back, my Son,
And see so little gain from threescore years.

These fields were burthened when they came to me;
Till I was forty years of age, not more
Than half of my inheritance was mine.
I toiled and toiled; God blessed me in my work,
And till these three weeks past the land was free.
—It looks as if it never could endure
Another Master. Heaven forgive me, Luke,
If I judge ill for thee, but it seems good
That thou shouldst go."
　　At this the old Man paused;
Then, pointing to the stones near which they stood,
Thus, after a short silence, he resumed:
"This was a work for us; and now, my Son,
It is a work for me. But, lay one stone—
Here, lay it for me, Luke, with thine own hands.
Nay, Boy, be of good hope;—we both may live
To see a better day. At eighty-four
I still am strong and hale;—do thou thy part;

I will do mine.—I will begin again
With many tasks that were resigned to thee:
Up to the heights, and in among the storms,
Will I without thee go again, and do
All works which I was wont to do alone,
Before I knew thy face.—Heaven bless thee, Boy!
Thy heart these two weeks has been beating fast
With many hopes; it should be so—yes—yes—
I knew that thou couldst never have a wish
To leave me, Luke: thou hast been bound to me
Only by links of love; when thou art gone,
What will be left to us!—But I forget
My purposes. Lay now the corner-stone,
As I requested; and hereafter, Luke,
When thou art gone away, should evil men
Be thy companions, think of me, my Son,
And of this moment; hither turn thy thoughts,
And God will strengthen thee: amid all fear
And all temptation, Luke, I pray that thou
May'st bear in mind the life thy Fathers lived,
Who, being innocent, did for that cause
Bestir them in good deeds. Now, fare thee well—
When thou return'st, thou in this place wilt see
A work which is not here: a covenant
'Twill be between us; but, whatever fate
Befall thee, I shall love thee to the last,
And bear thy memory with me to the grave."

The Shepherd ended here; and Luke stooped down,
And, as his Father had requested, laid
The first stone of the Sheep-fold. At the sight
The old Man's grief broke from him; to his heart
He pressed his Son, he kissed him and wept;
And to the house together they returned.
—Hushed was that House in peace, or seeming peace,
Ere the night fell:—with morrow's dawn the Boy
Began his journey, and, when he had reached
The public way, he put on a bold face;
And all the neighbours, as he passed their doors,
Came forth with wishes and with farewell prayers,
That followed him till he was out of sight.

A good report did from their Kinsman come,
Of Luke and his well-doing: and the Boy
Wrote loving letters, full of wondrous news,
Which, as the Housewife phrased it, were throughout
"The prettiest letters that were ever seen."
Both parents read them with rejoicing hearts.
So, many months passed on: and once again
The Shepherd went about his daily work
With confident and cheerful thoughts; and now
Sometimes when he could find a leisure hour
He to that valley took his way, and there
Wrought at the Sheep-fold. Meantime Luke began
To slacken in his duty; and, at length,
He in the dissolute city gave himself
To evil courses: ignominy and shame
Fell on him, so that he was driven at last
To seek a hiding-place beyond the seas.

There is a comfort in the strength of love;
'Twill make a thing endurable, which else
Would overset the brain, or break the heart:
I have conversed with more than one who well
Remember the old Man, and what he was
Years after he had heard this heavy news.
His bodily frame had been from youth to age
Of an unusual strength. Among the rocks
He went, and still looked up to sun and cloud,
And listened to the wind; and, as before,
Performed all kinds of labour for his sheep,
And for the land, his small inheritance.
And to that hollow dell from time to time
Did he repair, to build the Fold of which
His flock had need. 'Tis not forgotten yet
The pity which was then in every heart
For the old Man—and 'tis believed by all
That many and many a day he thither went,
And never lifted up a single stone.

There, by the Sheep-fold, sometimes was he seen
Sitting alone, or with his faithful Dog,
Then old, beside him, lying at his feet.

The length of full seven years, from time to time,
He at the building of this Sheep-fold wrought,
And left the work unfinished when he died.
Three years, or little more, did Isabel
Survive her Husband: at her death the estate
Was sold, and went into a stranger's hand.
The Cottage which was named the EVENING STAR
Is gone—the ploughshare has been through the ground
On which it stood; great changes have been wrought
In all the neighbourhood:—yet the oak is left
That grew beside their door; and the remains
Of the unfinished Sheep-fold may be seen
Beside the boisterous brook of Greenhead Ghyll.

THE PET-LAMB

A PASTORAL

[Composed 1800.—Published 1800.]

The dew was falling fast, the stars began to blink;
I heard a voice; it said, "Drink, pretty creature, drink!"
And, looking o'er the hedge, before me I espied
A snow-white mountain-lamb with a Maiden at its side.

Nor sheep nor kine were near; the lamb was all alone,
And by a slender cord was tethered to a stone;
With one knee on the grass did the little Maiden kneel,
While to that mountain-lamb she gave its evening meal.

The lamb, while from her hand he thus his supper took,
Seemed to feast with head and ears; and his tail with pleas-
    ure shook.
"Drink, pretty creature, drink," she said in such a tone
That I almost received her heart into my own.

'Twas little Barbara Lewthwaite, a child of beauty rare!
I watched them with delight, they were a lovely pair.
Now with her empty can the Maiden turned away:
But ere ten yards were gone her footsteps did she stay.

Right towards the lamb she looked; and from a shady place
I unobserved could see the workings of her face:
If Nature to her tongue could measured numbers bring,
Thus, thought I, to her lamb that little Maid might sing:

"What ails thee, young One? what? Why pull so at thy
          cord?
Is it not well with thee? well both for bed and board?
Thy plot of grass is soft, and green as grass can be;
Rest, little young One, rest; what is't that aileth thee?

"What is it thou wouldst seek? What is wanting in thy
          heart?
Thy limbs, are they not strong? And beautiful thou art:
This grass is tender grass; these flowers they have no peers;
And that green corn all day is rustling in thy ears!

"If the sun be shining hot, do but stretch thy woollen chain,
This beech is standing by, its covert thou canst gain;
For rain and mountain-storms! the like thou need'st not
          fear,
The rain and storm are things that scarcely can come here.

"Rest, little young One, rest; thou hast forgot the day
When my father found thee first in places far away;
Many flocks were on the hills, but thou were owned by
          none,
And thy mother from thy side for evermore was gone.

"He took thee in his arms, and in pity brought thee home:
A blessèd day for thee! then whither wouldst thou roam?
A faithful nurse thou hast; the dam that did thee yean
Upon the mountain-tops no kinder could have been.

"Thou know'st that twice a day I have brought thee in this
          can
Fresh water from the brook, as clear as ever ran;
And twice in the day, when the ground is wet with dew,
I bring thee draughts of milk, warm milk it is and new.

"Thy limbs will shortly be twice as stout as they are now,
Then I'll yoke thee to my cart like a pony in the plough;
My playmate thou shalt be; and when the wind is cold
Our hearth shall be thy bed, our house shall be thy fold.

"It will not, will not rest!—Poor creature, can it be
That 'tis thy mother's heart which is working so in thee?
Things that I know not of belike to thee are dear,
And dreams of things which thou canst neither see nor hear.

"Alas, the mountain-tops that look so green and fair!
I've heard of fearful winds and darkness that come there;
The little brooks that seem all pastime and all play,
When they are angry, roar like lions for their prey.

"Here thou need'st not dread the raven in the sky;
Night and day thou art safe,—our cottage is hard by.
Why bleat so after me? Why pull so at thy chain?
Sleep—and at break of day I will come to thee again!"

—As homeward through the lane I went with lazy feet,
This song to myself did I oftentimes repeat;
And it seemed, as I retraced the ballad line by line,
That but half of it was hers, and one half of it was *mine*.

Again, and once again, did I repeat the song;
"Nay," said I, "more than half to the damsel must belong,
For she looked with such a look, and she spake with such
          a tone,
That I almost received her heart into my own."

[Composed 1800.—Published 1800.]

'Tis said that some have died for love:
And here and there a church-yard grave is found
In the cold north's unhallowed ground,
Because the wretched man himself had slain,
His love was such a grievous pain.
And there is one whom I five years have known;
He dwells alone

Upon Helvellyn's side:
He loved—the pretty Barbara died;
And thus he makes his moan:
Three years had Barbara in her grave been laid
When thus his moan he made:

"Oh, move, thou Cottage, from behind that oak!
Or let the aged tree uprooted lie,
That in some other way yon smoke
May mount into the sky!
The clouds pass on; they from the heavens depart:
I look—the sky is empty space;
I know not what I trace;
But when I cease to look, my hand is on my heart.

"Oh, what a weight is in these shades! Ye leaves,
That murmur once so dear, when will it cease?
Your sound my heart of rest bereaves,
It robs my heart of peace.
Thou Thrush, that singest loud—and loud and free,
Into yon row of willows flit,
Upon that alder sit;
Or sing another song, or choose another tree.

"Roll back, sweet Rill! back to thy mountain-bounds,
And there for ever be thy waters chained!
For thou dost haunt the air with sounds
That cannot be sustained;
If still beneath that pine-tree's ragged bough
Headlong yon waterfall must come,
Oh let it then be dumb!
Be anything, sweet Rill, but that which thou art now.

"Thou Eglantine, so bright with sunny showers,
Proud as a rainbow spanning half the vale,
Thou one fair shrub, oh! shed thy flowers,
And stir not in the gale.
For thus to see thee nodding in the air,
To see thy arch thus stretch and bend,
Thus rise and thus descend,—
Disturbs me till the sight is more than I can bear."

The Man who makes this feverish complaint
Is one of giant stature, who could dance
Equipped from head to foot in iron mail.
Ah gentle Love! if ever thought was thine
To store up kindred hours for me, thy face
Turn from me, gentle Love! nor let me walk
Within the sound of Emma's voice, nor know
Such happiness as I have known to-day.

HART-LEAP WELL

[Composed January or February, 1800.—Published 1800.]

Hart-Leap Well is a small spring of water, about five miles from
Richmond in Yorkshire, and near the side of the road that leads
from Richmond to Askrigg. Its name is derived from a remarkable Chase, the memory of which is preserved by the monuments
spoken of in the second Part of the following Poem, which
monuments do now exist as I have there described them.

The Knight had ridden down from Wensley Moor
With the slow motion of a summer's cloud,
And now, as he approached a vassal's door,
"Bring forth another horse!" he cried aloud.

"Another horse!"—That shout the vassal heard
And saddled his best Steed, a comely grey;
Sir Walter mounted him; he was the third
Which he had mounted on that glorious day.

Joy sparkled in the prancing courser's eyes;
The horse and horseman are a happy pair;
But, though Sir Walter like a falcon flies,
There is a doleful silence in the air.

A rout this morning left Sir Walter's Hall,
That as they galloped made the echoes roar;
But horse and man are vanished, one and all;
Such race, I think, was never seen before.

Sir Walter, restless as a veering wind,
Calls to the few tired dogs that yet remain:
Blanch, Swift, and Music, noblest of their kind,
Follow, and up the weary mountain strain.

The Knight hallooed, he cheered and chid them on
With suppliant gestures and upbraidings stern;
But breath and eyesight fail; and, one by one,
The dogs are stretched among the mountain fern.

Where is the throng, the tumult of the race?
The bugles that so joyfully were blown?
—This chase it looks not like an earthly chase;
Sir Walter and the Hart are left alone.

The poor Hart toils along the mountain-side;
I will not stop to tell how far he fled,
Nor will I mention by what death he died;
But now the Knight beholds him lying dead.

Dismounting, then, he leaned against a thorn;
He had no follower, dog, nor man, nor boy:
He neither cracked his whip, nor blew his horn,
But gazed upon the spoil with silent joy.

Close to the thorn on which Sir Walter leaned
Stood his dumb partner in this glorious feat;
Weak as a lamb the hour that it is yeaned;
And white with foam as if with cleaving sleet.

Upon his side the Hart was lying stretched:
His nostril touched a spring beneath a hill,
And with the last deep groan his breath had fetched
The waters of the spring were trembling still.

And now, too happy for repose or rest,
(Never had living man such joyful lot!)
Sir Walter walked all round, north, south, and west,
And gazed and gazed upon that darling spot.

And climbing up the hill—(it was at least
Four roods of sheer ascent) Sir Walter found
Three several hoof-marks which the hunted Beast
Had left imprinted on the grassy ground.

Sir Walter wiped his face, and cried, "Till now
Such sight was never seen by human eyes:
Three leaps have borne him from this lofty brow
Down to the very fountain where he lies.

"I'll build a pleasure-house upon this spot,
And a small arbour, made for rural joy;
'Twill be the traveller's shed, the pilgrim's cot,
A place of love for damsels that are coy.

"A cunning artist will I have to frame
A basin for that fountain in the dell!
And they who do make mention of the same,
From this day forth, shall call it HART-LEAP WELL.

"And, gallant Stag! to make thy praises known,
Another monument shall here be raised;
Three several pillars, each a rough-hewn stone,
And planted where thy hoofs the turf have grazed.

"And in the summer-time, when days are long,
I will come hither with my Paramour;
And with the dancers and the minstrel's song
We will make merry in that pleasant bower.

"Till the foundations of the mountains fail
My mansion with its arbour shall endure;—
The joy of them who till the fields of Swale,
And them who dwell among the woods of Ure!"

Then home he went, and left the Hart stone-dead,
With breathless nostrils stretched above the spring.
—Soon did the Knight perform what he had said;
And far and wide the fame thereof did ring.

Ere thrice the Moon into her port had steered,
A cup of stone received the living well;
Three pillars of rude stone Sir Walter reared,
And built a house of pleasure in the dell.

And, near the fountain, flowers of stature tall
With trailing plants and trees were intertwined,—
Which soon composed a little sylvan hall,
A leafy shelter from the sun and wind.

And thither, when the summer days were long,
Sir Walter led his wondering Paramour;
And with the dancers and the minstrel's song
Made merriment within that pleasant bower.

The Knight, Sir Walter, died in course of time,
And his bones lie in his paternal vale.—
But there is matter for a second rhyme,
And I to this would add another tale.

PART SECOND

The moving accident is not my trade;
To freeze the blood I have no ready arts:
'Tis my delight, alone in summer shade,
To pipe a simple song for thinking hearts.

As I from Hawes to Richmond did repair,
It chanced that I saw standing in a dell
Three aspens at three corners of a square;
And one, not four yards distant, near a well.

What this imported I could ill divine:
And, pulling now the rein my horse to stop,
I saw three pillars standing in a line,—
The last stone-pillar on a dark hill-top.

The trees were grey, with neither arms nor head;
Half wasted the square mound of tawny green;
So that you just might say, as then I said,
"Here in old time the hand of man hath been."

I looked upon the hill both far and near,
More doleful place did never eye survey;
It seemed as if the spring-time came not here,
And Nature here were willing to decay.

I stood in various thoughts and fancies lost,
When one, who was in shepherd's garb attired,
Came up the hollow:—him did I accost,
And what this place might be I then enquired.

The Shepherd stopped, and that same story told
Which in my former rhyme I have rehearsed.
"A jolly place," said he, "in times of old!
But something ails it now: the spot is curst.

"You see these lifeless stumps of aspen wood—
Some say that they are beeches, others elms—
These were the bower; and here a mansion stood,
The finest palace of a hundred realms!

"The arbour does its own condition tell;
You see the stones, the fountain, and the stream;
But as to the great Lodge! you might as well
Hunt half a day for a forgotten dream.

"There's neither dog nor heifer, horse nor sheep,
Will wet his lips within that cup of stone;
And oftentimes, when all are fast asleep,
This water doth send forth a dolorous groan.

"Some say that here a murder has been done,
And blood cries out for blood: but, for my part,
I've guessed, when I've been sitting in the sun,
That it was all for that unhappy Hart.

"What thoughts must through the creature's brain have
    past!
Even from the topmost stone, upon the steep,
Are but three bounds—and look, Sir, at this last—
O Master! it has been a cruel leap.

"For thirteen hours he ran a desperate race;
And in my simple mind we cannot tell
What cause the Hart might have to love this place,
And come and make his death-bed near the well.

"Here on the grass perhaps asleep he sank,
Lulled by the fountain in the summer-tide;
This water was perhaps the first he drank
When he had wandered from his mother's side.

"In April here beneath the flowering thorn
He heard the birds their morning carols sing;
And he perhaps, for aught we know, was born
Not half a furlong from that self-same spring.

"Now, here is neither grass nor pleasant shade;
The sun on drearier hollow never shone;
So will it be, as I have often said,
Till trees, and stones, and fountain, all are gone."

"Grey-headed Shepherd, thou hast spoken well;
Small difference lies between thy creed and mine:
This Beast not unobserved by Nature fell;
His death was mourned by sympathy divine.

"The Being that is in the clouds and air,
That is in the green leaves among the groves,
Maintains a deep and reverential care
For the unoffending creatures whom he loves.

"The pleasure-house is dust:—behind, before,
This is no common waste, no common gloom;
But Nature, in due course of time, once more
Shall here put on her beauty and her bloom.

"She leaves these objects to a slow decay,
That what we are, and have been, may be known;
But at the coming of the milder day
These monuments shall all be overgrown.

"One lesson, Shepherd, let us two divide,
Taught both by what she shows, and what conceals;
Never to blend our pleasure or our pride
With sorrow of the meanest thing that feels."

THE SPARROW'S NEST

[Composed 1801.—Published 1807.]

Behold, within the leafy shade,
Those bright blue eggs together laid!
On me the chance-discovered sight
Gleamed like a vision of delight.
I started—seeming to espy
The home and sheltered bed,
The Sparrow's dwelling, which, hard by
My Father's house, in wet or dry
My sister Emmeline and I
    Together visited.

She looked at it and seemed to fear it;
Dreading, tho' wishing, to be near it:
Such heart was in her, being then
A little Prattler among men.
The Blessing of my later years
Was with me when a boy:
She gave me eyes, she gave me ears;
And humble cares, and delicate fears;
A heart, the fountain of sweet tears;
    And love, and thought, and joy.

LOUISA

AFTER ACCOMPANYING HER ON A MOUNTAIN EXCURSION

[Composed (probably) 1801.—Published 1807.]

I met Louisa in the shade,
And, having seen that lovely Maid,
Why should I fear to say
That, nymph-like, she is fleet and strong,
And down the rocks can leap along
Like rivulets in May?

And she hath smiles to earth unknown;
Smiles, that with motion of their own
Do spread, and sink, and rise;

That come and go with endless play,
And ever, as they pass away,
Are hidden in her eyes.

She loves her fire, her cottage-home;
Yet o'er the moorland will she roam
In weather rough and bleak;
And, when against the wind she strains,
Oh! might I kiss the mountain rains
That sparkle on her cheek.

Take all that's mine "beneath the moon,"
If I with her but half a noon
May sit beneath the walls
Of some old cave, or mossy nook,
When up she winds along the brook
To hunt the waterfalls.

TO A YOUNG LADY

WHO HAD BEEN REPROACHED FOR TAKING LONG WALKS IN THE COUNTRY

[Composed 1801 (?).—Published *Morning Post,* February 11, 1802; ed. 1807.]

Dear Child of Nature, let them rail!
—There is a nest in a green dale,
A harbour and a hold;
Where thou, a Wife and Friend, shalt see
Thy own heart-stirring days, and be
A light to young and old.

There, healthy as a shepherd boy,
And treading among flowers of joy
Which at no season fade,
Thou, while thy babes around thee cling,
Shalt show us how divine a thing
A Woman may be made.

Thy thoughts and feelings shall not die,
Nor leave thee, when grey hairs are nigh,

A melancholy slave;
But an old age serene and bright,
And lovely as a Lapland night,
Shall lead thee to thy grave.

THE SAILOR'S MOTHER

[Composed March 11, 12, 1802.—Published 1807.]

One morning (raw it was and wet—
A foggy day in winter time)
A Woman on the road I met,
Not old, though something past her prime:
Majestic in her person, tall and straight;
And like a Roman matron's was her mien and gait.

The ancient spirit is not dead;
Old times, thought I, are breathing there;
Proud was I that my country bred
Such strength, a dignity so fair:
She begged an alms, like one in poor estate;
I looked at her again, nor did my pride abate.

When from these lofty thoughts I woke,
"What is it," said I, "that you bear,
Beneath the covert of your Cloak,
Protected from this cold damp air?"
She answered, soon as she the question heard,
"A simple burthen, Sir, a little Singing-bird."

And, thus continuing, she said,
"I had a Son, who many a day
Sailed on the seas, but he is dead;
In Denmark he was cast away:
And I have travelled weary miles to see
If aught which he had owned might still remain for me.

"The bird and cage they both were his:
'Twas my Son's bird; and neat and trim
He kept it: many voyages
The singing-bird had gone with him;

When last he sailed, he left the bird behind;
From bodings, as might be, that hung upon his mind.

"He to a fellow-lodger's care
Had left it, to be watched and fed,
And pipe its song in safety;—there
I found it when my Son was dead;
And now; God help me for my little wit!
I bear it with me, Sir;—he took so much delight in it."

ALICE FELL;

OR, POVERTY.

[Composed March 12, 13, 1802, though probably conceived much earlier.
Published 1807.]

supposed to be Commons (handwritten annotation)

The post-boy drove with fierce career,
For threatening clouds the moon had drowned;
When, as we hurried on, my ear
Was smitten with a startling sound.

As if the wind blew many ways,
I heard the sound,—and more and more;
It seemed to follow with the chaise,
And still I heard it as before.

At length I to the boy called out;
He stopped his horses at the word,
But neither cry, nor voice, nor shout,
Nor aught else like it, could be heard.

The boy then smacked his whip, and fast
The horses scampered through the rain;
But, hearing soon upon the blast
The cry, I bade him halt again.

Forthwith alighting on the ground,
"Whence comes," said I, "this piteous moan?"
And there a little Girl I found,
Sitting behind the chaise, alone.

"My cloak!" no other word she spake,
But loud and bitterly she wept,
As if her innocent heart would break;
And down from off her seat she leapt.

"What ails you, child?"—she sobbed, "Look here!"
I saw it in the wheel entangled,
A weather-beaten rag as e'er
From any garden scare-crow dangled.

There, twisted between nave and spoke,
It hung, nor could at once be freed;
But our joint pains unloosed the cloak,
A miserable rag indeed!

"And whither are you going, child,
To-night along these lonesome ways?"
"To Durham," answered she, half wild—
"Then come with me into the chaise."

Insensible to all relief
Sat the poor girl, and forth did send
Sob after sob, as if her grief
Could never, never have an end.

"My child, in Durham do you dwell?"
She checked herself in her distress,
And said, "My name is Alice Fell;
I'm fatherless and motherless.

"And I to Durham, Sir, belong."
Again, as if the thought would choke
Her very heart, her grief grew strong;
And all was for her tattered cloak!

The chaise drove on; our journey's end
Was nigh; and, sitting by my side,
As if she had lost her only friend
She wept, nor would be pacified.

Up to the tavern-door we post;
Of Alice and her grief I told;
And I gave money to the host,
To buy a new cloak for the old.

"And let it be of duffil grey,
As warm a cloak as man can sell!"
Proud creature was she the next day,
The little orphan, Alice Fell!

BEGGARS

[Composed March 13, 14, 1802.—Published 1807.]

She had a tall man's height or more;
Her face from summer's noontide heat
No bonnet shaded, but she wore
A mantle, to her very feet
Descending with a graceful flow,
And on her head a cap as white as new-fallen snow.

Her skin was of Egyptian brown:
Haughty, as if her eye had seen
Its own light to a distance thrown,
She towered, fit person for a Queen
To lead those ancient Amazonian files;
Or ruling Bandit's wife among the Grecian isles.

Advancing, forth she stretched her hand
And begged an alms with doleful plea
That ceased not; on our English land
Such woes, I knew, could never be;
And yet a boon I gave her, for the creature
Was beautiful to see—a weed of glorious feature.

I left her, and pursued my way;
And soon before me did espy
A pair of little Boys at play,
Chasing a crimson butterfly;
The taller followed with his hat in hand,
Wreathed round with yellow flowers the gayest of the land.

The other wore a rimless crown
With leaves of laurel stuck about;
And while both followed up and down,
Each whooping with a merry shout,
In their fraternal features I could trace
Unquestionable lines of that wild Suppliant's face.

Yet *they*, so blithe of heart, seemed fit
For finest tasks of earth or air:
Wings let them have, and they might flit
Precursors to Aurora's car,
Scattering fresh flowers; though happier far, I ween,
To hunt their fluttering game o'er rock and level green.

They dart across my path—but lo,
Each ready with a plaintive whine!
Said I, "not half an hour ago
Your Mother has had alms of mine."
"That cannot be," one answered—"she is dead:"—
I looked reproof—they saw—but neither hung his head.

"She has been dead, Sir, many a day."—
"Hush, boys! you're telling me a lie;
It was your Mother, as I say!"
And, in the twinkling of an eye,
"Come! come!" cried one, and without more ado
Off to some other play the joyous Vagrants flew!

SEQUEL TO THE FOREGOING

COMPOSED MANY YEARS AFTER

[Composed 1817.—Published 1827.]

Where are they now, those wanton Boys?
For whose free range the dædal earth
Was filled with animated toys,
And implements of frolic mirth;
With tools for ready wit to guide;
And ornaments of seemlier pride,
More fresh, more bright, than princes wear;

For what one moment flung aside,
Another could repair;
What good or evil have they seen
Since I their pastime witnessed here,
Their daring wiles, their sportive cheer?
I ask—but all is dark between!

  They met me in a genial hour,
When universal nature breathed
As with the breath of one sweet flower,—
A time to overrule the power
Of discontent, and check the birth
Of thoughts with better thoughts at strife,
The most familiar bane of life
Since parting Innocence bequeathed
Mortality to Earth!
Soft clouds, the whitest of the year,
Sailed through the sky—the brooks ran clear;
The lambs from rock to rock were bounding;
With songs the budded groves resounding;
And to my heart are still endeared
The thoughts with which it then was cheered;
The faith which saw that gladsome pair
Walk through the fire with unsinged hair.
Or, if such faith must needs deceive—
Then, Spirits of beauty and of grace,
Associates in that eager chase;
Ye, who within the blameless mind
Your favourite seat of empire find—
Kind Spirits! may we not believe
That they, so happy and so fair
Through your sweet influence, and the care
Of pitying Heaven, at least were free
From touch of *deadly* injury?
Destined, whate'er their earthly doom,
For mercy and immortal bloom?

TO A BUTTERFLY

[Composed March 14, 1802.—Published 1807.]

Stay near me—do not take thy flight!
A little longer stay in sight!
Much converse do I find in thee,
Historian of my infancy!
Float near me; do not yet depart!
Dead times revive in thee:
Thou bring'st, gay creature as thou art!
A solemn image to my heart,
My father's family!

Oh! pleasant, pleasant were the days,
The time, when in our childish plays,
My sister Emmeline and I
Together chased the butterfly!
A very hunter did I rush
Upon the prey;—with leaps and springs
I followed on from brake to bush;
But she, God love her! feared to brush
The dust from off its wings.

TO THE CUCKOO

[Composed March 23-26, 1802.—Published 1807.]

O Blithe New-comer! I have heard,
    I hear thee and rejoice.
O Cuckoo! shall I call thee Bird,
    Or but a wandering Voice?

While I am lying on the grass
    Thy twofold shout I hear;
From hill to hill it seems to pass
    At once far off, and near.

Though babbling only to the Vale,
    Of sunshine and of flowers,
Thou bringest unto me a tale
    Of visionary hours.

Thrice welcome, darling of the Spring!
    Even yet thou art to me
No bird, but an invisible thing,
    A voice, a mystery;

The same whom in my schoolboy days
    I listened to; that Cry
Which made me look a thousand ways
    In bush, and tree, and sky.

To seek thee did I often rove
    Through woods and on the green;
And thou wert still a hope, a love;
    Still longed for, never seen.

And I can listen to thee yet;
    Can lie upon the plain
And listen, till I do beget
    That golden time again.

O blessèd Bird! the earth we pace
    Again appears to be
An unsubstantial, faery place;
    That is fit home for Thee!

[Composed March 26, 1802.—Published 1807.]

My heart leaps up when I behold
    A rainbow in the sky:
So was it when my life began;
So is it now I am a man;
So be it when I shall grow old,
    Or let me die!
The Child is father of the Man;
And I could wish my days to be
Bound each to each by natural piety.

AMONG ALL LOVELY THINGS MY LOVE HAD BEEN

[Composed April 12, 1802, though probably conceived much earlier.—
Published 1807; never reprinted by W.]

Among all lovely things my Love had been;
Had noted well the stars, all flowers that grew
About her home; but she had never seen
A Glow-worm, never one, and this I knew.

While riding near her home one stormy night
A single Glow-worm did I chance to espy;
I gave a fervent welcome to the sight,
And from my Horse I leapt; great joy had I.

Upon a leaf the Glow-worm did I lay,
To bear it with me through the stormy night:
And, as before, it shone without dismay;
Albeit putting forth a fainter light.

When to the Dwelling of my Love I came,
I went into the Orchard quietly;
And left the Glow-worm, blessing it by name,
Laid safely by itself, beneath a Tree.

The whole next day, I hoped, and hoped with fear;
At night the Glow-worm shone beneath the Tree:
I led my Lucy to the spot, "Look here!"
Oh! joy it was for her, and joy for me!

WRITTEN IN MARCH

WHILE RESTING ON THE BRIDGE AT THE FOOT OF BROTHER'S WATER

[Composed April 16, 1802.—Published 1807.]

The Cock is crowing,
The stream is flowing,
The small birds twitter,
The lake doth glitter,
The green field sleeps in the sun;

The oldest and youngest
Are at work with the strongest;
The cattle are grazing,
Their heads never raising;
There are forty feeding like one!

Like an army defeated
The snow hath retreated,
And now doth fare ill
On the top of the bare hill;
The Ploughboy is whooping—anon—anon:
There's joy in the mountains;
There's life in the fountains;
Small clouds are sailing,
Blue sky prevailing;
The rain is over and gone!

1947 —

TO A BUTTERFLY

[Composed April 30, 1802.—Published 1807.]

I've watched you now a full half-hour, *year*
Self-poised upon that yellow flower;
And, little Butterfly! indeed
I know not if you sleep or feed.
How motionless!—not frozen seas
More motionless! and then
What joy awaits you, when the breeze
Hath found you out among the trees,
And calls you forth again!

pine-tree
This plot of orchard-ground is ours;
My trees they are, my Sister's flowers;
Here rest your wings when they are weary;
Here lodge as in a sanctuary!
Come often to us, fear no wrong;   *me*
Sit near us on the bough!
We'll talk of sunshine and of song,
And summer days, when we were young;
Sweet childish days, that were as long
As twenty days are now.

years

TO THE SMALL CELANDINE

[Composed April 30, 1802.—Published 1807.]

Pansies, lilies, kingcups, daisies,
Let them live upon their praises;
Long as there's a sun that sets,
Primroses will have their glory;
Long as there are violets,
They will have a place in story:
There's a flower that shall be mine,
'Tis the little Celandine.

Eyes of some men travel far
For the finding of a star;
Up and down the heavens they go,
Men that keep a mighty rout!
I'm as great as they, I trow,
Since the day I found thee out,
Little Flower—I'll make a stir,
Like a sage astronomer.

Modest, yet withal an Elf
Bold, and lavish of thyself;
Since we needs must first have met
I have seen thee, high and low,
Thirty years or more, and yet
'Twas a face I did not know;
Thou hast now, go where I may,
Fifty greetings in a day.

Ere a leaf is on a bush,
In the time before the thrush
Has a thought about her nest,
Thou wilt come with half a call,
Spreading out thy glossy breast
Like a careless Prodigal;
Telling tales about the sun,
When we've little warmth, or none.

Poets, vain men in their mood!
Travel with the multitude:

Never heed them; I aver
That they all are wanton wooers;
But the thrifty cottager,
Who stirs little out of doors,
Joys to spy thee near her home;
Spring is coming, Thou art come!

Comfort have thou of thy merit,
Kindly, unassuming Spirit!
Careless of thy neighbourhood,
Thou dost show thy pleasant face
On the moor, and in the wood,
In the lane;—there's not a place,
Howsoever mean it be,
But 'tis good enough for thee.

Ill befall the yellow flowers,
Children of the flaring hours!
Buttercups, that will be seen,
Whether we will see or no;
Others, too, of lofty mien;
They have done as worldlings do,
Taken praise that should be thine,
Little, humble Celandine.

Prophet of delight and mirth,
Ill-requited upon earth;
Herald of a mighty band,
Of a joyous train ensuing,
Serving at my heart's command,
Tasks that are no tasks renewing,
I will sing, as doth behove,
Hymns in praise of what I love!

TO THE SAME FLOWER

[Composed May 1, 1802.—Published 1807.]

Pleasures newly found are sweet
When they lie about our feet:
February last, my heart

First at sight of thee was glad;
All unheard of as thou art,
Thou must needs, I think, have had,
Celandine! and long ago,
Praise of which I nothing know.

I have not a doubt but he,
Whosoe'er the man might be,
Who the first with pointed rays
(Workman worthy to be sainted)
Set the sign-board in a blaze,
When the rising sun he painted,
Took the fancy from a glance
At thy glittering countenance.

Soon as gentle breezes bring
News of winter's vanishing,
And the children build their bowers,
Sticking 'kerchief-plots of mould
All about with full-blown flowers,
Thick as sheep in shepherd's fold!
With the proudest thou art there,
Mantling in the tiny square.

Often have I sighed to measure
By myself a lonely pleasure,
Sighed to think I read a book
Only read, perhaps, by me;
Yet I long could overlook
Thy bright coronet and Thee,
And thy arch and wily ways,
And thy store of other praise.

Blithe of heart, from week to week
Thou dost play at hide-and-seek;
While the patient primrose sits
Like a beggar in the cold,
Thou, a flower of wiser wits,
Slip'st into thy sheltering hold;
Liveliest of the vernal train
When ye all are out again.

Drawn by what peculiar spell,
By what charm of sight or smell,
Does the dim-eyed curious Bee,
Labouring for her waxen cells,
Fondly settle upon Thee
Prized above all buds and bells
Opening daily at thy side,
By the season multiplied?

Thou art not beyond the moon,
But a thing "beneath our shoon:" *Milton's comma*
Let the bold Discoverer thrid
In his bark the polar sea;
Rear who will a pyramid;
Praise it is enough for me,
If there be but three or four
Who will love my little Flower.

RESOLUTION AND INDEPENDENCE

[Composed May 3–July 4, 1802.—Published 1807.]

I

There was a roaring in the wind all night;
The rain came heavily and fell in floods;
But now the sun is rising calm and bright;
The birds are singing in the distant woods;
Over his own sweet voice the Stock-dove broods;
The Jay makes answer as the Magpie chatters;
And all the air is filled with pleasant noise of waters.

II

All things that love the sun are out of doors;
The sky rejoices in the morning's birth;
The grass is bright with rain-drops;—on the moors
The hare is running races in her mirth;
And with her feet she from the plashy earth
Raises a mist; that, glittering in the sun,
Runs with her all the way, wherever she doth run.

III

I was a Traveller then upon the moor;
I saw the hare that raced about with joy;
I heard the woods and distant waters roar;
Or heard them not, as happy as a boy:
The pleasant season did my heart employ:
My old remembrances went from me wholly;
And all the ways of men, so vain and melancholy.

IV

But, as it sometimes chanceth, from the might
Of joy in minds that can no further go,
As high as we have mounted in delight
In our dejection do we sink as low;
To me that morning did it happen so;
And fears and fancies thick upon me came;
Dim sadness—and blind thoughts, I knew not, nor could
    name.

V

I heard the sky-lark warbling in the sky;
And I bethought me of the playful hare:
Even such a happy Child of earth am I;
Even as these blissful creatures do I fare;
Far from the world I walk, and from all care;
But there may come another day to me—
Solitude, pain of heart, distress, and poverty.

VI

My whole life I have lived in pleasant thought,
As if life's business were a summer mood;
As if all needful things would come unsought
To genial faith, still rich in genial good;
But how can He expect that others should
Build for him, sow for him, and at his call
Love him, who for himself will take no heed at all?

VII

I thought of Chatterton, the marvellous Boy,
The sleepless Soul that perished in his pride;
Of Him who walked in glory and in joy
Following his plough, along the mountain-side:
By our own spirits are we deified:
We Poets in our youth begin in gladness;
But thereof come in the end despondency and madness.

VIII

Now, whether it were by peculiar grace,
A leading from above, a something given,
Yet it befell that, in this lonely place,
When I with these untoward thoughts had striven,
Beside a pool bare to the eye of heaven
I saw a Man before me unawares:
The oldest man he seemed that ever wore grey hairs.

IX

As a huge stone is sometimes seen to lie
Couched on the bald top of an eminence;
Wonder to all who do the same espy,
By what means it could thither come, and whence;
So that it seems a thing endued with sense:
Like a sea-beast crawled forth, that on a shelf
Of rock or sand reposeth, there to sun itself;

X

Such seemed this Man, not all alive nor dead,
Nor all asleep—in his extreme old age:
His body was bent double, feet and head
Coming together in life's pilgrimage;
As if some dire constraint of pain, or rage
Of sickness felt by him in times long past,
A more than human weight upon his frame had cast.

XI

Himself he propped, limbs, body, and pale face,
Upon a long grey staff of shaven wood:
And, still as I drew near with gentle pace,
Upon the margin of that moorish flood
Motionless as a cloud the old Man stood,
That heareth not the loud winds when they call;
And moveth all together, if it move at all.

XII

At length, himself unsettling, he the pond
Stirred with his staff, and fixedly did look
Upon the muddy water, which he conned,
As if he had been reading in a book:
And now a stranger's privilege I took;
And, drawing to his side, to him did say,
"This morning gives us promise of a glorious day."

XIII

A gentle answer did the old Man make,
In courteous speech which forth he slowly drew:
And him with further words I thus bespake,
"What occupation do you there pursue?
This is a lonesome place for one like you."
Ere he replied, a flash of mild surprise
Broke from the sable orbs of his yet-vivid eyes.

XIV

His words came feebly, from a feeble chest,
But each in solemn order followed each,
With something of a lofty utterance drest—
Choice word and measured phrase, above the reach
Of ordinary men; a stately speech;
Such as grave Livers do in Scotland use,
Religious men, who give to God and man their dues.

XV

He told, that to these waters he had come
To gather leeches, being old and poor:
Employment hazardous and wearisome!
And he had many hardships to endure:
From pond to pond he roamed, from moor to moor;
Housing, with God's good help, by choice or chance;
And in this way he gained an honest maintenance.

XVI

The old Man still stood talking by my side;
But now his voice to me was like a stream
Scarce heard; nor word from word could I divide;
And the whole body of the Man did seem
Like one whom I had met with in a dream;
Or like a man from some far region sent,
To give me human strength, by apt admonishment.

XVII

My former thoughts returned: the fear that kills;
And hope that is unwilling to be fed;
Cold, pain, and labour, and all fleshly ills;
And mighty Poets in their misery dead.
—Perplexed, and longing to be comforted,
My question eagerly did I renew,
"How is it that you live, and what is it you do?"

XVIII

He with a smile did then his words repeat;
And said that, gathering leeches, far and wide
He travelled; stirring thus about his feet
The waters of the pools where they abide.
"Once I could meet with them on every side;
But they have dwindled long by slow decay;
Yet still I persevere, and find them where I may."

XIX

While he was talking thus, the lonely place,
The old Man's shape, and speech—all troubled me:
In my mind's eye I seemed to see him pace
About the weary moors continually,
Wandering about alone and silently.
While I these thoughts within myself pursued,
He, having made a pause, the same discourse renewed.

XX

And soon with this he other matter blended,
Cheerfully uttered, with demeanour kind,
But stately in the main; and, when he ended,
I could have laughed myself to scorn to find
In that decrepit Man so firm a mind.
"God," said I, "be my help and stay secure;
I'll think of the Leech-gatherer on the lonely moor!"

[Composed June 8, 1802.—Published 1807; omitted from ed. 1815–1832;
republished 1835.]

The sun has long been set,
    The stars are out by twos and threes,
The little birds are piping yet
    Among the bushes and trees;
There's a cuckoo, and one or two thrushes,
And a far-off wind that rushes,
And a sound of water that gushes,
And the cuckoo's sovereign cry
Fills all the hollow of the sky.
    Who would go "parading"
In London, "and masquerading,"
On such a night of June
With that beautiful soft half-moon,
And all these innocent blisses?
On such a night as this is!

TO H. C.

SIX YEARS OLD

[Composed 1802.—Published 1807.]

O thou! whose fancies from afar are brought;
Who of thy words dost make a mock apparel,
And fittest to unutterable thought
The breeze-like motion and the self-born carol;
Thou faery voyager! that dost float
In such clear water, that thy boat
May rather seem
To brood on air than on an earthly stream;
Suspended in a stream as clear as sky,
Where earth and heaven do make one imagery;
O blessed vision! happy child!
Thou art so exquisitely wild,
I think of thee with many fears
For what may be thy lot in future years.
    I thought of times when Pain might be thy guest,
Lord of thy house and hospitality;
And Grief, uneasy lover! never rest
But when she sate within the touch of thee.
O too industrious folly!
O vain and causeless melancholy!
Nature will either end thee quite;
Or, lengthening out thy season of delight,
Preserve for thee, by individual right,
A young lamb's heart among the full-grown flocks.
What hast thou to do with sorrow,
Or the injuries of to-morrow?
Thou art a dew-drop, which the morn brings forth,
Ill fitted to sustain unkindly shocks,
Or to be trailed along the soiling earth;
A gem that glitters while it lives,
And no forewarning gives;
But, at the touch of wrong, without a strife
Slips in a moment out of life.

STANZAS

WRITTEN IN MY POCKET-COPY OF THOMSON'S "CASTLE
OF INDOLENCE"

[Composed May 9–11, 1802.—Published 1815.]

Within our happy Castle there dwelt One
Whom without blame I may not overlook;
For never sun on living creature shone
Who more devout enjoyment with us took:
Here on his hours he hung as on a book,
On his own time here would he float away,
As doth a fly upon a summer brook;
But go to-morrow, or belike to-day,
Seek for him,—he is fled; and whither none can say.

Thus often would he leave our peaceful home,
And find elsewhere his business or delight;
Out of our Valley's limits did he roam:
Full many a time, upon a stormy night,
His voice came to us from the neighbouring height:
Oft could we see him driving full in view
At mid-day when the sun was shining bright;
What ill was on him, what he had to do,
A mighty wonder bred among our quiet crew.

Ah! piteous sight it was to see this Man
When he came back to us, a withered flower,—
Or like a sinful creature, pale and wan.
Down would he sit; and without strength or power
Look at the common grass from hour to hour:
And oftentimes, how long I fear to say,
Where apple-trees in blossom made a bower,
Retired in that sunshiny shade he lay;
And, like a naked Indian, slept himself away.

Great wonder to our gentle tribe it was
Whenever from our Valley he withdrew;
For happier soul no living creature has
Than he had, being here the long day through.
Some thought he was a lover, and did woo:

Some thought far worse of him, and judged him wrong;
But verse was what he had been wedded to;
And his own mind did like a tempest strong
Come to him thus, and drove the weary Wight along.

With him there often walked in friendly guise,
Or lay upon the moss by brook or tree,
A noticeable Man with large grey eyes,
And a pale face that seemed undoubtedly
As if a blooming face it ought to be;
Heavy his low-hung lip did oft appear,
Deprest by weight of musing Phantasy;
Profound his forehead was, though not severe;
Yet some did think that he had little business here:

Sweet heaven forefend! his was a lawful right;
Noisy he was, and gamesome as a boy;
His limbs would toss about him with delight,
Like branches when strong winds the trees annoy,
Nor lacked his calmer hours device or toy
To banish listlessness and irksome care;
He would have taught you how you might employ
Yourself; and many did to him repair,—
And certes not in vain; he had inventions rare.

Expedients, too, of simplest sort he tried:
Long blades of grass, plucked round him as he lay,
Made, to his ear attentively applied,
A pipe on which the wind would deftly play;
Glasses he had, that little things display,
The beetle panoplied in gems and gold,
A mailèd angel on a battle-day;
The mysteries that cups of flowers enfold,
And all the gorgeous sights which fairies do behold.

He would entice that other Man to hear
His music, and to view his imagery:
And, sooth, these two were each to the other dear:
No livelier love in such a place could be:
There did they dwell—from earthly labour free,
As happy spirits as were ever seen;

If but a bird, to keep them company,
Or butterfly sate down, they were, I ween,
As pleased as if the same had been a Maiden-queen.

TO THE DAISY

[Composed 1802.—Published 1807.]

"Her divine skill taught me this,
That from every thing I saw
I could some instruction draw,
And raise pleasure to the height
Through the meanest object's sight.
By the murmur of a spring,
Or the least bough's rustelling;
By a Daisy whose leaves spread
Shut when Titan goes to bed;
Or a shady bush or tree;
She could more infuse in me
Than all Nature's beauties can
In some other wiser man."

G. WITHER.

In youth from rock to rock I went,
From hill to hill in discontent
Of pleasure high and turbulent,
    Most pleased when most uneasy;
But now my own delights I make,—
My thirst at every rill can slake,
And gladly Nature's love partake
    Of Thee, sweet Daisy!

Thee Winter in the garland wears
That thinly decks his few grey hairs;
Spring parts the clouds with softest airs,
    That she may sun thee;
Whole Summer-fields are thine by right;
And Autumn, melancholy Wight!
Doth in thy crimson head delight
    When rains are on thee.

In shoals and bands, a morrice train,
Thou greet'st the traveller in the lane;
Pleased at his greeting thee again;
    Yet nothing daunted,
Nor grieved if thou be set at nought:

And oft alone in nooks remote
We meet thee, like a pleasant thought,
　When such are wanted.

Be violets in their secret mews
The flowers the wanton Zephyrs choose;
Proud be the rose, with rains and dews
　Her head impearling,
Thou liv'st with less ambitious aim,
Yet hast not gone without thy fame;
Thou art indeed by many a claim
　The Poet's darling.

If to a rock from rains he fly,
Or, some bright day of April sky,
Imprisoned by hot sunshine lie
　Near the green holly,
And wearily at length should fare;
He needs but look about, and there
Thou art!—a friend at hand, to scare
　His melancholy.

A hundred times, by rock or bower,
Ere thus I have lain couched an hour,
Have I derived from thy sweet power
　Some apprehension;
Some steady love; some brief delight;
Some memory that had taken flight;
Some chime of fancy wrong or right;
　Or stray invention.

If stately passions in me burn,
And one chance look to Thee should turn,
I drink out of an humbler urn
　A lowlier pleasure;
The homely sympathy that heeds
The common life our nature breeds;
A wisdom fitted to the needs
　Of hearts at leisure.

Fresh-smitten by the morning ray,
When thou art up, alert and gay,
Then, cheerful Flower! my spirits play
    With kindred gladness:
And when, at dusk, by dews opprest
Thou sink'st, the image of thy rest
Hath often eased my pensive breast
    Of careful sadness.

And all day long I number yet,
All seasons through, another debt,
Which I, wherever thou art met,
    To thee am owing;
An instinct call it, a blind sense;
A happy, genial influence,
Coming one knows not how, nor whence,
    Nor whither going.

Child of the Year! that round dost run
Thy pleasant course,—when day's begun
As ready to salute the sun
    As lark or leveret,
Thy long-lost praise thou shalt regain;
Nor be less dear to future men
Than in old time;—thou not in vain
    Art Nature's favourite.

TO THE SAME FLOWER

[Composed 1802.—Published 1807.]

With little here to do or see
Of things that in the great world be,
Daisy! again I talk to thee,
    For thou art worthy,
Thou unassuming Common-place
Of Nature, with that homely face,
And yet with something of a grace
    Which love makes for thee!

Oft on the dappled turf at ease
I sit, and play with similes,
Loose types of things through all degrees,
    Thoughts of thy raising:
And many a fond and idle name
I give to thee, for praise or blame,
As is the humour of the game,
    While I am gazing.

A nun demure of lowly port;
Or sprightly maiden, of Love's court,
In thy simplicity the sport
    Of all temptations;
A queen in crown of rubies drest;
A starveling in a scanty vest;
Are all, as seems to suit thee best,
    Thy appellations.

A little Cyclops with one eye
Staring to threaten and defy,
That thought comes next—and instantly
    The freak is over,
The shape will vanish—and behold
A silver shield with boss of gold,
That spreads itself, some faery bold
    In fight to cover!

I see thee glittering from afar—
And then thou art a pretty star;
Not quite so fair as many are
    In heaven above thee!
Yet like a star, with glittering crest,
Self-poised in air thou seem'st to rest;—
May peace come never to his nest,
    Who shall reprove thee!

Bright *Flower!* for by that name at last,
When all my reveries are past,
I call thee, and to that cleave fast,
    Sweet silent creature!
That breath'st with me in sun and air,

Do thou, as thou art wont, repair
My heart with gladness, and a share
　　Of thy meek nature!

TO THE DAISY

[Composed 1802.—Published 1807.]

Bright Flower! whose home is everywhere,
Bold in maternal Nature's care,
And all the long year through the heir
　　Of joy and sorrow;
Methinks that there abides in thee
Some concord with humanity,
Given to no other flower I see
　　The forest thorough!

Is it that Man is soon deprest?
A thoughtless Thing! who, once unblest,
Does little on his memory rest,
　　Or on his reason,
And Thou wouldst teach him how to find
A shelter under every wind,
A hope for times that are unkind
　　And every season?

Thou wander'st the wide world about,
Unchecked by pride or scrupulous doubt,
With friends to greet thee, or without,
　　Yet pleased and willing;
Meek, yielding to the occasion's call,
And all things suffering from all,
Thy function apostolical
　　In peace fulfilling.

[Begun August 29, 30, 1800.—Finished 1802.—Published 1815.]

When, to the attractions of the busy world
Preferring studious leisure, I had chosen

A habitation in this peaceful Vale,
Sharp season followed of continual storm
In deepest winter; and, from week to week,
Pathway, and lane, and public road, were clogged
With frequent showers of snow. Upon a hill,
At a short distance from my cottage, stands
A stately Fir-grove, whither I was wont
To hasten, for I found, beneath the roof
Of that perennial shade, a cloistral place
Of refuge, with an unincumbered floor.
Here, in safe covert, on the shallow snow,
And sometimes on a speck of visible earth,
The redbreast near me hopped; nor was I loth
To sympathize with vulgar coppice birds
That, for protection from the nipping blast,
Hither repaired.—A single beech-tree grew
Within this grove of firs! and, on the fork
Of that one beech, appeared a thrush's nest;
A last year's nest, conspicuously built
At such small elevation from the ground
As gave sure sign that they, who in that house
Of nature and of love had made their home
Amid the fir-trees, all the summer long
Dwelt in a tranquil spot. And oftentimes
A few sheep, stragglers from some mountain-flock,
Would watch my motions with suspicious stare,
From the remotest outskirts of the grove,—
Some nook where they had made their final stand,
Huddling together from two fears—the fear
Of me and of the storm. Full many an hour
Here did I lose. But in this grove the trees
Had been so thickly planted and had thriven
In such perplexed and intricate array,
That vainly did I seek beneath their stems
A length of open space, where to and fro
My feet might move without concern or care;
And, baffled thus, though earth from day to day
Was fettered, and the air by storm disturbed,
I ceased the shelter to frequent,—and prized,
Less than I wished to prize, that calm recess.

The snows dissolved, and genial Spring returned
To clothe the fields with verdure. Other haunts
Meanwhile were mine; till one bright April day,
By chance retiring from the glare of noon
To this forsaken covert, there I found
A hoary pathway traced between the trees,
And winding on with such an easy line
Along a natural opening, that I stood
Much wondering how I could have sought in vain
For what was now so obvious. To abide,
For an allotted interval of ease,
Under my cottage-roof, had gladly come
From the wild sea a cherished Visitant;
And with the sight of this same path—begun,
Begun and ended, in the shady grove,
Pleasant conviction flashed upon my mind
That, to this opportune recess allured,
He had surveyed it with a finer eye,
A heart more wakeful; and had worn the track
By pacing here, unwearied and alone,
In that habitual restlessness of foot
That haunts the Sailor, measuring o'er and o'er
His short domain upon the vessel's deck,
While she pursues her course through the dreary sea.

When thou hadst quitted Esthwaite's pleasant shore,
And taken thy first leave of those green hills
And rocks that were the play-ground of thy youth,
Year followed year, my Brother! and we two,
Conversing not, knew little in what mould
Each other's mind was fashioned; and at length
When once again we met in Grasmere Vale,
Between us there was little other bond
Than common feelings of fraternal love.
But thou, a School-boy, to the sea hadst carried
Undying recollections; Nature there
Was with thee; she, who loved us both, she still
Was with thee; and even so didst thou become
A *silent* Poet; from the solitude
Of the vast sea didst bring a watchful heart
Still couchant, an inevitable ear,

And an eye practised like a blind man's touch.
—Back to the joyless Ocean thou art gone;
Nor from this vestige of thy musing hours
Could I withhold thy honoured name,—and now
I love the fir-grove with a perfect love.
Thither do I withdraw when cloudless suns
Shine hot, or wind blows troublesome and strong;
And there I sit at evening, when the steep
Of Silver-how, and Grasmere's peaceful lake
And one green island, gleam between the stems
Of the dark firs, a visionary scene!
And while I gaze upon the spectacle
Of clouded splendour, on this dream-like sight
Of solemn loveliness, I think on thee,
My Brother, and on all which thou hast lost.
Nor seldom, if I rightly guess, while Thou,
Muttering the verses which I muttered first
Among the mountains, through the midnight watch
Art pacing thoughtfully the vessel's deck
In some far region, here, while o'er my head
At every impulse of the moving breeze,
The fir-grove murmurs with a sea-like sound,
Alone I tread this path;—for aught I know,
Timing my steps to thine; and, with a store
Of undistinguishable sympathies,
Mingling most earnest wishes for the day
When we, and others whom we love, shall meet
A second time, in Grasmere's happy Vale.

NOTE.—This wish was not granted; the lamented Person not long after
perished by shipwreck, in discharge of his duty as Commander of the
Honourable East India Company's Vessel, the Earl of Abergavenny.

A FAREWELL

[Finished May 29, 1802.—Published 1815.]

Farewell, thou little Nook of mountain-ground,
    Thou rocky corner in the lowest stair
Of that magnificent temple which doth bound
    One side of our whole vale with grandeur rare;

Sweet garden-orchard, eminently fair,
The loveliest spot that man hath ever found,
    Farewell!—we leave thee to Heaven's peaceful care,
Thee, and the Cottage which thou dost surround.

Our boat is safely anchored by the shore,
    And there will safely ride when we are gone;
The flowering shrubs that deck our humble door
    Will prosper, though untended and alone:
Fields, goods, and far-off chattels we have none:
These narrow bounds contain our private store
    Of things earth makes, and sun doth shine upon;
Here are they in our sight—we have no more.

Sunshine and shower be with you, bud and bell!
    For two months now in vain we shall be sought;
We leave you here in solitude to dwell
    With these our latest gifts of tender thought;
    Thou, like the morning, in thy saffron coat,
Bright gowan, and marsh-marigold, farewell!
    Whom from the borders of the Lake we brought,
And placed together near our rocky Well.

We go for One to whom ye will be dear;
    And she will prize this Bower, this Indian shed,
Our own contrivance, Building without peer!
    —A gentle Maid, whose heart is lowly bred,
    Whose pleasures are in wild fields gatherèd,
With joyousness, and with a thoughtful cheer,
    Will come to you; to you herself will wed;
And love the blessed life that we lead here.

Dear Spot! which we have watched with tender heed,
    Bringing thee chosen plants and blossoms blown
Among the distant mountains, flower and weed,
    Which thou hast taken to thee as thy own,
    Making all kindness registered and known;
Thou for our sakes, though Nature's child indeed,
    Fair in thyself and beautiful alone,
Hast taken gifts which thou dost little need.

And O most constant, yet most fickle Place
      That hast thy wayward moods, as thou dost show
To them who look not daily on thy face;
      Who, being loved, in love no bounds dost know,
      And say'st, when we forsake thee, "Let them go!"
Thou easy-hearted Thing, with thy wild race
      Of weeds and flowers, till we return be slow,
And travel with the year at a soft pace.

Help us to tell Her tales of years gone by,
      And this sweet spring, the best beloved and best;
Joy will be flown in its mortality;
      Something must stay to tell us of the rest.
      Here, thronged with primroses, the steep rock's
            breast
Glittered at evening like a starry sky;
      And in this bush our sparrow built her nest,
Of which I sang one song that will not die.

O happy Garden! whose seclusion deep
      Hath been so friendly to industrious hours;
And to soft slumbers, that did gently steep
      Our spirits, carrying with them dreams of flowers,
      And wild notes warbled among leafy bowers;
Two burning months let summer overleap,
      And, coming back with Her who will be ours,
Into thy bosom we again shall creep.

[Composed May 21, 1802.—Published September 6, 1802 (*Morning Post*);
            January 29, 1803 (*Ibid.*); 1807.]

I grieved for Buonaparté, with a vain
And an unthinking grief! The tenderest mood
Of that Man's mind—what can it be? what food
Fed his first hopes? what knowledge could *he* gain?
'Tis not in battles that from youth we train
The Governor who must be wise and good,
And temper with the sternness of the brain
Thoughts motherly, and meek as womanhood.
Wisdom doth live with children round her knees:

Books, leisure, perfect freedom, and the talk
Man holds with week-day man in the hourly walk
Of the mind's business: these are the degrees
By which true Sway doth mount; this is the stalk
True Power doth grow on; and her rights are these.

COMPOSED UPON WESTMINSTER BRIDGE

[Composed July 31, 1802.—Published 1807.]

Earth has not anything to show more fair:
Dull would he be of soul who could pass by
A sight so touching in its majesty:
This City now doth, like a garment, wear
The beauty of the morning; silent, bare,
Ships, towers, domes, theatres, and temples lie
Open unto the fields, and to the sky;
All bright and glittering in the smokeless air.
Never did sun more beautifully steep
In his first splendour, valley, rock, or hill;
Ne'er saw I, never felt, a calm so deep!
The river glideth at his own sweet will:
Dear God! the very houses seem asleep;
And all that mighty heart is lying still!

[Composed August, 1802.—Published 1807.]

It is a beauteous evening, calm and free;
The holy time is quiet as a Nun
Breathless with adoration; the broad sun
Is sinking down in its tranquillity;
The gentleness of heaven broods o'er the Sea:
Listen! the mighty Being is awake,
And doth with his eternal motion make
A sound like thunder—everlastingly.
Dear Child! dear Girl! that walkest with me here,
If thou appear untouched by solemn thought,
Thy nature is not therefore less divine:
Thou liest in Abraham's bosom all the year;
And worshipp'st at the Temple's inner shrine,
God being with thee when we know it not.

COMPOSED BY THE SEA-SIDE, NEAR CALAIS, AUGUST, 1802

[Composed August, 1802.—Published 1807.]

Fair Star of evening, Splendour of the west,
Star of my Country!—on the horizon's brink
Thou hangest, stooping, as might seem, to sink
On England's bosom; yet well pleased to rest,
Meanwhile, and be to her a glorious crest
Conspicuous to the Nations. Thou, I think,
Shouldst be my Country's emblem; and shouldst wink,
Bright Star! with laughter on her banners, drest
In thy fresh beauty. There! that dusky spot
Beneath thee, that is England; there she lies.
Blessings be on you both! one hope, one lot,
One life, one glory!—I, with many a fear
For my dear Country, many heartfelt sighs,
Among men who do not love her, linger here.

CALAIS, AUGUST, 1802

[Composed August, 1802.—Published January 29, 1803 (*Morning Post*);
1807.]

Is it a reed that's shaken by the wind,
Or what is it that ye go forth to see?
Lords, lawyers, statesmen, squires of low degree,
Men known, and men unknown, sick, lame, and blind,
Post forward all, like creatures of one kind,
With first-fruit offerings crowd to bend the knee
In France, before the new-born Majesty.
'Tis ever thus. Ye men of prostrate mind,
A seemly reverence may be paid to power;
But that's a loyal virtue, never sown
In haste, nor springing with a transient shower:
When truth, when sense, when liberty were flown,
What hardship had it been to wait an hour?
Shame on you, feeble Heads, to slavery prone!

COMPOSED NEAR CALAIS, ON THE ROAD LEADING TO ARDRES, AUGUST 7, 1802

[Composed August, 1802.—Published 1807.]

Jones! as from Calais southward you and I
Went pacing side by side, this public Way
Streamed with the pomp of a too-credulous day.
When faith was pledged to new-born Liberty:
A homeless sound of joy was in the sky:
From hour to hour the antiquated Earth
Beat like the heart of Man: songs, garlands, mirth,
Banners, and happy faces, far and nigh!
And now, sole register that these things were,
Two solitary greetings have I heard,
"Good morrow, Citizen!" a hollow word,
As if a dead man spake it! Yet despair
Touches me not, though pensive as a bird
Whose vernal coverts winter hath laid bare.

CALAIS, AUGUST 15, 1802

[Composed August 15, 1802.—Published February 26, 1803 (*Morning Post*); 1807.]

Festivals have I seen that were not names:
This is young Buonaparté's natal day,
And his is henceforth an established sway—
Consul for life. With worship France proclaims
Her approbation, and with pomps and games.
Heaven grant that other Cities may be gay!
Calais is not: and I have bent my way
To the sea-coast, noting that each man frames
His business as he likes. Far other show
My youth here witnessed, in a prouder time;
The senselessness of joy was then sublime!
Happy is he, who, caring not for Pope,
Consul, or King, can sound himself to know
The destiny of Man, and live in hope.

ON THE EXTINCTION OF THE VENETIAN REPUBLIC

[Composed probably August, 1802.—Published 1807.]

Once did She hold the gorgeous east in fee;
And was the safeguard of the west: the worth
Of Venice did not fall below her birth,
Venice, the eldest Child of Liberty.
She was a maiden City, bright and free;
No guile seduced, no force could violate;
And, when she took unto herself a Mate,
She must espouse the everlasting Sea.
And what if she had seen those glories fade,
Those titles vanish, and that strength decay;
Yet shall some tribute of regret be paid
When her long life hath reached its final day:
Men are we, and must grieve when even the Shade
Of that which once was great is passed away.

TO TOUSSAINT L'OUVERTURE

[Composed probably August, 1802.—Published February 2, 1803 (*Morning Post*); 1807.]

Toussaint, the most unhappy man of men!
Whether the whistling Rustic tend his plough
Within thy hearing, or thy head be now
Pillowed in some deep dungeon's earless den;—
O miserable Chieftain! where and when
Wilt thou find patience! Yet die not; do thou
Wear rather in thy bonds a cheerful brow:
Though fallen thyself, never to rise again,
Live, and take comfort. Thou hast left behind
Powers that will work for thee; air, earth, and skies:
There's not a breathing of the common wind
That will forget thee; thou hast great allies;
Thy friends are exultations, agonies,
And love, and man's unconquerable mind.

COMPOSED IN THE VALLEY NEAR DOVER, ON THE DAY OF LANDING

[Composed August 30, 1802.—Published 1807.]

Here, on our native soil, we breathe once more.
The cock that crows, the smoke that curls, that sound
Of bells;—those boys who in yon meadow-ground
In white-sleeved shirts are playing; and the roar
Of the waves breaking on the chalky shore;—
All, all are English. Oft have I looked round
With joy in Kent's green vales; but never found
Myself so satisfied in heart before.
Europe is yet in bonds; but let that pass,
Thought for another moment. Thou art free,
My Country! and 'tis joy enough and pride
For one hour's perfect bliss, to tread the grass
Of England once again, and hear and see,
With such a dear Companion at my side.

SEPTEMBER 1, 1802

[Composed September 1, 1802.—Published February 11, 1803 (*Morning Post*); 1807.]

Among the capricious acts of tyranny that disgraced those
times, was the chasing of all Negroes from France by
decree of the government: we had a Fellow-passenger
who was one of the expelled.

We had a female Passenger who came
From Calais with us, spotless in array,—
A white-robed Negro, like a lady gay,
Yet downcast as a woman fearing blame;
Meek, destitute, as seemed, of hope or aim
She sate, from notice turning not away,
But on all proffered intercourse did lay
A weight of languid speech, or to the same
No sign of answer made by word or face:
Yet still her eyes retained their tropic fire,
That, burning independent of the mind,
Joined with the lustre of her rich attire
To mock the Outcast—O ye Heavens, be kind!
And feel, thou Earth, for this afflicted Race!

SEPTEMBER, 1802. NEAR DOVER

[Composed September, 1802.—Published 1807.]

Inland, within a hollow vale, I stood;
And saw, while sea was calm and air was clear,
The coast of France—the coast of France how near!
Drawn almost into frightful neighbourhood.
I shrunk; for verily the barrier flood
Was like a lake, or river bright and fair,
A span of waters; yet what power is there!
What mightiness for evil and for good!
Even so doth God protect us if we be
Virtuous and wise. Winds blow, and waters roll,
Strength to the brave, and Power, and Deity;
Yet in themselves are nothing! One decree
Spake laws to *them*, and said that by the soul
Only, the Nations shall be great and free.

WRITTEN IN LONDON, SEPTEMBER, 1802

[Composed September, 1802.—Published 1807.]

O Friend! I know not which way I must look
For comfort, being, as I am, opprest,
To think that now our life is only drest
For show; mean handy-work of craftsman, cook,
Or groom!—We must run glittering like a brook
In the open sunshine, or we are unblest:
The wealthiest man among us is the best:
No grandeur now in nature or in book
Delights us. Rapine, avarice, expense,
This is idolatry; and these we adore:
Plain living and high thinking are no more:
The homely beauty of the good old cause
Is gone; our peace, our fearful innocence,
And pure religion breathing household laws.

LONDON, 1802

[Composed September, 1802.—Published 1807.]

Milton! thou shouldst be living at this hour:
England hath need of thee: she is a fen
Of stagnant waters: altar, sword, and pen,
Fireside, the heroic wealth of hall and bower,
Have forfeited their ancient English dower
Of inward happiness. We are selfish men;
Oh! raise us up, return to us again;
And give us manners, virtue, freedom, power.
Thy soul was like a Star, and dwelt apart;
Thou hadst a voice whose sound was like the sea:
Pure as the naked heavens, majestic, free,
So didst thou travel on life's common way,
In cheerful godliness; and yet thy heart
The lowliest duties on herself did lay.

[Composed probably 1802.—Published 1807.]

Great men have been among us; hands that penned
And tongues that uttered wisdom—better none:
The later Sidney, Marvel, Harrington,
Young Vane, and others who called Milton friend.
These moralists could act and comprehend:
They knew how genuine glory was put on;
Taught us how rightfully a nation shone
In splendour: what strength was, that would not bend
But in magnanimous meekness. France, 'tis strange,
Hath brought forth no such souls as we had then.
Perpetual emptiness! unceasing change!
No single volume paramount, no code,
No master spirit, no determined road;
But equally a want of books and men!

[Composed 1802 or 1803.—Published April 16, 1803 (*Morning Post*); 1807.]

It is not to be thought of that the Flood
Of British freedom, which, to the open sea

Of the world's praise, from dark antiquity
Hath flowed, "with pomp of waters, unwithstood,"
Roused though it be full often to a mood
Which spurns the check of salutary bands,
That this most famous Stream in bogs and sands
Should perish; and to evil and to good
Be lost for ever. In our halls is hung
Armoury of the invincible Knights of old:
We must be free or die, who speak the tongue
That Shakespeare spake; the faith and morals hold
Which Milton held.—In every thing we are sprung
Of Earth's first blood, have titles manifold.

[Composed 1802 or 1803.—Published September 17, 1803 (*Morning Post*);
1807.]

When I have borne in memory what has tamed
Great Nations, how ennobling thoughts depart
When men change swords for ledgers, and desert
The student's bower for gold, some fears unnamed
I had, my Country—am I to be blamed?
Now, when I think of thee, and what thou art,
Verily, in the bottom of my heart,
Of those unfilial fears I am ashamed.
For dearly must we prize thee; we who find
In thee a bulwark for the cause of men;
And I by my affection was beguiled:
What wonder if a Poet now and then,
Among the many movements of his mind,
Felt for thee as a lover or a child!

OCTOBER, 1803

[Composed October, 1803.—Published 1807.]

These times strike monied worldlings with dismay:
Even rich men, brave by nature, taint the air
With words of apprehension and despair:
While tens of thousands, thinking on the affray,
Men unto whom sufficient for the day

And minds not stinted or untilled are given,
Sound, healthy, children of the God of heaven,
Are cheerful as the rising sun in May.
What do we gather hence but firmer faith
That every gift of noble origin
Is breathed upon by Hope's perpetual breath;
That virtue and the faculties within
Are vital,—and that riches are akin
To fear, to change, to cowardice, and death?

OCTOBER, 1803

[Composed October, 1803.—Published 1807.]

When, looking on the present face of things,
I see one man, of men the meanest too!
Raised up to sway the world, to do, undo,
With mighty Nations for his underlings,
The great events with which old story rings
Seem vain and hollow; I find nothing great:
Nothing is left which I can venerate;
So that a doubt almost within me springs
Of Providence, such emptiness at length
Seems at the heart of all things. But, great God!
I measure back the steps which I have trod;
And tremble, seeing whence proceeds the strength
Of such poor Instruments, with thoughts sublime
I tremble at the sorrow of the time.

THE GREEN LINNET

[Composed 1803.—Published 1807.]

Beneath these fruit-tree boughs that shed
Their snow-white blossoms on my head,
With brightest sunshine round me spread
    Of spring's unclouded weather,
In this sequestered nook how sweet

To sit upon my orchard-seat!
And birds and flowers once more to greet,
  My last year's friends together.

One have I marked, the happiest guest
In all this covert of the blest:
Hail to Thee, far above the rest
  In joy of voice and pinion!
Thou, Linnet! in thy green array,
Presiding Spirit here to-day,
Dost lead the revels of the May;
  And this is thy dominion.

While birds, and butterflies, and flowers,
Make all one band of paramours,
Thou, ranging up and down the bowers,
  Art sole in thy employment:
A Life, a Presence like the Air,
Scattering thy gladness without care,
Too blest with any one to pair;
  Thyself thy own enjoyment.

Amid yon tuft of hazel trees,
That twinkle to the gusty breeze,
Behold him perched in ecstasies,
  Yet seeming still to hover;
There! where the flutter of his wings
Upon his back and body flings
Shadows and sunny glimmerings,
  That cover him all over.

My dazzled sight he oft deceives,
A Brother of the dancing leaves;
Then flits, and from the cottage eaves
  Pours forth his song in gushes;
As if by that exulting strain
He mocked and treated with disdain
The voiceless Form he chose to feign,
  While fluttering in the bushes.

YEW-TREES

[Composed 1803.—Published 1815.]

There is a Yew-tree, pride of Lorton Vale,
Which to this day stands single, in the midst
Of its own darkness, as it stood of yore;
Not loth to furnish weapons for the bands
Of Umfraville or Percy ere they marched
To Scotland's heaths; or those that crossed the sea
And drew their sounding bows at Azincour,
Perhaps at earlier Crecy, or Poictiers.
Of vast circumference and gloom profound
This solitary Tree! a living thing
Produced too slowly ever to decay;
Of form and aspect too magnificent
To be destroyed. But worthier still of note
Are those fraternal Four of Borrowdale,
Joined in one solemn and capacious grove;
Huge trunks! and each particular trunk a growth
Of intertwisted fibres serpentine
Up-coiling, and inveterately convolved;
Nor uninformed with Phantasy, and looks
That threaten the profane; a pillared shade,
Upon whose grassless floor of red-brown hue,
By sheddings from the pining umbrage tinged
Perennially—beneath whose sable roof
Of boughs, as if for festal purpose decked
With unrejoicing berries—ghostly Shapes
May meet at noontide; Fear and trembling Hope
Silence and Foresight; Death the Skeleton
And Time the Shadow;—there to celebrate,
As in a natural temple scattered o'er
With altars undisturbed of mossy stone,
United worship; or in mute repose
To lie, and listen to the mountain flood
Murmuring from Glaramara's inmost caves.

AT THE GRAVE OF BURNS

1803

SEVEN YEARS AFTER HIS DEATH

[Composed partly before 1807.—Published: vol. of 1842.]

I shiver, Spirit fierce and bold,
At thought of what I now behold:
As vapours breathed from dungeons cold
    Strike pleasure dead,
So sadness comes from out the mould
    Where Burns is laid.

And have I then thy bones so near,
And thou forbidden to appear?
As if it were thyself that's here
    I shrink with pain;
And both my wishes and my fear
    Alike are vain.

Off weight—nor press on weight!—away
Dark thoughts!—they came, but not to stay;
With chastened feelings would I pay
    The tribute due
To him, and aught that hides his clay
    From mortal view.

Fresh as the flower, whose modest worth
He sang, his genius "glinted" forth,
Rose like a star that touching earth,
    For so it seems,
Doth glorify its humble birth
    With matchless beams.

The piercing eye, the thoughtful brow,
The struggling heart, where be they now?—
Full soon the Aspirant of the plough,
    The prompt, the brave,
Slept, with the obscurest, in the low
    And silent grave.

I mourned with thousands, but as one
More deeply grieved, for He was gone
Whose light I hailed when first it shone,
        And showed my youth
How Verse may build a princely throne
        On humble truth.

Alas! where'er the current tends,
Regret pursues and with it blends,—
Huge Criffel's hoary top ascends
        By Skiddaw seen,—
Neighbours we were, and loving friends
        We might have been;

True friends though diversely inclined;
But heart with heart and mind with mind,
Where the main fibres are entwined,
        Through Nature's skill,
May even by contraries be joined,
        More closely still.

The tear will start, and let it flow;
Thou "poor Inhabitant below,"
At this dread moment—even so—
        Might we together
Have sate and talked where gowans blow,
        Or on wild heather.

What treasures would have then been placed
Within my reach; of knowledge graced
By fancy what a rich repast!
        But why go on?—
Oh! spare to sweep, thou mournful blast,
        His grave grass-grown.

There, too, a Son, his joy and pride,
(Not three weeks past the Stripling died,)
Lies gathered to his Father's side,
        Soul-moving sight!
Yet one to which is not denied
        Some sad delight.

For *he* is safe, a quiet bed
Hath early found among the dead,
Harboured where none can be misled,
    Wronged, or distrest;
And surely here it may be said
    That such are blest.

And oh for Thee, by pitying grace
Checked oft-times in a devious race,
May He, who halloweth the place
    Where Man is laid,
Receive thy Spirit in the embrace
    For which it prayed!

Sighing I turned away; but ere
Night fell I heard, or seemed to hear,
Music that sorrow comes not near,
    A ritual hymn,
Chanted in love that casts out fear
    By Seraphim.

THOUGHTS

SUGGESTED THE DAY FOLLOWING, ON THE BANKS OF NITH,
NEAR THE POET'S RESIDENCE

[Finished 1839.—Published: vol. of 1842.]

Too frail to keep the lofty vow
That must have followed when his brow
Was wreathed—"The Vision" tells us how—
    With holly spray,
He faltered, drifted to and fro,
    And passed away.

Well might such thoughts, dear Sister, throng
Our minds when, lingering all too long,
Over the grave of Burns we hung
    In social grief—
Indulged as if it were a wrong
    To seek relief.

But, leaving each unquiet theme
Where gentlest judgments may misdeem,
And prompt to welcome every gleam
    Of good and fair,
Let us beside the limpid Stream
    Breathe hopeful air.

Enough of sorrow, wreck, and blight;
Think rather of those moments bright
When to the consciousness of right
    His course was true,
When Wisdom prospered in his sight
    And virtue grew.

Yes, freely let our hearts expand,
Freely as in youth's season bland,
When side by side, his Book in hand,
    We wont to stray,
Our pleasure varying at command
    Of each sweet Lay.

How oft inspired must he have trod
These pathways, yon far-stretching road!
There lurks his home; in that Abode,
    With mirth elate,
Or in his nobly-pensive mood,
    The Rustic sate.

Proud thoughts that Image overawes,
Before it humbly let us pause,
And ask of Nature from what cause
    And by what rules
She trained her Burns to win applause
    That shames the Schools.

Through busiest street and loneliest glen
Are felt the flashes of his pen;
He rules 'mid winter snows, and when
    Bees fill their hives;
Deep in the general heart of men
    His power survives.

What need of fields in some far clime
Where Heroes, Sages, Bards sublime,
And all that fetched the flowing rhyme
    From genuine springs,
Shall dwell together till old Time
    Folds up his wings?

Sweet Mercy! to the gates of Heaven
This Minstrel lead, his sins forgiven;
The rueful conflict, the heart riven
    With vain endeavour,
And memory of Earth's bitter leaven,
    Effaced for ever.

But why to Him confine the prayer,
When kindred thoughts and yearnings **bear**
On the frail heart the purest share
    With all that live?—
The best of what we do and are,
    Just God, forgive!

GLEN ALMAIN

OR, THE NARROW GLEN

[Composed probably 1803.—Published 1807.]

In this still place, remote from men,
Sleeps Ossian, in the NARROW GLEN;
In this still place, where murmurs on
But one meek streamlet, only one:
He sang of battles, and the breath
Of stormy war, and violent death;
And should, methinks, when all was past,
Have rightfully been laid at last
Where rocks were rudely heaped, and rent
As by a spirit turbulent;
Where sights were rough, and sounds were wild,
And everything unreconciled;
In some complaining, dim retreat,

For fear and melancholy meet;
But this is calm; there cannot be
A more entire tranquillity.

Does then the Bard sleep here indeed?
Or is it but a groundless creed?
What matters it?—I blame them not
Whose Fancy in this lonely Spot
Was moved; and in such way expressed
Their notion of its perfect rest.
A convent, even a hermit's cell,
Would break the silence of this Dell:
It is not quiet, is not ease;
But something deeper far than these:
The separation that is here
Is of the grave; and of austere
Yet happy feelings of the dead:
And, therefore, was it rightly said
That Ossian, last of all his race!
Lies buried in this lonely place.

STEPPING WESTWARD

[Composed between 1803–1805.—Published 1807.]

While my Fellow-traveller and I were walking by the side of Lock Ket-
terine, one fine evening after sunset, in our road to a Hut where,
in the course of our Tour, we had been hospitably entertained some
weeks before, we met, in one of the loneliest parts of that solitary
region, two well-dressed Women, one of whom said to us, by way of
greeting, "What, you are stepping westward?"

"*What, you are stepping westward?*"—
      "*Yea.*"
—'Twould be a *wildish* destiny,
If we, who thus together roam
In a strange Land, and far from home,
Were in this place the guests of Chance:
Yet who would stop, or fear to advance,
Though home or shelter he had none,
With such a sky to lead him on?

The dewy ground was dark and cold;
Behind, all gloomy to behold;
And stepping westward seemed to be
A kind of *heavenly* destiny:
I liked the greeting; 'twas a sound
Of something without place or bound;
And seemed to give me spiritual right
To travel through that region bright.

The voice was soft, and she who spake
Was walking by her native lake:
The salutation had to me
The very sound of courtesy:
Its power was felt; and while my eye
Was fixed upon the glowing Sky,
The echo of the voice enwrought
A human sweetness with the thought
Of travelling through the world that lay
Before me in my endless way.

TO A HIGHLAND GIRL

AT INVERSNEYDE, UPON LOCH LOMOND

[Composed 1803.—Published 1807.]

Sweet Highland Girl, a very shower
Of beauty is thy earthly dower!
Twice seven consenting years have shed
Their utmost bounty on thy head:
And these grey rocks; that household lawn;
Those trees, a veil just half withdrawn;
This fall of water that doth make
A murmur near the silent lake;
This little bay; a quiet road
That holds in shelter thy Abode—
In truth together do ye seem
Like something fashioned in a dream;
Such Forms as from their covert peep
When earthly cares are laid asleep!

But, O fair Creature! in the light
Of common day, so heavenly bright,
I bless Thee, Vision as thou art,
I bless thee with a human heart;
God shield thee to thy latest years!
Thee, neither know I, nor thy peers;
And yet my eyes are filled with tears.

With earnest feeling I shall pray
For thee when I am far away:
For never saw I mien, or face,
In which more plainly I could trace
Benignity and home-bred sense
Ripening in perfect innocence.
Here scattered, like a random seed,
Remote from men, Thou dost not need
The embarrassed look of shy distress,
And maidenly shamefacedness:
Thou wear'st upon thy forehead clear
The freedom of a Mountaineer:
A face with gladness overspread!
Soft smiles, by human kindness bred!
And seemliness complete, that sways
Thy courtesies, about thee plays;
With no restraint, but such as springs
From quick and eager visitings
Of thoughts that lie beyond the reach
Of thy few words of English speech:
A bondage sweetly brooked, a strife
That gives thy gestures grace and life!
So have I, not unmoved in mind,
Seen birds of tempest-loving kind—
Thus beating up against the wind.

What hand but would a garland cull
For thee who art so beautiful?
O happy pleasure! here to dwell
Beside thee in some heathy dell;
Adopt your homely ways, and dress,
A Shepherd, thou a Shepherdess!
But I could frame a wish for thee

smoothness & buoyant

More like a grave reality:
Thou art to me but as a wave
Of the wild sea; and I would have
Some claim upon thee, if I could,
Though but of common neighbourhood.
What joy to hear thee, and to see!
Thy elder Brother I would be,
Thy Father—anything to thee!

Charleston!   *spouse?*

Now thanks to Heaven! that of its grace
Hath led me to this lonely place.
Joy have I had; and going hence
I bear away my recompense.
In spots like these it is we prize
Our Memory, feel that she hath eyes:
Then, why should I be loth to stir?
I feel this place was made for her;
To give new pleasure like the past,
Continued long as life shall last.
Nor am I loth, though pleased at heart,
Sweet Highland Girl! from thee to part;
For I, methinks, till I grow old,
As fair before me shall behold,
As I do now, the cabin small,
The lake, the bay, the waterfall;
And Thee, the Spirit of them all!

[Composed 1804.—Published 1807.]

She was a Phantom of delight
When first she gleamed upon my sight;
A lovely Apparition, sent
To be a moment's ornament;
Her eyes as stars of Twilight fair;
Like Twilight's, too, her dusky hair;
But all things else about her drawn
From May-time and the cheerful Dawn;
A dancing Shape, an Image gay,
To haunt, to startle, and way-lay.

I saw her upon nearer view,
A Spirit, yet a Woman too!
Her household motions light and free,
And steps of virgin-liberty;
A countenance in which did meet
Sweet records, promises as sweet;
A Creature not too bright or good
For human nature's daily food;
For transient sorrows, simple wiles,
Praise, blame, love, kisses, tears, and smiles.

And now I see with eye serene
The very pulse of the machine;
A Being breathing thoughtful breath,
A Traveller between life and death;
The reason firm, the temperate will,
Endurance, foresight, strength, and skill;
A perfect Woman, nobly planned,
To warn, to comfort, and command;
And yet a Spirit still, and bright
With something of angelic light.

THE SOLITARY REAPER

[Composed between 1803–1805.—Published 1807.]

Behold her, single in the field,
Yon solitary Highland Lass!
Reaping and singing by herself;
Stop here, or gently pass!
Alone she cuts and binds the grain,
And sings a melancholy strain;
O listen! for the Vale profound
Is overflowing with the sound.

No Nightingale did ever chaunt
More welcome notes to weary bands
Of travellers in some shady haunt,
Among Arabian sands:
A voice so thrilling ne'er was heard
In spring-time from the Cuckoo-bird,

Breaking the silence of the seas
Among the farthest Hebrides.

Will no one tell me what she sings!—
Perhaps the plaintive numbers flow
For old, unhappy, far-off things,
And battles long ago:
Or is it some more humble lay,
Familiar matter of to-day?
Some natural sorrow, loss, or pain,
That has been, and may be again?

Whate'er the theme, the Maiden sang
As if her song could have no ending;
I saw her singing at her work,
And o'er the sickle bending;—
I listened, motionless and still;
And, as I mounted up the hill,
The music in my heart I bore,
Long after it was heard no more.

ADDRESS TO KILCHURN CASTLE,
UPON LOCH AWE

[Composed ll. 1-3, 1803; finished "long after."—Published 1827.]

Child of loud-throated War! the mountain Stream
Roars in thy hearing; but thy hour of rest
Is come, and thou art silent in thy age;
Save when the wind sweeps by and sounds are
         caught
Ambiguous, neither wholly thine nor theirs.
Oh! there is life that breathes not; Powers there
         are
That touch each other to the quick in modes
Which the gross world no sense hath to perceive,
No soul to dream of. What art Thou, from care
Cast off—abandoned by thy rugged Sire,
Nor by soft Peace adopted; though, in place
And in dimension, such that thou might'st seem
But a mere footstool to yon sovereign Lord,

Huge Cruachan, (a thing that meaner hills
Might crush, nor know that it had suffered harm;)
Yet he, not loth, in favour of thy claims
To reverence, suspends his own; submitting
All that the God of Nature hath conferred,
All that he holds in common with the stars,
To the memorial majesty of Time
Impersonated in thy calm decay!
Take, then, thy seat, Vicegerent unreproved!
Now, while a farewell gleam of evening light
Is fondly lingering on thy shattered front,
Do thou, in turn, be paramount; and rule
Over the pomp and beauty of a scene
Whose mountains, torrents, lake, and woods, unite
To pay thee homage; and with these are joined,
In willing admiration and respect,
Two Hearts, which in thy presence might be called
Youthful as Spring.—Shade of departed Power,
Skeleton of unfleshed humanity,
The chronicle were welcome that should call
Into the compass of distinct regard
The toils and struggles of thy infant years!
Yon foaming flood seems motionless as ice;
Its dizzy turbulence eludes the eye,
Frozen by distance; so, majestic Pile,
To the perception of this Age, appear
Thy fierce beginnings, softened and subdued
And quieted in character—the strife,
The pride, the fury uncontrollable,
Lost on the aerial heights of the Crusades!

YARROW UNVISITED

[Composed 1803.—Published 1807.]

See the various Poems the scene of which is laid upon the banks of the
Yarrow; in particular, the exquisite Ballad of Hamilton beginning—
　　　"Busk ye, busk ye, my bonny, bonny Bride,
　　　Busk ye, busk ye, my winsome Marrow!"

From Stirling castle we had seen
　　The mazy Forth unravelled;

Had trod the banks of Clyde, and Tay,
  And with the Tweed had travelled;
And when we came to Clovenford,
  Then said my *"winsome Marrow,"*
"Whate'er betide, we'll turn aside,
  And see the Braes of Yarrow."

"Let Yarrow folk, *frae* Selkirk town,
  Who have been buying, selling,
Go back to Yarrow, 'tis their own;
  Each maiden to her dwelling!
On Yarrow's banks let herons feed,
  Hares couch, and rabbits burrow!
But we will downward with the Tweed,
  Nor turn aside to Yarrow.

"There's Galla Water, Leader Haughs,
  Both lying right before us;
And Dryborough, where with chiming Tweed
  The lintwhites sing in chorus;
There's pleasant Tiviot-dale, a land
  Made blithe with plough and harrow:
Why throw away a needful day
  To go in search of Yarrow?

"What's Yarrow but a river bare,
  That glides the dark hills under?
There are a thousand such elsewhere
  As worthy of your wonder."
—Strange words they seemed of slight and scorn;
  My True-love sighed for sorrow;
And looked me in the face, to think
  I thus could speak of Yarrow!

"Oh, green," said I, "are Yarrow's holms,
  And sweet is Yarrow flowing!
Fair hangs the apple frae the rock,
  But we will leave it growing.
O'er hilly path, and open Strath,
  We'll wander Scotland thorough;
But, though so near, we will not turn
  Into the dale of Yarrow.

"Let beeves and home-bred kine partake
   The sweets of Burn-mill meadow;
The swan on still St. Mary's Lake
   Float double, swan and shadow!
We will not see them; will not go,
   To-day, nor yet to-morrow;
Enough if in our hearts we know
   There's such a place as Yarrow.

"Be Yarrow stream unseen, unknown!
   It must, or we shall rue it:
We have a vision of our own;
   Ah! why should we undo it?
The treasured dreams of times long past,
   We'll keep them, winsome Marrow!
For when we're there, although 'tis fair,
   'Twill be another Yarrow!

"If Care with freezing years should come,
   And wandering seem but folly,—
Should we be loth to stir from home,
   And yet be melancholy;
Should life be dull, and spirits low,
   'Twill soothe us in our sorrow,
That earth hath something yet to show,
   The bonny holms of Yarrow!"

[Begun probably in the spring of 1802. Composed 1804.—Published 1807.]

I wandered lonely as a cloud
   That floats on high o'er vales and hills,
When all at once I saw a crowd,
   A host, of golden daffodils;
Beside the lake, beneath the trees,
Fluttering and dancing in the breeze.

Continuous as the stars that shine
   And twinkle on the milky way,
They stretched in never-ending line
   Along the margin of a bay:
Ten thousand saw I at a glance,
Tossing their heads in sprightly dance.

The waves beside them danced; but they
    Out-did the sparkling waves in glee:
A poet could not but be gay,
    In such a jocund company:
I gazed—and gazed—but little thought
What wealth the show to me had brought:

For oft, when on my couch I lie
    In vacant or in pensive mood,
They flash upon that inward eye
    Which is the bliss of solitude;
And then my heart with pleasure fills,
And dances with the daffodils.

VAUDRACOUR AND JULIA

[Composed probably before 1804.—Published 1820.]

The following tale was written as an Episode, in a work from which its
  length may perhaps exclude it. The facts are true; no invention as
  to these has been exercised, as none was needed.

O happy time of youthful lovers (thus
My story may begin) O balmy time,
In which a love-knot on a lady's brow
Is fairer than the fairest star in heaven!
To such inheritance of blessed fancy
(Fancy that sports more desperately with minds
Than ever fortune hath been known to do)
The high-born Vaudracour was brought, by years
Whose progress had a little overstepped
His stripling prime. A town of small repute,
Among the vine-clad mountains of Auvergne,
Was the Youth's birth-place. There he wooed a Maid
Who heard the heart-felt music of his suit
With answering vows. Plebeian was the stock,
Plebeian, though ingenuous, the stock,
From which her graces and her honours sprung:
And hence the father of the enamoured Youth,
With haughty indignation, spurned the thought
Of such alliance.—From their cradles up,
With but a step between their several homes,

Twins had they been in pleasure; after strife
And petty quarrels, had grown fond again;
Each other's advocate, each other's stay;
And, in their happiest moments, not content,
If more divided than a sportive pair
Of sea-fowl, conscious both that they are hovering
Within the eddy of a common blast,
Or hidden only by the concave depth
Of neighbouring billows from each other's sight.

Thus, not without concurrence of an age
Unknown to memory, was an earnest given
By ready nature for a life of love,
For endless constancy, and placid truth;
But whatsoe'er of such rare treasure lay
Reserved, had fate permitted, for support
Of their maturer years, his present mind
Was under fascination;—he beheld
A vision, and adored the thing he saw.
Arabian fiction never filled the world
With half the wonders that were wrought for him.
Earth breathed in one great presence of the spring;
Life turned the meanest of her implements,
Before his eyes, to price above all gold;
The house she dwelt in was a sainted shrine;
Her chamber-window did surpass in glory
The portals of the dawn; all Paradise
Could, by the simple opening of a door,
Let itself in upon him:—pathway, walks,
Swarmed with enchantment, till his spirit sank,
Surcharged, within him, overblest to move
Beneath a sun that wakes a weary world
To its dull round of ordinary cares;
A man too happy for mortality!

So passed the time, till, whether through effect
Of some unguarded moment that dissolved
Virtuous restraint—ah, speak it, think it, not!
Deem rather that the fervent Youth, who saw
So many bars between his present state
And the dear haven where he wished to be

In honourable wedlock with his Love,
Was in his judgment tempted to decline
To perilous weakness, and entrust his cause
To nature for a happy end of all;
Deem that by such fond hope the Youth was swayed,
And bear with their transgression, when I add
That Julia, wanting yet the name of wife,
Carried about her for a secret grief
The promise of a mother. To conceal
The threatened shame, the parents of the Maid
Found means to hurry her away by night,
And unforewarned, that in some distant spot
She might remain shrouded in privacy,
Until the babe was born. When morning came,
The Lover, thus bereft, stung with his loss,
And all uncertain whither he should turn,
Chafed like a wild beast in the toils; but soon
Discovering traces of the fugitives,
Their steps he followed to the Maid's retreat.
Easily may the sequel be divined—
Walks to and fro—watching at every hour;
And the fair Captive, who, whene'er she may,
Is busy at her casement as the swallow
Fluttering its pinions, almost within reach,
About the pendent nest, did thus espy
Her Lover!—thence a stolen interview,
Accomplished under friendly shade of night.

I pass the raptures of the pair;—such theme
Is, by innumerable poets, touched
In more delightful verse than skill of mine
Could fashion; chiefly by that darling bard
Who told of Juliet and her Romeo,
And of the lark's note heard before its time,
And of the streaks that laced the severing clouds
In the unrelenting east.—Through all her courts
The vacant city slept; the busy winds,
That keep no certain intervals of rest,
Moved not; meanwhile the galaxy displayed
Her fires, that like mysterious pulses beat
Aloft;—momentous but uneasy bliss!

To their full hearts the universe seemed hung
On that brief meeting's slender filament!

    They parted; and the generous Vaudracour
Reached speedily the native threshold bent
On making (so the Lovers had agreed)
A sacrifice of birthright to attain
A final portion from his father's hand;
Which granted, Bride and Bridegroom then would flee
To some remote and solitary place,
Shady as night, and beautiful as heaven,
Where they may live, with no one to behold
Their happiness, or to disturb their love.
But *now* of this no whisper; not the less,
If ever an obtrusive word were dropped
Touching the matter of his passion, still,
In his stern father's hearing, Vaudracour
Persisted openly that death alone
Should abrogate his human privilege
Divine, of swearing everlasting truth,
Upon the altar, to the Maid he loved.

    "You shall be baffled in your mad intent
If there be justice in the court of France,"
Muttered the Father.—From these words the Youth
Conceived a terror; and, by night or day
Stirred nowhere without weapons, that full soon
Found dreadful provocation: for at night,
When to his chamber he retired, attempt
Was made to seize him by three armèd men,
Acting, in furtherance of the Father's will,
Under a private signet of the State.
One the rash Youth's ungovernable hand
Slew, and as quickly to a second gave
A perilous wound—he shuddered to behold
The breathless corse; then peacefully resigned
His person to the law, was lodged in prison,
And wore the fetters of a criminal.

    Have you observed a tuft of wingèd seed
That, from the dandelion's naked stalk,

Mounted aloft, is suffered not to use
Its natural gifts for purposes of rest,
Driven by the autumnal whirlwind to and fro
Through the wide element? or have you marked
The heavier substance of a leaf-clad bough,
Within the vortex of a foaming flood,
Tormented? by such aid you may conceive
The perturbation that ensued;—ah, no!
Desperate the Maid—the Youth is stained with blood;
Unmatchable on earth is their disquiet!
Yet as the troubled seed and tortured bough
Is man, subjected to despotic sway.

For him, by private influence with the Court,
Was pardon gained, and liberty procured;
But not without exaction of a pledge,
Which liberty and love dispersed in air.
He flew to her from whom they would divide him—
He clove to her who could not give him peace—
Yea, his first word of greeting was,—"All right
Is gone from me; my lately-towering hopes,
To the least fibre of their lowest root,
Are withered; thou no longer canst be mine,
I thine—the conscience-stricken must not woo
The unruffled Innocent,—I see thy face,
Behold thee, and my misery is complete!"

"One, are we not?" exclaimed the Maiden—"One,
For innocence and youth, for weal and woe?"
Then with the father's name she coupled words
Of vehement indignation; but the Youth
Checked her with filial meekness; for no thought
Uncharitable crossed his mind, no sense
Of hasty anger, rising in the eclipse
Of true domestic loyalty, did e'er
Find place within his bosom.—Once again
The persevering wedge of tyranny
Achieved their separation: and once more
Were they united,—to be yet again
Disparted, pitiable lot! But here
A portion of the tale may well be left

In silence, though my memory could add
Much how the Youth, in scanty space of time,
Was traversed from without; much, too, of thoughts
That occupied his days in solitude
Under privation and restraint; and what,
Through dark and shapeless fear of things to come,
And what, through strong compunction for the past,
He suffered—breaking down in heart and mind!

Doomed to a third and last captivity,
His freedom he recovered on the eve
Of Julia's travail. When the babe was born,
Its presence tempted him to cherish schemes
Of future happiness. "You shall return,
Julia," said he, "and to your father's house
Go with the child.—You have been wretched; yet
The silver shower, whose reckless burthen weighs
Too heavily upon the lily's head,
Oft leaves a saving moisture at its root.
Malice, beholding you, will melt away.
Go!—'tis a town where both of us were born;
None will reproach you, for our truth is known;
And if, amid those once-bright bowers, our fate
Remain unpitied, pity is not in man.
With ornaments—the prettiest, nature yields
Or art can fashion, shall you deck our boy,
And feed his countenance with your own sweet looks,
Till no one can resist him.—Now, even now,
I see him sporting on the sunny lawn;
My father from the window sees him too;
Startled, as if some new-created thing
Enriched the earth, or Faery of the woods
Bounded before him;—but the unweeting Child
Shall by his beauty win his grandsire's heart,
So that it shall be softened, and our loves
End happily, as they began!" These gleams
Appeared but seldom; oftener was he seen
Propping a pale and melancholy face
Upon the Mother's bosom; resting thus
His head upon one breast, while from the other
The Babe was drawing in its quiet food.

—That pillow is no longer to be thine,
Fond Youth! that mournful solace now must pass
Into the list of things that cannot be!
Unwedded Julia, terror-smitten, hears
The sentence, by her mother's lip pronounced,
That dooms her to a convent.—Who shall tell,
Who dares report, the tidings to the lord
Of her affections? so they blindly asked
Who knew not to what quiet depths a weight
Of agony had pressed the Sufferer down:
The word, by others dreaded, he can hear
Composed and silent, without visible sign
Of even the least emotion. Noting this,
When the impatient object of his love
Upbraided him with slackness, he returned
No answer, only took the mother's hand
And kissed it; seemingly devoid of pain,
Or care, that what so tenderly he pressed
Was a dependant on the obdurate heart
Of one who came to disunite their lives
For ever—sad alternative! preferred,
By the unbending Parents of the Maid,
To secret 'spousals meanly disavowed.
—So be it!
                    In the city he remained
A season after Julia had withdrawn
To those religious walls. He, too, departs—
Who with him?—even the senseless Little-one.
With that sole charge he passed the city-gates,
For the last time, attendant by the side
Of a close chair, a litter, or sedan,
In which the Babe was carried. To a hill,
That rose a brief league distant from the town,
The dwellers in that house where he had lodged
Accompanied his steps, by anxious love
Impelled;—they parted from him there, and stood
Watching below till he had disappeared
On the hill top. His eyes he scarcely took,
Throughout that journey, from the vehicle
(Slow-moving ark of all his hopes!) that veiled
The tender infant: and at every inn,

And under every hospitable tree
At which the bearers halted or reposed,
Laid him with timid care upon his knees,
And looked, as mothers ne'er were known to look,
Upon the nursling which his arms embraced.

This was the manner in which Vaudracour
Departed with his infant; and thus reached
His father's house, where to the innocent child
Admittance was denied. The young man spake
No word of indignation or reproof.
But of his father begged, a last request,
That a retreat might be assigned to him,
Where in forgotten quiet he might dwell,
With such allowance as his wants required;
For wishes he had none. To a lodge that stood
Deep in a forest, with leave given, at the age
Of four-and-twenty summers he withdrew;
And thither took with him his motherless Babe,
And one domestic for their common needs,
An aged woman. It consoled him here
To attend upon the orphan, and perform
Obsequious service to the precious child,
Which, after a short time, by some mistake
Or indiscretion of the Father, died.—
The Tale I follow to its last recess
Of suffering or of peace, I know not which:
Theirs be the blame who caused the woe, not mine!

From this time forth he never shared a smile
With mortal creature. An Inhabitant
Of that same town, in which the pair had left
So lively a remembrance of their griefs,
By chance of business coming within reach
Of his retirement, to the forest lodge
Repaired, but only found the matron there,
Who told him that his pains were thrown away,
For that her Master never uttered word
To living thing—not even to her.—Behold!
While they were speaking, Vaudracour approached;
But seeing some one near, as on the latch

Of the garden-gate his hand was laid, he shrunk—
And, like a shadow, glided out of view.
Shocked at his savage aspect, from the place
The visitor retired.
                    Thus lived the Youth
Cut off from all intelligence with man,
And shunning even the light of common day;
Nor could the voice of Freedom, which through France
Full speedily resounded, public hope,
Or personal memory of his own deep wrongs,
Rouse him: but in those solitary shades
His days he wasted, an imbecile mind!

ADDRESS TO MY INFANT DAUGHTER, DORA

ON BEING REMINDED THAT SHE WAS A MONTH OLD THAT
DAY, SEPTEMBER 16

[Composed September 16, 1804.—Published 1815.]

————Hast thou then survived—
Mild Offspring of infirm humanity,
Meek Infant! among all forlornest things
The most forlorn—one life of that bright star,
The second glory of the Heavens?—Thou hast;
Already hast survived that great decay,
That transformation through the wide earth felt,
And by all nations. In that Being's sight
From whom the Race of human kind proceed,
A thousand years are but as yesterday;
And one day's narrow circuit is to Him
Not less capacious than a thousand years.
But what is time? What outward glory? Neither
A measure is of Thee, whose claims extend
Through "heaven's eternal year."—Yet hail to Thee,
Frail, feeble, Monthling!—by that name, methinks,
Thy scanty breathing-time is portioned out
Not idly.—Hadst thou been of Indian birth,
Couched on a casual bed of moss and leaves,
And rudely canopied by leafy boughs,
Or to the churlish elements exposed

On the blank plains,—the coldness of the night,
Or the night's darkness, or its cheerful face
Of beauty, by the changing moon adorned,
Would, with imperious admonition, then
Have scored thine age, and punctually timed
Thine infant history, on the minds of those
Who might have wandered with thee.—Mother's love,
Nor less than mother's love in other breasts,
Will, among us warm-clad and warmly housed,
Do for thee what the finger of the heavens
Doth all too often harshly execute
For thy unblest coevals, amid wilds
Where fancy hath small liberty to grace
The affections, to exalt them or refine;
And the maternal sympathy itself,
Though strong, is, in the main, a joyless tie
Of naked instinct, wound about the heart.
Happier, far happier is thy lot and ours!
Even now—to solemnise thy helpless state,
And to enliven in the mind's regard
Thy passive beauty—parallels have risen,
Resemblances, or contrasts, that connect,
Within the region of a father's thoughts,
Thee and thy mate and sister of the sky.
And first;—thy sinless progress, through a world
By sorrow darkened and by care disturbed,
Apt likeness bears to hers, through gathered clouds
Moving untouched in silver purity,
And cheering oft-times their reluctant gloom.
Fair are ye both, and both are free from stain:
But thou, how leisurely thou fill'st thy horn
With brightness! leaving her to post along,
And range about, disquieted in change,
And still impatient of the shape she wears.
Once up, once down the hill, one journey, Babe,
That will suffice thee; and it seems that now
Thou hast foreknowledge that such task is thine;
Thou travellest so contentedly, and sleep'st
In such a heedless peace. Alas! full soon
Hath this conception, grateful to behold,
Changed countenance, like an object sullied o'er

By breathing mist; and thine appears to be
A mournful labour, while to her is given
Hope, and a renovation without end.
—That smile forbids the thought; for on thy face
Smiles are beginning, like the beams of dawn,
To shoot and circulate; smiles have there been seen;
Tranquil assurances that Heaven supports
The feeble motions of thy life, and cheers
Thy loneliness: or shall those smiles be called
Feelers of love, put forth as if to explore
This untried world, and to prepare thy way
Through a strait passage intricate and dim?
Such are they; and the same are tokens, signs,
Which, when the appointed season hath arrived,
Joy, as her holiest language, shall adopt;
And Reason's godlike Power be proud to own.

THE SMALL CELANDINE

[Composed 1804.—Published 1807.]

There is a Flower, the lesser Celandine,
    That shrinks, like many more, from cold and rain;
And, the first moment that the sun may shine,
    Bright as the sun himself, 'tis out again!

When hailstones have been falling, swarm on swarm,
    Or blasts the green field and the trees distrest,
Oft have I seen it muffled up from harm,
    In close self-shelter, like a Thing at rest.

But lately, one rough day, this Flower I passed
    And recognised it, though an altered form,
Now standing forth an offering to the blast
    And buffeted at will by rain and storm.

I stopped, and said with inly-muttered voice,
    "It doth not love the shower, nor seek the cold:
This neither is its courage nor its choice,
    But its necessity in being old.

"The sunshine may not cheer it, nor the dew;
  It cannot help itself in its decay;
Stiff in its members, withered, changed of hue."
  And, in my spleen, I smiled that it was grey.

To be a Prodigal's Favourite—then, worse truth,
  A Miser's Pensioner—behold our lot!
O Man, that from thy fair and shining youth
  Age might but take the things Youth needed not!

TO A SKY-LARK

[Composed 1805.—Published 1807.]

Up with me! up with me into the clouds!
For thy song, Lark, is strong;
Up with me, up with me into the clouds!
Singing, singing,
With clouds and sky about thee ringing,
Lift me, guide me, till I find
That spot which seems so to thy mind!

I have walked through wildernesses dreary,
And to-day my heart is weary;
Had I now the wings of a Faery,
Up to thee would I fly.
There is madness about thee, and joy divine
In that song of thine;
Lift me, guide me, high and high
To thy banqueting place in the sky.

      Joyous as morning,
Thou art laughing and scorning;
Thou hast a nest for thy love and thy rest,
And, though little troubled with sloth,
Drunken Lark! thou wouldst be loth
To be such a traveller as I.
Happy, happy Liver,
With a soul as strong as a mountain river
Pouring out praise to the almighty Giver,
Joy and jollity be with us both!

Alas! my journey, rugged and uneven,
Through prickly moors or dusty ways must wind;
But hearing thee, or others of thy kind,
As full of gladness and as free of heaven,
I, with my fate contented, will plod on,
And hope for higher raptures, when life's day is
    done.

THE PRELUDE

SELECTIONS

BOOK FIRST

CHILDHOOD AND SCHOOL-TIME

(*Lines* 255–646)

Far better never to have heard the name
Of zeal and just ambition, than to live
Baffled and plagued by a mind that every hour
Turns recreant to her task; takes heart again,
Then feels immediately some hollow thought
Hang like an interdict upon her hopes.
This is my lot; for either still I find
Some imperfection in the chosen theme,

Or see of absolute accomplishment
Much wanting, so much wanting, in myself,
That I recoil and droop, and seek repose
In listlessness from vain perplexity,
Unprofitably travelling toward the grave,
Like a false steward who hath much received
And renders nothing back.
                              Was it for this
That one, the fairest of all rivers, loved
To blend his murmurs with my nurse's song,
And, from his alder shades and rocky falls,
And from his fords and shallows, sent a voice
That flowed along my dreams? For this, didst thou,

O Derwent! winding among grassy holms
Where I was looking on, a babe in arms,
Make ceaseless music that composed my thoughts
To more than infant softness, giving me
Amid the fretful dwellings of mankind
A foretaste, a dim earnest, of the calm
That Nature breathes among the hills and groves.

When he had left the mountains and received
On his smooth breast the shadow of those towers
That yet survive, a shattered monument
Of feudal sway, the bright blue river passed
Along the margin of our terrace walk;
A tempting playmate whom we dearly loved.
Oh, many a time have I, a five years' child,
In a small mill-race severed from his stream,
Made one long bathing of a summer's day;
Basked in the sun, and plunged and basked again
Alternate, all a summer's day, or scoured
The sandy fields, leaping through flowery groves
Of yellow ragwort; or when rock and hill,
The woods, and distant Skiddaw's lofty height,
Were bronzed with deepest radiance, stood alone
Beneath the sky, as if I had been born
On Indian plains, and from my mother's hut
Had run abroad in wantonness, to sport,
A naked savage, in the thunder shower.

Fair seed-time had my soul, and I grew up
Fostered alike by beauty and by fear:
Much favoured in my birthplace, and no less
In that beloved Vale to which erelong
We were transplanted—there were we let loose
For sports of wider range. Ere I had told
Ten birth-days, when among the mountain-slopes
Frost, and the breath of frosty wind, had snapped
The last autumnal crocus, 'twas my joy
With store of springes o'er my shoulder hung
To range the open heights where woodcocks run
Among the smooth green turf. Through half the night,
Scudding away from snare to snare, I plied

That anxious visitation;—moon and stars
Were shining o'er my head. I was alone,
And seemed to be a trouble to the peace
That dwelt among them. Sometimes it befell
In these night wanderings, that a strong desire
O'erpowered my better reason, and the bird
Which was the captive of another's toil
Became my prey; and when the deed was done
I heard among the solitary hills
Low breathings coming after me, and sounds
Of undistinguishable motion, steps
Almost as silent as the turf they trod.

Nor less when spring had warmed the cultured Vale,
Moved we as plunderers where the mother-bird
Had in high places built her lodge; though mean
Our object and inglorious, yet the end
Was not ignoble. Oh! when I have hung
Above the raven's nest, by knots of grass
And half-inch fissures in the slippery rock
But ill sustained, and almost (so it seemed)
Suspended by the blast that blew amain,
Shouldering the naked crag, oh, at that time
While on the perilous ridge I hung alone,
With what strange utterance did the loud dry wind
Blow through my ear! the sky seemed not a sky
Of earth—and with what motion moved the clouds!

Dust as we are, the immortal spirit grows
Like harmony in music; there is a dark
Inscrutable workmanship that reconciles
Discordant elements, makes them cling together
In one society. How strange that all
The terrors, pains, and early miseries,
Regrets, vexations, lassitudes interfused
Within my mind, should e'er have borne a part,
And that a needful part, in making up
The calm existence that is mine when I
Am worthy of myself! Praise to the end!
Thanks to the means which Nature deigned to employ;
Whether her fearless visitings, or those

That came with soft alarm, like hurtless light
Opening the peaceful clouds; or she may use
Severer interventions, ministry
More palpable, as best might suit her aim.

One summer evening (led by her) I found
A little boat tied to a willow tree
Within a rocky cave, its usual home.
Straight I unloosed her chain, and stepping in
Pushed from the shore. It was an act of stealth
And troubled pleasure, nor without the voice
Of mountain-echoes did my boat move on;
Leaving behind her still, on either side,
Small circles glittering idly in the moon,
Until they melted all into one track
Of sparkling light. But now, like one who rows,
Proud of his skill, to reach a chosen point
With an unswerving line, I fixed my view
Upon the summit of a craggy ridge,
The horizon's utmost boundary; far above
Was nothing but the stars and the grey sky.
She was an elfin pinnace; lustily
I dipped my oars into the silent lake,
And, as I rose upon the stroke, my boat
Went heaving through the water like a swan;
When, from behind that craggy steep till then
The horizon's bound, a huge peak, black and huge,
As if with voluntary power instinct
Upreared its head. I struck and struck again,
And growing still in stature the grim shape
Towered up between me and the stars, and still,
For so it seemed, with purpose of its own
And measured motion like a living thing,
Strode after me. With trembling oars I turned,
And through the silent water stole my way
Back to the covert of the willow tree;
There in her mooring-place I left my bark,—
And through the meadows homeward went, in grave
And serious mood; but after I had seen
That spectacle, for many days, my brain
Worked with a dim and undetermined sense

Of unknown modes of being; o'er my thoughts
There hung a darkness, call it solitude
Or blank desertion. No familiar shapes
Remained, no pleasant images of trees,
Of sea or sky, no colours of green fields;
But huge and mighty forms, that do not live
Like living men, moved slowly through the mind
By day, and were a trouble to my dreams.

Wisdom and Spirit of the universe!
Thou Soul that art the eternity of thought,
That givest to forms and images a breath
And everlasting motion, not in vain
By day or star-light thus from my first dawn
Of childhood didst thou intertwine for me
The passions that build up our human soul;
Not with the mean and vulgar works of man,
But with high objects, with enduring things—
With life and nature—purifying thus
The elements of feeling and of thought,
And sanctifying, by such discipline,
Both pain and fear, until we recognise
A grandeur in the beatings of the heart.
Nor was this fellowship vouchsafed to me
With stinted kindness. In November days,
When vapours rolling down the valley made
A lonely scene more lonesome, among woods,
At noon and mid the calm of summer nights,
When, by the margin of the trembling lake,
Beneath the gloomy hills homeward I went
In solitude, such intercourse was mine;
Mine was it in the fields both day and night,
And by the waters, all the summer long.

And in the frosty season, when the sun
Was set, and visible for many a mile
The cottage windows blazed through twilight gloom,
I heeded not their summons: happy time
It was indeed for all of us—for me
It was a time of rapture! Clear and loud
The village clock tolled six,—I wheeled about,

Proud and exulting like an untired horse
That cares not for his home. All shod with steel,
We hissed along the polished ice in games
Confederate, imitative of the chase
And woodland pleasures,—the resounding horn,
The pack loud chiming, and the hunted hare.
So through the darkness and the cold we flew,
And not a voice was idle; with the din
Smitten, the precipices rang aloud;
The leafless trees and every icy crag
Tinkled like iron; while far distant hills
Into the tumult sent an alien sound
Of melancholy not unnoticed, while the stars
Eastward were sparkling clear, and in the west
The orange sky of evening died away.
Not seldom from the uproar I retired
Into a silent bay, or sportively
Glanced sideway, leaving the tumultuous throng,
To cut across the reflex of a star
That fled, and, flying still before me, gleamed
Upon the glassy plain; and oftentimes,
When we had given our bodies to the wind,
And all the shadowy banks on either side
Came sweeping through the darkness, spinning still
The rapid line of motion, then at once
Have I, reclining back upon my heels,
Stopped short; yet still the solitary cliffs
Wheeled by me—even as if the earth had rolled
With visible motion her diurnal round!
Behind me did they stretch in solemn train,
Feebler and feebler, and I stood and watched
Till all was tranquil as a dreamless sleep.

Ye Presences of Nature in the sky
And on the earth! Ye Visions of the hills!
And Souls of lonely places! can I think
A vulgar hope was yours when ye employed
Such ministry, when ye through many a year
Haunting me thus among my boyish sports,
On caves and trees, upon the woods and hills,
Impressed upon all forms the characters

Of danger or desire; and thus did make
The surface of the universal earth
With triumph and delight, with hope and fear,
Work like a sea?

                Not uselessly employed,
Might I pursue this theme through every change
Of exercise and play, to which the year
Did summon us in his delightful round.

  We were a noisy crew; the sun in heaven
Beheld not vales more beautiful than ours;
Nor saw a band in happiness and joy
Richer, or worthier of the ground they trod.
I could record with no reluctant voice
The woods of autumn, and their hazel bowers
With milk-white clusters hung; the rod and line,
True symbol of hope's foolishness, whose strong
And unreproved enchantment led us on
By rocks and pools shut out from every star,
All the green summer, to forlorn cascades
Among the windings hid of mountain brooks.
—Unfading recollections! at this hour
The heart is almost mine with which I felt,
From some hill-top on sunny afternoons,
The paper kite high among fleecy clouds
Pull at her rein like an impetuous courser;
Or, from the meadows sent on gusty days,
Beheld her breast the wind, then suddenly
Dashed headlong, and rejected by the storm.

  Ye lowly cottages wherein we dwelt,
A ministration of your own was yours;
Can I forget you, being as you were
So beautiful among the pleasant fields
In which ye stood? or can I here forget
The plain and seemly countenance with which
Ye dealt out your plain comforts? Yet had ye
Delights and exultations of your own.
Eager and never weary we pursued
Our home-amusements by the warm peat-fire
At evening, when with pencil, and smooth slate

In square divisions parcelled out and all
With crosses and with cyphers scribbled o'er,
We schemed and puzzled, head opposed to head
In strife too humble to be named in verse:
Or round the naked table, snow-white deal,
Cherry or maple, sate in close array,
And to the combat, Loo or Whist, led on
A thick-ribbed army; not, as in the world,
Neglected and ungratefully thrown by
Even for the very service they had wrought,
But husbanded through many a long campaign.
Uncouth assemblage was it, where no few
Had changed their functions; some, plebeian cards
Which Fate, beyond the promise of their birth,
Had dignified, and called to represent
The persons of departed potentates.
Oh, with what echoes on the board they fell!
Ironic diamonds,—clubs, hearts, diamonds, spades,
A congregation piteously akin!
Cheap matter offered they to boyish wit,
Those sooty knaves, precipitated down
With scoffs and taunts, like Vulcan out of heaven:
The paramount ace, a moon in her eclipse,
Queens gleaming through their splendour's last decay,
And monarchs surly at the wrongs sustained
By royal visages. Meanwhile abroad
Incessant rain was falling, or the frost
Raged bitterly, with keen and silent tooth;
And, interrupting oft that eager game,
From under Esthwaite's splitting fields of ice
The pent-up air, struggling to free itself,
Gave out to meadow-grounds and hills a loud
Protracted yelling, like the noise of wolves
Howling in troops along the Bothnic Main.

Nor, sedulous as I have been to trace
How Nature by extrinsic passion first
Peopled the mind with forms sublime or fair,
And made me love them, may I here omit
How other pleasures have been mine, and joys
Of subtler origin; how I have felt,

Not seldom even in that tempestuous time,
Those hallowed and pure motions of the sense
Which seem, in their simplicity, to own
An intellectual charm; that calm delight
Which, if I err not, surely must belong
To those first-born affinities that fit
Our new existence to existing things,
And, in our dawn of being, constitute
The bond of union between life and joy.

Yes, I remember when the changeful earth,
And twice five summers on my mind had stamped
The faces of the moving year, even then
I held unconscious intercourse with beauty
Old as creation, drinking in a pure
Organic pleasure from the silver wreaths
Of curling mist, or from the level plain
Of waters coloured by impending clouds.

The sands of Westmoreland, the creeks and bays
Of Cumbria's rocky limits, they can tell
How, when the Sea threw off his evening shade
And to the shepherd's hut on distant hills
Sent welcome notice of the rising moon,
How I have stood, to fancies such as these
A stranger, linking with the spectacle
No conscious memory of a kindred sight,
And bringing with me no peculiar sense
Of quietness or peace; yet have I stood,
Even while mine eye hath moved o'er many a league
Of shining water, gathering as it seemed,
Through every hair-breadth in that field of light,
New pleasure like a bee among the flowers.

Thus oft amid those fits of vulgar joy
Which, through all seasons, on a child's pursuits
Are prompt attendants, 'mid that giddy bliss
Which, like a tempest, works along the blood
And is forgotten; even then I felt
Gleams like the flashing of a shield;—the earth
And common face of Nature spake to me

Rememerable things; sometimes, 'tis true,
By chance collisions and quaint accidents
(Like those ill-sorted unions, work supposed
Of evil-minded fairies), yet not vain
Nor profitless, if haply they impressed
Collateral objects and appearances,
Albeit lifeless then, and doomed to sleep
Until maturer seasons called them forth
To impregnate and to elevate the mind.
—And if the vulgar joy by its own weight
Wearied itself out of the memory,
The scenes which were a witness of that joy
Remained in their substantial lineaments
Depicted on the brain, and to the eye
Were visible, a daily sight; and thus
By the impressive discipline of fear,
By pleasure and repeated happiness,
So frequently repeated, and by force
Of obscure feelings representative
Of things forgotten, these same scenes so bright,
So beautiful, so majestic in themselves,
Though yet the day was distant, did become
Habitually dear, and all their forms
And changeful colours by invisible links
Were fastened to the affections.

                                 I began
My story early—not misled, I trust,
By an infirmity of love for days
Disowned by memory—ere the breath of spring
Planting my snowdrops among winter snows:
Nor will it seem to thee, O Friend! so prompt
In sympathy, that I have lengthened out
With fond and feeble tongue a tedious tale.
Meanwhile, my hope has been, that I might fetch
Invigorating thoughts from former years;
Might fix the wavering balance of my mind,
And haply meet reproaches too, whose power
May spur me on, in manhood now mature,
To honorable toil. Yet should these hopes
Prove vain, and thus should neither I be taught
To understand myself, nor thou to know

With better knowledge how the heart was framed
Of him thou lovest; need I dread from thee
Harsh judgments, if the song be loth to quit
Those recollected hours that have the charm
Of visionary things, those lovely forms
And sweet sensations that throw back our life,
And almost make remotest infancy
A visible scene, on which the sun is shining?

One end at least hath been attained; my mind
Hath been revived, and if this genial mood
Desert me not, forthwith shall be brought down
Through later years the story of my life.
The road lies plain before me;—'tis a theme
Single and of determined bounds; and hence
I choose it rather at this time, than work
Of ampler or more varied argument,
Where I might be discomfited and lost:
And certain hopes are with me, that to thee
This labour will be welcome, honoured Friend!

BOOK SECOND

SCHOOL-TIME—(Continued)

(Lines 1-197)

Thus far, O Friend! have we, though leaving much
Unvisited, endeavoured to retrace
The simple ways in which my childhood walked;
Those chiefly that first led me to the love
Of rivers, woods, and fields. The passion yet
Was in its birth, sustained as might befall
By nourishment that came unsought; for still
From week to week, from month to month, we lived
A round of tumult. Duly were our games
Prolonged in summer till the daylight failed.
No chair remained before the doors; the bench
And threshold steps were empty; fast asleep
The labourer, and the old man who had sate
A later lingerer; yet the revelry
Continued and the loud uproar; at last,

When all the ground was dark, and twinkling stars
Edged the black clouds, home and to bed we went,
Feverish with weary joints and beating minds.
Ah! is there one who ever has been young,
Nor needs a warning voice to tame the pride
Of intellect and virtue's self-esteem?
One is there, though the wisest and the best
Of all mankind, who covets not at times
Union that cannot be;—who would not give,
If so he might, to duty and to truth
The eagerness of infantine desire?
A tranquillising spirit presses now
On my corporeal frame, so wide appears
The vacancy between me and those days
Which yet have such self-presence in my mind,
That, musing on them, often do I seem
Two consciousnesses, conscious of myself
And of some other Being. A rude mass
Of native rock, left midway in the square
Of our small market village, was the goal
Or centre of these sports; and when, returned
After long absence, thither I repaired,
Gone was the old grey stone, and in its place
A smart Assembly-room usurped the ground
That had been ours. There let the fiddle scream,
And be ye happy! Yet, my Friends! I know
That more than one of you will think with me
Of those soft starry nights, and that old Dame
From whom the stone was named, who there had sate,
And watched her table with its huckster's wares
Assiduous, through the length of sixty years.

We ran a boisterous course; the year span round
With giddy motion. But the time approached
That brought with it a regular desire
For calmer pleasures, when the winning forms
Of Nature were collaterally attached
To every scheme of holiday delight
And every boyish sport, less grateful else
And languidly pursued.

When summer came,
Our pastime was, on bright half-holidays,
To sweep along the plain of Windermere
With rival oars; and the selected bourne
Was now an Island musical with birds
That sang and ceased not; now a Sister Isle
Beneath the oaks' umbrageous covert, sown
With lilies of the valley like a field;
And now a third small Island, where survived
In solitude the ruins of a shrine
Once to Our Lady dedicate, and served
Daily with chaunted rites. In such a race
So ended, disappointment could be none,
Uneasiness, or pain, or jealousy:
We rested in the shade, all pleased alike,
Conquered and conqueror. Thus the pride of strength,
And the vain-glory of superior skill,
Were tempered; thus was gradually produced
A quiet independence of the heart;
And to my Friend who knows me I may add,
Fearless of blame, that hence for future days
Ensued a diffidence and modesty,
And I was taught to feel, perhaps too much,
The self-sufficing power of Solitude.

Our daily meals were frugal, Sabine fare!
More than we wished we knew the blessing then
Of vigorous hunger—hence corporeal strength
Unsapped by delicate viands; for, exclude
A little weekly stipend, and we lived
Through three divisions of the quartered year
In penniless poverty. But now to school
From the half-yearly holidays returned,
We came with weightier purses, that sufficed
To furnish treats more costly than the Dame
Of the old grey stone, from her scant board, supplied.
Hence rustic dinners on the cool green ground,
Or in the woods, or by a river's side
Or shady fountain's, while among the leaves
Soft airs were stirring, and the mid-day sun
Unfelt shone brightly round us in our joy.
Nor is my aim neglected if I tell

How sometimes, in the length of those half-years,
We from our funds drew largely;—proud to curb,
And eager to spur on, the galloping steed;
And with the courteous inn-keeper, whose stud
Supplied our want, we haply might employ
Sly subterfuge, if the adventure's bound
Were distant: some famed temple where of yore
The Druids worshipped, or the antique walls
Of that large abbey, where within the Vale
Of Nightshade, to St. Mary's honour built,
Stands yet a mouldering pile with fractured arch,
Belfry, and images, and living trees;
A holy scene!—Along the smooth green turf
Our horses grazed. To more than inland peace,
Left by the west wind sweeping overhead
From a tumultuous ocean, trees and towers
In that sequestered valley may be seen,
Both silent and both motionless alike;
Such the deep shelter that is there, and such
The safeguard for repose and quietness.

Our steeds remounted and the summons given,
With whip and spur we through the chauntry flew
In uncouth race, and left the cross-legged knight,
And the stone-abbot, and that single wren
Which one day sang so sweetly in the nave
Of the old church, that—though from recent showers
The earth was comfortless, and, touched by faint
Internal breezes, sobbings of the place
And respirations, from the roofless walls
The shuddering ivy dripped large drops—yet still
So sweetly 'mid the gloom the invisible bird
Sang to herself, that there I could have made
My dwelling-place, and lived for ever there
To hear such music. Through the walls we flew
And down the valley, and, a circuit made
In wantonness of heart, through rough and smooth
We scampered homewards. Oh, ye rocks and streams,
And that still spirit shed from evening air!
Even in this joyous time I sometimes felt
Your presence, when with slackened step we breathed

Along the sides of the steep hills, or when
Lighted by gleams of moonlight from the sea
We beat with thundering hoofs the level sand.

Midway on long Winander's eastern shore,
Within the crescent of a pleasant bay,
A tavern stood; no homely-featured house,
Primeval like its neighbouring cottages,
But 'twas a splendid place, the door beset
With chaises, grooms, and liveries, and within
Decanters, glasses, and the blood-red wine.
In ancient times, and ere the Hall was built
On the large island, had this dwelling been
More worthy of a poet's love, a hut,
Proud of its own bright fire and sycamore shade.
But—though the rhymes were gone that once inscribed
The threshold, and large golden characters,
Spread o'er the spangled sign-board, had dislodged
The old Lion and usurped his place, in slight
And mockery of the rustic painter's hand—
Yet, to this hour, the spot to me is dear
With all its foolish pomp. The garden lay
Upon a slope surmounted by a plain
Of a small bowling-green; beneath us stood
A grove, with gleams of water through the trees
And over the tree-tops; nor did we want
Refreshment, strawberries and mellow cream.
There, while through half an afternoon we played
On the smooth platform, whether skill prevailed
Or happy blunder triumphed, bursts of glee
Made all the mountains ring. But, ere nightfall,
When in our pinnace we returned at leisure
Over the shadowy lake, and to the beach
Of some small island steered our course with one,
The Minstrel of the Troop, and left him there,
And rowed off gently, while he blew his flute
Alone upon the rock—oh, then, the calm
And dead still water lay upon my mind
Even with a weight of pleasure, and the sky,
Never before so beautiful, sank down
Into my heart, and held me like a dream!

Thus were my sympathies enlarged, and thus
Daily the common range of visible things
Grew dear to me: already I began
To love the sun; a boy I loved the sun,
Not as I since have loved him, as a pledge
And surety of our earthly life, a light
Which we behold and feel we are alive;
Nor for his bounty to so many worlds—
But for this cause, that I had seen him lay
His beauty on the morning hills, had seen
The western mountain touch his setting orb,
In many a thoughtless hour, when, from excess
Of happiness, my blood appeared to flow
For its own pleasure, and I breathed with joy.
And, from like feelings, humble though intense,
To patriotic and domestic love
Analogous, the moon to me was dear;
For I could dream away my purposes,
Standing to gaze upon her while she hung
Midway between the hills, as if she knew
No other region, but belonged to thee,
Yea, appertained by a peculiar right
To thee and thy grey huts, thou one dear Vale!

(*Lines* 352–471)

'Twere long to tell
What spring and autumn, what the winter snows,
And what the summer shade, what day and night,
Evening and morning, sleep and waking, thought
From sources inexhaustible, poured forth
To feed the spirit of religious love
In which I walked with Nature. But let this
Be not forgotten, that I still retained
My first creative sensibility;
That by the regular action of the world
My soul was unsubdued. A plastic power
Abode with me; a forming hand, at times
Rebellious, acting in a devious mood;
A local spirit of his own, at war
With general tendency, but, for the most,

Subservient strictly to external things
With which it communed. An auxiliar light
Came from my mind, which on the setting sun
Bestowed new splendour; the melodious birds,
The fluttering breezes, fountains that run on
Murmuring so sweetly in themselves, obeyed
A like dominion, and the midnight storm
Grew darker in the presence of my eye:
Hence my obeisance, my devotion hence,
And hence my transport.

              Nor should this, perchance,
Pass unrecorded, that I still had loved
The exercise and produce of a toil,
Than analytic industry to me
More pleasing, and whose character I deem
Is more poetic as resembling more
Creative agency. The song would speak
Of that interminable building reared
By observation of affinities
In objects where no brotherhood exists
To passive minds. My seventeenth year was come;
And, whether from this habit rooted now
So deeply in my mind, or from excess
In the great social principle of life
Coercing all things into sympathy,
To unorganic natures were transferred
My own enjoyments; or the power of truth
Coming in revelation, did converse
With things that really are; I, at this time,
Saw blessings spread around me like a sea.
Thus while the days flew by, and years passed on,
From Nature and her overflowing soul
I had received so much, that all my thoughts
Were steeped in feeling; I was only then
Contented, when with bliss ineffable
I felt the sentiment of Being spread
O'er all that moves and all that seemeth still;
O'er all that, lost beyond the reach of thought
And human knowledge, to the human eye
Invisible, yet liveth to the heart;
O'er all that leaps and runs, and shouts and sings,

Or beats the gladsome air; o'er all that glides
Beneath the wave, yea, in the wave itself,
And mighty depth of waters. Wonder not
If high the transport, great the joy I felt
Communing in this sort through earth and heaven
With every form of creature, as it looked
Towards the Uncreated with a countenance
Of adoration, with an eye of love.
One song they sang, and it was audible,
Most audible, then, when the fleshly ear,
O'ercome by humblest prelude of that strain,
Forgot her functions, and slept undisturbed.

If this be error, and another faith
Find easier access to the pious mind,
Yet were I grossly destitute of all
Those human sentiments that make this earth
So dear, if I should fail with grateful voice
To speak of you, ye mountains, and ye lakes
And sounding cataracts, ye mists and winds
That dwell among the hills where I was born.
If in my youth I have been pure in heart,
If, mingling with the world, I am content
With my own modest pleasures, and have lived
With God and Nature communing, removed
From little enmities and low desires,
The gift is yours; if in these times of fear
This melancholy waste of hopes o'erthrown,
If, 'mid indifference and apathy,
And wicked exultation when good men
On every side fall off, we know not how,
To selfishness, disguised in gentle names
Of peace and quiet and domestic love,
Yet mingled not unwillingly with sneers
On visionary minds; if, in this time
Of dereliction and dismay, I yet
Despair not of our nature, but retain
A more than Roman confidence, a faith
That fails not, in all sorrow my support,
The blessing of my life; the gift is yours,
Ye winds and sounding cataracts! 'tis yours,

Ye mountains! thine, O Nature! Thou hast fed
My lofty speculations; and in thee,
For this uneasy heart of ours, I find
A never-failing principle of joy
And purest passion.

                              Thou, my Friend! wert reared
In the great city, 'mid far other scenes;
But we, by different roads, at length have gained
The self-same bourne. And for this cause to thee
I speak, unapprehensive of contempt,
The insinuated scoff of coward tongues,
And all that silent language which so oft
In conversation between man and man
Blots from the human countenance all trace
Of beauty and of love. For thou hast sought
The truth in solitude, and, since the days
That gave thee liberty, full long desired,
To serve in Nature's temple, thou hast been
The most assiduous of her ministers;
In many things my brother, chiefly here
In this our deep devotion.

                              Fare thee well!
Health and the quiet of a healthful mind
Attend thee! seeking oft the haunts of men,
And yet more often living with thyself,
And for thyself, so haply shall thy days
Be many, and a blessing to mankind.

BOOK THIRD

RESIDENCE AT CAMBRIDGE

(*Lines* 1–82)

It was a dreary morning when the wheels
Rolled over a wide plain o'erhung with clouds,
And nothing cheered our way till first we saw
The long-roofed chapel of King's College lift
Turrets and pinnacles in answering files,

Extended high above a dusky grove.
  Advancing, we espied upon the road
A student clothed in gown and tasselled cap,
Striding along as if o'ertasked by Time,
Or covetous of exercise and air;
He passed—nor was I master of my eyes
Till he was left an arrow's flight behind.
As near and nearer to the spot we drew,
It seemed to suck us in with an eddy's force.
Onward we drove beneath the Castle; caught,
While crossing Magdalene Bridge, a glimpse of Cam;
And at the *Hoop* alighted, famous Inn.
  My spirit was up, my thoughts were full of hope;
Some friends I had, acquaintances who there
Seemed friends, poor simple schoolboys, now hung round
With honour and importance; in a world
Of welcome faces up and down I roved;
Questions, directions, warnings and advice,
Flowed in upon me, from all sides; fresh day
Of pride and pleasure! to myself I seemed
A man of business and expense, and went
From shop to shop about my own affairs,
To Tutor or to Tailor, as befell,
From street to street with loose and careless mind.

  I was the Dreamer, they the Dream; I roamed
Delighted through the motley spectacle;
Gowns grave, or gaudy, doctors, students, streets,
Courts, cloisters, flocks of churches, gateways, towers:
Migration strange for a stripling of the hills,
A northern villager.
                                As if the change
Had waited on some Fairy's wand, at once
Behold me rich in monies, and attired
In splendid garb, with hose of silk, and hair
Powdered like rimy trees, when frost is keen.
My lordly dressing-gown, I pass it by,
With other signs of manhood that supplied
The lack of beard.—The weeks went roundly on,
With invitations, suppers, wine and fruit,

Smooth housekeeping within, and all without
Liberal, and suiting gentleman's array.

The Evangelist St. John my patron was;
Three Gothic courts are his, and in the first
Was my abiding-place, a nook obscure;
Right underneath, the College kitchens made
A humming sound, less tuneable than bees,
But hardly less industrious; with shrill notes
Of sharp command and scolding intermixed.
Near me hung Trinity's loquacious clock,
Who never let the quarters, night or day,
Slip by him unproclaimed, and told the hours
Twice over with a male and female voice.
Her pealing organ was my neighbour too;
And from my pillow, looking forth by light
Of moon or favoring stars, I could behold
The antechapel where the statue stood
Of Newton with his prism and silent face,
The marble index of a mind for ever
Voyaging through strange seas of Thought, alone.

Of College labours, of the Lecturer's room
All studded round, as thick as chairs could stand,
With loyal students faithful to their books,
Half-and-half idlers, hardy recusants,
And honest dunces—of important days,
Examinations, when the man was weighed
As in a balance! of excessive hopes,
Tremblings withal and commendable fears,
Small jealousies, and triumphs good or bad—
Let others that know more speak as they know.
Such glory was but little sought by me,
And little won. Yet from the first crude days
Of settling time in this untried abode,
I was disturbed at times by prudent thoughts,
Wishing to hope without a hope, some fears
About my future worldly maintenance,
And, more than all, a strangeness in the mind,
A feeling that I was not for that hour,
Nor for that place.

(Lines 257-478)

Imagination slept,
And yet not utterly. I could not print
Ground where the grass had yielded to the steps
Of generations of illustrious men,
Unmoved. I could not always lightly pass
Through the same gateways, sleep where they had slept,
Wake where they waked, range that inclosure old,
That garden of great intellects, undisturbed.
Place also by the side of this dark sense
Of noble feeling, that those spiritual men,
Even the great Newton's own ethereal self,
Seemed humbled in these precincts thence to be
The more endeared. Their several memories here
(Even like their persons in their portraits clothed
With the accustomed garb of daily life)
Put on a lowly and a touching grace
Of more distinct humanity, that left
All genuine admiration unimpaired.

Beside the pleasant Mill of Trompington
I laughed with Chaucer in the hawthorn shade;
Heard him, while birds were warbling, tell his tales
Of amorous passion. And that gentle Bard,
Chosen by the Muses for their Page of State—
Sweet Spenser, moving through his clouded heaven
With the moon's beauty and the moon's soft pace,
I called him Brother, Englishman, and Friend!
Yea, our blind Poet, who, in his later day,
Stood almost single; uttering odious truth—
Darkness before, and danger's voice behind,
Soul awful—if the earth has ever lodged
An awful soul—I seemed to see him here
Familiarly, and in his scholar's dress
Bounding before me, yet a stripling youth—
A boy, no better, with his rosy cheeks
Angelical, keen eye, courageous look,
And conscious step of purity and pride.
Among the band of my compeers was one
Whom chance had stationed in the very room
Honoured by Milton's name. O temperate Bard!

Be it confest that, for the first time, seated
Within thy innocent lodge and oratory,
One of a festive circle, I poured out
Libations, to thy memory drank, till pride
And gratitude grew dizzy in a brain
Never excited by the fumes of wine
Before that hour, or since.   Then, forth I ran
From the assembly; through a length of streets,
Ran, ostrich-like, to reach our chapel door
In not a desperate or opprobrious time,
Albeit long after the importunate bell
Had stopped, with wearisome Cassandra voice
No longer haunting the dark winter night.
Call back, O Friend! a moment to thy mind,
The place itself and fashion of the rites.
With careless ostentation shouldering up
My surplice, through the inferior throng I clove
Of the plain Burghers, who in audience stood
On the last skirts of their permitted ground,
Under the pealing organ.   Empty thoughts!
I am ashamed of them; and that great Bard,
And thou, O Friend! who in thy ample mind
Hast placed me high above my best deserts,
Ye will forgive the weakness of that hour,
In some of its unworthy vanities,
Brother to many more.
                            In this mixed sort
The months passed on, remissly, not given up
To wilful alienation from the right,
Or walks of open scandal, but in vague
And loose indifference, easy likings, aims
Of a low pitch—duty and zeal dismissed,
Yet Nature, or a happy course of things
Not doing in their stead the needful work.
The memory languidly revolved, the heart
Reposed in noontide rest, the inner pulse
Of contemplation almost failed to beat.
Such life might not inaptly be compared
To a floating island, an amphibious spot
Unsound, of spongy texture, yet withal
Not wanting a fair face of water-weeds

And pleasant flowers. The thirst of living praise,
Fit reverence for the glorious Dead, the sight
Of those long vistas, sacred catacombs,
Where mighty *minds* lie visibly entombed,
Have often stirred the heart of youth, and bred
A fervent love of rigorous discipline.—
Alas! such high emotion touched not me.
Look was there none within these walls to shame
My easy spirits, and discountenance
Their light composure, far less to instil
A calm resolve of mind, firmly addressed
To puissant efforts. Nor was this the blame
Of others but my own; I should, in truth,
As far as doth concern my single self,
Misdeem most widely, lodging it elsewhere;
For I, bred up 'mid Nature's luxuries,
Was a spoiled child, and, rambling like the wind,
As I had done in daily intercourse
With those crystalline rivers, solemn heights,
And mountains, ranging like a fowl of the air,
I was ill-tutored for captivity;
To quit my pleasure, and, from month to month,
Take up a station calmly on the perch
Of sedentary peace. Those lovely forms
Had also left less space within my mind,
Which, wrought upon instinctively, had found
A freshness in those objects of her love,
A winning power, beyond all other power.
Not that I slighted books,—that were to lack
All sense,—but other passions in me ruled,
Passions more fervent, making me less prompt
To in-door study than was wise or well,
Or suited to those years. Yet I, though used
In magisterial liberty to rove,
Culling such flowers of learning as might tempt
A random choice, could shadow forth a place
(If now I yield not to a flattering dream)
Whose studious aspect should have bent me down
To instantaneous service; should at once
Have made me pay to science and to arts
And written lore, acknowledged my liege lord,

A homage frankly offered up, like that
Which I had paid to Nature. Toil and pains
In this recess, by thoughtful Fancy built,
Should spread from heart to heart; and stately groves,
Majestic edifices, should not want
A corresponding dignity within.
The congregating temper that pervades
Our unripe years, not wasted, should be taught
To minister to works of high attempt—
Works which the enthusiast would perform with love.
Youth should be awed, religiously possessed
With a conviction of the power that waits
On knowledge, when sincerely sought and prized
For its own sake, on glory and on praise
If but by labour won, and fit to endure
The passing day; should learn to put aside
Her trappings here, should strip them off abashed
Before antiquity and steadfast truth
And strong book-mindedness; and over all
A healthy sound simplicity should reign,
A seemly plainness, name it what you will,
Republican or pious.
                            If these thoughts
Are a gratuitous emblazonry
That mocks the recreant age *we* live in, then
Be Folly and False-seeming free to affect
Whatever formal gait of discipline
Shall raise them highest in their own esteem—
Let them parade among the Schools at will,
But spare the House of God. Was ever known
The witless shepherd who persists to drive
A flock that thirsts not to a pool disliked?
A weight must surely hang on days begun
And ended with such mockery. Be wise,
Ye Presidents and Deans, and, till the spirit
Of ancient times revive, and youth be trained
At home in pious service, to your bells
Give seasonable rest, for 'tis a sound
Hollow as ever vexed the tranquil air;
And your officious doings bring disgrace
On the plain steeples of our English Church,

Whose worship, 'mid remotest village trees,
Suffers for this. Even Science, too, at hand
In daily sight of this irreverence,
Is smitten thence with an unnatural taint,
Loses her just authority, falls beneath
Collateral suspicion, else unknown.
This truth escaped me not, and I confess,
That having 'mid my native hills given loose
To a schoolboy's vision, I had raised a pile
Upon the basis of the coming time,
That fell in ruins round me. Oh, what joy
To see a sanctuary for our country's youth
Informed with such a spirit as might be
Its own protection; a primeval grove
Where, though the shades with cheerfulness **were** filled,
Nor indigent of songs warbled from crowds
In under-coverts, yet the countenance
Of the whole place should bear a stamp of awe;
A habitation sober and demure
For ruminating creatures; a domain
For quiet things to wander in; a haunt
In which the heron should delight to feed
By the shy rivers, and the pelican
Upon the cypress spire in lonely thought
Might sit and sun himself.—Alas! alas!
In vain for such solemnity I looked;
Mine eyes were crossed by butterflies, ears **vexed**
By chattering popinjays; the inner heart
Seemed trivial, and the impresses without
Of a too gaudy region.
                          Different sight
Those venerable Doctors saw of old,
When all who dwelt within these famous walls
Led in abstemiousness a studious life;
When, in forlorn and naked chambers cooped
And crowded, o'er the ponderous books they **hung**
Like caterpillars eating out their way
In silence, or with keen devouring noise
Not to be tracked or fathered. Princes then
At matins froze, and couched at curfew-time,
Trained up through piety and zeal to prize

Spare diet, patient labour, and plain weeds.
O seat of Arts! renowned throughout the world!
Far different service in those homely days
The Muses' modest nurslings underwent
From their first childhood; in that glorious time
When Learning, like a stranger come from far,
Sounding through Christian lands her trumpet, roused
Peasant and king; when boys and youths, the growth
Of ragged villages and crazy huts,
Forsook their homes, and, errant in the quest
Of Patron, famous school or friendly nook,
Where, pensioned, they in shelter might sit down,
From town to town and through wide scattered realms
Journeyed with ponderous folios in their hands;
And often, starting from some covert place,
Saluted the chance comer on the road,
Crying, "An obolus, a penny give
To a poor scholar!"—when illustrious men,
Lovers of truth, by penury constrained,
Bucer, Erasmus, or Melancthon, read
Before the doors or windows of their cells
By moonshine through mere lack of taper light.

BOOK FOURTH

SUMMER VACATION

(*Lines* 1-92)

Bright was the summer's noon when quickening steps
Followed each other till a dreary moor
Was crossed, a bare ridge clomb, upon whose top,
Standing alone, as from a rampart's edge
I overlooked the bed of Windermere,
Like a vast river, stretching in the sun.
With exultation, at my feet I saw
Lake, islands, promontories, gleaming bays,
A universe of Nature's fairest forms
Proudly revealed with instantaneous burst,
Magnificent, and beautiful, and gay.

I bounded down the hill shouting amain
For the old Ferryman; to the shout the rocks
Replied, and when the Charon of the flood
Had staid his oars, and touched the jutting pier,
I did not step into the well-known boat
Without a cordial greeting. Thence with speed
Up the familiar hill I took my way
Towards that sweet Valley where I had been reared;
'Twas but a short hour's walk, ere veering round
I saw the snow-white church upon her hill
Sit like a thronèd Lady sending out
A gracious look all over her domain.
Yon azure smoke betrays the lurking town;
With eager footsteps I advance and reach
The cottage threshold where my journey closed.
Glad welcome had I, with some tears, perhaps,
From my old Dame, so kind and motherly,
While she perused me with a parent's pride.
The thoughts of gratitude shall fall like dew
Upon thy grave, good creature! While my heart
Can beat never will I forget thy name.
Heaven's blessing be upon thee where thou liest
After thy innocent and busy stir
In narrow cares, thy little daily growth
Of calm enjoyments, after eighty years,
And more than eighty, of untroubled life,
Childless, yet by the strangers to thy blood
Honoured with little less than filial love.
What joy was mine to see thee once again,
Thee and thy dwelling, and a crowd of things
About its narrow precincts all beloved,
And many of them seeming yet my own!
Why should I speak of what a thousand hearts
Have felt, and every man alive can guess?
The rooms, the court, the garden were not left
Long unsaluted, nor the sunny seat
Round the stone table under the dark pine,
Friendly to studious or to festive hours;
Nor that unruly child of mountain birth,
The famous brook, who, soon as he was boxed
Within our garden, found himself at once,

As if by trick insidious and unkind,
Stripped of his voice and left to dimple down
(Without an effort and without a will)
A channel paved by man's officious care.
I looked at him and smiled, and smiled again,
And in the press of twenty thousand thoughts,
"Ha," quoth I, "pretty prisoner, are you there!"
Well might sarcastic Fancy then have whispered,
"An emblem here behold of thy own life;
In its late course of even days with all
Their smooth enthralment;" but the heart was full,
Too full for that reproach. My aged Dame
Walked proudly at my side; she guided me;
I willing, nay—nay, wishing to be led.
—The face of every neighbour whom I met
Was like a volume to me; some were hailed
Upon the road, some busy at their work,
Unceremonious greetings interchanged
With half the length of a long field between.
Among my schoolfellows I scattered round
Like recognitions, but with some constraint
Attended, doubtless, with a little pride.
But with more shame, for my habiliments,
The transformation wrought by gay attire.
Not less delighted did I take my place
At our domestic table: and, dear Friend!
In this endeavour simply to relate
A Poet's history, may I leave untold
The thankfulness with which I laid me down
In my accustomed bed, more welcome now
Perhaps than if it had been more desired
Or been more often thought of with regret;
That lowly bed whence I had heard the wind
Roar, and the rain beat hard; where I so oft
Had lain awake on summer nights to watch
The moon in splendour couched among the leaves
Of a tall ash, that near our cottage stood;
Had watched her with fixed eyes while to and fro
In the dark summit of the waving tree
She rocked with every impulse of the breeze.

(*Lines* 277-338)

                                    Yet in spite
Of pleasure won, and knowledge not withheld,
There was an inner falling off—I loved,
Loved deeply all that had been loved before,
More deeply even than ever: but a swarm
Of heady schemes jostling each other, gawds,
And feast and dance, and public revelry,
And sports and games (too grateful in themselves,
Yet in themselves less grateful, I believe,
Than as they were a badge glossy and fresh
Of manliness and freedom) all conspired
To lure my mind from firm habitual quest
Of feeding pleasures, to depress the zeal
And damp those yearnings which had once been mine—
A wild, unworldly-minded youth, given up
To his own eager thoughts. It would demand
Some skill, and longer time than may be spared,
To paint these vanities, and how they wrought
In haunts where they, till now, had been unknown.
It seemed the very garments that I wore
Preyed on my strength, and stopped the quiet stream
Of self-forgetfulness.

                              Yes, that heartless chase
Of trivial pleasures was a poor exchange
For books and nature at that early age.
'Tis true, some casual knowledge might be gained
Of character or life; but at that time,
Of manners put to school I took small note,
And all my deeper passions lay elsewhere.
Far better had it been to exalt the mind
By solitary study, to uphold
Intense desire through meditative peace;
And yet, for chastisement of these regrets,
The memory of one particular hour
Doth here rise up against me. 'Mid a throng
Of maids and youths, old men, and matrons staid,
A medley of all tempers, I had passed
The night in dancing, gaiety, and mirth,
With din of instruments and shuffling feet,
And glancing forms, and tapers glittering,

And unaimed prattle flying up and down;
Spirits upon the stretch, and here and there
Slight shocks of young love-liking interspersed,
Whose transient pleasure mounted to the head,
And tingled through the veins. Ere we retired,
The cock had crowed, and now the eastern sky
Was kindling, not unseen, from humble copse
And open field, through which the pathway wound,
And homeward led my steps. Magnificent
The morning rose, in memorable pomp,
Glorious as e'er I had beheld—in front,
The sea lay laughing at a distance; near,
The solid mountains shone, bright as the clouds,
Grain-tinctured, drenched in empyrean light;
And in the meadows and the lower grounds
Was all the sweetness of a common dawn—
Dews, vapours, and the melody of birds,
And labourers going forth to till the fields.
Ah! need I say, dear Friend! that to the brim
My heart was full; I made no vows, but vows
Were then made for me; bond unknown to me
Was given, that I should be, else sinning greatly,
A dedicated Spirit. On I walked
In thankful blessedness, which yet survives.

BOOK FIFTH

BOOKS

(*Lines* 361 425)

There was a Boy: ye knew him well, ye cliffs
And islands of Winander!—many a time
At evening, when the earliest stars began
To move along the edges of the hills,
Rising or setting, would he stand alone
Beneath the trees or by the glimmering lake,
And there, with fingers interwoven, both hands
Pressed closely palm to palm, and to his mouth
Uplifted, he, as through an instrument,

Blew mimic hootings to the silent owls,
That they might answer him; and they would shout
Across the watery vale, and shout again,
Responsive to his call, with quivering peals,
And long halloos and screams, and echoes loud,
Redoubled and redoubled, concourse wild
Of jocund din; and, when a lengthened pause
Of silence came and baffled his best skill,
Then sometimes, in that silence while he hung
Listening, a gentle shock of mild surprise
Has carried far into his heart the voice
Of mountain torrents; or the visible scene
Would enter unawares into his mind,
With all its solemn imagery, its rocks,
Its woods, and that uncertain heaven, received
Into the bosom of the steady lake.

This Boy was taken from his mates, and died
In childhood, ere he was full twelve years old.
Fair is the spot, most beautiful the vale
Where he was born; the grassy church-yard hangs
Upon a slope above the village school,
And through that churchyard when my way has led
On summer evenings, I believe that there
A long half hour together I have stood
Mute, looking at the grave in which he lies!
Even now appears before the mind's clear eye
That self-same village church; I see her sit
(The thronèd Lady whom erewhile we hailed)
On her green hill, forgetful of this Boy
Who slumbers at her feet,—forgetful, too,
Of all her silent neighbourhood of graves,
And listening only to the gladsome sounds
That, from the rural school ascending, play
Beneath her and about her. May she long
Behold a race of young ones like to those
With whom I herded!—(easily, indeed,
We might have fed upon a fatter soil
Of arts and letters—but be that forgiven)—
A race of real children; not too wise,
Too learned, or too good; but wanton, fresh,

And bandied up and down by love and hate;
Not unresentful where self-justified;
Fierce, moody, patient, venturous, modest, shy;
Mad at their sports like withered leaves in winds;
Though doing wrong and suffering, and full oft
Bending beneath our life's mysterious weight
Of pain, and doubt, and fear, yet yielding not
In happiness to the happiest upon earth.
Simplicity in habit, truth in speech,
Be these the daily strengtheners of their minds;
May books and Nature be their early joy!
And knowledge, rightly honoured with that name—
Knowledge not purchased by the loss of power!

BOOK SIXTH

CAMBRIDGE AND THE ALPS

(*Lines* 1-65)

The leaves were fading when to Esthwaite's banks
And the simplicities of cottage life
I bade farewell; and, one among the youth
Who, summoned by that season, reunite
As scattered birds troop to the fowler's lure,
Went back to Granta's cloisters, not so prompt
Or eager, though as gay and undepressed
In mind, as when I thence had taken flight
A few short months before. I turned my face
Without repining from the coves and heights
Clothed in the sunshine of the withering fern;
Quitted, not loth, the mild magnificence
Of calmer lakes and louder streams; and you,
Frank-hearted maids of rocky Cumberland,
You and your not unwelcome days of mirth
Relinquished, and your nights of revelry,
And in my own unlovely cell sate down
In lightsome mood—such privilege has youth
That cannot take long leave of pleasant thoughts.

The bonds of indolent society
Relaxing in their hold, henceforth I lived
More to myself. Two winters may be passed
Without a separate notice: many books
Were skimmed, devoured, or studiously perused,
But with no settled plan. I was detached
Internally from academic cares;
Yet independent study seemed a course
Of hardy disobedience towards friends
And kindred, proud rebellion and unkind.
This spurious virtue, rather let it bear
A name it now deserves, this cowardice,
Gave treacherous sanction to that over-love
Of freedom which encouraged me to turn
From regulations even of my own
As from restraints and bonds. Yet who can tell—
Who knows what thus may have been gained, both then
And at a later season, or preserved;
What love of nature, what original strength
Of contemplation, what intuitive truths,
The deepest and the best, what keen research,
Unbiassed, unbewildered, and unawed?

The Poet's soul was with me at that time;
Sweet meditations, the still overflow
Of present happiness, while future years
Lacked not anticipations, tender dreams,
No few of which have since been realised;
And some remain, hopes for my future life.
Four years and thirty, told this very week,
Have I been now a sojourner on earth,
By sorrow not unsmitten; yet for me
Life's morning radiance hath not left the hills,
Her dew is on the flowers. Those were the days
Which also first emboldened me to trust
With firmness, hitherto but slightly touched
By such a daring thought, that I might leave
Some monument behind me which pure hearts
Should reverence. The instinctive humbleness,
Maintained even by the very name and thought
Of printed books and authorship, began,

To melt away; and further, the dread awe
Of mighty names was softened down and seemed
Approachable, admitting fellowship
Of modest sympathy. Such aspect now,
Though not familiarly, my mind put on,
Content to observe, to achieve, and to enjoy.

(Lines 322–408)

When the third summer freed us from restraint,
A youthful friend, he too a mountaineer,
Not slow to share my wishes, took his staff,
And sallying forth, we journeyed side by side,
Bound to the distant Alps. A hardy slight
Did this unprecedented course imply
Of college studies and their sad rewards;
Nor had, in truth, the scheme been formed by me
Without uneasy forethought of the pain,
The censures, and ill-omening of those
To whom my worldly interests were dear.
But nature then was sovereign in my mind,
And mighty forms, seizing a youthful fancy,
Had given a charter to irregular hopes.
In any age of uneventful calm
Among the nations, surely would my heart
Have been possessed by similar desire;
But Europe at that time was thrilled with joy,
France standing on the top of golden hours,
And human nature seeming born again.

Lightly equipped, and but a few brief looks
Cast on the white cliffs of our native shore
From the receding vessel's deck, we chanced
To land at Calais on the very eve
Of that great federal day; and there we saw,
In a mean city, and among a few,
How bright a face is worn when joy of one
Is joy for tens of millions. Southward thence
We held our way, direct through hamlets, towns,
Gaudy with reliques of that festival,

Flowers left to wither on triumphal arcs,
And window-garlands. On the public roads,
And, once, three days successively, through paths
By which our toilsome journey was abridged,
Among sequestered villages we walked
And found benevolence and blessedness
Spread like a fragrance everywhere, when spring
Hath left no corner of the land untouched:
Where elms for many and many a league in files
With their thin umbrage, on the stately roads
Of that great kingdom, rustled o'er our heads,
For ever near us as we paced along:
How sweet at such a time, with such delight
On every side, in prime of youthful strength,
To feed a Poet's tender melancholy
And fond conceit of sadness, with the sound
Of undulations varying as might please
The wind that swayed them; once, and more than once,
Unhoused beneath the evening star we saw
Dances of liberty, and, in late hours
Of darkness, dances in the open air
Deftly prolonged, though grey-haired lookers on
Might waste their breath in chiding.
                                        Under hills—
The vine-clad hills and slopes of Burgundy,
Upon the bosom of the gentle Saone
We glided forward with the flowing stream.
Swift Rhone! thou wert the *wings* on which we cut
A winding passage with majestic ease
Between thy lofty rocks. Enchanting show
Those woods and farms and orchards did present,
And single cottages and lurking towns,
Reach after reach, succession without end
Of deep and stately vales! A lonely pair
Of strangers, till day closed, we sailed along,
Clustered together with a merry crowd
Of those emancipated, a blithe host
Of travellers, chiefly delegates returning
From the great spousals newly solemnized
At their chief city, in the sight of Heaven.
Like bees they swarmed, gaudy and gay as bees;

Some vapoured in the unruliness of joy,
And with their swords flourished as if to fight
The saucy air. In this proud company
We landed—took with them our evening meal,
Guests welcome almost as the angels were
To Abraham of old. The supper done,
With flowing cups elate and happy thoughts
We rose at signals given, and formed a ring
And, hand in hand, danced round and round the board;
All hearts were open, every tongue was loud
With amity and glee; we bore a name
Honoured in France, the name of Englishmen,
And hospitably did they give us hail,
As their forerunners in a glorious course;
And round and round the board we danced again.
With these blithe friends our voyage we renewed
At early dawn.

(Lines 489–499)

'Tis not my present purpose to retrace
That variegated journey step by step.
A march it was of military speed,
And Earth did change her images and forms
Before us, fast as clouds are changed in heaven.
Day after day, up early and down late,
From hill to vale we dropped, from vale to hill
Mounted—from province on to province swept,
Keen hunters in a chase of fourteen weeks,
Eager as birds of prey, or as a ship
Upon the stretch, when winds are blowing fair:

(Lines 754–778)

Oh, most beloved Friend! a glorious time,
A happy time that was; triumphant looks
Were then the common language of all eyes;
As if awaked from sleep, the Nations hailed
Their great expectancy: the fife of war
Was then a spirit-stirring sound indeed,
A blackbird's whistle in a budding grove.

We left the Swiss exulting in the fate
Of their near neighbours; and, when shortening fast
Our pilgrimage, nor distant far from home,
We crossed the Brabant armies on the fret
For battle in the cause of Liberty.
A stripling, scarcely of the household then
Of social life, I looked upon these things
As from a distance; heard, and saw, and felt,
Was touched, but with no intimate concern;
I seemed to move along them, as a bird
Moves through the air, or as a fish pursues
Its sport, or feeds in its proper element;
I wanted not that joy, I did not need
Such help; the ever-living universe,
Turn where I might, was opening out its glories,
And the independent spirit of pure youth
Called forth, at every season, new delights
Spread round my steps like sunshine o'er green fields.

BOOK EIGHTH

RETROSPECT—LOVE OF NATURE LEADING TO LOVE OF MAN

(*Lines* 173–339)

Smooth life had flock and shepherd in old time,
Long springs and tepid winters, on the banks
Of delicate Galesus; and no less
Those scattered along Adria's myrtle shores:
Smooth life had herdsman, and his snow-white herd
To triumphs and to sacrificial rites
Devoted, on the inviolable stream
Of rich Clitumnus; and the goat-herd lived
As calmly, underneath the pleasant brows
Of cool Lucretilis, where the pipe was heard
Of Pan, Invisible God, thrilling the rocks
With tutelary music, from all harm
The fold protecting. I myself, mature
In manhood then, have seen a pastoral tract

Like one of these, where Fancy might run wild,
Though under skies less generous, less serene:
There, for her own delight had Nature framed
A pleasure-ground, diffused a fair expanse
Of level pasture, islanded with groves
And banked with woody risings; but the Plain
Endless, here opening widely out, and there
Shut up in lesser lakes or beds of lawn
And intricate recesses, creek or bay
Sheltered within a shelter, where at large
The shepherd strays, a rolling hut his home.
Thither he comes with spring-time, there abides
All summer, and at sunrise ye may hear
His flageolet to liquid notes of love
Attuned, or sprightly fife resounding far.
Nook is there none, nor tract of that vast space
Where passage opens, but the same shall have
In turn its visitant, telling there his hours
In unlaborious pleasure, with no task
More toilsome than to carve a beechen bowl
For spring or fountain, which the traveller finds,
When through the region he pursues at will
His devious course. A glimpse of such sweet life
I saw when, from the melancholy walls
Of Goslar, once imperial, I renewed
My daily walk along that wide champaign,
That, reaching to her gates, spreads east and west,
And northwards, from beneath the mountainous verge
Of the Hercynian forest. Yet, hail to you
Moors, mountains, headlands, and ye hollow vales,
Ye long deep channels for the Atlantic's voice,
Powers of my native region! Ye that seize
The heart with firmer grasp! Your snows and streams
Ungovernable, and your terrifying winds,
That howl so dismally for him who treads
Companionless your awful solitudes!
There, 'tis the shepherd's task the winter long
To wait upon the storms: of their approach
Sagacious, into sheltering coves he drives
His flock, and thither from the homestead bears
A toilsome burden up the craggy ways,

And deals it out, their regular nourishment
Strewn on the frozen snow. And when the spring
Looks out, and all the pastures dance with lambs,
And when the flock, with warmer weather, climbs
Higher and higher, him his office leads
To watch their goings, whatsoever track
The wanderers choose. For this he quits his home
At day-spring, and no sooner doth the sun
Begin to strike him with a fire-like heat,
Than he lies down upon some shining rock,
And breakfasts with his dog. When they have stolen,
As is their wont, a pittance from strict time,
For rest not needed or exchange of love,
Then from his couch he starts; and now his feet
Crush out a livelier fragrance from the flowers
Of lowly thyme, by Nature's skill enwrought
In the wild turf: the lingering dews of morn
Smoke round him, as from hill to hill he hies,
His staff protending like a hunter's spear,
Or by its aid leaping from crag to crag,
And o'er the brawling beds of unbridged streams.
Philosophy, methinks, at Fancy's call,
Might deign to follow him through what he does
Or sees in his day's march; himself he feels,
In those vast regions where his service lies,
A freeman, wedded to his life of hope
And hazard, and hard labour inter-changed
With that majestic indolence so dear
To native man. A rambling schoolboy, thus
I felt his presence in his own domain,
As of a lord and master, or a power,
Or genius, under Nature, under God,
Presiding; and severest solitude
Had more commanding looks when he was there.
When up the lonely brooks on rainy days
Angling I went, or trod the trackless hills
By mists bewildered, suddenly mine eyes
Have glanced upon him distant a few steps,
In size a giant, stalking through thick fog,
His sheep like Greenland bears; or, as he stepped
Beyond the boundary line of some hill-shadow,

His form hath flashed upon me, glorified
By the deep radiance of the setting sun:
Or him have I descried in distant sky,
A solitary object and sublime,
Above all height! like an aerial cross
Stationed alone upon a spiry rock
Of the Chartreuse, for worship. Thus was man
Ennobled outwardly before my sight,
And thus my heart was early introduced
To an unconscious love and reverence
Of human nature; hence the human form
To me became an index of delight,
Of grace and honour, power and worthiness.
Meanwhile this creature—spiritual almost
As those of books, but more exalted far;
Far more of an imaginative form
Than the gay Corin of the groves, who lives
For his own fancies, or to dance by the hour,
In coronal, with Phyllis in the midst—
Was, for the purposes of kind, a man
With the most common; husband, father; learned,
Could teach, admonish; suffered with the rest
From vice and folly, wretchedness and fear;
Of this I little saw, cared less for it,
But something must have felt.
                              Call ye these appearances—
Which I beheld of shepherds in my youth,
This sanctity of Nature given to man—
A shadow, a delusion, ye who pore
On the dead letter, miss the spirit of things;
Whose truth is not a motion or a shape
Instinct with vital functions, but a block
Or waxen image which yourselves have made,
And ye adore! But blessèd be the God
Of Nature and of Man that this was so;
That men before my inexperienced eyes
Did first present themselves thus purified,
Removed, and to a distance that was fit:
And so we all of us in some degree
Are led to knowledge, wheresoever led,
And howsoever; were it otherwise,

And we found evil fast as we find good
In our first years, or think that it is found,
How could the innocent heart bear up and live!
But doubly fortunate my lot; not here
Alone, that something of a better life
Perhaps was round me than it is the privilege
Of most to move in, but that first I looked
At man through objects that were great or fair;
First communed with him by their help. And thus
Was founded a sure safeguard and defence
Against the weight of meanness, selfish cares,
Coarse manners, vulgar passions, that beat in
On all sides from the ordinary world
In which we traffic. Starting from this point
I had my face turned toward the truth, began
With an advantage furnished by that kind
Of prepossession, without which the soul
Receives no knowledge that can bring forth good,
No genuine insight ever comes to her.
From the restraint of over-watchful eyes
Preserved, I moved about, year after year,
Happy, and now most thankful that my walk
Was guarded from too early intercourse
With the deformities of crowded life,
And those ensuing laughters and contempts,
Self-pleasing, which, if we would wish to think
With a due reverence on earth's rightful lord,
Here placed to be the inheritor of heaven,
Will not permit us; but pursue the mind,
That to devotion willingly would rise,
Into the temple and the temple's heart.

BOOK NINTH

RESIDENCE IN FRANCE

(*Lines* 23–430)

Free as a colt at pasture on the hill,
I ranged at large, through London's wide domain,
Month after month. Obscurely did I live,

Not seeking frequent intercourse with men,
By literature, or elegance, or rank,
Distinguished. Scarcely was a year thus spent
Ere I forsook the crowded solitude,
With less regret for its luxurious pomp,
And all the nicely-guarded shows of art,
Than for the humble book-stalls in the streets,
Exposed to eye and hand where'er I turned.

France lured me forth; the realm that I had crossed
So lately, journeying toward the snow-clad Alps.
But now, relinquishing the scrip and staff,
And all enjoyment which the summer sun
Sheds round the steps of those who meet the day
With motion constant as his own, I went
Prepared to sojourn in a pleasant town,
Washed by the current of the stately Loire.

Through Paris lay my readiest course, and there
Sojourning a few days, I visited
In haste, each spot of old or recent fame,
The latter chiefly; from the field of Mars
Down to the suburbs of St. Antony,
And from Mont Martre southward to the Dome
Of Geneviève. In both her clamorous Halls,
The National Synod and the Jacobins,
I saw the Revolutionary Power
Toss like a ship at anchor, rocked by storms;
The Arcades I traversed, in the Palace huge
Of Orleans; coasted round and round the line
Of Tavern, Brothel, Gaming-house, and Shop,
Great rendezvous of worst and best, the walk
Of all who had a purpose, or had not:
I stared and listened, with a stranger's ears,
To Hawkers and Haranguers, hubbub wild!
And hissing Factionists with ardent eyes,
In knots, or pairs, or single. Not a look
Hope takes, or Doubt or Fear is forced to wear,
But seemed there present; and I scanned them all,
Watched every gesture uncontrollable,
Of anger, and vexation, and despite,

All side by side, and struggling face to face,
With gaiety and dissolute idleness.

Where silent zephyrs sported with the dust
Of the Bastille, I sate in the open sun,
And from the rubbish gathered up a stone,
And pocketed the relic, in the guise
Of an enthusiast; yet, in honest truth,
I looked for something that I could not find,
Affecting more emotion than I felt;
For 'tis most certain, that these various sights,
However potent their first shock, with me
Appeared to recompense the traveller's pains
Less than the painted Magdalene of Le Brun,
A beauty exquisitely wrought, with hair
Dishevelled, gleaming eyes, and rueful cheek
Pale and bedropped with everflowing tears.

But hence to my more permanent abode
I hasten; there, by novelties in speech,
Domestic manners, customs, gestures, looks,
And all the attire of ordinary life,
Attention was engrossed; and, thus amused,
I stood, 'mid those concussions, unconcerned,
Tranquil almost, and careless as a flower
Glassed in a greenhouse, or a parlour shrub
That spreads its leaves in unmolested peace,
While every bush and tree, the country through,
Is shaking to the roots: indifference this
Which may seem strange: but I was unprepared
With needful knowledge, had abruptly passed
Into a theatre, whose stage was filled
And busy with an action far advanced.
Like others, I had skimmed, and sometimes read
With care, the master-pamphlets of the day;
Nor wanted such half-insight as grew wild
Upon that meagre soil, helped out by talk
And public news; but having never seen
A chronicle that might suffice to show
Whence the main organs of the public power
Had sprung, their transmigrations, when and how

Accomplished, giving thus unto events
A form and body; all things were to me
Loose and disjointed, and the affections left
Without a vital interest. At that time,
Moreover, the first storm was overblown,
And the strong hand of outward violence
Locked up in quiet. For myself, I fear
Now in connection with so great a theme
To speak (as I must be compelled to do)
Of one so unimportant; night by night
Did I frequent the formal haunts of men,
Whom, in the city, privilege of birth
Sequestered from the rest, societies
Polished in arts, and in punctilio versed;
Whence, and from deeper causes, all discourse
Of good and evil of the time was shunned
With scrupulous care; but these restrictions soon
Proved tedious, and I gradually withdrew
Into a noisier world, and thus ere long
Became a patriot; and my heart was all
Given to the people, and my love was theirs.

A band of military Officers,
Then stationed in the city, were the chief
Of my associates: some of these wore swords
That had been seasoned in the wars, and all
Were men well-born; the chivalry of France.
In age and temper differing, they had yet
One spirit ruling in each heart; alike
(Save only one, hereafter to be named)
Were bent upon undoing what was done;
This was their rest and only hope; therewith
No fear had they of bad becoming worse,
For worst to them was come; nor would have stirred,
Or deemed it worth a moment's thought to stir,
In anything, save only as the act
Looked thitherward. One, reckoning by years,
Was in the prime of manhood, and erewhile
He had sate lord in many tender hearts;
Though heedless of such honours now, and changed;
His temper was quite mastered by the times,

And they had blighted him, had eaten away
The beauty of his person, doing wrong
Alike to body and to mind: his port,
Which once had been erect and open, now
Was stooping and contracted, and a face,
Endowed by Nature with her fairest gifts
Of symmetry and light and bloom, expressed,
As much as any that was ever seen,
A ravage out of season, made by thoughts
Unhealthy and vexatious. With the hour,
That from the press of Paris duly brought
Its freight of public news, the fever came,
A punctual visitant, to shake this man,
Disarmed his voice and fanned his yellow cheek
Into a thousand colours; while he read,
Or mused, his sword was haunted by his touch
Continually, like an uneasy place
In his own body. 'Twas in truth an hour
Of universal ferment; mildest men
Were agitated; and commotions, strife
Of passions and opinions, filled the walls
Of peaceful houses with unquiet sounds.
The soil of common life, was, at that time,
Too hot to tread upon. Oft said I then,
And not then only, "What a mockery this
Of history, the past and that to come!
Now do I feel how all men are deceived,
Reading of nations and their works, in faith,
Faith given to vanity and emptiness;
Oh! laughter for the page that would reflect
To future times the face of what now is!"
The land all swarmed with passion, like a plain
Devoured by locusts,—Carra, Gorsas,—add
A hundred other names, forgotten now,
Nor to be heard of more; yet, they were powers,
Like earthquakes, shocks repeated day by day,
And felt through every nook of town and field.

Such was the state of things. Meanwhile the chief
Of my associates stood prepared for flight
To augment the band of emigrants in arms

Upon the borders of the Rhine, and leagued
With foreign foes mustered for instant war.
This was their undisguised intent, and they
Were waiting with the whole of their desires
The moment to depart.
                    An Englishman,
Born in a land whose very name appeared
To license some unruliness of mind;
A stranger, with youth's further privilege,
And the indulgence that a half-learnt speech
Wins from the courteous; I, who had been else
Shunned and not tolerated, freely lived
With these defenders of the Crown, and talked,
And heard their notions; nor did they disdain
The wish to bring me over to their cause.

But though untaught by thinking or by books
To reason well of polity or law,
And nice distinctions, then on every tongue,
Of natural rights and civil; and to acts
Of nations and their passing interests,
(If with unworldly ends and aims compared)
Almost indifferent, even the historian's tale
Prizing but little otherwise than I prized
Tales of the poets, as it made the heart
Beat high, and filled the fancy with fair forms,
Old heroes and their sufferings and their deeds;
Yet in the regal sceptre, and the pomp
Of orders and degrees, I nothing found
Then, or had ever, even in crudest youth,
That dazzled me, but rather what I mourned
And ill could brook, beholding that the best
Ruled not, and feeling that they ought to rule.

For, born in a poor district, and which yet
Retaineth more of ancient homeliness
Than any other nook of English ground,
It was my fortune scarcely to have seen,
Through the whole tenour of my schoolday time,
The face of one, who, whether boy or man,

Was vested with attention or respect
Through claims of wealth or blood; nor was it least
Of many benefits, in later years
Derived from academic institutes
And rules, that they held something up to view
Of a Republic, where all stood thus far
Upon equal ground; that we were brothers all
In honour, as in one community,
Scholars and gentlemen; where, furthermore,
Distinction open lay to all that came,
And wealth and titles were in less esteem
Than talents, worth, and prosperous industry.
Add unto this, subservience from the first
To presences of God's mysterious power
Made manifest in Nature's sovereignty,
And fellowship with venerable books,
To sanction the proud workings of the soul,
And mountain liberty. It could not be
But that one tutored thus should look with awe
Upon the faculties of man, receive
Gladly the highest promises, and hail,
As best, the government of equal rights
And individual worth. And hence, O Friend!
If at the first great outbreak I rejoiced
Less than might well befit my youth, the cause
In part lay here, that unto me the events
Seemed nothing out of nature's certain course,
A gift that was come rather late than soon.
No wonder, then, if advocates like these,
Inflamed by passion, blind with prejudice,
And stung with injury, at this riper day,
Were impotent to make my hopes put on
The shape of theirs, my understanding bend
In honour to their honour: zeal, which yet
Had slumbered, now in opposition burst
Forth like a Polar summer: every word
They uttered was a dart, by counterwinds
Blown back upon themselves; their reason seemed
Confusion-stricken by a higher power
Than human understanding, their discourse

Maimed, spiritless: and, in their weakness strong,
I triumphed.
       Meantime, day by day, the roads
Were crowded with the bravest youth of France,
And all the promptest of her spirits, linked
In gallant soldiership, and posting on
To meet the war upon her frontier bounds.
Yet at this very moment do tears start
Into mine eyes: I do not say I weep—
I wept not then,—but tears have dimmed my sight,
In memory of the farewells of that time,
Domestic severings, female fortitude
At dearest separations, patriot love
And self-devotion, and terrestrial hope,
Encouraged with a martyr's confidence;
Even files of strangers merely seen but once,
And for a moment, men from far with sound
Of music, martial tunes, and banners spread,
Entering the city, here and there a face,
Or person singled out among the rest,
Yet still a stranger and beloved as such;
Even by these passing spectacles my heart
Was oftentimes uplifted, and they seemed
Arguments sent from Heaven to prove the cause
Good, pure, which no one could stand up against,
Who was not lost, abandoned, selfish, proud,
Mean, miserable, wilfully depraved,
Hater perverse of equity and truth.

  Among that band of Officers was one,
Already hinted at, of other mould—
A patriot, thence rejected by the rest,
And with an oriental loathing spurned,
As of a different caste. A meeker man
Than this lived never, nor a more benign,
Meek though enthusiastic. Injuries
Made *him* more gracious, and his nature then
Did breathe its sweetness out most sensibly,
As aromatic flowers on Alpine turf,
When foot hath crushed them. He through the events
Of that great change wandered in perfect faith,

As through a book, an old romance, or tale
Of Fairy, or some dream of actions wrought
Behind the summer clouds. By birth he ranked
With the most noble, but unto the poor
Among mankind he was in service bound,
As by some tie invisible, oaths professed
To a religious order. Man he loved
As man; and, to the mean and the obscure,
And all the homely in their homely works,
Transferred a courtesy which had no air
Of condescension; but did rather seem
A passion and a gallantry, like that
Which he, a soldier, in his idler day
Had paid to woman: somewhat vain he was,
Or seemed so, yet it was not vanity,
But fondness, and a kind of radiant joy
Diffused around him, while he was intent
On works of love or freedom, or revolved
Complacently the progress of a cause,
Whereof he was a part: yet this was meek
And placid, and took nothing from the man
That was delightful. Oft in solitude
With him did I discourse about the end
Of civil government, and its wisest forms;
Of ancient loyalty, and chartered rights,
Custom and habit, novelty and change;
Of self-respect, and virtue in the few
For patrimonial honour set apart,
And ignorance in the labouring multitude.
For he, to all intolerance indisposed,
Balanced these contemplations in his mind;
And I, who at that time was scarcely dipped
Into the turmoil, bore a sounder judgment
Than later days allowed; carried about me,
With less alloy to its integrity,
The experience of past ages, as, through help
Of books and common life, it makes sure way
To youthful minds, by objects over near
Not pressed upon, nor dazzled or misled
By struggling with the crowd for present ends.

But though not deaf, nor obstinate to find
Error without excuse upon the side
Of them who strove against us, more delight
We took, and let this freely be confessed,
In painting to ourselves the miseries
Of royal courts, and that voluptuous life
Unfeeling, where the man who is of soul
The meanest thrives the most; where dignity,
True personal dignity, abideth not;
A light, a cruel, and vain world cut off
From the natural inlets of just sentiment,
From lowly sympathy and chastening truth:
Where good and evil interchange their names,
And thirst for bloody spoils abroad is paired
With vice at home. We added dearest themes—
Man and his noble nature, as it is
The gift which God has placed within his power,
His blind desires and steady faculties
Capable of clear truth, the one to break
Bondage, the other to build liberty
On firm foundations, making social life,
Through knowledge spreading and imperishable,
As just in regulations, and as pure
As individual in the wise and good.

We summoned up the honorable deeds
Of ancient Story, thought of each bright spot,
That would be found in all recorded time,
Of truth preserved and error passed away;
Of single spirits that catch the flame from Heaven,
And how the multitudes of men will feed
And fan each other; thought of sects, how keen
They are to put the appropriate nature on,
Triumphant over every obstacle
Of custom, language, country, love, or hate,
And what they do and suffer for their creed;
How far they travel, and how long endure;
How quickly mighty Nations have been formed,
From least beginnings; how, together locked
By new opinions, scattered tribes have made
One body, spreading wide as clouds in heaven.

To aspirations then of our own minds
Did we appeal; and, finally, beheld
A living confirmation of the whole
Before us, in a people from the depth
Of shameful imbecility uprisen,
Fresh as the morning star. Elate we looked
Upon their virtues; saw, in rudest men,
Self-sacrifice the firmest; generous love,
And continence of mind, and sense of right,
Uppermost in the midst of fiercest strife.

  Oh, sweet it is, in academic groves,
Or such retirement, Friend! as we have known
In the green dales beside our Rotha's stream,
Greta, or Derwent, or some nameless rill,
To ruminate, with interchange of talk,
On rational liberty, and hope in man,
Justice and peace. But far more sweet such toil—
Toil, say I, for it leads to thoughts abstruse—
If nature then be standing on the brink
Of some great trial, and we hear the voice
Of one devoted,—one whom circumstance
Hath called upon to embody his deep sense
In action, give it outwardly a shape,
And that of benediction, to the world.
Then doubt is not, and truth is more than truth,—
A hope it is, and a desire; a creed
Of zeal, by an authority Divine
Sanctioned, of danger, difficulty, or death.
Such conversation, under Attic shades,
Did Dion hold with Plato; ripened thus
For a deliverer's glorious task,—and such
He, on that ministry already bound,
Held with Eudemus and Timonides,
Surrounded by adventurers in arms,
When those two vessels with their daring freight,
For the Sicilian Tyrant's overthrow,
Sailed from Zacynthus,—philosophic war,
Led by Philosophers. With harder fate,
Though like ambition, such was he, O Friend!
Of whom I speak. So BEAUPUY (let the name

Stand near the worthiest of Antiquity)
Fashioned his life; and many a long discourse,
With like persuasion honoured, we maintained:
He, on his part, accoutred for the worst,
He perished fighting, in supreme command,
Upon the borders of the unhappy Loire,
For liberty, against deluded men,
His fellow country-men; and yet most blessed
In this, that he the fate of later times
Lived not to see, nor what we now behold,
Who have as ardent hearts as he had then.

(*Lines* 502-532)

Hatred of absolute rule, where will of one
Is law for all, and of that barren pride
In them who, by immunities unjust,
Between the sovereign and the people stand,
His helper and not theirs, laid stronger hold
Daily upon me, mixed with pity too
And love; for where hope is, there love will be
For the abject multitude. And when we chanced
One day to meet a hunger-bitten girl,
Who crept along fitting her languid gait
Unto a heifer's motion, by a cord
Tied to her arm, and picking thus from the lane
Its sustenance, while the girl with pallid hands
Was busy knitting in a heartless mood
Of solitude, and at the sight my friend
In agitation said, " 'Tis against *that*
That we are fighting," I with him believed
That a benignant spirit was abroad
Which might not be withstood, that poverty
Abject as this would in a little time
Be found no more, that we should see the earth
Unthwarted in her wish to recompense
The meek, the lowly, patient child of toil,
All institutes for ever blotted out
That legalised exclusion, empty pomp
Abolished, sensual state and cruel power,
Whether by edict of the one or few;

And finally, as sum and crown of all,
Should see the people having a strong hand
In framing their own laws; whence better days
To all mankind.

BOOK TENTH

RESIDENCE IN FRANCE—(Continued)

(*Lines* 1–415)

It was a beautiful and silent day
That overspread the countenance of earth,
Then fading with unusual quietness,—
A day as beautiful as e'er was given
To soothe regret, though deepening what it soothed,
When by the gliding Loire I paused, and cast
Upon his rich domains, vineyard and tilth,
Green meadow-ground, and many-coloured woods,
Again, and yet again, a farewell look;
Then from the quiet of that scene passed on,
Bound to the fierce Metropolis. From his throne
The King had fallen, and that invading host—
Presumptuous cloud, on whose black front was written
The tender mercies of the dismal wind
That bore it—on the plains of Liberty
Had burst innocuous. Say in bolder words,
They—who had come elate as eastern hunters
Banded beneath the Great Mogul, when he
Erewhile went forth from Agra or Lahore,
Rajahs and Omrahs in his train, intent
To drive their prey enclosed within a ring
Wide as a province, but, the signal given,
Before the point of the life-threatening spear
Narrowing itself by moments—they, rash men,
Had seen the anticipated quarry turned
Into avengers, from whose wrath they fled
In terror. Disappointment and dismay
Remained for all whose fancies had run wild

With evil expectations; confidence
And perfect triumph for the better cause.

   The State, as if to stamp the final seal
On her security, and to the world
Show what she was, a high and fearless soul,
Exulting in defiance, or heart-stung
By sharp resentment, or belike to taunt
With spiteful gratitude the baffled League,
That had stirred up her slackening faculties
To a new transition, when the King was crushed,
Spared not the empty throne, and in proud haste
Assumed the body and venerable name
Of a Republic. Lamentable crimes,
'Tis true, had gone before this hour, dire work
Of massacre, in which the senseless sword
Was prayed to as a judge; but these were past,
Earth free from them for ever, as was thought,—
Ephemeral monsters, to be seen but once!
Things that could only show themselves and die.

   Cheered with this hope, to Paris I returned,
And ranged, with ardour heretofore unfelt,
The spacious city, and in progress passed
The prison where the unhappy Monarch lay,
Associate with his children and his wife
In bondage; and the palace, lately stormed
With roar of cannon by a furious host.
I crossed the square (an empty area then!)
Of the Carrousel, where so late had lain
The dead, upon the dying heaped, and gazed
On this and other spots, as doth a man
Upon a volume whose contents he knows
Are memorable, but from him locked up,
Being written in a tongue he cannot read,
So that he questions the mute leaves with pain,
And half upbraids their silence. But that night
I felt most deeply in what world I was,
What ground I trod on, and what air I breathed.
High was my room and lonely, near the roof
Of a large mansion or hotel, a lodge

That would have pleased me in more quiet times;
Nor was it wholly without pleasure then.
With unextinguished taper I kept watch,
Reading at intervals; the fear gone by
Pressed on me almost like a fear to come.
I thought of those September massacres,
Divided from me by one little month,
Saw them and touched: the rest was conjured up
From tragic fictions or true history,
Remembrances and dim admonishments.
The horse is taught his manage, and no star
Of wildest course but treads back his own steps;
For the spent hurricane the air provides
As fierce a successor; the tide retreats
But to return out of its hiding-place
In the great deep; all things have second birth;
The earthquake is not satisfied at once;
And in this way I wrought upon myself,
Until I seemed to hear a voice that cried,
To the whole city, "sleep no more." The trance
Fled with the voice to which it had given birth;
But vainly comments of a calmer mind
Promised soft peace and sweet forgetfulness.
The place, all hushed and silent as it was,
Appeared unfit for the repose of night,
Defenceless as a wood where tigers roam.

With early morning towards the Palace-walk
Of Orleans eagerly I turned; as yet
The streets were still; not so those long Arcades;
There, 'mid a peal of ill-matched sounds and cries,
That greeted me on entering, I could hear
Shrill voices from the hawkers in the throng,
Bawling, "Denunciation of the Crimes
Of Maximilian Robespierre;" the hand,
Prompt as the voice, held forth a printed speech,
The same that had been recently pronounced,
When Robespierre, not ignorant for what mark
Some words of indirect reproof had been
Intended, rose in hardihood, and dared
The man who had an ill surmise of him
To bring his charge in openness; whereat,

When a dead pause ensued, and no one stirred,
In silence of all present, from his seat
Louvet walked single through the avenue,
And took his station in the Tribune, saying,
"I, Robespierre, accuse thee!"   Well is known
The inglorious issue of that charge, and how
He, who had launched the startling thunderbolt,
The one bold man, whose voice the attack had sounded,
Was left without a follower to discharge
His perilous duty, and retire lamenting
That Heaven's best aid is wasted upon men
Who to themselves are false.
                              But these are things
Of which I speak, only as they were storm
Or sunshine to my individual mind,
No further. Let me then relate that now—
In some sort seeing with my proper eyes
That Liberty, and Life, and Death would soon
To the remotest corners of the land
Lie in the arbitrement of those who ruled
The capital City; what was struggled for,
And by what combatants victory must be won;
The indecision on their part whose aim
Seemed best, and the straightforward path of those
Who in attack or in defence were strong
Through their impiety—my inmost soul
Was agitated; yea, I could almost
Have prayed that throughout earth upon all men,
By patient exercise of reason made
Worthy of liberty, all spirits filled
With zeal expanding in Truth's holy light,
The gift of tongues might fall, and power arrive
From the four quarters of the winds to do
For France, what without help she could not do,
A work of honour; think not that to this
I added, work of safety: from all doubt
Or trepidation for the end of things
Far was I, far as angels are from guilt.

Yet did I grieve, nor only grieved, but thought
Of opposition and of remedies:

An insignificant stranger and obscure,
And one, moreover, little graced with power
Of eloquence even in my native speech,
And all unfit for tumult or intrigue,
Yet would I at this time with willing heart
Have undertaken for a cause so great
Service however dangerous. I revolved,
How much the destiny of Man had still
Hung upon single persons; that there was,
Transcendent to all local patrimony,
One nature, as there is one sun in heaven;
That objects, even as they are great, thereby
Do come within the reach of humblest eyes;
That Man is only weak through his mistrust
And want of hope where evidence divine
Proclaims to him that hope should be most sure;
Nor did the inexperience of my youth
Preclude conviction, that a spirit strong
In hope, and trained to noble aspirations,
A spirit thoroughly faithful to itself,
Is for Society's unreasoning herd
A domineering instinct, serves at once
For way and guide, a fluent receptacle
That gathers up each petty straggling rill
And vein of water, glad to be rolled on
In safe obedience; that a mind, whose rest
Is where it ought to be, in self-restraint,
In circumspection and simplicity,
Falls rarely in entire discomfiture
Below its aim, or meets with, from without,
A treachery that foils it or defeats;
And, lastly, if the means on human will,
Frail human will, dependent should betray
Him who too boldly trusted them, I felt
That 'mid the loud distractions of the world
A sovereign voice subsists within the soul,
Arbiter undisturbed of right and wrong,
Of life and death, in majesty severe
Enjoining, as may best promote the aims
Of truth and justice, either* sacrifice,

*Utter?

From whatsoever region of our cares
Or our infirm affections Nature pleads,
Earnest and blind, against the stern decree.

On the other side, I called to mind those truths
That are the commonplaces of the schools—
(A theme for boys, too hackneyed for their sires,)
Yet, with a revelation's liveliness,
In all their comprehensive bearings known
And visible to philosophers of old,
Men who, to business of the world untrained,
Lived in the shade; and to Harmodius known
And his compeer Aristogiton, known
To Brutus—that tyrannic power is weak,
Hath neither gratitude, nor faith, nor love,
Nor the support of good or evil men
To trust in; that the godhead which is ours
Can never utterly be charmed or stilled;
That nothing hath a natural right to last
But equity and reason; that all else
Meets foes irreconcilable, and at best
Lives only by variety of disease.

Well might my wishes be intense, my thoughts
Strong and perturbed, not doubting at that time
But that the virtue of one paramount mind
Would have abashed those impious crests—have quelled
Outrage and bloody power, and—in despite
Of what the People long had been and were
Through ignorance and false teaching, sadder proof
Of immaturity, and—in the teeth
Of desperate opposition from without—
Have cleared a passage for just government,
And left a solid birthright to the State,
Redeemed, according to example given
By ancient lawgivers.
                    In this frame of mind,
Dragged by a chain of harsh necessity,
So seemed it,—now I thankfully acknowledge,
Forced by the gracious providence of Heaven,—
To England I returned, else (though assured

That I both was and must be of small weight,
No better than a landsman on the deck
Of a ship struggling with a hideous storm)
Doubtless, I should have then made common cause
With some who perished; haply perished too,
A poor mistaken and bewildered offering,—
Should to the breast of Nature have gone back,
With all my resolutions, all my hopes,
A Poet only to myself, to men
Useless, and even, beloved Friend! a soul
To thee unknown!
              Twice had the trees let fall
Their leaves, as often Winter had put on
His hoary crown, since I had seen the surge
Beat against Albion's shore, since ear of mine
Had caught the accents of my native speech
Upon our native country's sacred ground.
A patriot of the world, how could I glide
Into communion with her sylvan shades,
Erewhile my tuneful haunt? It pleased me more
To abide in the great City, where I found
The general air still busy with the stir
Of that first memorable onset made
By a strong levy of humanity
Upon the traffickers in Negro blood;
Effort which, though defeated, had recalled
To notice old forgotten principles,
And through the nation spread a novel heat
Of virtuous feeling. For myself, I own
That this particular strife had wanted power
To rivet my affections; nor did now
Its unsuccessful issue much excite
My sorrow; for I brought with me the faith
That, if France prospered, good men would not long
Pay fruitless worship to humanity,
And this most rotten branch of human shame,
Object, so seemed it, of superfluous pains,
Would fall together with its parent tree.
What, then, were my emotions, when in arms
Britain put forth her freeborn strength in league,
Oh, pity and shame! with those confederate Powers!

Not in my single self alone I found,
But in the minds of all ingenuous youth,
Change and subversion from that hour. No shock
Given to my moral nature had I known
Down to that very moment; neither lapse
Nor turn of sentiment that might be named
A revolution, save at this one time;
All else was progress on the self-same path
On which, with a diversity of pace,
I had been travelling: this a stride at once
Into another region. As a light
And pliant harebell, swinging in the breeze
On some grey rock—its birthplace—so had I
Wantoned, fast rooted on the ancient tower
Of my beloved country, wishing not
A happier fortune than to wither there:
Now was I from that pleasant station torn
And tossed about in whirlwind. I rejoiced,
Yea, afterwards—truth most painful to record!—
Exulted, in the triumph of my soul,
When Englishmen by thousands were o'erthrown,
Left without glory on the field, or driven,
Brave hearts! to shameful flight. It was a grief,—
Grief call it not, 'twas anything but that,—
A conflict of sensations without name,
Of which *he* only, who may love the sight
Of a village steeple, as I do, can judge,
When, in the congregation bending all
To their great Father, prayers were offered up,
Or praises for our country's victories;
And, 'mid the simple worshippers, perchance
I only, like an uninvited guest
Whom no one owned, sate silent, shall I add,
Fed on the day of vengeance yet to come.

Oh! much have they to account for, who could tear,
By violence, at one decisive rent,
From the best youth in England their dear pride,
Their joy, in England; this, too, at a time
In which worst losses easily might wear
The best of names, when patriotic love

Did of itself in modesty give way,
Like the Precursor when the Deity
Is come Whose harbinger he was; a time
In which apostasy from ancient faith
Seemed but conversion to a higher creed;
Withal a season dangerous and wild,
A time when sage Experience would have snatched
Flowers out of any hedge-row to compose
A chaplet in contempt of his grey locks.

When the proud fleet that bears the red-cross flag
In that unworthy service was prepared
To mingle, I beheld the vessels lie,
A brood of gallant creatures, on the deep;
I saw them in their rest, a sojourner
Through a whole month of calm and glassy days
In that delightful island which protects
Their place of convocation—there I heard,
Each evening, pacing by the still seashore,
A monitory sound that never failed,—
The sunset cannon. While the orb went down
In the tranquillity of nature, came
That voice, ill requiem! seldom heard by me
Without a spirit overcast by dark
Imaginations, sense of woes to come,
Sorrow for human kind, and pain of heart.

In France, the men, who, for their desperate ends,
Had plucked up mercy by the roots, were glad
Of this new enemy. Tyrants, strong before
In wicked pleas, were strong as demons now;
And thus, on every side beset with foes,
The goaded land waxed mad; the crimes of few
Spread into madness of the many; blasts
From hell came sanctified like airs from heaven.
The sterness of the just, the faith of those
Who doubted not that Providence had times
Of vengeful retribution, theirs who throned
The human Understanding paramount
And made of that their God, the hopes of men
Who were content to barter short-lived pangs

For a paradise of ages, the blind rage
Of insolent tempers, the light vanity
Of intermeddlers, steady purposes
Of the suspicious, slips of the indiscreet,
And all the accidents of life were pressed
Into one service, busy with one work.
The Senate stood aghast, her prudence quenched,
Her wisdom stifled, and her justice scared,
Her frenzy only active to extol
Past outrages, and shape the way for new,
Which no one dared to oppose or mitigate.

Domestic carnage now filled the whole year
With feast-days; old men from the chimney-nook,
The maiden from the bosom of her love,
The mother from the cradle of her babe,
The warrior from the field—all perished, all—
Friends, enemies, of all parties, ages, ranks,
Head after head, and never heads enough
For those that bade them fall. They found their joy,
They made it proudly, eager as a child,
(If like desires of innocent little ones
May with such heinous appetites be compared),
Pleased in some open field to exercise
A toy that mimics with revolving wings
The motion of a wind-mill; though the air
Do of itself blow fresh, and make the vanes
Spin in his eyesight, *that* contents him not,
But, with the plaything at arm's length, he sets
His front against the blast, and runs amain,
That it may whirl the faster.
                          Amid the depth
Of those enormities, even thinking minds
Forgot, at seasons, whence they had their being;
Forgot that such a sound was ever heard
As Liberty upon earth: yet all beneath
Her innocent authority was wrought,
Nor could have been, without her blessed name.
The illustrious wife of Roland, in the hour
Of her composure, felt that agony,
And gave it vent in her last words. O Friend!

It was a lamentable time for man,
Whether a hope had e'er been his or not!
A woeful time for them whose hopes survived
The shock; most woeful for those few who still
Were flattered, and had trust in human kind:
They had the deepest feeling of the grief.
Meanwhile the Invaders fared as they deserved:
The Herculean Commonwealth had put forth her arms,
And throttled with an infant godhead's might
The snakes about her cradle; that was well,
And as it should be; yet no cure for them
Whose souls were sick with pain of what would be
Hereafter brought in charge against mankind.
Most melancholy at that time, O Friend!
Were my day-thoughts,—my nights were miserable;
Through months, through years, long after the last beat
Of those atrocities, the hour of sleep
To me came rarely charged with natural gifts,
Such ghastly visions had I of despair
And tyranny, and implements of death;
And innocent victims sinking under fear,
And momentary hope, and worn-out prayer,
Each in his separate cell, or penned in crowds
For sacrifice, and struggling with fond mirth
And levity in dungeons, where the dust
Was laid with tears. Then suddenly the scene
Changed, and the unbroken dream entangled me
In long orations, which I strove to plead
Before unjust tribunals,—with a voice
Labouring, a brain confounded, and a sense,
Death-like, of treacherous desertion, felt
In the last place of refuge—my own soul.

(*Lines* 464-480)

Then was the truth received into my heart,
That, under heaviest sorrow earth can bring,
If from the affliction somewhere do not grow
Honour which could not else have been, a faith,
An elevation, and a sanctity,
If new strength be not given nor old restored,

The blame is ours, not Nature's. When a taunt
Was taken up by scoffers in their pride,
Saying, "Behold the harvest that we reap
From popular government and equality,"
I clearly saw that neither these nor aught
Of wild belief engrafted on their names
By false philosophy had caused the woe,
But a terrific reservoir of guilt
And ignorance filled up from age to age,
That could no longer hold its loathsome charge,
But burst and spread in deluge through the land.

BOOK ELEVENTH

FRANCE—(Concluded)

(*Lines* 1–73)

From that time forth, Authority in France
Put on a milder face; Terror had ceased,
Yet everything was wanting that might give
Courage to them who looked for good by light
Of rational Experience, for the shoots
And hopeful blossoms of a second spring:
Yet, in me, confidence was unimpaired;
The Senate's language, and the public acts
And measures of the Government, though both
Weak, and of heartless omen, had not power
To daunt me; in the People was my trust,
And in the virtues which mine eyes had seen.
I knew that wound external could not take
Life from the young Republic; that new foes
Would only follow, in the path of shame,
Their brethren, and her triumphs be in the end
Great, universal, irresistible.
This intuition led me to confound
One victory with another, higher far,—
Triumphs of unambitious peace at home,

And noiseless fortitude. Beholding still
Resistance strong as heretofore, I thought
That what was in degree the same was likewise
The same in quality,—that, as the worse
Of the two spirits then at strife remained
Untired, the better, surely, would preserve
The heart that first had roused him. Youth maintains,
In all conditions of society,
Communion more direct and intimate
With Nature,—hence, ofttimes, with reason too—
Than age or manhood, even. To Nature, then,
Power had reverted: habit, custom, law,
Had left an interregnum's open space
For *her* to move about in, uncontrolled.
Hence could I see how Babel-like their task,
Who, by the recent deluge stupefied,
With their whole souls went culling from the day
Its petty promises, to build a tower
For their own safety; laughed with my compeers
At gravest heads, by enmity to France
Distempered, till they found, in every blast
Forced from the street-disturbing newsman's horn,
For her great cause record or prophecy
Of utter ruin. How might we believe
That wisdom could, in any shape, come near
Men clinging to delusions so insane?
And thus, experience proving that no few
Of our opinions had been just, we took
Like credit to ourselves where less was due,
And thought that other notions were as sound,
Yea, could not but be right, because we saw
That foolish men opposed them.
                    To a strain
More animated I might here give way,
And tell, since juvenile errors are my theme,
What in those days through Britain was performed
To turn *all* judgments out of their right course;
But this is passion over-near ourselves,
Reality too close and too intense,
And intermixed with something, in my mind,
Of scorn and condemnation personal,

That would profane the sanctity of verse.
Our Shepherds, this say merely, at that time
Acted, or seemed at least to act, like men
Thirsting to make the guardian crook of law
A tool of murder; they who ruled the State,—
Though with such awful proof before their eyes
That he, who would sow death, reaps death, or worse,
And can reap nothing better,—child-like longed
To imitate, not wise enough to avoid;
Or left (by mere timidity betrayed)
The plain straight road, for one no better chosen
Than if their wish had been to undermine
Justice, and make an end of Liberty.

(*Lines* 105–144)

O pleasant exercise of hope and joy!
For mighty were the auxiliars which then stood
Upon our side, us who were strong in love!
Bliss was it in that dawn to be alive,
But to be young was very Heaven! O times,
In which the meagre, stale, forbidding ways
Of custom, law, and statute, took at once
The attraction of a country in romance!
When Reason seemed the most to assert her rights
When most intent on making of herself
A prime enchantress—to assist the work,
Which then was going forward in her name!
Not favoured spots alone, but the whole Earth,
The beauty wore of promise—that which sets
(As at some moments might not be unfelt
Among the bowers of Paradise itself)
The budding rose above the rose full blown.
What temper at the prospect did not wake
To happiness unthought of? The inert
Were roused, and lively natures rapt away!
They who had fed their childhood upon dreams,
The play-fellows of fancy, who had made
All powers of swiftness, subtilty, and strength
Their ministers,—who in lordly wise had stirred
Among the grandest objects of the sense,

And dealt with whatsoever they found there
As if they had within some lurking right
To wield it;—they, too, who of gentle mood
Had watched all gentle motions, and to these
Had fitted their own thoughts, schemers more mild,
And in the region of their peaceful selves;—
Now was it that *both* found, the meek and lofty
Did both find, helpers to their hearts' desire,
And stuff at hand, plastic as they could wish,—
Were called upon to exercise their skill,
Not in Utopia,—subterranean fields,—
Or some secreted island, Heaven knows where!
But in the very world, which is the world
Of all of us,—the place where, in the end,
We find our happiness, or not at all!

(*Lines* 209-222)

But now, become oppressors in their turn,
Frenchmen had changed a war of self-defence
For one of conquest, losing sight of all
Which they had struggled for: up mounted now,
Openly in the eye of earth and heaven,
The scale of liberty. I read her doom,
With anger vexed, with disappointment sore,
But not dismayed, nor taking to the shame
Of a false prophet. While resentment rose
Striving to hide, what nought could heal, the wounds
Of mortified presumption, I adhered
More firmly to old tenets, and, to prove
Their temper, strained them more; and thus, in heat
Of contest, did opinions every day
Grow into consequence, till round my mind
They clung, as if they were its life, nay more,
The very being of the immortal soul.

(*Lines* 333-374)

Then it was—
Thanks to the bounteous Giver of all good!—
That the beloved Sister in whose sight

Those days were passed, now speaking in a voice
Of sudden admonition—like a brook
That did but *cross* a lonely road, and now
Is seen, heard, felt, and caught at every turn,
Companion never lost through many a league—
Maintained for me a saving intercourse
With my true self; for, though bedimmed and changed
Much, as it seemed, I was no further changed
Than as a clouded and a waning moon:
She whispered still that brightness would return,
She, in the midst of all, preserved me still
A Poet, made me seek beneath that name,
And that alone, my office upon earth;
And, lastly, as hereafter will be shown,
If willing audience fail not, Nature's self,
By all varieties of human love
Assisted, led me back through opening day
To those sweet counsels between head and heart
Whence grew that genuine knowledge, fraught with peace,
Which, through the later sinkings of this cause,
Hath still upheld me, and upholds me now
In the catastrophe (for so they dream,
And nothing less), when, finally to close
And seal up all the gains of France, a Pope
Is summoned in to crown an Emperor—
This last opprobrium, when we see a people,
That once looked up in faith, as if to Heaven
For manna, take a lesson from the dog
Returning to his vomit; when the sun
That rose in splendour, was alive, and moved
In exultation with a living pomp
Of clouds—his glory's natural retinue—
Hath dropped all functions by the gods bestowed,
And, turned into a gewgaw, a machine,
Sets like an Opera phantom.
                          Thus, O Friend!
Through times of honour and through times of shame
Descending, have I faithfully retraced
The perturbations of a youthful mind
Under a long-lived storm of great events—

ELEGIAC STANZAS

SUGGESTED BY A PICTURE OF PEELE CASTLE, IN A STORM,
PAINTED BY SIR GEORGE BEAUMONT

[Composed 1805.—Published 1807.]

I was thy neighbour once, thou rugged Pile!
   Four summer weeks I dwelt in sight of thee:
I saw thee every day; and all the while
   Thy Form was sleeping on a glassy sea.

So pure the sky, so quiet was the air!
   So like, so very like, was day to day!
Whene'er I looked, thy Image still was there;
   It trembled, but it never passed away.

How perfect was the calm! it seemed no sleep;
   No mood, which season takes away, or brings:
I could have fancied that the mighty Deep
   Was even the gentlest of all gentle Things.

Ah! then, if mine had been the Painter's hand,
   To express what then I saw; and add the gleam,
The light that never was, on sea or land,
   The consecration, and the Poet's dream;

I would have planted thee, thou hoary Pile,
   Amid a world how different from this!
Beside a sea that could not cease to smile;
   On tranquil land, beneath a sky of bliss.

Thou shouldst have seemed a treasure-house divine
   Of peaceful years; a chronicle of heaven;—
Of all the sunbeams that did ever shine
   The very sweetest had to thee been given.

A Picture had it been of lasting ease,
   Elysian quiet, without toil or strife;
No motion but the moving tide, a breeze,
   Or merely silent Nature's breathing life.

Such, in the fond illusion of my heart,
  Such Picture would I at that time have made:
And seen the soul of truth in every part,
  A steadfast peace that might not be betrayed.

So once it would have been,—'tis so no more;
  I have submitted to a new control:
A power is gone, which nothing can restore;
  A deep distress hath humanised my Soul.

Not for a moment could I now behold
  A smiling sea, and be what I have been:
The feeling of my loss will ne'er be old;
  This, which I know, I speak with mind serene.

Then, Beaumont, Friend! who would have been the
      Friend,
  If he had lived, of Him whom I deplore,
This work of thine I blame not, but commend;
  This sea in anger, and that dismal shore.

O 'tis a passionate Work!—yet wise and well,
  Well chosen is the spirit that is here;
That Hulk which labours in the deadly swell,
  This rueful sky, this pageantry of fear!

And this huge Castle, standing here sublime,
  I love to see the look with which it braves,
Cased in the unfeeling armour of old time,
  The lightning, the fierce wind, and trampling waves.

Farewell, farewell the heart that lives alone,
  Housed in a dream, at distance from the Kind!
Such happiness, wherever it be known,
  Is to be pitied; for 'tis surely blind.

But welcome fortitude, and patient cheer,
  And frequent sights of what is to be borne!
Such sights, or worse, as are before me here.—
  Not without hope we suffer and we mourn.

ODE TO DUTY

[Composed 1805.—Published 1807.]

"Jam non consilio bonus sed more eo perductus, ut non tantum recte facere possim, sed nisi recte facere non possim."

Stern Daughter of the Voice of God!
O Duty! if that name thou love
Who art a light to guide, a rod
To check the erring, and reprove;
Thou, who art victory and law
When empty terrors overawe;
From vain temptations dost set free;
And calm'st the weary strife of frail humanity!

There are who ask not if thine eye
Be on them; who, in love and truth,
Where no misgivings is, rely
Upon the genial sense of youth:
Glad Hearts! without reproach or blot;
Who do thy work, and know it not:
Oh! if through confidence misplaced
They fail, thy saving arms, dread Power! around
      them cast.

Serene will be our days and bright,
And happy will our nature be,
When love is an unerring light,
And joy its own security.
And they a blissful course may hold
Even now, who, not unwisely bold,
Live in the spirit of this creed;
Yet seek thy firm support, according to their need.

I, loving freedom, and untried;
No sport of every random gust,
Yet being to myself a guide,
Too blindly have reposed my trust:
And oft, when in my heart was heard
Thy timely mandate, I deferred
The task, in smoother walks to stray;
But thee I now would serve more strictly, if I may.

Through no disturbance of my soul,
Or strong compunction in me wrought,
I supplicate for thy control;
But in the quietness of thought:
Me this unchartered freedom tires;
I feel the weight of chance-desires:
My hopes no more must change their name,
I long for a repose that ever is the same.

[Yet not the less would I throughout
Still act according to the voice
Of my own wish; and feel past doubt
That my submissiveness was choice:
Not seeking in the school of pride
For "precepts over dignified,"
Denial and restraint I prize
No farther than they breed a second Will more
          wise.]

apprendre

Stern Lawgiver! yet thou dost wear
The Godhead's most benignant grace;
Nor know we anything so fair
As is the smile upon thy face:
Flowers laugh before thee on their beds
And fragrance in thy footing treads;
Thou dost preserve the stars from wrong;
And the most ancient heavens, through Thee, are
          fresh and strong.

To humbler functions, awful Power!
I call thee: I myself commend
Unto thy guidance from this hour;
Oh, let my weakness have an end!
Give unto me, made lowly wise,
The spirit of self-sacrifice;
The confidence of reason give;
And in the light of truth thy Bondman let me live!

CHARACTER OF THE HAPPY WARRIOR

[Composed December, 1805, or January, 1806.—Published 1807.]

Who is the happy Warrior? Who is he
That every man in arms should wish to be?
—It is the generous Spirit, who, when brought
Among the tasks of real life, hath wrought
Upon the plan that pleased his boyish thought:
Whose high endeavors are an inward light
That makes the path before him always bright:
Who, with a natural instinct to discern
What knowledge can perform, is diligent to learn;
Abides by this resolve, and stops not there,
But makes his moral being his prime care;
Who, doomed to go in company with Pain,
And Fear, and Bloodshed, miserable train!
Turns his necessity to glorious gain;
In face of these doth exercise a power
Which is our human nature's highest dower;
Controls them and subdues, transmutes, bereaves
Of their bad influence, and their good receives:
By objects, which might force the soul to abate
Her feeling, rendered more compassionate;
Is placable—because occasions rise
So often that demand such sacrifice;
More skilful in self-knowledge, even more pure,
As tempted more; more able to endure,
As more exposed to suffering and distress;
Thence, also, more alive to tenderness.
—'Tis he whose law is reason; who depends
Upon that law as on the best of friends;
Whence, in a state where men are tempted still
To evil for a guard against worse ill,
And what in quality or act is best
Doth seldom on a right foundation rest,
He labours good on good to fix, and owes
To virtue every triumph that he knows:
—Who, if he rise to station of command,
Rises by open means; and there will stand
On honourable terms, or else retire,

And in himself possess his own desire;
Who comprehends his trust, and to the same
Keeps faithful with a singleness of aim;
And therefore does not stoop, nor lie in wait
For wealth, or honours, or for worldly state;
Whom they must follow; on whose head must fall,
Like showers of manna, if they come at all:
Whose powers shed round him in the common strife,
Or mild concerns of ordinary life,
A constant influence, a peculiar grace;
But who, if he be called upon to face
Some awful moment to which Heaven has joined
Great issues, good or bad for human kind,
Is happy as a Lover; and attired
With sudden brightness, like a Man inspired;
And, through the heat of conflict, keeps the law
In calmness made, and sees what he foresaw;
Or if an unexpected call succeed,
Come when it will, is equal to the need:
—He who, though thus endued as with a sense
And faculty for storm and turbulence,
Is yet a Soul whose master-bias leans
To homefelt pleasures and to gentle scenes;
Sweet images! which, wheresoe'er he be,
Are at his heart; and such fidelity
It is his darling passion to approve;
More brave for this, that he hath much to love:——
'Tis, finally, the Man, who, lifted high,
Conspicuous object in a Nation's eye,
Or left unthought-of in obscurity,—
Who, with a toward or untoward lot,
Prosperous or adverse, to his wish or not—
Plays, in the many games of life, that one
Where what he most doth value must be won:
Whom neither shape of danger can dismay,
Nor thought of tender happiness betray;
Who, not content that former worth stand fast,
Looks forward, persevering to the last,
From well to better, daily self-surpast:
Who, whether praise of him must walk the earth
For ever, and to noble deeds give birth,

Or he must fall, to sleep without his fame,
And leave a dead unprofitable name—
Finds comfort in himself and in his cause;
And, while the mortal mist is gathering, draws
His breath in confidence of Heaven's applause:
This is the happy Warrior; this is He
That every Man in arms should wish to be.

A COMPLAINT

[Composed 1806.—Published 1807.]

There is a change—and I am poor;
 Your love hath been, nor long ago,
A fountain at my fond heart's door,
 Whose only business was to flow;
And flow it did; not taking heed
Of its own bounty, or my need.

What happy moments did I count!
 Blest was I then all bliss above!
Now, for that consecrated fount
 Of murmuring, sparkling, living love,
What have I? shall I dare to tell?
A comfortless and hidden well.

A well of love—it may be deep—
 I trust it is,—and never dry:
What matter? if the waters sleep
 In silence and obscurity.
—Such change, and at the very door
Of my fond heart, hath made me poor.

[Composed ?.—Published 1807.]

Nuns fret not at their convent's narrow room;
And hermits are contented with their cells;
And students with their pensive citadels;
Maids at the wheel, the weaver at his loom,
Sit blithe and happy; bees that soar for bloom,

High as the highest Peak of Furness-fells,
Will murmur by the hour in foxglove bells:
In truth the prison, unto which we doom
Ourselves, no prison is: and hence for me,
In sundry moods, 'twas pastime to be bound
Within the Sonnet's scanty plot of ground;
Pleased if some Souls (for such there needs must be)
Who have felt the weight of too much liberty,
Should find brief solace there, as I have found.

God give me strength to keep my big mouth shut until I know what I'm talking about, + why? is living hell

PERSONAL TALK

[Composed ?.—Published 1807.]

I

I am not One who much or oft delight
To season my fireside with personal talk,—
Of friends, who live within an easy walk,
Or neighbours, daily, weekly, in my sight:
And, for my chance-acquaintance, ladies bright,
Sons, mothers, maidens withering on the stalk,
These all wear out of me, like Forms with chalk
Painted on rich men's floors, for one feast-night.
Better than such discourse doth silence long,
Long, barren silence, square with my desire;
To sit without emotion, hope, or aim,
In the loved presence of my cottage-fire,
And listen to the flapping of the flame,
Or kettle whispering its faint undersong.

II

"Yet life," you say, "is life; we have seen and see,
And with a living pleasure we describe;
And fits of sprightly malice do but bribe
The languid mind into activity.
Sound sense, and love itself, and mirth and glee
Are fostered by the comment and the gibe."
Even be it so: yet still among your tribe,

Our daily world's true Worldlings, rank not me!
Children are blest, and powerful; their world lies
More justly balanced; partly at their feet,
And part far from them:—sweetest melodies
Are those that are by distance made more sweet;
Whose mind is but the mind of his own eyes,
He is a Slave; the meanest we can meet!

III

Wings have we,—and as far as we can go
We may find pleasure: wilderness and wood,
Blank ocean and mere sky, support that mood
Which with the lofty sanctifies the low.
Dreams, books, are each a world; and books, we know,
Are a substantial world, both pure and good:
Round these, with tendrils strong as flesh and blood,
Our pastime and our happiness will grow.
There find I personal themes, a plenteous store,
Matter wherein right voluble I am,
To which I listen with a ready ear;
Two shall be named, pre-eminently dear,—
The gentle Lady married to the Moor;
And heavenly Una with her milk-white Lamb.

IV

Nor can I not believe but that hereby
Great gains are mine; for thus I live remote
From evil-speaking; rancour, never sought,
Comes to me not; malignant truth, or lie.
Hence have I genial seasons, hence have I
Smooth passions, smooth discourse, and joyous
         thought:
And thus from day to day my little boat
Rocks in its harbour, lodging peaceably.
Blessings be with them—and eternal praise,
Who gave us nobler loves, and nobler cares—
The Poets, who on earth have made us heirs
Of truth and pure delight by heavenly lays!
Oh! might my name be numbered among theirs,
Then gladly would I end my mortal days.

ADMONITION

Intended more particularly for the perusal of those who may have happened to be enamoured of some beautiful place of Retreat, in the Country of the Lakes.

[Composed ?.—Published 1807.]

Well may'st thou halt—and gaze with brightening eye!
The lovely Cottage in the guardian nook
Hath stirred thee deeply; with its own dear brook,
Its own small pasture, almost its own sky!
But covet not the Abode;—forbear to sigh,
As many do, repining while they look;
Intruders—who would tear from Nature's book
This precious leaf, with harsh impicty.
Think what the Home must be if it were thine,
Even thine, though few thy wants!—Roof, window,
          door,
The very flowers are sacred to the Poor,
The roses to the porch which they entwine:
Yea, all, that now enchants thee, from the day
On which it should be touched, would melt away.

[Composed 1806.—Published 1807.]

Yes, it was the mountain Echo,
    Solitary, clear, profound,
Answering to the shouting Cuckoo,
    Giving to her sound for sound!

Unsolicited reply
    To a babbling wanderer sent;
Like her ordinary cry,
    Like—but oh, how different!

Hears not also mortal Life?
    Hear not we, unthinking Creatures!
Slaves of folly, love, or strife—
    Voices of two different natures?

Have not *we* too?—yes, we have
    Answers, and we know not whence;
Echoes from beyond the grave,
    Recognised intelligence!

Such rebounds our inward ear
    Catches sometimes from afar—
Listen, ponder, hold them dear;
    For of God,—of God they are.

STRAY PLEASURES

[Composed 1806.—Published 1807.]

"——Pleasure is spread through the earth
In stray gifts to be claimed by whoever shall find."

By their floating mill,
    That lies dead and still,
Behold yon Prisoners three,
The Miller with two Dames, on the breast of the
      Thames!
The platform is small, but gives room for them all;
And they're dancing merrily.

From the shore come the notes
    To their mill where it floats,
To their house and their mill tethered fast:
To the small wooden isle where, their work to beguile,
They from morning to even take whatever is given;—
And many a blithe day they have past.

In sight of the spires,
    All alive with the fires
Of the sun going down to his rest,
In the broad open eye of the solitary sky,
They dance,—there are three, as jocund as free,
While they dance on the calm river's breast.

Man and Maidens wheel,
    They themselves make the reel,
And their music's a prey which they seize;

It plays not for them,—what matter? 'tis theirs;
And if they had care, it has scattered their cares
While they dance, crying, "Long as ye please!'

They dance not for me,
Yet mine is their glee!
Thus pleasure is spread through the earth
In stray gifts to be claimed by whoever shall find;
Thus a rich loving-kindness, redundantly kind,
Moves all nature to gladness and mirth.

The showers of the spring
Rouse the birds, and they sing;
If the wind do but stir for his proper delight,
Each leaf, that and this, his neighbour will kiss;
Each wave, one and t'other, speeds after his brother;
They are happy, for that is their right!

[Composed December, 1806.—Published 1807.]

How sweet it is, when mother Fancy rocks
The wayward brain, to saunter through a wood!
An old place, full of many a lovely brood,
Tall trees, green arbours, and ground-flowers in flocks;
And wild rose tip-toe upon hawthorn stocks.
Like a bold Girl, who plays her agile pranks
At Wakes and Fairs with wandering Mountebanks,—
When she stands cresting the Clown's head, and mocks
The crowd beneath her. Verily I think,
Such place to me is sometimes like a dream
Or map of the whole world: thoughts, link by link,
Enter through ears and eyesight, with such gleam
Of all things, that at last in fear I shrink,
And leap at once from the delicious stream.

[Composed ?.—Published 1807.]

The world is too much with us; late and soon,
Getting and spending, we lay waste our powers:
Little we see in Nature that is ours;

We have given our hearts away, a sordid boon!
This Sea that bares her bosom to the moon;
The winds that will be howling at all hours,
And are up-gathered now like sleeping flowers;
For this, for everything, we are out of tune;
It moves us not.—Great God! I'd rather be
A Pagan suckled in a creed outworn;
So might I, standing on this pleasant lea,
Have glimpses that would make me less forlorn;
Have sight of Proteus rising from the sea;
Or hear old Triton blow his wreathèd horn.

[Composed ?.—Published 1807.]

With Ships the sea was sprinkled far and nigh,
Like stars in heaven, and joyously it showed;
Some lying fast at anchor in the road,
Some veering up and down, one knew not why.
A goodly Vessel did I then espy
Come like a giant from a haven broad;
And lustily along the bay she strode,
Her tackling rich, and of apparel high.
This Ship was nought to me, nor I to her,
Yet I pursued her with a Lover's look;
This Ship to all the rest did I prefer:
When will she turn, and whither? She will brook
No tarrying; where She comes the winds must stir:
On went She, and due north her journey took.

[Composed ?.—Published 1807.]

Where lies the Land to which yon Ship must go?
Fresh as a lark mounting at break of day,
Festively she puts forth in trim array;
Is she for tropic suns, or polar snow?
What boots the enquiry?—Neither friend nor foe
She cares for; let her travel where she may,
She finds familiar names, a beaten way
Ever before her, and a wind to blow.
Yet still I ask, what haven is her mark?

And, almost as it was when ships were rare,
(From time to time, like Pilgrims, here and there
Crossing the waters) doubt, and something dark,
Of the old Sea some reverential fear,
Is with me at thy farewell, joyous Bark!

TO SLEEP

[Composed ?.—Published 1807.]

A flock of sheep that leisurely pass by,
One after one; the sound of rain, and bees
Murmuring; the fall of rivers, winds and seas,
Smooth fields, white sheets of water, and pure sky;
I have thought of all by turns, and yet do lie
Sleepless! and soon the small birds' melodies
Must hear, first uttered from my orchard trees;
And the first cuckoo's melancholy cry.
Even thus last night, and two nights more, I lay
And could not win thee, Sleep! by any stealth:
So do not let me wear to-night away:
Without Thee what is all the morning's wealth?
Come, blessed barrier between day and day,
Dear mother of fresh thoughts and joyous health!

[Composed ?.—Published 1807.]

Methought I saw the footsteps of a throne
Which mists and vapours from mine eyes did shroud—
Nor view of who might sit thereon allowed;
But all the steps and ground about were strown
With sights the ruefullest that flesh and bone
Ever put on; a miserable crowd,
Sick, hale, old, young, who cried before that cloud,
"Thou art our king, O Death! to thee we groan."
Those steps I clomb; the mists before me gave
Smooth way; and I beheld the face of one
Sleeping alone within a mossy cave,
With her face up to heaven; that seemed to have
Pleasing remembrance of a thought foregone;
A lovely Beauty in a summer grave!

LINES

Composed at Grasmere, during a walk one Evening, after a stormy day,
the Author having just read in a Newspaper that the dissolution of Mr.
Fox was hourly expected.

[Composed September (?), 1806.—Published 1807.]

Loud is the Vale! the Voice is up
    With which she speaks when storms are gone,
A mighty unison of streams!
    Of all her Voices, One!

Loud is the Vale;—this inland Depth
    In peace is roaring like the Sea;
Yon star upon the mountain-top
    Is listening quietly.

Sad was I, even to pain deprest,
    Importunate and heavy load!
The Comforter hath found me here,
    Upon this lonely road;

And many thousands now are sad—
    Wait the fulfilment of their fear;
For he must die who is their stay,
    Their glory disappear.

A Power is passing from the earth
    To breathless Nature's dark abyss;
But when the great and good depart
    What is it more than this—

That Man, who is from God sent forth,
    Doth yet again to God return?—
Such ebb and flow must ever be,
    Then wherefore should we mourn?

NOVEMBER, 1806

[Composed 1806.—Published 1807.]

Another year!—another deadly blow!
Another mighty Empire overthrown!
And We are left, or shall be left, alone;
The last that dare to struggle with the Foe.
'Tis well! from this day forward we shall know
That in ourselves our safety, must be sought;
That by our own right hands it must be wrought;
That we must stand unpropped, or be laid low.
O dastard whom such foretaste doth not cheer!
We shall exult, if they who rule the land
Be men who hold its many blessings dear,
Wise, upright, valiant; not a servile band,
Who are to judge of danger which they fear,
And honour which they do not understand.

ODE

INTIMATIONS OF IMMORTALITY
FROM RECOLLECTIONS OF
EARLY CHILDHOOD

The Child is father of the Man;
And I could wish my days to be
Bound each to each by natural piety.

[Composed 1802–1806.—Published 1807.]

I

There was a time when meadow, grove, and stream,
The earth, and every common sight,
          To me did seem
      Apparelled in celestial light,
The glory and the freshness of a dream.
It is not now as it hath been of yore;—
      Turn wheresoe'er I may,
          By night or day,
The things which I have seen I now can see no
          more.

II

The Rainbow comes and goes,
　　And lovely is the Rose,
　　The Moon doth with delight
Look round her when the heavens are bare,
　　Waters on a starry night
　　Are beautiful and fair;
　The sunshine is a glorious birth;
　But yet I know, where'er I go,
That there hath past away a glory from the earth.

III

Now, while the birds thus sing a joyous song,
　　And while the young lambs bound
　　As to the tabor's sound,
To me alone there came a thought of grief:
A timely utterance gave that thought relief,
　　And I again am strong:
The cataracts blow their trumpets from the steep;
No more shall grief of mine the season wrong;
I hear the Echoes through the mountains throng.
The Winds come to me from the fields of sleep,
　　And all the earth is gay;
　　　Land and sea
　Give themselves up to jollity,
　　And with the heart of May
　Doth every Beast keep holiday;—
　　　Thou Child of Joy,
Shout round me, let me hear thy shouts, thou
　　happy Shepherd-boy!

IV

Ye blessed Creatures, I have heard the call
　　Ye to each other make; I see
The heavens laugh with you in your jubilee;
　　My heart is at your festival,
　　My head hath its coronal,
The fulness of your bliss, I feel—I feel it all.
　　Oh evil day! if I were sullen
　　While Earth herself is adorning,

This sweet May-morning,
And the Children are culling
On every side,
In a thousand valleys far and wide,
Fresh flowers; while the sun shines warm,
And the Babe leaps up on his Mother's arm:—
I hear, I hear, with joy I hear!
—But there's a Tree, of many, one,
A single Field which I have looked upon,
Both of them speak of something that is gone:
The Pansy at my feet
Doth the same tale repeat:
Whither is fled the visionary gleam?
Where is it now, the glory and the dream?

v

Our birth is but a sleep and a forgetting:
The Soul that rises with us, our life's Star,
Hath had elsewhere its setting,
And cometh from afar:
Not in entire forgetfulness,
And not in utter nakedness,
But trailing clouds of glory do we come
From God, who is our home:
Heaven lies about us in our infancy!
Shades of the prison-house begin to close
Upon the growing Boy,
But He beholds the light, and whence it flows,
He sees it in his joy;
The Youth, who daily farther from the east
Must travel, still is Nature's Priest,
And by the vision splendid
Is on his way attended;
At length the Man perceives it die away,
And fade into the light of common day.

VI

Earth fills her lap with pleasures of her own;
Yearnings she hath in her own natural kind,

And, even with something of a Mother's mind,
        And no unworthy aim,
    The homely Nurse doth all she can
To make her Foster-child, her Inmate Man,
        Forget the glories he hath known,
And that imperial palace whence he came.

VII

Behold the Child among his new-born blisses,
A six years' Darling of a pigmy size!
See, where 'mid work of his own hand he lies,
Fretted by sallies of his mother's kisses,
With light upon him from his father's eyes!
See, at his feet, some little plan or chart,
Some fragment from his dream of human life,
Shaped by himself with newly-learned art;
        A wedding or a festival,
        A mourning or a funeral;
            And this hath now his heart,
        And unto this he frames his song:
            Then will he fit his tongue
To dialogues of business, love, or strife;
        But it will not be long
        Ere this be thrown aside,
        And with new joy and pride
The little Actor cons another part;
Filling from time to time his "humorous stage"
With all the Persons, down to palsied Age,
That Life brings with her in her equipage;
        As if his whole vocation
        Were endless imitation.

VIII

Thou, whose exterior semblance doth belie
        Thy Soul's immensity;
Thou best Philosopher, who yet dost keep
Thy heritage, thou Eye among the blind,
That, deaf and silent, read'st the eternal deep,

Haunted for ever by the eternal mind,—
    Mighty Prophet! Seer blest!
    On whom those truths do rest,
Which we are toiling all our lives to find,
In darkness lost, the darkness of the grave;
Thou, over whom thy Immortality
Broods like the Day, a Master o'er a Slave,
A Presence which is not to be put by;
Thou little Child, yet glorious in the might
Of heaven-born freedom on thy being's height,
Why with such earnest pains dost thou provoke
The years to bring the inevitable yoke,
Thus blindly with thy blessedness at strife?
Full soon thy Soul shall have her earthly freight,
And custom lie upon thee with a weight,
Heavy as frost, and deep almost as life!

           IX

    O joy! that in our embers
    Is something that doth live,
    That nature yet remembers
    What was so fugitive!
The thought of our past years in me doth breed
Perpetual benediction: not indeed
For that which is most worthy to be blest;
Delight and liberty, the simple creed
Of Childhood, whether busy or at rest,
With new-fledged hope still fluttering in his
        breast:—
    Not for these I raise
    The song of thanks and praise;
  But for those obstinate questionings
    Of sense and outward things,
    Fallings from us, vanishings;
    Blank misgivings of a Creature
Moving about in worlds not realised,
High instincts before which our mortal Nature
Did tremble like a guilty Thing surprised:
    But for those first affections,
    Those shadowy recollections,

Which, be they what they may,
Are yet the fountain-light of all our day,
Are yet a master-light of all our seeing;
  Uphold us, cherish, and have power to make
Our noisy years seem moments in the being
Of the eternal Silence: truths that wake,
  To perish never:
Which neither listlessness, nor mad endeavour,
  Nor Man nor Boy,
Nor all that is at enmity with joy,
Can utterly abolish or destroy!
  Hence in a season of calm weather
   Though inland far we be,
Our Souls have sight of that immortal sea
   Which brought us hither,
  Can in a moment travel thither,
And see the Children sport upon the shore,
And hear the mighty waters rolling evermore.

     x

Then sing, ye Birds, sing, sing a joyous song!
   And let the young Lambs bound
   As to the tabor's sound!
We in thought will join your throng,
   Ye that pipe and ye that play,
   Ye that through your hearts today
   Feel the gladness of the May!
What though the radiance which was once so bright
Be now for ever taken from my sight,
  Though nothing can bring back the hour
Of splendour in the grass, of glory in the flower;
   We will grieve not, rather find
   Strength in what remains behind;
   In the primal sympathy
   Which having been must ever be;
   In the soothing thoughts that spring
   Out of human suffering;
   In the faith that looks through death,
In years that bring the philosophic mind.

XI

And O, ye Fountains, Meadows, Hills, and Groves,
Forebode not any severing of our loves!
Yet in my heart of hearts I feel your might;
I only have relinquished one delight
To live beneath your more habitual sway.
I love the Brooks which down their channels fret,
Even more than when I tripped lightly as they;
The innocent brightness of a new-born Day
    Is lovely yet;
The Clouds that gather round the setting sun
Do take a sober colouring from an eye
That hath kept watch o'er man's mortality;
Another race hath been, and other palms are won.
Thanks to the human heart by which we live,
Thanks to its tenderness, its joys, and fears,
To me the meanest flower that blows can give
Thoughts that do often lie too deep for tears.

THOUGHT OF A BRITON ON THE SUBJUGATION OF
SWITZERLAND

[Composed probably early in 1807.—Published 1807.]

Two Voices are there; one is of the sea,
One of the mountains; each a mighty Voice;
In both from age to age thou didst rejoice,
They were thy chosen music, Liberty!
There came a Tyrant, and with holy glee
Thou fought'st against him; but hast vainly
        striven:
Thou from thy Alpine holds at length art driven,
Where not a torrent murmurs heard by thee.
Of one deep bliss thine ear hath been bereft:
Then cleave, O cleave to that which still is left;
For, high-souled Maid, what sorrow would it be
That Mountain floods should thunder as before,
And Ocean bellow from his rocky shore,
And neither awful Voice be heard by thee!

TO THOMAS CLARKSON, ON THE FINAL PASSING OF THE BILL
FOR THE ABOLITION OF THE SLAVE TRADE.   MARCH, 1807

[Composed March, 1807.—Published 1807.]

Clarkson! it was an obstinate hill to climb:
How toilsome—nay, how dire—it was, by thee
Is known; by none, perhaps, so feelingly:
But thou, who, starting in thy fervent prime,
Didst first lead forth that enterprise sublime,
Hast heard the constant Voice its charge repeat,
Which, out of thy young heart's oracular seat,
First roused thee.—O true yoke-fellow of Time,
Duty's intrepid liegeman, see, the palm
Is won, and by all Nations shall be worn!
The blood-stained Writing is for ever torn;
And thou henceforth wilt have a good man's calm,
A great man's happiness; thy zeal shall find
Repose at length, firm friend of human kind!

GIPSIES.

[Composed 1807.—Published 1807.]

Yet are they here the same unbroken knot
Of human Beings, in the self-same spot!
    Men, women, children, yea the frame
    Of the whole spectacle the same!
Only their fire seems bolder, yielding light,
Now deep and red, the colouring of night;
    That on their Gipsy-faces falls,
    Their bed of straw and blanket-walls.
—Twelve hours, twelve bounteous hours are gone,
    while I
Have been a traveller under open sky,
    Much witnessing of change and cheer,
    Yet as I left I find them here!
The weary Sun betook himself to rest;—
Then issued Vesper from the fulgent west,
    Outshining like a visible God
    The glorious path in which he trod.

And now, ascending, after one dark hour
And one night's diminution of her power,
    Behold the mighty Moon! this way
    She looks as if at them—but they
Regard not her:—oh, better wrong and strife
(By nature transient) than this torpid life;
    Life which the very stars reprove
    As on their silent tasks they move!
Yet, witness all that stirs in heaven or earth!
In scorn I speak not;—they are what their birth
    And breeding suffer them to be;
    Wild outcasts of society!

[Composed 1806.—Published 1807.]

O Nightingale! thou surely art
A creature of a "fiery heart":—
These notes of thine—they pierce and pierce;
Tumultuous harmony and fierce!
Thou sing'st as if the God of wine
Had helped thee to a Valentine;
A song in mockery and despite
Of shades, and dews, and silent night;
And steady bliss, and all the loves
Now sleeping in these peaceful groves.

I heard a Stock-dove sing or say
His homely tale, this very day;
His voice was buried among trees,
Yet to be come-at by the breeze:
He did not cease; but coocd—and cooed;
And somewhat pensively he wooed:
He sang of love, with quiet blending,
Slow to begin, and never ending;
Of serious faith, and inward glee;
That was the song—the song for me!

SONG AT THE FEAST OF BROUGHAM CASTLE

UPON THE RESTORATION OF LORD CLIFFORD, THE SHEPHERD,
TO THE ESTATES AND HONOURS OF HIS ANCESTORS

[Composed 1807.—Published 1807.]

High in the breathless Hall the Minstrel sate,
And Emont's murmur mingled with the Song.—
The words of ancient time I thus translate,
A festal strain that hath been silent long:—

"From town to town, from tower to tower,
The red rose is a gladsome flower.
Her thirty years of winter past,
The red rose is revived at last;
She lifts her head for endless spring,
For everlasting blossoming:
Both roses flourish, red and white:
In love and sisterly delight
The two that were at strife are blended,
And all old troubles now are ended.—
Joy! joy to both! but most to her
Who is the flower of Lancaster!
Behold her how She smiles to-day
On this great throng, this bright array!
Fair greeting doth she send to all
From every corner of the hall;
But chiefly from above the board
Where sits in state our rightful Lord,
A Clifford to his own restored!

"They came with banner, spear, and shield;
And it was proved in Bosworth-field.
Not long the Avenger was withstood—
Earth helped him with the cry of blood:
St. George was for us, and the might
Of blessed Angels crowned the right.
Loud voice the Land has uttered forth,
We loudest in the faithful north:
Our fields rejoice, our mountains ring,
Our streams proclaim a welcoming;

Our strong-abodes and castles see
The glory of their loyalty.

"How glad is Skipton at this hour—
Though lonely, a deserted Tower;
Knight, squire, and yeoman, page and groom:
We have them at the feast of Brough'm.
How glad Pendragon—though the sleep
Of years be on her!—She shall reap
A taste of this great pleasure, viewing
As in a dream her own renewing.
Rejoiced is Brough, right glad, I deem,
Beside her little humble stream;
And she that keepeth watch and ward
Her statelier Eden's course to guard;
They both are happy at this hour,
Though each is but a lonely Tower:—
But here is perfect joy and pride
For one fair House by Emont's side,
This day, distinguished without peer,
To see her Master and to cheer—
Him, and his Lady-mother dear!

"Oh! it was a time forlorn
When the fatherless was born—
Give her wings that she may fly,
Or she sees her infant die!
Swords that are with slaughter wild
Hunt the Mother and the Child.
Who will take them from the light?
—Yonder is a man in sight—
Yonder is a house—but where?
No, they must not enter there.
To the caves, and to the brooks,
To the clouds of heaven she looks;
She is speechless, but her eyes
Pray in ghostly agonies.
Blissful Mary, Mother mild,
Maid and Mother undefiled,
Save a Mother and her Child!

"Now Who is he that bounds with joy
On Carrock's side, a Shepherd-boy?
No thoughts hath he but thoughts that pass
Light as the wind along the grass.
Can this be He who hither came
In secret, like a smothered flame?
O'er whom such thankful tears were shed
For shelter, and a poor man's bread!
God loves the Child; and God hath willed
That those dear words should be fulfilled,
The Lady's words, when forced away
The last she to her Babe did say:
'My own, my own, thy Fellow-guest
I may not be; but rest thee, rest,
For lowly shepherd's life is best!'

"Alas! when evil men are strong
No life is good, no pleasure long.
The Boy must part from Mosedale's groves,
And leave Blencathara's rugged coves,
And quit the flowers that summer brings
To Glenderamakin's lofty springs;
Must vanish, and his careless cheer
Be turned to heaviness and fear.
—Give Sir Lancelot Threlkeld praise!
Hear it, good man, old in days!
Thou tree of covert and of rest
For this young Bird that is distrest;
Among thy branches safe he lay,
And he was free to sport and play,
When falcons were abroad for prey.

"A recreant harp, that sings of fear
And heaviness in Clifford's ear!
I said, when evil men are strong,
No life is good, no pleasure long,
A weak and cowardly untruth!
Our Clifford was a happy Youth,
And thankful through a weary time,
That brought him up to manhood's prime.
—Again he wanders forth at will,
And tends a flock from hill to hill:

His garb is humble; ne'er was seen
Such garb with such a noble mien;
Among the shepherd-grooms no mate
Hath he, a Child of strength and state!
Yet lacks not friends for simple glee,
Nor yet for higher sympathy.
To his side the fallow-deer
Came, and rested without fear;
The eagle, lord of land and sea,
Stooped down to pay him fealty;
And both the undying fish that swim
Through Bowscale-tarn did wait on him;
The pair were servants of his eye
In their immortality;
And glancing, gleaming, dark or bright,
Moved to and fro, for his delight.
He knew the rocks which Angels haunt
Upon the mountains visitant;
He hath kenned them taking wing:
And into caves where Faeries sing
He hath entered; and been told
By Voices how men lived of old.
Among the heavens his eye can see
The face of thing that is to be;
And, if that men report him right,
His tongue could whisper words of might.
—Now another day is come,
Fitter hope, and nobler doom;
He hath thrown aside his crook,
And hath buried deep his book;
Armour rusting in his halls
On the blood of Clifford calls:—
'Quell the Scot,' exclaims the Lance—
Bear me to the heart of France,
Is the longing of the Shield—
Tell thy name, thou trembling Field;
Field of death, where'er thou be,
Groan thou with our victory!
Happy day, and mighty hour,
When our Shepherd in his power,
Mailed and horsed, with lance and sword,

To his ancestors restored
Like a re-appearing Star,
Like a glory from afar,
First shall head the flock of war!"

Alas! the impassioned minstrel did not know
    How, by Heaven's grace, this Clifford's heart
        was framed:
How he, long forced in humble walks to go,
    Was softened into feeling, soothed, and tamed.

Love had he found in huts where poor men lie;
    His daily teachers had been woods and rills,
The silence that is in the starry sky,
    The sleep that is among the lonely hills.

In him the savage virtue of the Race,
    Revenge, and all ferocious thoughts were
        dead:
Nor did he change; but kept in lofty place
    The wisdom which adversity had bred.

Glad were the vales, and every cottage-hearth;
    The Shepherd-lord was honoured more and
        more;
And, ages after he was laid in earth,
    "The good Lord Clifford" was the name he
        bore.

THE FORCE OF PRAYER

OR
THE FOUNDING OF BOLTON PRIORY
A TRADITION

[Composed 1807.—Published 1815.]

"What is good for a bootless bene?"
    With these dark words begins my Tale;
And their meaning is, whence can comfort spring
    When Prayer is of no avail?

"What is good for a bootless bene?"
    The Falconer to the Lady said;
And she made answer "ENDLESS SORROW!"
    For she knew that her Son was dead.

She knew it by the Falconer's words,
    And from the look of the Falconer's eye;
And from the love which was in her soul
    For her youthful Romilly.

—Young Romilly through Barden woods
    Is ranging high and low;
And holds a greyhound in a leash,
    To let slip upon buck or doe.

The pair have reached that fearful chasm,
    How tempting to bestride!
For lordly Wharf is there pent in
    With rocks on either side.

The striding-place is called THE STRID,
A name which it took of yore:
A thousand years hath it borne that name,
And shall a thousand more.

And thither is young Romilly come,
And what may now forbid
That he, perhaps for the hundredth time,
Shall bound across THE STRID?

He sprang in glee,—for what cared he
That the river was strong, and the rocks were
        steep?—
But the greyhound in the leash hung back,
And checked him in his leap.

The Boy is in the arms of Wharf,
And strangled by a merciless force;
For never more was young Romilly seen
Till he rose a lifeless corse.

Now there is stillness in the vale,
And long, unspeaking, sorrow:
Wharf shall be to pitying hearts
A name more sad than Yarrow.

If for a Lover the Lady wept,
A solace she might borrow
From death, and from the passion of death:—
Old Wharf might heal her sorrow.

She weeps not for the wedding-day
Which was to be to-morrow:
Her hope was a further-looking hope,
And hers is a mother's sorrow.

He was a tree that stood alone,
And proudly did its branches wave;
And the root of this delightful tree
Was in her husband's grave!

Long, long in darkness did she sit,
And her first words were, "Let there be
In Bolton, on the field of Wharf,
A stately Priory!"

The stately Priory was reared;
And Wharf, as he moved along,
To matins joined a mournful voice,
Nor failed at even-song.

And the Lady prayed in heaviness
That looked not for relief!
But slowly did her succour come,
And a patience to her grief.

Oh! there is never sorrow of heart
That shall lack a timely end,
If but to God we turn, and ask
Of Him to be our friend!

GEORGE AND SARAH GREEN

[Composed 1808.—Published September, 1839 (*Tait's Edinburgh Magazine*);
never printed by W.]

Who weeps for strangers? Many wept
  For George and Sarah Green;
Wept for that pair's unhappy fate,
  Whose grave may here be seen.

By night, upon these stormy fells,
  Did wife and husband roam;
Six little ones at home had left,
  And could not find that home.

For *any* dwelling-place of man
  As vainly did they seek.
He perish'd; and a voice was heard—
  The widow's lonely shriek.

Not many steps, and she was left
  A body without life—
A few short steps were the chain that bound
  The husband to the wife.

Now do those sternly-featured hills
  Look gently on this grave;
And quiet *now* are the depths of air,
  As a sea without a wave.

But deeper lies the heart of peace
  In quiet more profound;
The heart of quietness is here
  Within this churchyard bound.

And from all agony of mind
  It keeps them safe, and far
From fear and grief, and from all need
  Of sun or guiding star.

O darkness of the grave! how deep,
  After that living night—

That last and dreary living one
  Of sorrow and affright?

O sacred marriage-bed of death,
  That keeps them side by side
In bond of peace, in bond of love,
  That may not be untied!

CHARACTERISTICS OF A CHILD THREE YEARS OLD

[Composed 1811.—Published 1815.]

Loving she is, and tractable, though wild;
And Innocence hath privilege in her
To dignify arch looks and laughing eyes;
And feats of cunning; and the pretty round
Of trespasses, affected to provoke
Mock-chastisement and partnership in play.
And, as a faggot sparkles on the hearth,
Not less if unattended and alone
Than when both young and old sit gathered round
And take delight in its activity;
Even so this happy Creature of herself
Is all-sufficient; solitude to her
Is blithe society, who fills the air
With gladness and involuntary songs.
Light are her sallies as the tripping fawn's
Forth-startled from the fern where she lay couched;
Unthought-of, unexpected, as the stir
Of the soft breeze ruffling the meadow-flowers,
Or from before it chasing wantonly
The many-coloured images imprest
Upon the bosom of a placid lake.

[Composed 1811.—Published 1815.]

The power of Armies is a visible thing,
  Formal, and circumscribed in time and space;

But who the limits of that power shall trace
Which a brave People into light can bring
Or hide, at will,—for freedom combating
By just revenge inflamed? No foot may chase,
No eye can follow, to a fatal place
That power, that spirit, whether on the wing
Like the strong wind, or sleeping like the wind
Within its awful caves.—From year to year
Springs this indigenous produce far and near;
No craft this subtle element can bind,
Rising like water from the soil, to find
In every nook a lip that it may cheer.

SONG FOR THE SPINNING WHEEL

FOUNDED UPON A BELIEF PREVALENT AMONG THE PASTORAL
VALES OF WESTMORELAND

[Composed 1812.—Published 1820.]

Swiftly turn the murmuring wheel!
  Night has brought the welcome hour,
When the weary fingers feel
  Help, as if from faery power;
Dewy night o'ershades the ground;
Turn the swift wheel round and round!

Now, beneath the starry sky,
  Couch the widely-scattered sheep;—
Ply the pleasant labour, ply!
  For the spindle, while they sleep,
Runs with speed more smooth and fine,
Gathering up a trustier line.

Short-lived likings may be bred
  By a glance from fickle eyes;
But true love is like the thread
  Which the kindly wool supplies,
When the flocks are all at rest,
Sleeping on the mountain's breast.

THE EXCURSION

SELECTIONS

BOOK FIRST

(Lines 438–956)

Supine the Wanderer lay,
His eyes as if in drowsiness half shut,
The shadows of the breezy elms above
Dappling his face. He had not heard the sound
Of my approaching steps, and in the shade
Unnoticed did I stand some minutes' space.
At length I hailed him, seeing that his hat
Was moist with water-drops, as if the brim
Had newly scooped a running stream. He rose,
And ere our lively greeting into peace
Had settled, " 'Tis," said I, "a burning day:
My lips are parched with thirst, but you, it seems,
Have somewhere found relief." He, at the word,
Pointing towards a sweet-briar, bade me climb
The fence where that aspiring shrub looked out
Upon the public way. It was a plot
Of garden ground run wild, its matted weeds
Marked with the steps of those, whom, as they passed,
The gooseberry trees that shot in long lank slips,
Or currants, hanging from their leafless stems,
In scanty strings, had tempted to o'erleap
The broken wall. I looked around, and there,
Where two tall hedge-rows of thick alder boughs
Joined in a cold damp nook, espied a well
Shrouded with willow-flowers and plumy fern.
My thirst I slaked, and, from the cheerless spot
Withdrawing, straightway to the shade returned
Where sate the old Man on the cottage bench;
And, while, beside him, with uncovered head,
I yet was standing, freely to respire,
And cool my temples in the fanning air,
Thus did he speak. "I see around me here

Things which you cannot see: we die, my Friend,
Nor we alone, but that which each man loved
And prized in his peculiar nook of earth
Dies with him, or is changed; and very soon
Even of the good is no memorial left.
—The Poets, in their elegies and songs
Lamenting the departed, call the groves,
They call upon the hills and streams to mourn,
And senseless rocks; nor idly; for they speak,
In these their invocations, with a voice
Obedient to the strong creative power
Of human passion. Sympathies there are
More tranquil, yet perhaps of kindred birth,
That steal upon the meditative mind,
And grow with thought. Beside yon spring I stood,
And eyed its waters till we seemed to feel
One sadness, they and I. For them a bond
Of brotherhood is broken: time has been
When, every day, the touch of human hand
Dislodged the natural sleep that binds them up
In mortal stillness; and they ministered
To human comfort! Stooping down to drink,
Upon the slimy foot-stone I espied
The useless fragment of a wooden bowl,
Green with the moss of years, and subject only
To the soft handling of the elements:
There let it lie—how foolish are such thoughts!
Forgive them;—never—never did my steps
Approach this door but she who dwelt within
A daughter's welcome gave me, and I loved her
As my own child. Oh, Sir! the good die first,
And they whose hearts are dry as summer dust
Burn to the socket. Many a passenger
Hath blessed poor Margaret for her gentle looks,
When she upheld the cool refreshment drawn
From that forsaken spring; and no one came
But he was welcome; no one went away
But that it seemed she loved him. She is dead,
The light extinguished of her lonely hut,
The hut itself abandoned to decay,
And she forgotten in the quiet grave.

"I speak," continued he, "of One whose stock
Of virtues bloomed beneath this lowly roof.
She was a Woman of a steady mind,
Tender and deep in her excess of love;
Not speaking much, pleased rather with the joy
Of her own thoughts: by some especial care
Her temper had been framed, as if to make
A Being, who by adding love to peace
Might live on earth a life of happiness.
Her wedded Partner lacked not on his side
The humble worth that satisfied her heart:
Frugal, affectionate, sober, and withal
Keenly industrious. She with pride would tell
That he was often seated at his loom,
In summer, ere the mower was abroad
Among the dewy grass,—in early spring,
Ere the last star had vanished.—They who passed
At evening, from behind the garden fence
Might hear his busy spade, which he would ply,
After his daily work, until the light
Had failed, and every leaf and flower were lost
In the dark hedges. So their days were spent
In peace and comfort; and a pretty boy
Was their best hope, next to the God in heaven.

"Not twenty years ago, but you I think
Can scarcely bear it now in mind, there came
Two blighting seasons, when the fields were left
With half a harvest. It pleased Heaven to add
A worse affliction in the plague of war:
This happy Land was stricken to the heart!
A Wanderer then among the cottages,
I, with my freight of winter raiment, saw
The hardships of that season: many rich
Sank down, as in a dream, among the poor;
And of the poor did many cease to be,
And their place knew them not. Meanwhile, abridged
Of daily comforts, gladly reconciled
To numerous self-denials, Margaret
Went struggling on through those calamitous years
With cheerful hope, until the second autumn,

When her life's Helpmate on a sick-bed lay,
Smitten with perilous fever. In disease
He lingered long; and, when his strength returned,
He found the little he had stored, to meet
The hour of accident or crippling age,
Was all consumed. A second infant now
Was added to the troubles of a time
Laden, for them and all of their degree,
With care and sorrow: shoals of artisans
From ill-requited labour turned adrift
Sought daily bread from public charity,
They, and their wives and children—happier far
Could they have lived as do the little birds
That peck along the hedge-rows, or the kite
That makes her dwelling on the mountain rocks!
    "A sad reverse it was for him who long
Had filled with plenty, and possessed in peace,
This lonely Cottage. At the door he stood,
And whistled many a snatch of merry tunes
That had no mirth in them; or with his knife
Carved uncouth figures on the heads of sticks—
Then, not less idly, sought, through every nook
In house or garden, any casual work
Of use or ornament; and with a strange,
Amusing, yet uneasy, novelty,
He mingled, where he might, the various tasks
Of summer, autumn, winter, and of spring.
But this endured not; his good humour soon
Became a weight in which no pleasure was:
And poverty brought on a petted mood
And a sore temper: day by day he drooped,
And he would leave his work—and to the town
Would turn without an errand his slack steps;
Or wander here and there among the fields.
One while he would speak lightly of his babes,
And with a cruel tongue: at other times
He tossed them with a false unnatural joy:
And 'twas a rueful thing to see the looks
Of the poor innocent children. 'Every smile,'
Said Margaret to me, here beneath these trees,
'Made my heart bleed.' "

                              At this the Wanderer paused;
And, looking up to those enormous elms,
He said, " 'Tis now the hour of deepest noon.
At this still season of repose and peace,
This hour when all things which are not at rest
Are cheerful; while this multitude of flies
With tuneful hum is filling all the air;
Why should a tear be on an old Man's cheek
Why should we thus, with an untoward mind,
And in the weakness of humanity,
From natural wisdom turn our hearts away;
To natural comfort shut our eyes and ears;
And, feeding on disquiet, thus disturb
The calm of nature with our restless thoughts?"
He spake with somewhat of a solemn tone:
But, when he ended, there was in his face
Such easy cheerfulness, a look so mild,
That for a little time it stole away
All recollection; and that simple tale
Passed from my mind like a forgotten sound.
A while on trivial things we held discourse,
To me soon tasteless. In my own despite,
I thought of that poor Woman as of one
Whom I had known and loved. He had rehearsed
Her homely tale with such familiar power,
With such an active countenance, an eye
So busy, that the things of which he spake
Seemed present; and, attention now relaxed,
A heart-felt chilliness crept along my veins.
I rose; and, having left the breezy shade,
Stood drinking comfort from the warmer sun,
That had not cheered me long—ere, looking round
Upon that tranquil Ruin, I returned,
And begged of the old Man that, for my sake,
He would resume his story.

                              He replied,
"It were a wantonness, and would demand
Severe reproof, if we were men whose hearts
Could hold vain dalliance with the misery
Even of the dead; contented thence to draw

A momentary pleasure, never marked
By reason, barren of all future good.
But we have known that there is often found
In mournful thoughts, and always might be found
A power to virtue friendly; were't not so,
I am a dreamer among men, indeed
An idle dreamer! 'Tis a common tale,
An ordinary sorrow of man's life,
A tale of silent suffering, hardly clothed
In bodily form.—But without further bidding
I will proceed.

           While thus it fared with them,
To whom this cottage, till those hapless years,
Had been a blessèd home, it was my chance
To travel in a country far remote;
And when these lofty elms once more appeared
What pleasant expectations lured me on
O'er the flat Common!—With quick step I reached
The threshold, lifted with light hand the latch;
But, when I entered, Margaret looked at me
A little while; then turned her head away
Speechless,—and, sitting down upon a chair,
Wept bitterly. I wist not what to do,
Nor how to speak to her. Poor Wretch! at last
She rose from off her seat, and then,—O Sir!
I cannot *tell* how she pronounced my name:—
With fervent love, and with a face of grief
Unutterably helpless, and a look
That seemed to cling upon me, she enquired
If I had seen her husband. As she spake
A strange surprise and fear came to my heart,
Nor had I power to answer ere she told
That he had disappeared—not two months gone.
He left his house: two wretched days had past,
And on the third, as wistfully she raised
Her head from off her pillow, to look forth,
Like one in trouble, for returning light,
Within her chamber-casement she espied
A folded paper, lying as if placed
To meet her waking eyes. This tremblingly
She opened—found no writing, but beheld

Pieces of money carefully enclosed,
Silver and gold. 'I shuddered at the sight,'
Said Margaret, 'for I knew it was his hand
That must have placed it there; and ere that day
Was ended, that long anxious day, I learned,
From one who by my husband had been sent
With the sad news, that he had joined a troop
Of soldiers, going to a distant land.
—He left me thus—he could not gather heart
To take a farewell of me; for he feared
That I should follow with my babes, and sink
Beneath the misery of that wandering life.'

"This tale did Margaret tell with many tears:
And, when she ended, I had little power
To give her comfort, and was glad to take
Such words of hope from her own mouth as served
To cheer us both. But long we had not talked
Ere we built up a pile of better thoughts,
And with a brighter eye she looked around
As if she had been shedding tears of joy.
We parted.—'Twas the time of early spring;
I left her busy with her garden tools;
And well remember, o'er that fence she looked,
And, while I paced along the foot-way path,
Called out, and sent a blessing after me,
With tender cheerfulness, and with a voice
That seemed the very sound of happy thoughts.

"I roved o'er many a hill and many a dale,
With my accustomed load; in heat and cold,
Through many a wood and many an open ground,
In sunshine and in shade, in wet and fair,
Drooping or blithe of heart, as might befall;
My best companions now the driving winds,
And now the 'trotting brooks' and whispering trees,
And now the music of my own sad steps,
With many a short-lived thought that passed between,
And disappeared.
                    I journeyed back this way,
When, in the warmth of midsummer, the wheat

Was yellow; and the soft and bladed grass,
Springing afresh, had o'er the hay-field spread
Its tender verdure. At the door arrived,
I found that she was absent. In the shade,
Where now we sit, I waited her return.
Her cottage, then a cheerful object, wore
Its customary look,—only, it seemed,
The honeysuckle, crowding round the porch,
Hung down in heavier tufts; and that bright weed,
The yellow stone-crop, suffered to take root
Along the window's edge, profusely grew
Blinding the lower panes. I turned aside,
And strolled into her garden. It appeared
To lag behind the season, and had lost
Its pride of neatness. Daisy-flowers and thrift
Had broken their trim border-lines, and straggled
O'er paths they used to deck; carnations, once
Prized for surpassing beauty, and no less
For the peculiar pains they had required,
Declined their languid heads, wanting support.
The cumbrous bind-weed, with its wreaths and bells,
Had twined about her two small rows of peas,
And dragged them to the earth.
                              Ere this an hour
Was wasted.—Back I turned my restless steps;
A stranger passed; and, guessing whom I sought,
He said that she was used to ramble far.—
The sun was sinking in the west; and now
I sate with sad impatience. From within
Her solitary infant cried aloud;
Then, like a blast that dies away self-stilled,
The voice was silent. From the bench I rose;
But neither could divert nor soothe my thoughts.
The spot, though fair, was very desolate—
The longer I remained, more desolate:
And, looking round me, now I first observed
The corner stones, on either side the porch,
With dull red stains discoloured, and stuck o'er
With tufts and hairs of wool, as if the sheep,
That fed upon the Common, thither came
Familiarly, and found a couching-place

Even at her threshold. Deeper shadows fell
From these tall elms; the cottage-clock struck
    eight;—
I turned, and saw her distant a few steps.
Her face was pale and thin—her figure, too,
Was changed. As she unlocked the door, she said,
'It grieves me you have waited here so long,
But, in good truth, I've wandered much of late;
And, sometimes—to my shame I speak—have need
Of my best prayers to bring me back again.'
While on the board she spread our evening meal,
She told me—interrupting not the work
Which gave employment to her listless hands—
That she had parted with her elder child;
To a kind master on a distant farm
Now happily apprenticed.—'I perceive
You look at me, and you have cause; to-day
I have been travelling far; and many days
About the fields I wander, knowing this
Only, that what I seek I cannot find;
And so I waste my time: for I am changed;
And to myself,' said she, 'have done much wrong
And to this helpless infant. I have slept
Weeping, and weeping have I waked; my tears
Have flowed as if my body were not such
As others are; and I could never die.
But I am now in mind and in my heart
More easy; and I hope,' said she, 'that God
Will give me patience to endure the things
Which I behold at home.'
                              It would have grieved
Your very soul to see her. Sir, I feel
The story linger in my heart; I fear
'Tis long and tedious; but my spirit clings
To that poor Woman:—so familiarly
Do I perceive her manner, and her look,
And presence; and so deeply do I feel
Her goodness, that, not seldom, in my walks
A momentary trance comes over me;
And to myself I seem to muse on One
By sorrow laid asleep; or borne away,

A human being destined to awake
To human life, or something very near
To human life, when he shall come again
For whom she suffered. Yes, it would have grieved
Your very soul to see her: evermore
Her eyelids drooped, her eyes downward were cast;
And, when she at her table gave me food,
She did not look at me. Her voice was low,
Her body was subdued. In every act
Pertaining to her home-affairs, appeared
The careless stillness of a thinking mind
Self-occupied; to which all outward things
Are like an idle matter. Still she sighed,
But yet no motion of the breast was seen,
No heaving of the heart. While by the fire
We sate together, sighs came on my ear,
I knew not how, and hardly whence they came.

"Ere my departure, to her care I gave,
For her son's use, some tokens of regard,
Which with a look of welcome she received;
And I exhorted her to place her trust
In God's good love, and seek his help by prayer.
I took my staff, and, when I kissed her babe,
The tears stood in her eyes. I left her then
With the best hope and comfort I could give;
She thanked me for my wish;—but for my hope
It seemed she did not thank me.
                                 I returned,
And took my rounds along this road again
When on its sunny bank the primrose flower
Peeped forth, to give an earnest of the Spring.
I found her sad and drooping: she had learned
No tidings of her husband; if he lived,
She knew not that he lived; if he were dead,
She knew not he was dead. She seemed the same
In person and appearance; but her house
Bespake a sleepy hand of negligence;
The floor was neither dry nor neat, the hearth
Was comfortless, and her small lot of books,
Which, in the cottage-window, heretofore

Had been piled up against the corner panes
In seemly order, now, with straggling leaves
Lay scattered here and there, open or shut,
As they had chanced to fall. Her infant Babe
Had from its mother caught the trick of grief,
And sighed among its playthings. I withdrew,
And once again entering the garden saw,
More plainly still, that poverty and grief
Were now come nearer to her: weeds defaced
The hardened soil, and knots of withered grass:
No ridges there appeared to clear black mould,
No winter greenness; of her herbs and flowers,
It seemed the better part were gnawed away
Or trampled into earth; a chain of straw,
Which had been twined about the slender stem
Of a young apple-tree, lay at its root;
The bark was nibbled round by truant sheep.
—Margaret stood near, her infant in her arms,
And, noting that my eye was on the tree,
She said, 'I fear it will be dead and gone
Ere Robert come again.' When to the House
We had returned together, she enquired
If I had any hope:—But for her babe
And for her little orphan boy, she said,
She had no wish to live, that she must die
Of sorrow. Yet I saw the idle loom
Still in its place; his Sunday garments hung
Upon the self-same nail; his very staff
Stood undisturbed behind the door.
　　　　　　　　　　　　　　　And when,
In bleak December, I retraced this way,
She told me that her little babe was dead,
And she was left alone. She now, released
From her maternal cares, had taken up
The employment common through these wilds, and
　　　gained,
By spinning hemp, a pittance for herself;
And for this end had hired a neighbour's boy
To give her needful help. That very time
Most willingly she put her work aside,
And walked with me along the miry road,

Heedless how far; and, in such piteous sort
That any heart had ached to hear her, begged
That, whersoe'er I went, I still would ask
For him whom she had lost. We parted then—
Our final parting; for from that time forth
Did many seasons pass ere I returned
Into this tract again.

                  Nine tedious years;
From their first separation, nine long years,
She lingered in unquiet widowhood;
A Wife and Widow. Needs must it have been
A sore heart-wasting! I have heard, my Friend,
That in yon arbour oftentimes she sate
Alone, through half the vacant sabbath day;
And, if a dog passed by, she still would quit
The shade, and look abroad. On this old bench
For hours she sate; and evermore her eye
Was busy in the distance, shaping things
That made her heart beat quick. You see that path,
Now faint,—the grass has crept o'er its grey line;
There, to and fro, she paced through many a day
Of the warm summer, from a belt of hemp
That girt her waist, spinning the long-drawn thread
With backward steps. Yet ever as there passed
A man whose garments showed the soldier's red,
Or crippled mendicant in soldier's garb,
The little child who sate to turn the wheel
Ceased from his task; and she with faltering voice
Made many a fond enquiry; and when they,
Whose presence gave no comfort, were gone by,
Her heart was still more sad. And by yon gate,
That bars the traveller's road, she often stood,
And when a stranger horseman came, the latch
Would lift, and in his face look wistfully:
Most happy, if, from aught discovered there
Of tender feeling, she might dare repeat
The same sad question. Meanwhile her poor Hut
Sank to decay; for he was gone, whose hand,
At the first nipping of October frost,
Closed up each chink, and with fresh bands of straw
Chequered the green-grown thatch. And so she lived

Through the long winter, reckless and alone;
Until her house by frost, and thaw, and rain,
Was sapped; and while she slept, the nightly damps
Did chill her breast; and in the stormy day
Her tattered clothes were ruffled by the wind,
Even at the side of her own fire.   Yet still
She loved this wretched spot, nor would for worlds
Have parted hence; and still that length of road,
And this rude bench, one torturing hope endeared,
Fast rooted at her heart; and here, my Friend,—
In sickness she remained; and here she died;
Last human tenant of these ruined walls!"

The old Man ceased: he saw that I was moved;
From that low bench, rising instinctively
I turned aside in weakness, nor had power
To thank him for the tale which he had told
I stood, and leaning o'er the garden wall
Reviewed that Woman's sufferings; and it seemed
To comfort me while with a brother's love
I blessed her in the impotence of grief.
Then towards the cottage I returned; and traced
Fondly, though with an interest more mild,
That secret spirit of humanity
Which, 'mid the calm oblivious tendencies
Of nature, 'mid her plants, and weeds, and flowers,
And silent overgrowings, still survived.
The old Man, noting this, resumed, and said,
"My Friend! enough to sorrow you have given,
The purposes of wisdom ask no more:
Nor more would she have craved as due to One
Who, in her worst distress, had ofttimes felt
The unbounded might of prayer; and learned with
        soul
Fixed on the Cross, that consolation springs,
From sources deeper far than deepest pain,
For the meek Sufferer.   Why then should we read
The forms of things with an unworthy eye?
She sleeps in the calm earth, and peace is here.
I well remember that those very plumes,
Those weeds, and the high spear-grass on that wall,

By mist and silent rain-drops silvered o'er,
As once I passed, into my heart conveyed
So still an image of tranquillity,
So calm and still, and looked so beautiful
Amid the uneasy thoughts which filled my mind,
That what we feel of sorrow and despair
From ruin and from change, and all the grief
That passing shows of Being leave behind,
Appeared an idle dream, that could maintain,
Nowhere, dominion o'er the enlightened spirit
Whose meditative sympathies repose
Upon the breast of Faith. I turned away,
And walked along my road in happiness."

BOOK FOURTH

(Lines 8–331)

A pause of silence followed; then, with voice
That did not falter though the heart was moved,
The Wanderer said:—

                One adequate support
For the calamities of mortal life
Exists—one only; an assured belief
That the procession of our fate, howe'er
Sad or disturbed, is ordered by a Being
Of infinite benevolence and power;
Whose everlasting purposes embrace
All accidents, converting them to good.
—The darts of anguish *fix* not where the seat
Of suffering hath been thoroughly fortified
By acquiescence in the Will supreme
For time and for eternity; by faith,
Faith absolute in God, including hope,
And the defence that lies in boundless love
Of his perfections; with habitual dread
Of aught unworthily conceived, endured
Impatiently, ill-done, or left undone,
To the dishonour of his holy name.
Soul of our Souls, and safeguard of the world!

Sustain, thou only canst, the sick of heart;
Restore their languid spirits, and recall
Their lost affections unto thee and thine!"

Then, as we issued from that covert nook,
He thus continued, lifting up his eyes
To heaven:—"How beautiful this dome of sky;
And the vast hills, in fluctuation fixed
At thy command, how awful! Shall the Soul,
Human and rational, report of thee
Even less than these!—Be mute who will, who can,
Yet I will praise thee with impassioned voice:
My lips, that may forget thee in the crowd,
Cannot forget thee here; where thou hast built,
For thy own glory, in the wilderness!
Me didst thou constitute a priest of thine,
In such a temple as we now behold
Reared for thy presence: therefore am I bound
To worship, here, and everywhere—as one
Not doomed to ignorance, though forced to tread,
From childhood up, the ways of poverty,
From unreflecting ignorance preserved,
And from debasement rescued.—By thy grace
The particle divine remained unquenched;
And, 'mid the wild weeds of a rugged soil,
Thy bounty caused to flourish deathless flowers,
From paradise transplanted: wintry age
Impends; the frost will gather round my heart;
If the flowers wither, I am worse than dead!
—Come, labour, when the worn-out frame requires
Perpetual sabbath; come, disease and want;
And sad exclusion through decay of sense;
But leave me unabated trust in thee—
And let thy favour, to the end of life,
Inspire me with ability to seek
Repose and hope among eternal things—
Father of heaven and earth! and I am rich,
And will possess my portion in content!

"And what are things eternal?—powers depart,"
The grey-haired Wanderer steadfastly replied,

Answering the question which himself had asked,
"Possessions vanish, and opinions change,
And passions hold a fluctuating seat:
But, by the storms of circumstance unshaken,
And subject neither to eclipse nor wane,
Duty exists;—immutably survive,
For our support, the measures and the forms,
Which an abstract intelligence supplies;
Whose kingdom is, where time and space are not.
Of other converse which mind, soul, and heart,
Do, with united urgency, require,
What more that may not perish?—Thou, dread
    source,
Prime, self-existing cause and end of all
That in the scale of being fill their place;
Above our human region, or below,
Set and sustained;—thou, who didst wrap the cloud
Of infancy around us, that thyself,
Therein, with our simplicity awhile
Might'st hold, on earth, communion undisturbed;
Who from the anarchy of dreaming sleep,
Or from its death-like void, with punctual care,
And touch as gentle as the morning light,
Restor'st us, daily, to the powers of sense
And reason's steadfast rule—thou, thou alone
Art everlasting, and the blessed Spirits,
Which thou includest, as the sea her waves:
For adoration thou endur'st; endure
For consciousness the motions of thy will;
For apprehension those transcendent truths
Of the pure intellect, that stand as laws
(Submission constituting strength and power)
Even to thy Being's infinite majesty!
This universe shall pass away—a work
Glorious! because the shadow of thy might,
A step, or link, for intercourse with thee.
Ah! if the time must come, in which my feet
No more shall stray where meditation leads,
By flowing stream, through wood, or craggy wild,
Loved haunts like these; the unimprisoned Mind
May yet have scope to range among her own,

Her thoughts, her images, her high desires.
If the dear faculty of sight should fail,
Still, it may be allowed me to remember
What visionary powers of eye and soul
In youth were mine; when, stationed on the top
Of some huge hill, expectant, I beheld
The sun rise up, from distant climes returned
Darkness to chase, and sleep; and bring the day
His bounteous gift! or saw him toward the deep
Sink, with a retinue of flaming clouds
Attended; then, my spirit was entranced
With joy exalted to beatitude;
The measure of my soul was filled with bliss,
And holiest love; as earth, sea, air, with light,
With pomp, with glory, with magnificence!

"Those fervent raptures are for ever flown;
And, since their date, my soul hath undergone
Change manifold, for better or for worse:
Yet cease I not to struggle, and aspire
Heavenward; and chide the part of me that flags,
Through sinful choice; or dread necessity
On human nature from above imposed.
'Tis, by comparison, an easy task
Earth to despise; but, to converse with heaven—
This is not easy:—to relinquish all
We have, or hope, of happiness and joy,
And stand in freedom loosened from this world,
I deem not arduous; but must needs confess
That 'tis a thing impossible to frame
Conceptions equal to the soul's desires;
And the most difficult of tasks to *keep*
Heights which the soul is competent to gain.
—Man is of dust: ethereal hopes are his,
Which, when they should sustain themselves aloft,
Want due consistence; like a pillar of smoke,
That with majestic energy from earth
Rises; but, having reached the thinner air,
Melts, and dissolves, and is no longer seen.
From this infirmity of mortal kind
Sorrow proceeds, which else were not; at least,

If grief be something hallowed and ordained,
If, in proportion, it be just and meet,
Yet, through this weakness of the general heart,
Is it enabled to maintain its hold
In that excess which conscience disapproves.
For who could sink and settle to that point
Of selfishness; so senseless who could be
As long and perseveringly to mourn
For any object of his love, removed
From this unstable world, if he could fix
A satisfying view upon that state
Of pure, imperishable, blessedness,
Which reason promises, and holy writ
Ensures to all believers?—Yet mistrust
Is of such incapacity, methinks,
No natural branch; despondency far less;
And, least of all, is absolute despair.
—And, if there be whose tender frames have drooped
Even to the dust; apparently, through weight
Of anguish unrelieved, and lack of power
An agonizing sorrow to transmute;
Deem not that proof is here of hope withheld
When wanted most; a confidence impaired
So pitiably, that, having ceased to see
With bodily eyes, they are borne down by love
Of what is lost, and perish through regret.
Oh! no, the innocent Sufferer often sees
Too clearly; feels too vividly; and longs
To realize the vision, with intense
And over-constant yearning;—there—there lies
The excess, by which the balance is destroyed.
Too, too contracted are these walls of flesh,
This vital warmth too cold, these visual orbs,
Though inconceivably endowed, too dim
For any passion of the soul that leads
To ecstasy; and all the crooked paths
Of time and change disdaining, takes its course
Along the line of limitless desires.
I, speaking now from such disorder free,
Nor rapt, nor craving, but in settled peace,
I cannot doubt that they whom you deplore

Are glorified; or, if they sleep, shall wake
From sleep, and dwell with God in endless love.
Hope, below this, consists not with belief
In mercy, carried infinite degrees
Beyond the tenderness of human hearts:
Hope, below this, consists not with belief
In perfect wisdom, guiding mightiest power,
That finds no limits but her own pure will.

"Here then we rest; not fearing for our creed
The worst that human reasoning can achieve,
To unsettle or perplex it: yet with pain
Acknowledging, and grievous self-reproach,
That, though immovably convinced, we want
Zeal, and the virtue to exist by faith
As soldiers live by courage; as, by strength
Of heart, the sailor fights with roaring seas.
Alas! the endowment of immortal power
Is matched unequally with custom, time,
And domineering faculties of sense
In *all*; in most with superadded foes,
Idle temptations; open vanities,
Ephemeral offspring of the unblushing world;
And, in the private regions of the mind,
Ill-governed passions, ranklings of despite,
Immoderate wishes, pining discontent,
Distress and care. What then remains?—To seek
Those helps for his occasions ever near
Who lacks not will to use them; vows, renewed
On the first motion of a holy thought;
Vigils of contemplation; praise; and prayer—
A stream, which, from the fountain of the heart
Issuing, however feebly, nowhere flows
Without access of unexpected strength.
But, above all, the victory is most sure
For him, who, seeking faith by virtue, strives
To yield entire submission to the law
Of conscience—conscience reverenced and obeyed,
As God's most intimate presence in the soul,
And his most perfect image in the world.

—Endeavour thus to live; these rules regard;
These helps solicit; and a steadfast seat
Shall then be yours among the happy few
Who dwell on earth, yet breathe empyreal air,
Sons of the morning. For your nobler part,
Ere disencumbered of her mortal chains,
Doubt shall be quelled and trouble chased away;
With only such degree of sadness left
As may support longings of pure desire;
And strengthen love, rejoicing secretly
In the sublime attractions of the grave."

    While, in this strain, the venerable Sage
Poured forth his aspirations, and announced
His judgments, near that lonely house we paced
A plot of green-sward, seemingly preserved
By nature's care from wreck of scattered stones,
And from encroachment of encircling heath:
Small space! but, for reiterated steps,
Smooth and commodious; as a stately deck
Which to and fro the mariner is used
To tread for pastime, talking with his mates,
Or haply thinking of far-distant friends,
While the ship glides before a steady breeze.
Stillness prevailed around us: and the voice
That spake was capable to lift the soul
Toward regions yet more tranquil. But, methought,
That he, whose fixed despondency had given
Impulse and motive to that strong discourse,
Was less upraised in spirit than abashed;
Shrinking from admonition, like a man
Who feels that to exhort is to reproach.
Yet not to be diverted from his aim,
The Sage continued:—

                              "For that other loss,
The loss of confidence in social man,
By the unexpected transports of our age
Carried so high, that every thought, which looked
Beyond the temporal destiny of the Kind,
To many seemed superfluous—as, no cause

Could e'er for such exalted confidence
Exist; so, none is now for fixed despair:
The two extremes are equally disowned
By reason: if, with sharp recoil, from one
You have been driven far as its opposite,
Between them seek the point whereon to build
Sound expectations. So doth he advise
Who shared at first the illusion; but was soon
Cast from the pedestal of pride by shocks
Which Nature gently gave, in woods and fields;
Nor unreproved by Providence, thus speaking
To the inattentive children of the world:
'Vain-glorious Generation! what new powers
On you have been conferred? what gifts, withheld
From your progenitors, have ye received,
Fit recompense of new desert? what claim
Are ye prepared to urge, that my decrees
For you should undergo a sudden change;
And the weak functions of one busy day,
Reclaiming and extirpating, perform
What all the slowly-moving years of time,
With their united force, have left undone?
By nature's gradual processes be taught;
By story be confounded! Ye aspire
Rashly, to fall once more; and that false fruit,
Which, to your overweening spirits, yields
Hope of a flight celestial, will produce
Misery and shame. But Wisdom of her sons
Shall not the less, though late, be justified.'

"Such timely warning," said the Wanderer, "gave
That visionary voice; and, at this day,
When a Tartarean darkness overspreads
The groaning nations; when the impious rule,
By will or by established ordinance,
Their own dire agents, and constrain the good
To acts which they abhor; though I bewail
This triumph, yet the pity of my heart
Prevents me not from owning, that the law,
By which mankind now suffers, is most just.

For by superior energies; more strict
Affiance in each other; faith more firm
In their unhallowed principles; the bad
Have fairly earned a victory o'er the weak,
The vacillating, inconsistent good.
Therefore, not unconsoled, I wait—in hope
To see the moment, when the righteous cause
Shall gain defenders zealous and devout
As they who have opposed her; in which Virtue
Will, to her efforts, tolerate no bounds
That are not lofty as her rights; aspiring
By impulse of her own ethereal zeal.
That spirit only can redeem mankind;
And when that sacred spirit shall appear,
Then shall *our* triumph be complete as theirs.
Yet, should this confidence prove vain, the wise
Have still the keeping of their proper peace;
Are guardians of their own tranquillity."

(*Lines* 1132–1150)

                                    "I have seen
A curious child, who dwelt upon a tract
Of inland ground, applying to his ear
The convolutions of a smooth-lipped shell;
To which, in silence hushed, his very soul
Listened intensely; and his countenance soon
Brightened with joy; for from within were heard
Murmurings, whereby the monitor expressed
Mysterious union with its native sea.
Even such a shell the universe itself
Is to the ear of Faith; and there are times,
I doubt not, when to you it doth impart
Authentic tidings of invisible things;
Of ebb and flow, and ever-during power;
And central peace, subsisting at the heart
Of endless agitation. Here you stand.
Adore, and worship, when you know it not;
Pious beyond the intention of your thought;
Devout above the meaning of your will."

YARROW VISITED

SEPTEMBER, 1814

[Composed 1814.—Published 1815.]

And is this—Yarrow?—*This* the Stream
Of which my fancy cherished,
So faithfully, a waking dream?
An image that hath perished!
O that some Minstrel's harp were near,
To utter notes of gladness,
And chase this silence from the air,
That fills my heart with sadness!

Yet why?—a silvery current flows
With uncontrolled meanderings;
Nor have these eyes by greener hills
Been soothed, in all my wanderings.
And, through her depths, Saint Mary's Lake
Is visibly delighted;
For not a feature of those hills
Is in the mirror slighted.

A blue sky bends o'er Yarrow vale,
Save where that pearly whiteness
Is round the rising sun diffused,
A tender hazy brightness;
Mild dawn of promise! that excludes
All profitless dejection;
Though not unwilling here to admit
A pensive recollection.

Where was it that the famous Flower
Of Yarrow Vale lay bleeding?
His bed perchance was yon smooth mound
On which the herd is feeding:
And haply from this crystal pool,
Now peaceful as the morning,
The water-wraith ascended thrice—
And gave his doleful warning.

Delicious is the Lay that sings
The haunts of happy Lovers,
The path that leads them to the grove,
The leafy grove that covers:
And Pity sanctifies the Verse
That paints, by strength of sorrow,
The unconquerable strength of love;
Bear witness, rueful Yarrow!

But thou, that didst appear so fair
To fond imagination,
Dost rival in the light of day
Her delicate creation:
Meek loveliness is round thee spread,
A softness still and holy;
The grace of forest charms decayed,
And pastoral melancholy.

That region left, the vale unfolds
Rich groves of lofty stature,
With Yarrow winding through the pomp
Of cultivated nature;
And, rising from those lofty groves,
Behold a Ruin hoary!
The shattered front of Newark's Towers,
Renowned in Border story.

Fair scenes for childhood's opening bloom,
For sportive youth to stray in;
For manhood to enjoy his strength;
And age to wear away in!
Yon cottage seems a bower of bliss,
A covert for protection
Of tender thoughts, that nestle there—
The brood of chaste affection.

How sweet, on this autumnal day,
The wild-wood fruits to gather,
And on my True-love's forehead plant
A crest of blooming heather!
And what if I enwreathed my own!

'Twere no offence to reason;
The sober Hills thus deck their brows
To meet the wintry season.

I see—but not by sight alone,
Loved Yarrow, have I won thee;
A ray of fancy still survives—
Her sunshine plays upon thee!
Thy ever-youthful waters keep
A course of lively pleasure;
And gladsome notes my lips can breathe
Accordant to the measure.

The vapours linger round the Heights,
They melt, and soon must vanish;
One hour is theirs, nor more is mine—
Sad thought, which I would banish,
But that I know, where'er I go,
Thy genuine image, Yarrow!
Will dwell with me—to heighten joy,
And cheer my mind in sorrow.

LAODAMIA

[Composed 1814.—Published 1815.]

"With sacrifice before the rising morn
Vows have I made by fruitless hope inspired;
And from the infernal Gods, 'mid shades forlorn
Of night, my slaughtered Lord have I required:
Celestial pity I again implore;—
Restore him to my sight—great Jove, restore!"

So speaking, and by fervent love endowed
With faith, the Suppliant heavenward lifts her hands;
While, like the sun emerging from a cloud,
Her countenance brightens—and her eye expands;
Her bosom heaves and spreads, her stature grows;
And she expects the issue in repose.

O terror! what hath she perceived?—O joy!
What doth she look on?—whom doth she behold?
Her Hero slain upon the beach of Troy?
His vital presence? his corporeal mould?
It is—if sense deceive her not—'tis He!
And a God leads him, wingèd Mercury!

Mild Hermes spake—and touched her with his wand
That calms all fear; "Such grace hath crowned thy
    prayer,
Laodamía! that at Jove's command
Thy Husband walks the paths of upper air:
He comes to tarry with thee three hours' space;
Accept the gift, behold him face to face!"

Forth sprang the impassioned Queen her Lord to
    clasp;
Again that consummation she essayed;
But unsubstantial Form eludes her grasp
As often as that eager grasp was made.
The Phantom parts—but parts to re-unite,
And re-assume his place before her sight.

"Protesiláus, lo! thy guide is gone!
Confirm, I pray, the vision with thy voice:
This is our palace,—yonder is thy throne;
Speak, and the floor thou tread'st on will rejoice.
Not to appal me have the gods bestowed
This precious boon; and blest a sad abode."

"Great Jove, Laodamía! doth not leave
His gifts imperfect:—Spectre though I be,
I am not sent to scare thee or deceive;
But in reward of thy fidelity.
And something also did my worth obtain;
For fearless virtue bringeth boundless gain.

"Thou knowest, the Delphic oracle foretold
That the first Greek who touched the Trojan strand
Should die; but me the threat could not withhold:
A generous cause a victim did demand;
And forth I leapt upon the sandy plain;
A self-devoted chief—by Hector slain."

"Supreme of Heroes—bravest, noblest, best!
Thy matchless courage I bewail no more,
Which then, when tens of thousands were deprest
By doubt, propelled thee to the fatal shore;
Thou found'st—and I forgive thee—here thou art—
A nobler counsellor than my poor heart.

"But thou, though capable of sternest deed,
Wert kind as resolute, and good as brave;
And he, whose power restores thee, hath decreed
Thou shouldest elude the malice of the grave:
Redundant are thy locks, thy lips as fair
As when their breath enriched Thessalian air.

"No Spectre greets me,—no vain Shadow this;
Come, blooming Hero, place thee by my side!
Give, on this well-known couch, one nuptial kiss
To me, this day, a second time thy bride!"
Jove frowned in heaven: the conscious Parcæ threw
Upon those roseate lips a Stygian hue.

"This visage tells thee that my doom is past:
Nor should the change be mourned, even if the joys
Of sense were able to return as fast
And surely as they vanish. Earth destroys
Those raptures duly—Erebus disdains:
Calm pleasures there abide—majestic pains.

"Be taught, O faithful Consort, to control
Rebellious passion: for the Gods approve
The depth, and not the tumult, of the soul;
A fervent, not ungovernable, love.
Thy transports moderate; and meekly mourn
When I depart, for brief is my sojourn—"

"Ah wherefore?—Did not Hercules by force
Wrest from the guardian Monster of the tomb
Alcestis, a reanimated corse,
Given back to dwell on earth in vernal bloom?
Medea's spells dispersed the weight of years,
And Æson stood a youth 'mid youthful peers.

"The Gods to us are merciful—and they
Yet further may relent: for mightier far
Than strength of nerve and sinew, or the sway
Of magic potent over sun and star,
Is love, though oft to agony distrest,
And though his favourite seat be feeble woman's
  breast.

"But if thou goest, I follow—" "Peace!" he said,—
She looked upon him and was calmed and cheered;
The ghastly colour from his lips had fled;
In his deportment, shape, and mien, appeared
Elysian beauty, melancholy grace,
Brought from a pensive though a happy place.

He spake of love, such love as Spirits feel
In worlds whose course is equable and pure;
No fears to beat away—no strife to heal—
The past unsighed for, and the future sure;
Spake of heroic arts in graver mood
Revived, with finer harmony pursued;

Of all that is most beauteous—imaged there
In happier beauty; more pellucid streams,
An ampler ether, a diviner air,
And fields invested with purpureal gleams;
Climes which the sun, who sheds the brightest day
Earth knows, is all unworthy to survey.

Yet there the Soul shall enter which hath earned
That privilege by virtue.—"Ill," said he,
"The end of man's existence I discerned,
Who from ignoble games and revelry
Could draw, when we had parted, vain delight,
While tears were thy best pastime, day and night;

"And while my youthful peers before my eyes
(Each hero following his peculiar bent)
Prepared themselves for glorious enterprise
By martial sports,—or, seated in the tent,
Chieftains and kings in council were detained;
What time the fleet at Aulis lay enchained.

"The wished-for wind was given:—I then revolved
The oracle, upon the silent sea;
And, if no worthier led the way, resolved
That, of a thousand vessels, mine should be
The foremost prow in pressing to the strand,—
Mine the first blood that tinged the Trojan sand.

"Yet bitter, oft-times bitter, was the pang
When of thy loss I thought, belovèd Wife!
On thee too fondly did my memory hang,
And on the joys we shared in mortal life,—
The paths which we had trod—these fountains,
    flowers;
My new-planned cities, and unfinished towers.

"But should suspense permit the Foe to cry,
'Behold they tremble!—haughty their array,
Yet of their number no one dares to die?'
In soul I swept the indignity away:
Old frailties then recurred:—but lofty thought,
In act embodied, my deliverance wrought.

"And Thou, though strong in love, art all too weak
In reason, in self-government too slow;
I counsel thee by fortitude to seek
Our blest re-union in the shades below.
The invisible world with thee hath sympathised;
Be thy affections raised and solemnised.

"Learn, by a mortal yearning, to ascend—
Seeking a higher object. Love was given,
Encouraged, sanctioned, chiefly for that end;
For this the passion to excess was driven—
That self might be annulled: her bondage prove
The fetters of a dream opposed to love."—

Aloud she shrieked! for Hermes reappears!
Round the dear Shade she would have clung—'tis
    vain:
The hours are past—too brief had they been years;
And him no mortal effort can detain:

Swift, toward the realms that know not earthly day,
He through the portal takes his silent way,
And on the palace-floor a lifeless corse She lay.

Thus, all in vain exhorted and reproved,
She perished; and, as for a wilful crime,
By the just Gods whom no weak pity moved,
Was doomed to wear out her appointed time,
Apart from happy Ghosts, that gather flowers
Of blissful quiet 'mid unfading bowers.

—Yet tears to human suffering are due;
And mortal hopes defeated and o'erthrown
Are mourned by man, and not by man alone,
As fondly he believes.—Upon the side
Of Hellespont (such faith was entertained)
A knot of spiry trees for ages grew
From out the tomb of him for whom she died;
And ever, when such stature they had gained
That Ilium's walls were subject to their view,
The trees' tall summits withered at the sight;
A constant interchange of growth and blight!

TO B. R. HAYDON

[Composed December, 1815.—Published February 4, 1816 (*The Champion*);
March 31, 1816 (*The Examiner*); vol. of 1816.]

High is our calling, Friend!—Creative Art
(Whether the instrument of words she use,
Or pencil pregnant with ethereal hues,)
Demands the service of a mind and heart,
Though sensitive, yet, in their weakest part,
Heroically fashioned——to infuse
Faith in the whispers of the lonely Muse,
While the whole world seems adverse to desert.
And, oh! when Nature sinks, as oft she may,
Through long-lived pressure of obscure distress,
Still to be strenuous for the bright reward,
And in the soul admit of no decay,
Brook no continuance of weak-mindedness—
Great is the glory, for the strife is hard!

[The reference is to Wordsworth's three-year-old daughter, Catherine, who died June 5, 1812.—Published 1815.]

Surprised by joy—impatient as the Wind
I turned to share the transport—Oh! with whom
But Thee, deep buried in the silent tomb,
That spot which no vicissitude can find?
Love, faithful love, recalled thee to my mind—
But how could I forget thee? Through what power,
Even for the least division of an hour,
Have I been so beguiled as to be blind
To my most grievous loss!—That thought's return
Was the worst pang that sorrow ever bore,
Save one, one only, when I stood forlorn,
Knowing my heart's best treasure was no more;
That neither present time, nor years unborn
Could to my sight that heavenly face restore.

DION

[Composed 1816.—Published 1820.]

I

Serene, and fitted to embrace,
Where'er he turned, a swan-like grace
Of haughtiness without pretence,
And to unfold a still magnificence,
Was princely Dion, in the power
And beauty of his happier hour.
And what pure homage *then* did wait
On Dion's virtues, while the lunar beam
Of Plato's genius, from its lofty sphere,
Fell round him in the grove of Academe,
Softening their inbred dignity austere—
    That he, not too elate
    With self-sufficing solitude,
But with majestic lowliness endued,
Might in the universal bosom reign,
And from affectionate observance gain
Help, under every change of adverse fate.

II

Five thousand warriors—O the rapturous day!
Each crowned with flowers, and armed with spear
  and shield,
Or ruder weapon which their course might yield,
To Syracuse advance in bright array.
Who leads them on?—The anxious people see
Long-exiled Dion marching at their head,
He also crowned with flowers of Sicily,
And in a white, far-beaming, corselet clad!
Pure transport undisturbed by doubt or fear
The gazers feel; and, rushing to the plain,
Salute those strangers as a holy train
Or blest procession (to the Immortals dear)

That brought their precious liberty again.
Lo! when the gates are entered, on each hand,
Down the long street, rich goblets filled with wine
  In seemly order stand,
On tables set, as if for rites divine;—
And, as the great Deliverer marches by,
He looks on festal ground with fruits bestrown;
And flowers are on his person thrown
  In boundless prodigality;
Nor doth the general voice abstain from prayer,
Invoking Dion's tutelary care,
As if a very Deity he were!

III

Mourn, hills and groves of Attica! and mourn
Ilissus, bending o'er thy classic urn!
Mourn, and lament for him whose spirit dreads
Your once sweet memory, studious walks and shades!
For him who to divinity aspired,
Not on the breath of popular applause,
But through dependence on the sacred laws
Framed in the schools where Wisdom dwelt retired,
Intent to trace the ideal path of right
(More fair than heaven's broad causeway paved with
  stars)

Which Dion learned to measure with sublime
   delight,—
But He hath overleaped the eternal bars;
And, following guides whose craft holds no consent
With aught that breathes the ethereal element,
Hath stained the robes of civil power with blood,
Unjustly shed, though for the public good.
Whence doubts that came too late, and wishes vain,
Hollow excuses, and triumphant pain;
And oft his cogitations sink as low
As, through the abysses of a joyless heart,
The heaviest plummet of despair can go—
But whence that sudden check? that fearful start!
   He hears an uncouth sound—
   Anon his lifted eyes
Saw, at a long-drawn gallery's dusky bound,
A Shape of more than mortal size
And hideous aspect, stalking round and round!
   A woman's garb the Phantom wore,
   And fiercely swept the marble floor,—
   Like Auster whirling to and fro,
   His force on Caspian foam to try;
Or Boreas when he scours the snow
That skins the plains of Thessaly,
Or when aloft on Mænalus he stops
His flight, 'mid eddying pine-tree tops!

IV

So, but from toil less sign of profit reaping,
The sullen Spectre to her purpose bowed,
   Sweeping—vehemently sweeping—
No pause admitted, no design avowed!
"Avaunt, inexplicable Guest!—avaunt,"
Exclaimed the Chieftain—"let me rather see
The coronal that coiling vipers make!
The torch that flames with many a lurid flake,
And the long train of doleful pageantry
Which they behold, whom vengeful Furies haunt;
Who, while they struggle from the scourge to flee,
Move where the blasted soil is not unworn,

And, in their anguish, bear what other minds have
    borne!"

v

But Shapes, that come not at an earthly call,
Will not depart when mortal voices bid;
Lords of the visionary eye whose lid,
Once raised, remains aghast, and will not fall!
Ye Gods, thought He, that servile Implement
    Obeys a mystical intent!
Your Minister would brush away
The spots that to my soul adhere;
But should she labour night and day,
They will not, cannot disappear;
Whence angry perturbations,—and that look
Which no philosophy can brook!

vi

Ill-fated Chief! there are whose hopes are built
Upon the ruins of thy glorious name;
Who, through the portal of one moment's guilt,
Pursue thee with their deadly aim!
O matchless perfidy! portentous lust
Of monstrous crime!—that horror-striking blade,
Drawn in defiance of the Gods, hath laid
The noble Syracusan low in dust!
Shuddered the walls—the marble city wept—
And sylvan places heaved a pensive sigh;
But in calm peace the appointed Victim slept,
As he had fallen in magnanimity;
Of spirit too capacious to require
That Destiny her course should change; too just
To his own native greatness to desire
That wretched boon, days lengthened by mistrust.
So were the hopeless troubles, that involved
The soul of Dion, instantly dissolved.
Released from life and cares of princely state,
He left this moral grafted on his Fate;
"Him only pleasure leads, and peace attends,
Him, only him, the shield of Jove defends,
Whose means are fair and spotless as his ends."

[Composed 1816.—Published 1820, as the first stanza of *Dion*, but afterwards withdrawn.]

Fair is the Swan, whose majesty, prevailing
O'er breezeless water, on Locarno's lake,
Bears him on while proudly sailing
He leaves behind a moon-illumined wake:
Behold! the mantling spirit of reserve
Fashions his neck into a goodly curve;
An arch thrown back between luxuriant wings
Of whitest garniture, like fir-tree boughs
To which, on some unruffled morning, clings
A flaky weight of winter's purest snows!
—Behold!—as with a gushing impulse heaves
That downy prow, and softly cleaves
The mirror of the crystal flood,
Vanish inverted hill, and shadowy wood,
And pendent rocks, where'er, in gliding state,
Winds the mute Creature without visible Mate
Or Rival, save the Queen of night
Showering down a silver light,
From heaven, upon her chosen Favourite!

[Composed September, 1819.—Published 1820.]

Departing summer hath assumed
An aspect tenderly illumed,
The gentlest look of spring;
That calls from yonder leafy shade
Unfaded, yet prepared to fade,
A timely carolling.

No faint and hesitating trill,
Such tribute as to winter chill
The lonely redbreast pays!
Clear, loud, and lively is the din,
From social warblers gathering in
Their harvest of sweet lays.

Nor doth the example fail to cheer
Me, conscious that my leaf is sere,
And yellow on the bough:—
Fall, rosy garlands, from my head!

Ye myrtle wreaths, your fragrance shed
Around a younger brow!

Yet will I temperately rejoice;
Wide is the range, and free the choice
Of undiscordant themes;
Which, haply, kindred souls may prize
Not less than vernal ecstasies,
And passion's feverish dreams.

For deathless powers to verse belong,
And they like Demi-gods are strong
On whom the Muses smile;
But some their function have disclaimed,
Best pleased with what is aptlicst framed
To enervate and defile.

Not such the initiatory strains
Committed to the silent plains
In Britain's earliest dawn:
Trembled the groves, the stars grew pale,
While all-too-daringly the veil
Of nature was withdrawn!

Nor such the spirit-stirring note
When the live chords Alcæus smote,
Inflamed by sense of wrong;
Woe! woe to Tyrants! from the lyre
Broke threateningly, in sparkles dire
Of fierce vindictive song.

And not unhallowed was the page
By wingèd Love inscribed, to assuage
The pangs of vain pursuit;
Love listening while the Lesbian Maid
With finest touch of passion swayed
Her own Aeolian lute.

O ye, who patiently explore
The wreck of Herculanean lore,
What rapture! could ye seize

Some Theban fragment, or unroll
One precious, tender-hearted, scroll
Of pure Simonides.

That were, indeed, a genuine birth
Of poesy; a bursting forth
Of genius from the dust:
What Horace gloried to behold,
What Maro loved, shall we enfold?
Can haughty Time be just!

OXFORD, MAY 30, 1820

[Composed 1820.—Published 1820.]

Ye sacred Nurseries of blooming Youth!
In whose collegiate shelter England's Flowers
Expand, enjoying through their vernal hours
The air of liberty, the light of truth;
Much have ye suffered from Time's gnawing tooth:
Yet, O ye spires of Oxford! domes and towers!
Gardens and groves! your presence overpowers
The soberness of reason; till, in sooth,
Transformed, and rushing on a bold exchange
I slight my own beloved Cam, to range
Where silver Isis leads my stripling feet;
Pace the long avenue, or glide adown
The stream-like windings of that glorious street—
An eager Novice robed in fluttering gown!

FIVE SONNETS FROM THE SERIES ON THE RIVER DUDDON

[Published 1820.]

What aspect bore the Man who roved or fled,
First of his tribe, to this dark dell—who first
In this pellucid Current slaked his thirst?
What hopes came with him? what designs were spread
Along his path? His unprotected bed
What dreams encompassed? Was the intruder nursed
In hideous usages, and rights accursed,

That thinned the living and disturbed the dead?
No voice replies;—both air and earth are mute;
And Thou, blue Streamlet, murmuring yield'st no
    more
Than a soft record, that, whatever fruit
Of ignorance thou might'st witness heretofore,
Thy function was to heal and to restore,
To soothe and cleanse, not madden and pollute!

SEATHWAITE CHAPEL

Sacred Religion! "mother of form and fear,"
Dread arbitress of mutable respect,
New rites ordaining when the old are wrecked,
Or cease to please the fickle worshipper;
Mother of Love! (that name best suits thee here)
Mother of Love! for this deep vale, protect
Truth's holy lamp, pure source of bright effect,
Gifted to purge the vapoury atmosphere
That seeks to stifle it;—as in those days
When this low Pile a Gospel Teacher knew,
Whose good works formed an endless retinue:
A Pastor such as Chaucer's verse portrays;
Such as the heaven-taught skill of Herbert drew;
And tender Goldsmith crowned with deathless praise!

Return, Content! for fondly I pursued,
Even when a child, the Streams—unheard, unseen;
Through tangled woods, impending rocks between;
Or, free as air, with flying inquest viewed
The sullen reservoirs whence their bold brood—
Pure as the morning, fretful, boisterous, keen,
Green as the salt-sea billows, white and green—
Poured down the hills, a choral multitude!
Nor have I tracked their course for scanty gains;
They taught me random cares and truant joys,
That shield from mischief and preserve from stains
Vague minds, while men are growing out of boys;
Maturer Fancy owes to their rough noise
Impetuous thoughts that brook not servile reins.

Not hurled precipitous from steep to steep;
Lingering no more 'mid flower-enamelled lands
And blooming thickets; nor by rocky bands
Held; but in radiant progress toward the Deep
Where mightiest rivers into powerless sleep
Sink, and forget their nature—*now* expands
Majestic Duddon, over smooth flat sands
Gliding in silence with unfettered sweep!
Beneath an ampler sky a region wide
Is opened round him:—hamlets, towers, and towns,
And blue-topped hills, behold him from afar;
In stately mien to sovereign Thames allied
Spreading his bosom under Kentish downs,
With commerce freighted, or triumphant war.

AFTER-THOUGHT

I thought of Thee, my partner and my guide,
As being past away.—Vain smypathies!
For, backward, Duddon! as I cast my eyes,
I see what was, and is, and will abide;
Still glides the Stream, and shall for ever glide;
The Form remains, the Function never dies;
While we, the brave, the mighty, and the wise,
We Men, who in our morn of youth defied
The elements, must vanish;—be it so!
Enough, if something from our hands have power
To live, and act, and serve the future hour;
And if, as toward the silent tomb we go,
Through love, through hope, and faith's transcendent
    dower,
We feel that we are greater than we know.

TWELVE OF THE ECCLESIASTICAL SONNETS

[Composed mostly in 1821.—Published 1822.]

I saw the figure of a lovely Maid
Seated alone beneath a darksome tree,
Whose fondly-overhanging canopy

Set off her brightness with a pleasing shade.
No Spirit was she; *that* my heart betrayed,
For she was one I loved exceedingly;
But while I gazed in tender reverie
(Or was it sleep that with my Fancy played?)
The bright corporeal presence—form and face—
Remaining still distinct grew thin and rare,
Like sunny mist;—at length the golden hair,
Shape, limbs, and heavenly features, keeping pace
Each with the other in a lingering race
Of dissolution, melted into air.

WALTON'S BOOK OF LIVES

There are no colours in the fairest sky
So fair as these. The feather, whence the pen
Was shaped that traced the lives of these good men,
Dropped from an Angel's wing. With moistened eye
We read of faith and purest charity
In Statesman, Priest, and humble Citizen;
Oh could we copy their mild virtues, then
What joy to live, what blessedness to die!
Methinks their very names shine still and bright;
Apart—like glow-worms on a summer night;
Or lonely tapers when from far they fling
A guiding ray; or seen—like stars on high,
Satellites burning in a lucid ring
Around meek Walton's heavenly memory.

PLACES OF WORSHIP

As star that shines dependent upon star
Is to the sky while we look up in love;
As to the deep fair ships which though they move
Seem fixed, to eyes that watch them from afar;
As to the sandy desert fountains are,
With palm-groves shaded at wide intervals,
Whose fruit around the sun-burnt Native falls
Of roving tired or desultory war—
Such to this British Isle her christian Fanes,

Each linked to each for kindred services;
Her Spires, her Steeple-towers with glittering vanes
Far-kenned, her Chapels lurking among trees,
Where a few villagers on bended knees
Find solace which a busy world disdains.

PASTORAL CHARACTER

A genial hearth, a hospitable board,
And a refined rusticity, belong
To the neat mansion, where, his flock among,
The learned Pastor dwells, their watchful Lord.
Though meek and patient as a sheathèd sword;
Though pride's least lurking thought appear a wrong
To human kind; though peace be on his tongue,
Gentleness in his heart—can earth afford
Such genuine state, pre-eminence so free,
As when, arrayed in Christ's authority,
He from the pulpit lifts his awful hand;
Conjures, implores, and labours all he can
For re-subjecting to divine command
The stubborn spirit of rebellious man?

CATECHISING

From Little down to Least, in due degree,
Around the Pastor, each in new-wrought vest,
Each with a vernal posy at his breast,
We stood, a trembling, earnest Company!
With low soft murmur, like a distant bee,
Some spake, by thought-perplexing fears betrayed;
And some a bold unerring answer made:
How fluttered then thy anxious heart for me,
Belovèd Mother! Thou whose happy hand
Had bound the flowers I wore, with faithful tie:
Sweet flowers! at whose inaudible command
Her countenance, phantom-like, doth re-appear:
O lost too early for the frequent tear,
And ill requited by this heartfelt sigh.

RURAL CEREMONY

Closing the sacred Book which long has fed
Our meditations, give we to a day
Of annual joy one tributary lay;
This day, when, forth by rustic music led,
The village Children, while the sky is red
With evening lights, advance in long array
Through the still churchyard, each with garland gay,
That, carried sceptre-like, o'ertops the head
Of the proud Bearer. To the wide church-door,
Charged with these offerings which their fathers bore
For decoration in the Papal time,
The innocent Procession softly moves:—
The spirit of Laud is pleased in heaven's pure clime,
And Hooker's voice the spectacle approves!

MUTABILITY

From low to high doth dissolution climb,
And sink from high to low, along a scale
Of awful notes, whose concord shall not fail;
A musical but melancholy chime,
Which they can hear who meddle not with crime,
Nor avarice, nor over-anxious care.
Truth fails not; but her outward forms that bear
The longest date do melt like frosty rime,
That in the morning whitened hill and plain
And is no more; drop like the tower sublime
Of yesterday, which royally did wear
His crown of weeds, but could not even sustain
Some casual shout that broke the silent air,
Or the unimaginable touch of Time.

OLD ABBEYS

Monastic Domes! following my downward way,
Untouched by due regret I marked your fall!
Now, ruin, beauty, ancient stillness, all
Dispose to judgments temperate as we lay

On our past selves in life's declining day:
For as, by discipline of Time made wise,
We learn to tolerate the infirmities
And faults of others—gently as he may,
So with our own the mild Instructor deals,
Teaching us to forget them or forgive.
Perversely curious, then, for hidden ill
Why should we break Time's charitable seals?
Once ye were holy, ye are holy still;
Your spirit freely let me drink, and live.

CATHEDRALS, ETC.

Open your gates, ye everlasting Piles!
Types of the spiritual Church which God hath reared;
Not loth we quit the newly-hallowed sward
And humble altar, 'mid your sumptuous aisles
To kneel, or thrid your intricate defiles,
Or down the nave to pace in motion slow;
Watching, with upward eye, the tall tower grow
And mount, at every step, with living wiles
Instinct—to rouse the heart and lead the will
By a bright ladder to the world above.
Open your gates, ye Monuments of love
Divine! thou Lincoln, on thy sovereign hill!
Thou, stately York! and Ye, whose splendours cheer
Isis and Cam, to patient Science dear!

INSIDE OF KING'S COLLEGE CHAPEL, CAMBRIDGE

Tax not the royal Saint with vain expense,
With ill-matched aims the Architect who planned—
Albeit labouring for a scanty band
Of white-robed Scholars only—this immense
And glorious Work of fine intelligence!
Give all thou canst; high Heaven rejects the lore
Of nicely-calculated less or more;
So deemed the man who fashioned for the sense
These lofty pillars, spread that branching roof
Self-poised, and scooped into ten thousand cells,

Where light and shade repose, where music dwells
Lingering—and wandering on as loth to die;
Like thoughts whose very sweetness yieldeth proof
That they were born for immortality.

THE SAME

What awful perspective! while from our sight
With gradual stealth the lateral windows hide
Their Portraitures, their stone-work glimmers, dyed
In the soft chequerings of a sleepy light.
Martyr, or King, or sainted Eremite,
Whoe'er ye be, that thus, yourselves unseen,
Imbue your prison-bars with solemn sheen,
Shine on, until ye fade with coming Night!—
But, from the arms of silence—list! O list!
The music bursteth into second life;
The notes luxuriate, every stone is kissed
By sound, or ghost of sound, in mazy strife;
Heart-thrilling strains, that cast, before the eye
Of the devout, a veil of ecstasy!

CONTINUED

They dreamt not of a perishable home
Who thus could build. Be mine, in hours of fear
Or grovelling thought, to seek a refuge here;
Or through the aisles of Westminster to roam;
Where bubbles burst, and folly's dancing foam
Melts, if it cross the threshold; where the wreath
Of awe-struck wisdom droops: or let my path
Lead to that younger Pile, whose sky-like dome
Hath typified by reach of daring art
Infinity's embrace; whose guardian crest,
The silent Cross, among the stars shall spread
As now, when She hath also seen her breast
Filled with mementos, satiate with its part
Of grateful England's overflowing Dead.

MEMORY

[Composed 1823.—Published 1827.]

A pen—to register; a key—
That winds through secret wards;
Are well assigned to Memory
By allegoric Bards.

As aptly, also, might be given
A Pencil to her hand;
That, softening objects, sometimes even
Outstrips the heart's demand;

That smoothes foregone distress, the lines
Of lingering care subdues,
Long-vanished happiness refines,
And clothes in brighter hues;

Yet, like a tool of Fancy, works
Those Spectres to dilate
That startle Conscience, as she lurks
Within her lonely seat.

O! that our lives, which flee so fast,
In purity were such,
That not an image of the past
Should fear that pencil's touch!

Retirement then might hourly look
Upon a soothing scene,
Age steal to his allotted nook
Contented and serene;

With heart as calm as lakes that sleep,
In frosty moonlight glistening;
Or mountain rivers, where they creep
Along a channel smooth and deep,
To their own far-off murmurs listening.

TO ——

[Composed 1824.—Published 1827.]

O dearer far than light and life are dear,
Full oft our human foresight I deplore;
Trembling, through my unworthiness, with fear
That friends, by death disjoined, may meet no more!

Misgivings, hard to vanquish or control,
Mix with the day, and cross the hour of rest;
While all the future, for thy purer soul,
With "sober certainties" of love is blest.

That sigh of thine, not meant for human ear,
Tells that these words thy humbleness offend;
Yet bear me up—else faltering in the rear
Of a steep march: support me to the end.

Peace settles where the intellect is meek,
And Love is dutiful in thought and deed;
Through Thee communion with that Love I seek:
The faith Heaven strengthens where *he* moulds the
       Creed.

TO A SKYLARK

[Composed 1825.—Published 1827.]

Ethereal minstrel! pilgrim of the sky!
Dost thou despise the earth where cares abound?
Or, while the wings aspire, are heart and eye
Both with thy nest upon the dewy ground?
Thy nest which thou canst drop into at will,
Those quivering wings composed, that music still!
Leave to the nightingale her shady wood;
A privacy of glorious light is thine;
Whence thou dost pour upon the world a flood
Of harmony, with instinct more divine;
Type of the wise who soar, but never roam;
True to the kindred points of Heaven and Home!

THE PILLAR OF TRAJAN

[Composed 1825.—Published 1827.]

Where towers are crushed, and unforbidden weeds
O'er mutilated arches shed their seeds;
And temples, doomed to milder change, unfold
A new magnificence that vies with old;
Firm in its pristine majesty hath stood
A votive Column, spared by fire and flood:—
And, though the passions of man's fretful race
Have never ceased to eddy round its base,
Not injured more by touch of meddling hands
Than a lone obelisk, 'mid Nubian sands,
Or aught in Syrian deserts left to save
From death the memory of the good and brave.
Historic figures round the shaft embost
Ascend, with lineaments in air not lost:
Still as he turns, the charmed spectator sees
Group winding after group with dreamlike ease;
Triumphs in sun-light gratitude displayed,
Or softly stealing into modest shade.
—So, pleased with purple clusters to entwine
Some lofty elm-tree, mounts the daring vine;
The woodbine so, with spiral grace, and breathes
Wide-spreading odours from her flowery wreaths.

Borne by the Muse from rills in shepherd's ears
Murmuring but one smooth story for all years,
I gladly commune with the mind and heart
Of him who thus survives by classic art,
His actions witness, venerate his mien,
And study Trajan as by Pliny seen;
Behold how fought the Chief whose conquering sword
Stretched far as earth might own a single lord;
In the delight of moral prudence schooled,
How feelingly at home the Sovereign ruled;
Best of the good—in pagan faith allied
To more than Man, by virtue deified.

Memorial Pillar! 'mid the wrecks of Time
Preserve thy charge with confidence sublime—

The exultations, pomps, and cares of Rome,
Whence half the breathing world received its doom;
Things that recoil from language; that, if shown
By apter pencil, from the light had flown.
A Pontiff, Trajan *here* the Gods implores,
There greets an Embassy from Indian shores;
Lo! he harangues his cohorts—*there* the storm
Of battle meets him in authentic form!
Unharnessed, naked, troops of Moorish horse
Sweep to the charge; more high, the Dacian force,
To hoof and finger mailed;—yet, high or low,
None bleed, and none lie prostrate but the foe;
In every Roman, through all turns of fate,
Is Roman dignity inviolate;
Spirit in him pre-eminent, who guides,
Supports, adorns, and over all presides;
Distinguished only by inherent state
From honoured Instruments that round him wait;
Rise as he may, his grandeur scorns the test
Of outward symbol, nor will deign to rest
On aught by which another is deprest.
—Alas! that One thus disciplined could toil
To enslave whole nations on their native soil;
So emulous of Macedonian fame,
That, when his age was measured with his aim,
He drooped, 'mid else unclouded victories,
And turned his eagles back with deep-drawn sighs:
O weakness of the Great! O folly of the Wise!

Where now the haughty Empire that was spread
With such fond hope? her very speech is dead;
Yet glorious Art the power of Time defies,
And Trajan still, through various enterprise,
Mounts, in this fine illusion, toward the skies:
Still are we present with the imperial Chief,
Nor cease to gaze upon the bold Relief
Till Rome, to silent marble unconfined,
Becomes with all her years a vision of the Mind.

[Composed ?.—Published 1827.]

Scorn not the Sonnet; Critic, you have frowned,
Mindless of its just honours; with this key
Shakespeare unlocked his heart; the melody
Of this small lute gave ease to Petrarch's wound;
A thousand times this pipe did Tasso sound;
With it Camöens soothed an exile's grief;
The Sonnet glittered a gay myrtle leaf
Amid the cypress with which Dante crowned
His visionary brow; a glow-worm lamp,
It cheered mild Spenser, called from Faery-land
To struggle through dark ways; and when a damp
Fell round the path of Milton, in his hand
The Thing became a trumpet; whence he blew
Soul-animating strains—alas, too few!

[Composed 1830 (? 1831).—Published 1835.]

In these fair vales hath many a Tree
　　At Wordsworth's suit been spared;
And from the builder's hand this Stone,
　　For some rude beauty of its own,
　　　　Was rescued by the Bard:
So let it rest; and time will come
　　When here the tender-hearted
May heave a gentle sigh for him,
　　As one of the departed.

YARROW REVISITED

The following Stanzas are a memorial of a day passed with Sir Walter
Scott and other Friends visiting the Banks of the Yarrow under his
guidance, immediately before his departure from Abbotsford, for Naples.

[Composed 1831.—Published 1835.]

The gallant Youth, who may have gained,
　　Or seeks, a "winsome Marrow,"
Was but an Infant in the lap
　　When first I looked on Yarrow;
Once more, by Newark's Castle-gate
　　Long left without a warder,
I stood, looked, listened, and with Thee
　　Great Minstrel of the Border!

Grave thoughts ruled wide on that sweet day,
  Their dignity installing
In gentle bosoms, while sere leaves
  Were on the bough, or falling;
But breezes played, and sunshine gleamed—
  The forest to embolden;
Reddened the fiery hues, and shot
  Transparence through the golden.

For busy thoughts the Stream flowed on
  In foamy agitation;
And slept in many a crystal pool
  For quiet contemplation:
No public and no private care
  The freeborn mind enthralling,
We made a day of happy hours,
  Our happy days recalling.

Brisk Youth appeared, the Morn of Youth,
  With freaks of graceful folly,—
Life's temperate Noon, her sober Eve,
  Her Night not melancholy;
Past, present, future, all appeared
  In harmony united,
Like guests that meet, and some from far,
  By cordial love invited.

And if, as Yarrow, through the woods
  And down the meadow ranging,
Did meet us with unaltered face,
  Though we were changed and changing;
If, *then*, some natural shadows spread
  Our inward prospect over,
The soul's deep valley was not slow
  Its brightness to recover.

Eternal blessings on the Muse,
  And her divine employment!
The blameless Muse, who trains her Sons
  For hope and calm enjoyment;
Albeit sickness, lingering yet,
  Has o'er their pillow brooded;

And Care waylays their steps—a Sprite
    Not easily eluded.

For thee, O Scott! compelled to change
    Green Eildon-hill and Cheviot
For warm Vesuvio's vine-clad slopes;
    And leave thy Tweed and Tiviot
For mild Sorrento's breezy waves;
    May classic Fancy, linking
With native Fancy her fresh aid,
    Preserve thy heart from sinking!

Oh! while they minister to thee,
    Each vying with the other,
May Health return to mellow Age,
    With Strength, her venturous brother;
And Tiber, and each brook and rill
    Renowned in song and story,
With unimagined beauty shine,
    Nor lose one ray of glory!

For Thou, upon a hundred streams,
    By tales of love and sorrow,
Of faithful love, undaunted truth,
    Hast shed the power of Yarrow;
And streams unknown, hills yet unseen,
    Wherever they invite Thee,
At parent Nature's grateful call,
    With gladness must requite Thee.

A gracious welcome shall be thine,
    Such looks of love and honour
As thy own Yarrow gave to me
    When first I gazed upon her;
Beheld what I had feared to see,
    Unwilling to surrender
Dreams treasured up from early days,
    The holy and the tender.

And what, for this frail world, were all
    That mortals do or suffer,

Did no responsive harp, no pen
    Memorial tribute offer?
Yea, what were mighty Nature's self?
    Her features, could they win us,
Unhelped by the poetic voice
    That hourly speaks within us?

Nor deem that localised Romance
    Plays false with our affections;
Unsanctifies our tears—made sport
    For fanciful dejections:
Ah, no! the visions of the past
    Sustain the heart in feeling
Life as she is—our changeful Life,
    With friends and kindred dealing.

Bear witness, Ye, whose thoughts that day
    In Yarrow's groves were centred;
Who through the silent portal arch
    Of mouldering Newark entered;
And clomb the winding stair that once
    Too timidly was mounted
By the "last Minstrel," (not the last!)
    Ere he his Tale recounted.

Flow on for ever, Yarrow Stream!
    Fulfil thy pensive duty,
Well pleased that future Bards should chant
    For simple hearts thy beauty;
To dream-light dear while yet unseen,
    Dear to the common sunshine,
And dearer still, as now I feel,
    To memory's shadowy moonshine!

ON THE DEPARTURE OF SIR WALTER SCOTT FROM
ABBOTSFORD, FOR NAPLES

[Composed September, 1831.—Published 1833 (*Literary Souvenir* of Alaric
Watts); vol. of 1835.]

A trouble, not of clouds, or weeping rain,
    Nor of the setting sun's pathetic light

Engendered, hangs o'er Eildon's triple height:
Spirits of Power, assembled there, complain
For kindred Power departing from their sight;
While Tweed, best pleased in chanting a blithe
    strain,
Saddens his voice again, and yet again.
Lift up your hearts, ye Mourners! for the might
Of the whole world's good wishes with him goes;
Blessings and prayers in nobler retinue
Than sceptred king or laurelled conqueror knows,
Follow this wondrous Potentate. Be true,
Ye winds of ocean, and the midland sea,
Wafting your Charge to soft Parthenope!

DEVOTIONAL INCITEMENTS

[Composed 1832.—Published 1835.]

"Not to the earth confined,
Ascend to heaven."

Where will they stop, those breathing Powers,
The Spirits of the new-born flowers?
They wander with the breeze, they wind
Where'er the streams a passage find;
Up from their native ground they rise
In mute aerial harmonies;
From humble violet—modest thyme—
Exhaled, the essential odours climb,
As if no space below the sky
Their subtle flight could satisfy:
Heaven will not tax our thoughts with pride
If like ambition be *their* guide.

Roused by this kindliest of May-showers,
The spirit-quickener of the flowers,
That with moist virtue softly cleaves
The buds, and freshens the young leaves,
The birds pour forth their souls in notes
Of rapture from a thousand throats—
Here checked by too impetuous haste,
While there the music runs to waste,

With bounty more and more enlarged,
Till the whole air is overcharged;
Give ear, O Man! to their appeal,
And thirst for no inferior zeal,
Thou, who canst *think*, as well as feel.

Mount from the earth; aspire! aspire!
So pleads the town's cathedral quire,
In strains that from their solemn height
Sink, to attain a loftier flight;
While incense from the altar breathes
Rich fragrance in embodied wreaths;
Or, flung from swinging censer, shrouds
The taper-lights, and curls in clouds
Around angelic Forms, the still
Creation of the painter's skill,
That on the service next concealed
One moment, and the next revealed.
—Cast off your bonds, awake, arise,
And for no transient ecstasies!
What else can mean the visual plea
Of still or moving imagery—
The iterated summons loud,
Not wasted on the attendant crowd,
Nor wholly lost upon the throng
Hurrying the busy streets along?

Alas! the sanctities combined
By art to unsensualise the mind
Decay and languish; or, as creeds
And humours change, are spurned like weeds:
The priests are from their altars thrust;
Temples are levelled with the dust;
And solemn rites and awful forms
Founder amid fanatic storms.
Yet evermore, through years renewed
In undisturbed vicissitude
Of seasons balancing their flight
On the swift wings of day and night,
Kind Nature keeps a heavenly door
Wide open for the scattered Poor,

Where flower-breathed incense to the skies
Is wafted in mute harmonies;
And ground fresh-cloven by the plough
Is fragrant with a humbler vow;
Where birds and brooks from leafy dells
Chime forth unwearied canticles,
And vapours magnify and spread
The glory of the sun's bright head—
Still constant in her worship, still
Conforming to the eternal Will,
Whether men sow or reap the fields,
Divine monition Nature yields,
That not by bread alone we live,
Or what a hand of flesh can give;
That every day should leave some part
Free for a sabbath of the heart:
So shall the seventh be truly blest,
From morn to eve, with hallowed rest.

[Composed 1833.—Published 1835.]

Calm is the fragrant air, and loth to lose
Day's grateful warmth, tho' moist with falling dews.
Look for the stars, you'll say that there are none;
Look up a second time, and, one by one,
You mark them twinkling out with silvery light,
And wonder how they could elude the sight!
The birds, of late so noisy in their bowers,
Warbled a while with faint and fainter powers,
But now are silent as the dim-seen flowers:
Nor does the village Church-clock's iron tone
The time's and season's influence disown;
Nine beats distinctly to each other bound
In drowsy sequence—how unlike the sound
That, in rough winter, oft inflicts a fear
On fireside listeners, doubting what they hear!
The shepherd, bent on rising with the sun,
Had closed his door before the day was done,
And now with thankful heart to bed doth creep,
And joins his little children in their sleep.
The bat, lured forth where trees the lane o'ershade,

Flits and reflits along the close arcade;
The busy dor-hawk chases the white moth
With burring note, which Industry and Sloth
Might both be pleased with, for it suits them both.
A stream is heard—I see it not, but know
By its soft music whence the waters flow:
    Wheels and the tread of hoofs are heard no more;
One boat there was, but it will touch the shore
With the next dipping of its slackened oar;
Faint sound, that, for the gayest of the gay,
Might give to serious thought a moment's sway,
As a last token of man's toilsome day!

    .

THE WARNING

[These are the concluding lines of a poem composed in 1833 and published in 1835, entitled *The Warning*.]

Who shall preserve or prop the tottering Realm?
What hand suffice to govern the state-helm?
If in the aims of men the surest test
Of good or bad (whate'er be sought for or profest)
Lie in the means required, or ways ordained,
For compassing the end, else never gained;
Yet governors and governed both are blind
To this plain truth, or fling it to the wind;
If to expedience principle must bow;
Past, future, shrinking up beneath the incumbent
    Now;
If cowardly concession still must feed
The thirst for power in men who ne'er concede;
Nor turn aside, unless to shape a way
For domination at some riper day;
If generous Loyalty must stand in awe
Of subtle Treason, in his mask of law.
Or with bravado insolent and hard.
Provoking punishment, to win reward;
If office help the factions to conspire,

And they who *should* extinguish, fan the fire—
Then, will the sceptre be a straw, the crown
Sit loosely, like the thistle's crest of down;
To be blown off at will, by Power that spares it
In cunning patience, from the head that wears it.

Lost people, trained to theoretic feud!
Lost above all, ye labouring multitude!
Bewildered whether ye, by slanderous tongues
Deceived, mistake calamities for wrongs;
And over fancied usurpations brood.
Oft snapping at revenge in sullen mood;
Or, from long stress of real injuries fly.
To desperation for a remedy;
In bursts of outrage spread your judgments wide,
And to your wrath cry out, "Be thou our guide;"
Or, bound by oaths, come forth to tread earth's floor
In marshalled thousands, darkening street and moor
With the worst shape mock-patience ever wore;
Or, to the giddy top of self-esteem
By Flatterers carried, mount into a dream
Of boundless suffrage, at whose sage behest
Justice shall rule, disorder be supprest,
And every man sit down as Plenty's Guest!
—O for a bridle bitted with remorse
To stop your Leaders in their headstrong course!
Oh may the Almighty scatter with His grace
These mists, and lead you to a safer place,
By paths no human wisdom can foretrace!
May He pour round you, from worlds far above
Man's feverish passions, His pure light of love,
That quietly restores the natural mien
To hope, and makes truth willing to be seen!
Else shall your blood-stained hands in frenzy reap
Fields gaily sown when promises were cheap.—
Why is the Past belied with wicked art,
The Future made to play so false a part,
Among a people famed for strength of mind,
Foremost in freedom, noblest of mankind?
We act as if we joyed in the sad tune

Storms make in rising, valued in the moon
Nought but her changes. Thus, ungrateful Nation!
If thou persist, and, scorning moderation,
Spread for thyself the snares of tribulation,
Whom, then, shall meekness guard? What saving skill
Lie in forbearance, strength in standing still?
—Soon shall the widow (for the speed of Time
Nought equals when the hours are winged with crime)
Widow, or wife, implore on tremulous knee,
From him who judged her lord, a like decree;
The skies will weep o'er old men desolate:
Ye little-ones! Earth shudders at your fate,
Outcasts and homeless orphans——

But turn, my Soul, and from the sleeping pair
Learn thou the beauty of omniscient care!
Be strong in faith, bid anxious thoughts lie still;
Seek for the good and cherish it—the ill
Oppose, or bear with a submissive will.

IN SIGHT OF THE TOWN OF COCKERMOUTH

(Where the Author was born, and his Father's remains are laid.)

[Composed 1833.—Published 1835.]

A point of life between my Parent's dust,
And yours, my buried Little-ones! am I;
And to those graves looking habitually
In kindred quiet I repose my trust.
Death to the innocent is more than just,
And, to the sinner, mercifully bent;
So may I hope, if truly I repent
And meekly bear the ills which bear I must:
And You, my Offspring! that do still remain,
Yet may outstrip me in the appointed race,
If e'er, through fault of mine, in mutual pain
We breathed together for a moment's space,
The wrong, by love provoked, let love arraign,
And only love keep in your hearts a place.

ON A HIGH PART OF THE COAST OF CUMBERLAND

Easter Sunday, April 7

THE AUTHOR'S SIXTY-THIRD BIRTHDAY

[Composed April 7, 1833.—Published 1835.]

The Sun, that seemed so mildly to retire,
Flung back from distant climes a streaming fire,
Whose blaze is now subdued to tender gleams,
Prelude of night's approach with soothing dreams.
Look round;—of all the clouds not one is moving;
'Tis the still hour of thinking, feeling, loving.
Silent, and steadfast as the vaulted sky,
The boundless plain of waters seems to lie:—
Comes that low sound from breezes rustling o'er
The grass-crowned headland that conceals the shore?
No; 'tis the earth-voice of the mighty sea,
Whispering how meek and gentle he *can* be!
Thou Power supreme! who, arming to rebuke
Offenders, dost put off the gracious look,
And clothe thyself with terrors like the flood
Of Ocean roused into his fiercest mood,
Whatever discipline thy Will ordain
For the brief course that must for me remain;
Teach me with quick-eared spirit to rejoice
In admonitions of thy softest voice!
Whate'er the path these mortal feet may trace,
Breathe through my soul the blessing of thy grace,
Glad, through a perfect love, a faith sincere
Drawn from the wisdom that begins with fear,
Glad to expand; and, for a season, free
From finite cares, to rest absorbed in Thee!

BY THE SEA-SIDE

[Composed 1833.—Published 1835.]

The sun is couched, the sea-fowl gone to rest,
And the wild storm hath somewhere found a nest;
Air slumbers—wave with wave no longer strives,

Only a heaving of the deep survives,
A tell-tale motion! soon will it be laid,
And by the tide alone the water swayed.
Stealthy withdrawings, interminglings mild
Of light with shade in beauty reconciled—
Such is the prospect far as sight can range,
The soothing recompense, the welcome change.
Where now the ships that drove before the blast,
Threatened by angry breakers as they passed;
And by a train of flying clouds bemocked;
Or, in the hollow surge, at anchor rocked
As on a bed of death? Some lodge in peace,
Saved by His care who bade the tempest cease;
And some, too heedless of past danger, court
Fresh gales to waft them to the far-off port;
But near, or hanging sea and sky between,
Not one of all those wingèd powers is seen,
Seen in her course, nor 'mid this quiet heard;
Yet oh! how gladly would the air be stirred
By some acknowledgment of thanks and praise
Soft in its temper as those vesper lays
Sung to the Virgin while accordant oars
Urge the slow bark along Calabrian shores;
A sea-born service through the mountains felt
Till into one loved vision all things melt:
Or like those hymns that soothe with graver sound
The gulfy coast of Norway iron-bound;
And, from the wide and open Baltic, rise
With punctual care, Lutherian harmonies.
Hush, not a voice is here! but why repine,
Now when the star of eve comes forth to shine
On British waters with that look benign?
Ye mariners, that plough your onward way,
Or in the haven rest, or sheltering bay,
May silent thanks at least to God be given
With a full heart; "our thoughts are *heard* in
    heaven!"

[Composed 1833.—Published 1835.]

"There!" said a Stripling, pointing with meet pride
Towards a low roof with green trees half concealed,

"Is Mosgiel Farm; and that's the very field
Where Burns ploughed up the Daisy." Far and wide
A plain below stretched seaward, while, descried
Above sea-clouds, the Peaks of Arran rose;
And, by that simple notice, the repose
Of earth, sky, sea, and air, was vivified.
Beneath "the random *bield* of clod or stone"
Myriads of daisies have shone forth in flower
Near the lark's nest, and in their natural hour
Have passed away; less happy than the One
That, by the unwilling ploughshare, died to prove
The tender charm of poetry and love.

THE LABOURER'S NOON-DAY HYMN

[Composed 1834.—Published 1835.]

Up to the throne of God is borne
The voice of praise at early morn,
And he accepts the punctual hymn
Sung as the light of day grows dim:

Nor will he turn his ear aside
From holy offerings at noontide.
Then here reposing let us raise
A song of gratitude and praise.

What though our burthen be not light
We need not toil from morn to night;
The respite of the mid-day hour
Is in the thankful Creature's power.

Blest are the moments, doubly blest,
That, drawn from this one hour of rest,
Are with a ready heart bestowed
Upon the service of our God!

Each field is then a hallowed spot,
An altar is in each man's cot,
A church in every grove that spreads
Its living roof above our heads.

Look up to Heaven! the industrious Sun
Already half his race hath run;
He cannot halt nor go astray,
But our immortal Spirits may.

Lord! since his rising in the East,
If we have faltered or transgressed,
Guide, from thy love's abundant source,
What yet remains of this day's course:

Help with thy grace, through life's short day,
Our upward and our downward way;
And glorify for us the west,
When we shall sink to final rest.

WRITTEN AFTER THE DEATH OF CHARLES LAMB

[Composed November, 1835.—Published 1837.]

To a good Man of most dear memory
This Stone is sacred. Here he lies apart
From the great city where he first drew breath,
Was reared and taught; and humbly earned his bread,
To the strict labours of the merchant's desk
By duty chained. Not seldom did those tasks
Tease, and the thought of time so spent depress,
His spirit, but the recompense was high;
Firm Independence, Bounty's rightful sire;
Affections, warm as sunshine, free as air;
And when the precious hours of leisure came,
Knowledge and wisdom, gained from converse sweet
With books, or while he ranged the crowded streets
With a keen eye, and overflowing heart:
So genius triumphed over seeming wrong,
And poured out truth in works by thoughtful love
Inspired—works potent over smiles and tears.
And as round mountain-tops the lightning plays,
Thus innocently sported, breaking forth
As from a cloud of some grave sympathy,

Humour and wild instinctive wit, and all
The vivid flashes of his spoken words.
From the most gentle creature nursed in fields
Had been derived the name he bore—a name,
Wherever Christian altars have been raised,
Hallowed to meekness and to innocence;
And if in him meekness at times gave way,
Provoked out of herself by troubles strange,
Many and strange, that hung about his life;
Still, at the centre of his being, lodged
A soul by resignation sanctified:
And if too often, self-reproached, he felt
That innocence belongs not to our kind,
A power that never ceased to abide in him,
Charity, 'mid the multitude of sins
That she can cover, left not his exposed
To an unforgiving judgment from just Heaven.
O, he was good, if e'er a good Man lived!

　　.　　　.　　　.　　　.　　　.　　　.

From a reflecting mind and sorrowing heart
Those simple lines flowed with an earnest wish,
Though but a doubting hope, that they might serve
Fitly to guard the precious dust of him
Whose virtues called them forth. That aim is missed;
For much that truth most urgently required
Had from a faltering pen been asked in vain:
Yet, haply, on the printed page received,
The imperfect record, there, may stand unblamed
As long as verse of mine shall breathe the air
Of memory, or see the light of love.

　Thou wert a scorner of the fields, my Friend,
But more in show than truth; and from the fields,
And from the mountains, to thy rural grave
Transported, my soothed spirit hovers o'er
Its green untrodden turf, and blowing flowers;
And taking up a voice shall speak (tho' still
Awed by the theme's peculiar sanctity
Which words less free presumed not even to touch)

Of that fraternal love, whose heaven-lit lamp
From infancy, through manhood, to the last
Of threescore years, and to thy latest hour,
Burnt on with ever-strengthening light, enshrined
Within thy bosom.
                           "Wonderful" hath been
The love established between man and man,
"Passing the love of women;" and between
Man and his help-mate in fast wedlock joined
Through God, is raised a spirit and soul of love
Without whose blissful influence Paradise
Had been no Paradise; and earth were now
A waste where creatures bearing human form,
Direst of savage beasts, would roam in fear,
Joyless and comfortless. Our days glide on;
And let him grieve who cannot choose but grieve
That he hath been an Elm without his Vine,
And her bright dower of clustering charities,
That, round his trunk and branches, might have clung
Enriching and adorning. Unto thee,
Not so enriched, not so adorned, to thee
Was given (say rather thou of later birth
Wert given to her) a Sister—'tis a word
Timidly uttered, for she *lives*, the meek,
The self-restraining, and the ever-kind;
In whom thy reason and intelligent heart
Found—for all interests, hopes, and tender cares,
All softening, humanising, hallowing powers,
Whether withheld, or for her sake unsought—
More than sufficient recompense!
                                      Her love
(What weakness prompts the voice to tell it here?)
Was as the love of mothers; and when years,
Lifting the boy to man's estate, had called
The long-protected to assume the part
Of a protector, the first filial tie
Was undissolved; and, in or out of sight,
Remained imperishably interwoven
With life itself. Thus, 'mid a shifting world,
Did they together testify of time

And season's difference—a double tree
With two collateral stems sprung from one root;
Such were they—such thro' life they *might* have been
In union, in partition only such;
Otherwise wrought the will of the Most High;
Yet, thro' all visitations and all trials,
Still they were faithful; like two vessels launched
From the same beach one ocean to explore
With mutual help, and sailing—to their league
True, as inexorable winds, or bars
Floating or fixed of polar ice, allow.

But turn we rather, let my spirit turn
With thine, O silent and invisible Friend!
To those dear intervals, nor rare nor brief,
When reunited, and by choice withdrawn
From miscellaneous converse, ye were taught
That the remembrance of foregone distress,
And the worse fear of future ill (which oft
Doth hang around it, as a sickly child
Upon its mother) may be both alike
Disarmed of power to unsettle present good
So prized, and things inward and outward held
In such an even balance, that the heart
Acknowledges God's grace, his mercy feels,
And in its depth of gratitude is still.

O gift divine of quiet sequestration!
The hermit, exercised in prayer and praise,
And feeding daily on the hope of heaven,
Is happy in his vow, and fondly cleaves
To life-long singleness; but happier far
Was to your souls, and to the thoughts of others,
A thousand times more beautiful appeared,
Your *dual* loneliness. The sacred tie
Is broken; yet why grieve? for Time but holds
His moiety in trust, till Joy shall lead
To the blest world where parting is unknown.

EXTEMPORE EFFUSION UPON THE DEATH OF
JAMES HOGG

[Composed November, 1835.—Published December 12, 1835 (*The Athenæum*);
ed. 1837. James Hogg, the Ettrick Shepherd, and Felicia Hemans died
1835, Coleridge and Lamb, 1834; Scott and Crabbe, 1832.]

When first, descending from the moorlands,
    I saw the Stream of Yarrow glide
Along a bare and open valley,
    The Ettrick Shepherd was my guide.

When last along its banks I wandered,
    Through groves that had begun to shed
Their golden leaves upon the pathways,
    My steps the Border-minstrel led.

The mighty Minstrel breathes no longer,
    'Mid mouldering ruins low he lies;
And death upon the braes of Yarrow,
    Has closed the Shepherd-poet's eyes:

Nor has the rolling year twice measured,
    From sign to sign, its steadfast course,
Since every mortal power of Coleridge
    Was frozen at its marvellous source;

The rapt One, of the godlike forehead,
    The heaven-eyed creature sleeps in earth:
And Lamb, the frolic and the gentle,
    Has vanished from his lonely hearth.

Like clouds that rake the mountain-summits,
    Or waves that own no curbing hand,
How fast has brother followed brother,
    From sunshine to the sunless land!

Yet I, whose lids from infant slumber
    Were earlier raised, remain to hear
A timid voice, that asks in whispers,
    "Who next will drop and disappear?"

Our haughty life is crowned with darkness,
    Like London with its own black wreath,
On which with thee, O Crabbe! forthlooking,
    I gazed from Hampstead's breezy heath.

As if but yesterday departed,
    Thou too art gone before; but why,
O'er ripe fruit, reasonably gathered,
    Should frail survivors heave a sigh?

Mourn rather for that holy Spirit,
    Sweet as the spring, as ocean deep;
For Her who, ere her summer faded,
    Has sunk into a breathless sleep.

No more of old romantic sorrows,
    For slaughtered Youth or love-lorn Maid!
With sharper grief is Yarrow smitten,
    And Ettrick mourns with her their Poet dead.

[Composed 1846.—Published 1850.]

I know an aged Man constrained to dwell
    In a large house of public charity,
Where he abides, as in a Prisoner's cell,
    With numbers near, alas! no company.

When he could creep about, at will, though poor
    And forced to live on alms, this old Man fed
A Redbreast, one that to his cottage door
    Came not, but in a lane partook his bread.

There, at the root of one particular tree,
    An easy seat this worn-out Labourer found
While Robin pecked the crumbs upon his knee
    Laid one by one, or scattered on the ground.

Dear intercourse was theirs, day after day;
    What signs of mutual gladness when they met!
Think of their common peace, their simple play,
    The parting moment and its fond regret.

Months passed in love that failed not to fulfil,
  In spite of season's change, its own demand,
By fluttering pinions here and busy bill;
  There by caresses from a tremulous hand.

Thus in the chosen spot a tie so strong
  Was formed between the solitary pair,
That when his fate had housed him 'mid a throng
  The Captive shunned all converse proffered there.

Wife, children, kindred, they were dead and gone;
  But, if no evil hap his wishes crossed,
One living Stay was left, and on that one
  Some recompense for all that he had lost.

O that the good old Man had power to prove,
  By message sent through air or visible token,
That still he loves the Bird, and still must love;
  That friendship lasts though fellowship is broken!

APPENDIX

APPENDIX "A"

MY LORD,

Reputation may not improperly be termed the moral life
of man. Alluding to our natural existence, Addison, in a
sublime allegory well known to your Lordship, has represented us as crossing an immense bridge, from whose surface
from a variety of causes we disappear one after another,
and are seen no more. Every one who enters upon public
life has such a bridge to pass. Some slip through at the
very commencement of their career from thoughtlessness,
others pursue their course a little longer, till, misled by the
phantoms of avarice and ambition, they fall victims to
their delusion. Your Lordship was either seen, or supposed
to be seen, continuing your way for a long time unseduced
and undismayed; but those who now look for you will look
in vain, and it is feared you have at last fallen, through
one of the numerous trap-doors, into the tide of contempt,
to be swept down to the ocean of oblivion.

It is not my intention to be illiberal; these latter expressions have been forced from me by indignation. Your
Lordship has given a proof that even religious controversy
may be conducted without asperity; I hope I shall profit
by your example. At the same time, with a spirit which
you may not approve—for it is a republican spirit—I shall
not preclude myself from any truths, however severe, which
I may think beneficial to the cause which I have undertaken to defend. You will not, then, be surprised when
I inform you that it is only the name of its author which
has induced me to notice an Appendix to a Sermon which

you have lately given to the world, with a hope that it may have some effect in calming a perturbation which, you say, has been excited in the minds of the lower orders of the community. While, with a servility which has prejudiced many people against religion itself, the ministers of the Church of England have appeared as writers upon public measures only to be the advocates of slavery civil and religious, your Lordship stood almost alone as the defender of truth and political charity. The names of levelling prelate, bishop of the Dissenters, which were intended as a dishonour to your character, were looked upon by your friends—perhaps by yourself—as an acknowledgment of your possessing an enlarged and philosophical mind; and, like the generals in a neighbour-country, if it had been equally becoming your profession, you might have adopted, as an honourable title, a denomination intended as a stigma.

On opening your Appendix, your admirers will naturally expect to find an impartial statement of the grievances which harass this Nation, and a sagacious inquiry into the proper modes of redress. They will be disappointed. Sensible how large a portion of mankind receive opinions upon authority, I am apprehensive lest the doctrines which they will there find should derive a weight from your name to which they are by no means intrinsically entitled. I will therefore examine what you have advanced, from a hope of being able to do away any impression left on the minds of such as may be liable to confound with argument a strong prepossession for your Lordship's talents, experience, and virtues.

Before I take notice of what you appear to have laid down as principles, it may not be improper to advert to some incidental opinions found at the commencement of your political confession of faith.

At a period big with the fate of the human race I am sorry that you attach so much importance to the personal sufferings of the late royal martyr, and that an anxiety for the issue of the present convulsions should not have prevented you from joining in the idle cry of modish lamentation which has resounded from the Court to the cottage. You wish it to be supposed you are one of those who are unpersuaded of the guilt of Louis XVI. If you had attended to the history of the French Revolution as minutely as its importance demands, so far from stopping to bewail his death, you would rather have regretted that the blind fondness of his people had placed a human being in that monstrous situation which rendered him unaccountable before a human tribunal. A bishop (M. Grégoire), a man of philosophy and humanity as distinguished as your Lordship, declared at the opening of the National Convention—and twenty-five millions of men were convinced of the truth of the assertion—that there was not a citizen on the tenth of August who, if he could have dragged before the eyes of Louis the corpse of one of his murdered brothers, might not have exclaimed to him: "Tyran, voilà ton ouvrage." Think of this, and you will not want consolation under any depression your spirits may feel at the contrast exhibited by Louis on the most splendid throne of the universe, and Louis alone in the tower of the Temple or on the scaffold. But there is a class of men who received the news of the late execution with much more heartfelt sorrow than that which you, among such a multitude, so officiously express. The passion of pity is one of which, above all others, a Christian teacher should be cautious of cherishing the abuse when, under the influence of reason, it is regulated by the disproportion of the pain suffered to the guilt incurred. It is from the passion thus directed that the men of whom I have just spoken are afflicted by the catastrophe of the fallen monarch. They are sorry that the prejudice and weakness of mankind have made it necessary to force an individual into an unnatural situation, which requires more than human talents and human virtues, and at the same time precludes him from attaining even a moderate knowledge of common life, and from feeling a particular share in the interests of mankind. But, above all, these men lament that any combination of circumstances should have rendered it necessary or advisable to veil for a moment the statues of the laws, and that by such emergency the cause of twenty-five millions of people, I may say of the whole human race, should have been so materially injured. Any other sorrow for the death of Louis is irrational and weak.

In France royalty is no more. The person of the last anointed is no more also; and I flatter myself I am not alone, even in this kingdom, when I wish that it may please the Almighty neither by the hands of His priests nor His nobles (I allude to a striking passage of Racine) to raise his posterity to the rank of his ancestors, and reillume the torch of extinguished David. [Here Wordsworth appends a quotation from "Athalie," Act I, sc. 2.]

You say: "I fly with terror and abhorrence even from the altar of Liberty, when I see it stained with the blood of the aged, of the innocent, of the defenceless sex, of the ministers of religion, and of the faithful adherents of a fallen monarch." What! have you so little knowledge of the nature of man as to be ignorant that a time of revolution is not the season of true Liberty? Alas, the obstinacy and perversion of man is such that she is too often obliged to borrow the very arms of Despotism to overthrow him, and, in order to reign in peace, must establish herself by violence. She deplores such stern necessity, but the safety of the people, her supreme law, is her consolation. This apparent contradiction between the principles of liberty and the march of revolutions; this spirit of jealousy, of severity, of disquietude, of vexation, indispensable from a state of war between the oppressors and oppressed, must of necessity confuse the ideas of morality, and contract the benign exertion of the best affections of the human heart. Political virtues are developed at the expense of moral ones; and the sweet emotions of compassion, evidently dangerous when traitors are to be punished, are too often altogether smothered. But is this a sufficient reason to reprobate a conclusion from which is to spring a fairer order of things? It is the province of education to rectify the erroneous notions which a habit of oppression, and even of resistance, may have created, and to soften this ferocity of character, proceeding from a necessary suspension of the mild and social virtues; it belongs to her to create a race of men who, truly free, will look upon their fathers as only enfranchised.

I proceed to the sorrow you express for the fate of the French priesthood. The measure by which that body was immediately stripped of part of its possessions, and a more equal distribution enjoined of the rest, does not meet with your Lordship's approbation. You do not question the right of the Nation over ecclesiastical wealth; you have

voluntarily abandoned a ground which you were conscious
was altogether untenable. Having allowed this right, can
you question the propriety of exerting it at that particular
period? The urgencies of the State were such as required
the immediate application of a remedy. Even the clergy
were conscious of such necessity; and aware, from the
immunities they had long enjoyed, that the people would
insist upon their bearing some share of the burden, offered
of themselves a considerable portion of their superfluities.
The Assembly was true to justice, and refused to com-
promise the interests of the Nation by accepting as a
satisfaction the insidious offerings of compulsive charity.
They enforced their right. They took from the clergy
a large share of their wealth, and applied it to the allevia-
tion of the national misery. Experience shows daily the
wise employment of the ample provision which yet remains
to them. While you reflect on the vast diminution which
some men's fortunes must have undergone, your sorrow for
these individuals will be diminished by recollecting the
unworthy motives which induced the bulk of them to
undertake the office, and the scandalous arts which enabled
so many to attain the rank and enormous wealth which it
has seemed necessary to annex to the charge of a Christian
pastor. You will rather look upon it as a signal act of
justice that they should thus unexpectedly be stripped of
the rewards of their vices and their crimes. If you should
lament the sad reverse by which the hero of the necklace
(Prince de Rohan) has been divested of about 1,300,000
livres of annual revenue, you may find some consolation
that a part of this prodigious mass of riches is gone to
preserve from famine some thousands of curés, who were
pining in villages unobserved by Courts.

I now proceed to principles. Your Lordship very properly asserts that "the liberty of man in a state of society
consists in his being subject to no law but the law enacted
by the general will of the society to which he belongs."
You approve of the object which the French had in view
when, in the infancy of the Revolution, they were attempting to destroy arbitrary power, and to erect a temple to
Liberty on its remains. It is with surprise, then, that I
find you afterwards presuming to dictate to the world

a servile adoption of the British constitution. It is with indignation I perceive you "reprobate" a people for having imagined happiness and liberty more likely to flourish in the open field of a Republic than under the shade of Monarchy. You are therefore guilty of a most glaring contradiction. Twenty-five millions of Frenchmen have felt that they could have no security for their liberties under any modification of monarchical power. They have in consequence unanimously chosen a Republic. You cannot but observe that they have only exercised that right in which, by your own confession, liberty essentially resides.

As to your arguments, by which you pretend to justify your anathemas of a Republic—if arguments they may be called—they are so concise, that I cannot but transcribe them. "I dislike a Republic for this reason, because of all forms of government, scarcely excepting the most despotic, I think a Republic the most oppressive to the bulk of the people; they are deceived in it with a show of liberty, but they live in it under the most odious of all tyrannies—the tyranny of their equals."

This passage is a singular proof of that fatality by which the advocates of error furnish weapons for their own destruction: while it is merely assertion in respect to a justification of your aversion to Republicanism, a strong argument may be drawn from it in its favour. Mr. Burke, in a philosophic lamentation over the extinction of chivalry, told us that in those times vice lost half its evil by losing all its grossness. Infatuated moralist! Your Lordship excites compassion as labouring under the same delusion. Slavery is a bitter and a poisonous draught. We have but one conclusion under it, that a Nation may dash the cup to the ground when she pleases. Do not imagine that by taking from its bitterness you weaken its deadly quality; no, by rendering it more palatable you contribute to its power of destruction. We submit without repining to the chastisements of Providence, aware that we are creatures, that opposition is vain and remonstrance impossible. But when redress is in our own power and resistance is rational, we suffer with the same humility from beings like ourselves, because we are taught from infancy that we were born in a state of inferiority to our oppressors, that they were sent into the world to scourge, and we to be scourged. Accordingly we see the bulk of mankind, actuated by these fatal prejudices, even more ready to lay themselves under the feet of the great than the great are to trample upon them. Now taking for granted, that in Republics men live under the tyranny of what you call their equals, the circumstance of this being the most odious of all tyrannies is what a Republican would boast of; as soon as tyranny becomes odious, the principal step is made towards its destruction. Reflecting on the degraded state of the mass of mankind, a philosopher will lament that oppression is not odious to them, that the iron, while it eats the soul, is not felt to enter into it. "Tout homme né dans l'esclavage naît pour l'esclavage, rien n'est plus certain; les esclaves perdent tout dans leurs fers, jusqu'au désir d'en sortir; ils aiment leur servitude, comme les compagnons d'Ulysse aimaient leur abrutissement."

I return to the quotation in which you reprobate Republicanism. Relying upon the temper of the times, you have surely thought little argument necessary to contest what few will be hardy enough to support; the strongest of auxiliaries, imprisonment and the pillory, has left your arm little to perform. But the happiness of mankind is so closely connected with this subject, that I cannot suffer such considerations to deter me from throwing out a few hints, which may lead to a conclusion that a Republic legitimately constructed contains less of an oppressive principle than any other form of government.

Your Lordship will scarcely question that much of human misery, that the great evils which desolate States, proceed from the governors' having an interest distinct from that of the governed. It should seem a natural deduction, that whatever has a tendency to identify the two must also in the same degree promote the general welfare. As the magnitude of almost all States prevents the possibility of their enjoying a pure democracy, philosophers—from a wish, as far as is in their power, to make the governors and the governed one—will turn their thoughts to the system of universal representation, and will annex an equal importance to the suffrage of every individual. Jealous of giving up no more of the authority of the people than is necessary, they will be solicitous of finding out some method by which the office of their delegates may be confined as much as is practicable to the proposing and deliberating upon laws rather than to enacting them; reserving to the people the power of finally inscribing them in the national code. Unless this is attended to, as soon as a people has chosen representatives it no longer has a political existence, except as it is understood to retain the privilege of annihiliating the trust when it shall think proper, and of resuming its original power. Sensible that at the moment of election an interest distinct from that of the general body is created, an enlightened legislator will endeavour by every possible method to diminish the operation of such interest. The first and most natural mode that presents itself is that of shortening the regular duration of this trust, in order that the man who has betrayed it may soon be superseded by a more worthy successor. But this is not enough; aware of the possibility of imposition, and of the natural tendency of power to corrupt the heart of man, a sensible Republican will think it essential that the office of legislator be not intrusted to the same man for a succession of years. He will also be induced to this wise restraint by the grand principle of identification; he will be more sure of the virtue of the legislator by knowing that, in the capacity of private citizen, tomorrow he must either smart under the oppression or bless the justice of the law which he has enacted to-day.

Perhaps in the very outset of this inquiry the principle on which I proceed will be questioned, and I shall be told that the people are not the proper judges of their own welfare. But because under every government of modern times, till the foundation of the American Republic, the bulk of mankind have appeared incapable of discerning their true interests, no conclusion can be drawn against my principle. At this moment have we not daily the strongest proofs of the success with which, in what you call the best of all monarchical governments, the popular mind may be debauched? Left to the quiet exercise of their own judgment, do you think that the people would have thought it necessary to set fire to the house of the

philosophic Priestley, and to hunt down his life like that
of a traitor or a parricide? that, deprived almost of the
necessaries of existence by the burden of their taxes, they
would cry out, as with one voice, for a war from which
not a single ray of consolation can visit them to compensate for the additional keenness with which they are about
to smart under the scourge of labour, of cold, and of
hunger?

Appearing, as I do, the advocate of Republicanism, let me
not be misunderstood. I am well aware from the abuse
of the executive power in States, that there is not a single
European nation but what affords a melancholy proof that
if, at this moment, the original authority of the people
should be restored, all that could be expected from such
restoration would in the beginning be but change of
tyranny. Considering the nature of a Republic in reference
to the present condition of Europe, your Lordship stops
here; but a philosopher will extend his views much farther;
having dried up the source from which flows the corruption
of the public opinion, he will be sensible that the stream
will go on gradually refining itself. I must add also that
the coercive power is of necessity so strong in all the old
governments, that a people could not at first make an
abuse of that liberty which a legitimate Republic supposes.
The animal just released from its stall will exhaust the
overflow of its spirits in a round of wanton vagaries;
but it will soon return to itself, and enjoy its freedom in
moderate and regular delight.

But, to resume the subject of universal representation, I
ought to have mentioned before that in the choice of its
representatives a people will not immorally hold out wealth
as a criterion of integrity, nor lay down as a fundamental
rule, that to be qualified for the trying duties of legislation
a citizen should be possessed of a certain fixed property.
Virtues, talents, and acquirements are all that it will look
for.

Having destroyed every external object of delusion, let us
now see what makes the supposition necessary that the people will mislead themselves. Your Lordship respects "peas-
ants and mechanics when they intrude not themselves into
concerns for which their education has not fitted them."

Setting aside the idea of a peasant or mechanic being a legislator, what vast education is requisite to enable him to judge amongst his neighbours which is most qualified by his industry and integrity to be intrusted with the care of the interests of himself and of his fellow-citizens? But leaving this ground, as governments formed on such a plan proceed in a plain and open manner, their administration would require much less of what is called talents and experience, that is, of disciplined treachery and hoary Machiavelism; and at the same time, as it would no longer be their interest to keep the mass of the nation in ignorance, a moderate portion of useful knowledge would be universally disseminated. If your Lordship has travelled in the democratic cantons of Switzerland, you must have seen the herdsmen with the staff in one hand and the book in the other. In the constituent Assembly of France was found a peasant whose sagacity was as distinguished as his integrity, whose blunt honesty overawed and baffled the refinements of hypocritical patriots. The people of Paris followed him with acclamations, and the name of Père Gérard will long be mentioned with admiration and respect through the eighty-three departments.

From these hints, if pursued further, might be demonstrated the expediency of the whole people "intruding themselves" on the office of legislation, and the wisdom of putting into force what they may claim as a right. But government is divided into two parts—the legislative and executive. The executive power you would lodge in the hands of an individual. Before we inquire into the propriety of this measure, it will be necessary to state the proper objects of the executive power in governments where the principle of universal representation is admitted. With regard to that portion of this power which is exerted in the application of the laws, it may be observed that much of it would be superseded. As laws, being but the expression of the general will, would be enacted only from an almost universal conviction of their utility, any resistance to such laws, any desire of eluding them, must proceed from a few refractory individuals. As far, then, as relates to the internal administration of the country, a Republic has a manifest advantage over a Monarchy, inasmuch as less force is requisite to compel obedience to its laws.

From the judicial tribunals of our own country, though we labour under a variety of partial and oppressive laws, we have an evident proof of the nullity of regal interference, as the king's name is confessedly a mere fiction, and justice is known to be most equitably administered when the judges are least dependent on the crown.

I have spoken of laws partial and oppressive; our penal code is so crowded with disproportioned penalties and indiscriminate severity that a conscientious man would sacrifice, in many instances, his respect for the laws to the common feelings of humanity; and there must be a strange vice in that legislation from which can proceed laws in whose execution a man cannot be instrumental without forfeiting his self-esteem and incurring the contempt of his fellow-citizens.

But to return from this digression; with regard to the other branches of the executive government, which relate rather to original measures than to administering the law, it may be observed that the power exercised in conducting them is distinguished by almost imperceptible shades from the legislative, and that all such as admit of open discussion and of the delay attendant on public deliberations are properly the province of the representative assembly. If this observation be duly attended to, it will appear that this part of the executive power will be extremely circumscribed, will be stripped almost entirely of a deliberative capacity, and will be reduced to a mere hand or instrument. As a Republican government would leave this power to a select body destitute of the means of corruption, and whom the people, continually contributing, could at all times bring to account or dismiss, will it not necessarily ensue that a body so selected and supported would perform their simple functions with greater efficacy and fidelity than the complicated concerns of royalty can be expected to meet with in the councils of princes; of men who from their wealth and interest have forced themselves into trust; and of statesmen, whose constant object is to exalt themselves by laying pitfalls for their colleagues and for their country.

I shall pursue this subject no further; but adopting your Lordship's method of argument, instead of continuing to demonstrate the superiority of a Republican executive government, I will repeat some of the objections which have been often made to monarchy, and have not been answered.

My first objection to regal government is its instability, proceeding from a variety of causes. Where monarchy is found in its greatest intensity, as in Morocco and Turkey, this observation is illustrated in a very pointed manner, and indeed is more or less striking as governments are more or less despotic. The reason is obvious: as the monarch is the chooser of his ministers, and as his own passions and caprice are in general the sole guides of his conduct, these ministers, instead of pursuing directly the one grand object of national welfare, will make it their chief study to vary their measures according to his humours. But a minister may be refractory: his successor will naturally run headlong into plans totally the reverse of the former system; for if he treads in the same path, he is well aware that a similar fate will attend him. This observation will apply to each succession of kings, who, from vanity and a desire of distinction, will in general studiously avoid any step which may lead to a suspicion that they are so spiritless as to imitate their predecessor. That a similar instability is not incident to Republics is evident from their very constitution.

As from the nature of monarchy, particularly of hereditary monarchy, there must always be a vast disproportion between the duties to be performed and the powers that are to perform them; and as the measures of government, far from gaining additional vigour, are, on the contrary, enfeebled by being intrusted to one hand, what arguments can be used for allowing to the will of a single being a weight which, as history shows, will subvert that of the whole body politic? And this brings me to my grand objection to monarchy, which is drawn from THE ETERNAL NATURE OF MAN. The office of king is a trial to which human virtue is not equal. Pure and universal representation, by which alone liberty can be secured, cannot, I think, exist together with monarchy. It seems madness to expect a manifestation of the general will, at the same time that we allow to a particular will that weight which it must obtain in all governments that can with any propriety be called monarchical. They must war with each other till one of them is extinguished. It was so in France and . . .

I shall not pursue this topic further, but, as you are a teacher of purity of morals, I cannot but remind you of that atmosphere of corruption without which it should seem that courts cannot exist.

You seem anxious to explain what ought to be understood by the equality of men in a state of civil society; but your Lordship's success has not answered your trouble. If you had looked in the articles of the Rights of Man, you would have found your efforts superseded: "Equality, without which liberty cannot exist, is to be met with in perfection in that State in which no distinctions are admitted but such as have evidently for their object the general good;" "The end of government cannot be attained without authorising some members of the society to command, and of course without imposing on the rest the necessity of obedience."

Here, then, is an inevitable inequality, which may be denominated that of power. In order to render this as small as possible, a legislator will be careful not to give greater force to such authority than is essential to its due execution. Government is at best but a necessary evil. Compelled to place themselves in a state of subordination, men will obviously endeavour to prevent the abuse of that superiority to which they submit; accordingly they will cautiously avoid whatever may lead those in whom it is acknowledged to suppose they hold it as a right. Nothing will more effectually contribute to this than that the person in whom authority has been lodged should occasionally descend to the level of private citizen; he will learn from it a wholesome lesson, and the people will be less liable to confound the person with the power. On this principle hereditary authority will be prescribed; and on another also—that in such a system as that of hereditary authority, no security can be had for talents adequate to the discharge of the office, and consequently the people can only feel the mortification of being humbled without having protected themselves.

Another distinction will arise amongst mankind, which, though it may be easily modified by government, exists independent of it; I mean the distinction of wealth, which always will attend superior talents and industry. It cannot be denied that the security of individual property is one of the strongest and most natural motives to induce men to bow their necks to the yoke of civil government. In order to attain this end of security to property, a legislator will proceed with impartiality. He should not suppose that, when he has insured to their proprietors the possession of lands and movables against the depredation of the necessitous, nothing remains to be done. The history of all ages has demonstrated that wealth not only can secure itself, but includes even an oppressive principle. Aware of this, and that the extremes of poverty and riches have a necessary tendency to corrupt the human heart, he will banish from his code all laws such as the unnatural monster of primogeniture, such as encourage associations against labour in the form of corporate bodies, and indeed all that monopolising system of legislation, whose baleful influence is shown in the depopulation of the country and in the necessity which reduces the sad relicks to owe their very existence to the ostentatious bounty of their oppressors. If it is true in common life, it is still more true in governments, that we should be just before we are generous; but our legislators seem to have forgotten or despised this homely maxim. They have unjustly left unprotected that most important part of property, not less real because it has no material existence, that which ought to enable the labourer to provide food for himself and his family. I appeal to innumerable statutes, whose constant and professed object it is to lower the price of labour, to compel the workman to be content with arbitrary wages, evidently too small from the necessity of legal enforcement of the acceptance of them. Even from the astonishing amount of the sums raised for the support of one description of the poor may be concluded the extent and greatness of that oppression, whose effects have rendered it possible for the few to afford so much, and have shown us that such a multitude of our brothers exist in even helpless indigence. Your Lordship tells us that the science of civil government has received all the perfection of which it is capable. For my part, I am more enthusiastic. The sorrow I feel from the contemplation of this melancholy picture is not unconsoled by a comfortable hope that the class of wretches called mendicants will not much longer shock the feelings of humanity; that the miseries entailed upon the marriage of those who are not rich will no longer tempt the bulk of mankind to fly to that promiscuous intercourse to which they are impelled by the instincts of nature and the dreadful satisfaction of escaping the prospect of infants, sad fruit of such intercourse, whom they are unable to support. If these flattering prospects be ever realised, it must be owing to some wise and salutary regulations counteracting that inequality among mankind which proceeds from the present fixed disproportion of their possessions.

I am not an advocate for the agrarian law nor for sumptuary regulations, but I contend that the people amongst whom the law of primogeniture exists, and among whom corporate bodies are encouraged, and immense salaries annexed to useless and indeed hereditary offices, is oppressed by an inequality in the distribution of wealth which does not necessarily attend men in a state of civil society.

Thus far we have considered inequalities inseparable from civil society. But other arbitrary distinctions exist among mankind, either from choice or usurpation. I allude to titles, to stars, ribbons, and garters, and other badges of fictitious superiority. Your Lordship will not question the grand principle on which this inquiry set out; I look upon it, then, as my duty to try the propriety of these distinctions by that criterion, and think it will be no difficult task to prove that these separations among mankind are absurd, impolitic, and immoral. Considering hereditary nobility as a reward for services rendered to the State—and it is to my charity that you owe the permission of taking up the question on this ground—what services can a man render to the State adequate to such a compensation that the making of laws, upon which the happiness of millions is to depend, shall be lodged in him and

his posterity, however depraved may be their principles,
however contemptible their understandings?

But here I may be accused of sophistry; I ought to sub-
tract every idea of power from such distinction, though
from the weakness of mankind it is impossible to discon-
nect them. What services then, can a man render to
society to compensate for the outrage done to the dignity
of our nature when we bind ourselves to address him and
his posterity with humiliating circumlocutions, calling him
most noble, most honourable, most high, most august,
serene, excellent, eminent, and so forth; when it is more
than probable that such unnatural flattery will but generate
vices which ought to consign him to neglect and solitude,
or make him the perpetual object of the finger of scorn?
And does not experience justify the observation, that where
titles—a thing very rare—have been conferred as the
rewards of merit, those to whom they have descended, far
from being thereby animated to imitate their ancestor,
have presumed upon that lustre which they supposed
thrown round them, and, prodigally relying on such re-
sources, lavished what alone was their own, their personal
reputation?

It would be happy if this delusion were confined to themselves; but, alas, the world is weak enough to grant the
indulgence which they assume. Vice, which is forgiven
in one character, will soon cease to meet with sternness
of rebuke when found in others. Even at first she will
entreat pardon with confidence, assured that ere long
she will be charitably supposed to stand in no need of it.

But let me ask you seriously, from the mode in which
these distinctions are originally conferred, is it not almost
necessary that, far from being the rewards of services rendered to the State, they should usually be the recompense of
an industrious sacrifice of the general welfare to the particular aggrandisement of that power by which they are bestowed? Let us even alter their source, and consider them
as proceeding from the Nation itself, and deprived of that
hereditary quality; even here I should proscribe them, and
for the most evident reason—that a man's past services
are no sufficient security for his future character; he who
to-day merits the civic wreath may to-morrow deserve

the Tarpeian rock. Besides, where respect is not perverted, where the world is not taught to reverence men without regarding their conduct, the esteem of mankind will have a very different value, and, when a proper independence is secured, will be regarded as a sufficient recompense for services however important, and will be a much surer guarantee of the continuance of such virtues as may deserve it.

I have another strong objection to nobility, which is that it has a necessary tendency to dishonour labour, a prejudice which extends far beyond its own circle; that it binds down whole ranks of men to idleness, while it gives the enjoyment of a reward which exceeds the hopes of the most active exertions of human industry. The languid tedium of this noble repose must be dissipated, and gaming, with the tricking manoeuvres of the horse-race, afford occupation to hours which it would be happy for mankind had they been totally unemployed.

Reflecting on the corruption of the public manners, does your Lordship shudder at the prostitution which miserably deluges our streets? You may find the cause in our aristocratical prejudices. Are you disgusted with the hypocrisy and sycophancy of our intercourse in private life? You may find the cause in the necessity of dissimulation which we have established by regulations which oblige us to address as our superiors, indeed as our masters, men whom we cannot but internally despise. Do you lament that such large portions of mankind should stoop to occupations unworthy the dignity of their nature? You may find in the pride and luxury thought necessary to nobility how such servile arts are encouraged. Besides, where the most honourable of the Land do not blush to accept such offices as groom of the bedchamber, master of the hounds, lords in waiting, captain of the honourable band of gentlemen-pensioners, is it astonishing that the bulk of the people should not ask of an occupation, what is it? but what may be gained by it?

If the long equestrian train of equipage should make your Lordship sigh for the poor who are pining in hunger, you will find that little is thought of snatching the bread from their mouths to eke out the "necessary splendour" of nobility.

I have not time to pursue this subject further, but am so strongly impressed with the baleful influence of aristocracy and nobility upon human happiness and virtue, that if, as I am persuaded, monarchy cannot exist without such supporters, I think that reason sufficient for the preference I have given to the Republican system.

It is with reluctance that I quit the subjects I have just touched upon; but the nature of this Address does not permit me to continue the discussion. I proceed to what more immediately relates to this Kingdom at the present crisis.

You ask with triumphant confidence, to what other law are the people of England subject than the general will of the society to which they belong? Is your Lordship to be told that acquiescence is not choice, and that obedience is not freedom? If there is a single man in Great Britain who has no suffrage in the election of a representative, the will of the society of which he is a member is not generally expressed; he is a Helot in that society. You answer the question, so confidently put, in this singular manner: "The King, we are all justly persuaded, has not the inclination—and we all know that, if he had the inclination, he has not the power—to substitute his will in the place of law. The House of Lords has no such power. The House of Commons has no such power." This passage, so artfully and unconstitutionally framed to agree with the delusions of the moment, cannot deceive a thinking reader. The expression of your full persuasion of the upright intentions of the King can only be the language of flattery. You are not to be told that it is constitutionally a maxim not to attribute to the person of the King the measures and misconduct of government. Had you chosen to speak, as you ought to have done, openly and explicitly, you must have expressed your just persuasion and implicit confidence in the integrity, moderation, and wisdom of his Majesty's ministers. Have you forgot the avowed ministerial maxim of Sir Robert Walpole? Are you ignorant of the overwhelming corruption of the present day?

You seem unconscious of the absurdity of separating what is inseparable even in imagination. Would it have been any consolation to the miserable Romans under the second triumvirate to have been asked insultingly, Is it Octavius, is it Anthony, or is it Lepidus that has caused this bitterness of affliction? and when the answer could not be returned with certainty, to have been reproached that their sufferings were imaginary? The fact is that the King *and* Lords *and* Commons, by what is termed the omnipotence of Parliament, have constitutionally the right of enacting whatever laws they please in defiance of the petitions or remonstrances of the nation. They have the power of doubling our enormous debt of 240 million, and *may* pursue measures which could never be supposed the emanation of the general will without concluding the people stripped of reason, of sentiment, and even of that first instinct which prompts them to preserve their own existence.

I congratulate your Lordship upon your enthusiastic fondness for the judicial proceedings of this country. I am happy to find you have passed through life without having your fleece torn from your back in the thorny labyrinth of litigation. But you have not lived always in colleges, and must have passed by some victims, whom it cannot be supposed, without a reflection on your heart, that you have forgotten. Here I am reminded of what I have said on the subject of representation—to be qualified for the office of the legislation you should have felt like the bulk of mankind; their sorrows should be familiar to you, of which, if you are ignorant, how can you redress them? As a member of the assembly which, from a confidence in its experience, sagacity, and wisdom, the constitution has invested with the supreme appellant jurisdiction to determine the most doubtful points of an intricate jurisprudence, your Lordship cannot, I presume, be ignorant of the consuming expense of our never-ending process, the verbosity of unintelligible statutes, and the perpetual contrariety in our judicial decisions.

"The greatest freedom that can be enjoyed by man in a state of civil society, the greatest security that can be given with respect to the protection of his character, property, personal liberty, limb, and life, is afforded to every individual by our present constitution."

"Let it never be forgotten by ourselves, and let us impress the observation upon the hearts of our children, that we are in possession of both (liberty and equality), of as much of both as can be consistent with the end for which civil society was introduced among mankind."

Many of my readers will hardly believe me when I inform them that these passages are copied verbatim from your Appendix. Mr. Burke roused the indignation of all ranks of men when, by a refinement in cruelty superior to that which in the East yokes the living to the dead, he strove to persuade us that we and our posterity to the end of time were riveted to a constitution by the indissoluble compact of—a dead parchment, and were bound to cherish a corse at the bosom when reason might call aloud that it should be entombed. Your Lordship aims at the same detestable object by means more criminal, because more dangerous and insidious. Attempting to lull the people of England into a belief that any inquiries directed towards the nature of liberty and equality can in no other way lead to their happiness than by convincing them that they have already arrived at perfection in the science of government, what is your object but to exclude them for ever from the most fruitful field of human knowledge? Besides, it is another cause to execrate this doctrine that the consequence of such fatal delusion would be that they must entirely draw off their attention, not only from the government, but from their governors; that the stream of public vigilance, far from clearing and enriching the prospect of society, would by its stagnation consign it to barrenness, and by its putrefaction infect it with death. You have aimed an arrow at liberty and philosophy, the eyes of the human race; why, like the inveterate enemy of Philip, in putting your name to the shaft, did you not declare openly its destination?

As a teacher of religion, your Lordship cannot be ignorant of a class of breaches of duty which may be denominated faults of omission. You profess to give your opinions upon the present turbulent crisis, expressing a wish that they may have some effect in tranquillising the minds of the people. Whence comes it, then, that the two grand causes in this working of the popular mind are passed over in silence? Your Lordship's conduct may bring to mind the story of a company of strolling comedians, who gave out the play of Hamlet as the performance of the evening. The audience were not a little surprised to be told, on the drawing up of the curtain, that from circumstances of particular convenience it was hoped that they would dispense with the omission of the character of—Hamlet! But to be serious—for the subject is serious in the extreme—from your silence respecting the general call for a PARLIAMENTARY REFORM, supported by your assertion that we at present enjoy as great a portion of liberty and equality as is consistent with civil society, what can be supposed but that you are a determined enemy to the redress of what the people of England call and feel to be grievances?

From your omitting to speak upon the war, and your general disapprobation of French measures and French principles, expressed particularly at this moment, we are necessarily led also to conclude that you have no wish to dispel an infatuation which is now giving up to the sword so large a portion of the poor, and consigning the rest to the more slow and more painful consumption of want. I could excuse your silence on this point, as it would ill become an English bishop at the close of the eighteenth century to make the pulpit the vehicle of exhortations which would have disgraced the incendiary of the Crusades, the hermit Peter. But you have deprived yourself of the plea of decorum by giving no opinion on the REFORM OF THE LEGISLATURE. As undoubtedly you have some secret reason for the reservation of your sentiments on this latter head, I cannot but apply the same reason to the former. Upon what principle is your conduct to be explained? In some parts of England it is quaintly said, when a drunken man is seen reeling towards his home, that he has business on both sides of the road. Observing your Lordship's tortuous path, the spectators will be far from insinuating that you have partaken of Mr. Burke's intoxicating bowl; they will content themselves, shaking their heads as you stagger along, with remarking that you have business on both sides of the road.

The friends of Liberty congratulate themselves upon

the odium under which they are at present labouring, as
the causes which have produced it have obliged so many
of her false adherents to disclaim with officious earnestness
aṇy desire to promote her interests; nor are they disheart-
ened by the diminution which their body is supposed already
to have sustained. Conscious that an enemy lurking in
our ranks is ten times more formidable than when drawn
out against us, that the unblushing aristocracy of a Maury
or a Cazalès is far less dangerous than the insidious mask
of patriotism assumed by a La Fayette or a Mirabeau,
we thank you for your desertion. Political convulsions
have been said particularly to call forth concealed abilities,
but it has been seldom observed how vast is their consumption of them. Reflecting upon the fate of the greatest portion of the members of the constituent and legislative
assemblies, we must necessarily be struck with a prodigious
annihilation of human talents. Aware that this necessity
is attached to a struggle for Liberty, we are the less sorry
that we can expect no advantage from the mental endow-
ments of your Lordship. Besides the names which I—[Here
the manuscript breaks off.]

APPENDIX "B"

PREFACE TO THE SECOND EDITION OF "LYRICAL BALLADS,"
1800

The first Volume of these Poems has already been submitted to general perusal. It was published, as an experi-
ment, which, I hoped, might be of some use to ascertain,
how far, by fitting to metrical arrangement a selection of
the real language of men in a state of vivid sensation, that
sort of pleasure and that quantity of pleasure may be
imparted, which a Poet may rationally endeavour to impart.

I had formed no very inaccurate estimate of the probable
effect of those Poems: I flattered myself that they who
should be pleased with them would read them with more
than common pleasure: and, on the other hand, I was well
aware, that by those who should dislike them, they would
be read with more than common dislike. The result has
differed from my expectation in this only, that a greater
number have been pleased than I ventured to hope I should
please.

. . . .

Several of my Friends are anxious for the success of these
Poems, from a belief, that, if the views with which they
were composed were indeed realised, a class of Poetry would
be produced, well adapted to interest mankind permanently,
and not unimportant in the quality, and in the multiplicity
of its moral relations: and on this account they have advised
me to prefix a systematic defence of the theory upon which
the Poems were written. But I was unwilling to undertake
the task, knowing that on this occasion the Reader would
look coldly upon my arguments, since I might be suspected
of having been principally influenced by the selfish and
foolish hope of *reasoning* him into an approbation of these

particular Poems: and I was still more unwilling to undertake the task, because, adequately to display the opinions, and fully to enforce the arguments, would require a space wholly disproportionate to a preface. For, to treat the subject with the clearness and coherence of which it is susceptible, it would be necessary to give a full account of the present state of the public taste in this country, and to determine how far this taste is healthy or depraved; which, again, could not be determined, without pointing out in what manner language and the human mind act and re-act on each other, and without retracing the revolutions, not of literature alone, but likewise of society itself. I have therefore altogether declined to enter regularly upon this defence; yet I am sensible, that there would be something like impropriety in abruptly obtruding upon the Public, without a few words of introduction, Poems so materially different from those upon which general approbation is at present bestowed.

It is supposed, that by the act of writing in verse an Author makes a formal engagement that he will gratify certain known habits of association; that he not only thus apprises the Reader that certain classes of ideas and expressions will be found in his book, but that others will be carefully excluded. This exponent or symbol held forth by metrical language must in different eras of literature have excited very different expectations: for example, in the age of Catullus, Terence, and Lucretius, and that of Statius or Claudian; and in our own country, in the age of Shakespeare and Beaumont and Fletcher, and that of Donne and Cowley, or Dryden, or Pope. I will not take upon me to determine the exact import of the promise which, by the act of writing in verse, an Author in the present day makes to his reader: but it will undoubtedly appear to many persons that I have not fulfilled the terms of an engagement thus voluntarily contracted. They who have been accustomed to the gaudiness and inane phraseology of many modern writers, if they persist in reading this book to its conclusion, will, no doubt, frequently have to struggle with feelings of strangeness and awkwardness: they will look round for poetry, and will be induced to inquire by what species of courtesy these attempts can be permitted to assume that title. I hope therefore the reader will not censure me for attempting to state what I have proposed to myself to perform; and also (as far as the limits of a preface will permit) to explain some of the chief reasons which have determined me in the choice of my purpose: that at least he may be spared any unpleasant feeling of disappointment, and that I myself may be protected from one of the most dishonourable accusations which can be brought against an Author; namely, that of an indolence which prevents him from endeavouring to ascertain what is his duty, or, when his duty is ascertained, prevents him from performing it.

The principal object, then, proposed in these Poems was to choose incidents and situations from common life, and to relate or describe them, throughout, as far as was possible in a selection of language really used by men, and, at the same time, to throw over them a certain colouring of imagination, whereby ordinary things should be presented to the mind in an unusual aspect; and, further, and above all, to make these incidents and situations interesting by tracing in them, truly though not ostentatiously, the primary laws of our nature: chiefly, as far as regards the manner in which we associate ideas in a state of excitement. Humble and rustic life was generally chosen, because, in that condition, the essential passions of the heart find a better soil in which they can attain their maturity, are less under restraint, and speak a plainer and more emphatic language; because in that condition of life our elementary feelings coexist in a state of greater simplicity, and, consequently, may be more accurately contemplated, and more forcibly communicated; because the manners of rural life germinate from those elementary feelings, and, from the necessary character of rural occupations, are more easily comprehended, and are more durable; and, lastly, because in that condition the passions of men are incorporated with the beautiful and permanent forms of nature. The language, too, of these men has been adopted (purified indeed from what appear to be its real defects, from all lasting and rational causes of dislike or disgust) because such men hourly communicate with the best objects from which the best part of language is originally derived; and because, from their rank in society and the sameness and narrow circle of their intercourse, being less under the influence of social vanity, they convey their feelings and notions in simple and unelaborated expressions. Accordingly, such a language, arising out of repeated experience and regular feelings, is a more permanent, and a far more philosophical language, than that which is frequently substituted for it by Poets, who think that they are conferring honour upon themselves and their art, in proportion as they separate themselves from the sympathies of men, and indulge in arbitrary and capricious habits of expression, in order to furnish food for fickle tastes, and fickle appetites, of their own creation.*

I cannot, however, be insensible to the present outcry against the triviality and meanness, both of thought and language, which some of my contemporaries have occasionally introduced into their metrical compositions; and I acknowledge that this defect, where it exists, is more dishonourable to the Writer's own character than false refinement or arbitrary innovation, though I should contend at the same time, that it is far less pernicious in the sum of its consequences. From such verses the Poems in these volumes will be found distinguished at least by one mark of difference, that each of them has a worthy *purpose*. Not that I always began to write with a distinct purpose formally conceived; but habits of meditation have, I trust, so prompted and regulated my feelings, that my descriptions of such objects as strongly excite those feelings, will be found to carry along with them a *purpose*. If this opinion be erroneous, I can have little right to the name of a Poet. For all good poetry is the spontaneous overflow of powerful feelings: and though this be true, Poems to which any value can be attached were never produced on any variety of subjects but by a man who, being possessed of more than usual organic sensibility, had also thought long and deeply. For our continued influxes of feeling are modified and directed by our thoughts, which are indeed the representatives of all our past feelings; and, as by contemplating the relation of these general representatives to each other, we discover what is really important to men, so, by the repeti-

---

* It is worth while here to observe, that the affecting parts of Chaucer are almost always expressed in language pure and universally intelligible even to this day.

tion and continuance of this act, our feelings will be connected with important subjects, till at length, if we be originally possessed of much sensibility, such habits of mind will be produced, that, by obeying blindly and mechanically the impulses of those habits, we shall describe objects, and utter sentiments, of such a nature, and in such connection with each other, that the understanding of the Reader must necessarily be in some degree enlightened, and his affections strengthened and purified.

It has been said that each of these poems has a purpose. Another circumstance must be mentioned which distinguishes these Poems from the popular Poetry of the day; it is this, that the feeling therein developed gives importance to the action and situation, and not the action and situation to the feeling.

A sense of false modesty shall not prevent me from asserting, that the Reader's attention is pointed to this mark of distinction, far less for the sake of these particular Poems than from the general importance of the subject. The subject is indeed important! For the human mind is capable of being excited without the application of gross and violent stimulants; and he must have a very faint perception of its beauty and dignity who does not know this, and who does not further know, that one being is elevated above another, in proportion as he possesses this capability. It has therefore appeared to me, that to endeavour to produce or enlarge this capability is one of the best services in which, at any period, a Writer can be engaged; but this service, excellent at all times, is especially so at the present day. For a multitude of causes, unknown to former times, are now acting with a combined force to blunt the discriminating powers of the mind, and, unfitting it for all voluntary exertion, to reduce it to a state of almost savage torpor. The most effective of these causes are the great national events which are daily taking place, and the increasing accumulation of men in cities, where the uniformity of their occupations produces a craving for extraordinary incident, which the rapid communication of intelligence hourly gratifies. To this tendency of life and manners the literature and theatrical exhibitions of the country have conformed themselves. The invaluable works of our elder writers, I had almost said the works of Shakespeare and Milton, are driven into neglect by frantic novels, sickly and stupid German Tragedies, and deluges of idle and extravagant stories in verse.—When I think upon this degrading thirst after outrageous stimulation, I am almost ashamed to have spoken of the feeble endeavour made in these volumes to counteract it; and, reflecting upon the magnitude of the general evil, I should be oppressed with no dishonourable melancholy, had I not a deep impression of certain inherent and indestructible qualities of the human mind, and likewise of certain powers in the great and permanent objects that act upon it, which are equally inherent and indestructible; and were there not added to this impression a belief, that the time is approaching when the evil will be systematically opposed, by men of greater powers, and with far more distinguished success.

Having dwelt thus long on the subjects and aim of these Poems, I shall request the Reader's permission to apprise him of a few circumstances relating to their *style*, in order, among other reasons, that he may not censure me for not having performed what I never attempted. The Reader will find that personifications of abstract ideas rarely occur in these volumes; and are utterly rejected, as an ordinary device to elevate the style, and raise it above prose. My purpose was to imitate, and, as far as possible, to adopt the very language of men; and assuredly such personifications do not make any natural or regular part of that language. They are, indeed, a figure of speech occasionally prompted by passion, and I have made use of them as such; but have endeavoured utterly to reject them as a mechanical device of style, or as a family language which Writers in metre seem to lay claim to by prescription. I have wished to keep the Reader in the company of flesh and blood, persuaded that by so doing I shall interest him. Others who pursue a different track will interest him likewise; I do not interfere with their claim, but wish to prefer a claim of my own. There will also be found in these volumes little of what is usually called poetic diction; as much pains has been taken to avoid it as is ordinarily taken to produce it; this has been done for the reason already alleged, to bring my language near to the language of men; and further, because the pleasure which I have proposed to myself to impart, is of a kind very different from that which is supposed by many persons to be the proper object of poetry. Without being culpably particular, I do not know how to give my Reader a more exact notion of the style in which it was my wish and intention to write, than by informing him that I have at all times endeavoured to look steadily at my subject; consequently, there is, I hope, in these Poems little falsehood of description, and my ideas are expressed in language fitted to their respective importance. Something must have been gained by this practice, as it is friendly to one property of all good poetry, namely, good sense: but it has necessarily cut me off from a large portion of phrases and figures of speech which from father to son have long been regarded as the common inheritance of Poets. I have also thought it expedient to restrict myself still further, having abstained from the use of many expressions, in themselves proper and beautiful, but which have been foolishly repeated by bad Poets, till such feelings of disgust are connected with them as it is scarcely possible by any art of association to overpower.

If in a poem there should be found a series of lines, or even a single line, in which the language, though naturally arranged, and according to the strict laws of metre, does not differ from that of prose, there is a numerous class of critics, who, when they stumble upon these prosaisms, as they call them, imagine that they have made a notable discovery, and exult over the Poet as over a man ignorant of his own profession. Now these men would establish a canon of criticism which the Reader will conclude he must utterly reject, if he wishes to be pleased with these volumes. And it would be a most easy task to prove to him, that not only the language of a large portion of every good poem, even of the most elevated character, must necessarily, except with reference to the metre, in no respect differ from that of good prose, but likewise that some of the most interesting parts of the best poems will be found to be strictly the language of prose when prose is well written. The truth of this assertion might be demonstrated by innumerable passages from almost all the poetical writings, even of Milton himself. To illustrate the subject in a general manner, I will here adduce a short composition of Gray, who was at the head of those who, by their reasonings, have attempted to widen the space of separation betwixt Prose and Metrical composition, and was more than any other man curiously elaborate in the structure of his own poetic diction.

> "In vain to me the smiling mornings shine,
> And reddening Phoebus lifts his golden fire:
> The birds in vain their amorous descant join,
> Or cheerful fields resume their green attire.
> These ears, alas! for other notes repine;
> *A different object do these eyes require;*
> *My lonely anguish melts no heart but mine;*
> *And in my breast the imperfect joys expire;*
> Yet morning smiles the busy race to cheer,
> And new-born pleasure brings to happier men;
> The fields to all their wonted tribute bear;
> To warm their little loves the birds complain,
> *I fruitless mourn to him that cannot hear,*
> *And weep the more because I weep in vain."*

It will easily be perceived, that the only part of this Sonnet which is of any value is the lines printed in Italics; it is equally obvious, that, except in the rhyme, and in the use of the single word "fruitless" for fruitlessly, which is so far a defect, the language of these lines does in no respect differ from that of prose.

By the foregoing quotation it has been shown that the language of Prose may yet be well adapted to Poetry; and it was previously asserted, that a large portion of the language of every good poem can in no respect differ from that of good Prose. We will go further. It may be safely affirmed, that there neither is, nor can be, any *essential* difference between the language of prose and metrical composition. We are fond of tracing the resemblance between Poetry and Painting, and, accordingly, we call them Sisters: but where shall we find bonds of connection sufficiently strict to typify the affinity betwixt metrical and prose composition? They both speak by and to the same organs; the bodies in which both of them are clothed may be said to be of the same substance, their affections are kindred, and almost identical, not necessarily differing even in degree; Poetry* sheds no tears "such as Angels weep," but natural and human tears; she can boast of no celestial ichor that distinguishes her vital juices from those of prose; the same human blood circulates through the veins of them both.

If it be affirmed that rhyme and metrical arrangement of themselves constitute a distinction which overturns what has just been said on the strict affinity of metrical language with that of prose, and paves the way for other artificial distinctions which the mind voluntarily admits, I answer that the language of such Poetry as is here recommended is, as far as is possible, a selection of the language really spoken by men; that this selection, wherever it is made with true taste and feeling, will of itself form a distinction far greater than would at first be imagined, and will entirely separate the composition from the vulgarity and meanness of ordinary life; and, if metre be superadded thereto, I believe that a dissimilitude will be produced altogether sufficient for the gratification of a rational mind. What other distinction would we have? Whence is it to come? And where is it to exist? Not, surely, where the Poet speaks through the mouths of his characters: it cannot be necessary here, either for elevation of style, or any of its supposed ornaments: for, if the Poet's subject be judiciously chosen, it will naturally, and upon fit occasion, lead him to passions the language of which, if selected truly and judiciously, must necessarily be dignified and variegated, and alive with metaphors and figures. I forbear to speak of an incongruity which would shock the intelligent Reader, should the Poet interweave any foreign splendour of his own with that which the passion naturally suggests: it is sufficient to say that such addition is unnecessary. And, surely, it is more probable that those passages, which with propriety abound with metaphors and figures, will have

* I here use the word "Poetry" (though against my own judgment) as opposed to the word Prose, and synonymous with metrical composition. But much confusion has been introduced into criticism by this contradistinction of Poetry and Prose, instead of the more philosophical one of Poetry and Matter of Fact, or Science. The only strict antithesis to Prose is Metre; nor is this, in truth, a *strict* antithesis, because lines and passages of metre so naturally occur in writing prose, that it would be scarcely possible to avoid them, even were it desirable.

their due effect, if, upon other occasions where the passions are of a milder character, the style also be subdued and temperate.

But, as the pleasure which I hope to give by the Poems now presented to the Reader must depend entirely on just notions upon this subject, and, as it is in itself of high importance to our taste and moral feelings, I cannot content myself with these detached remarks. And if, in what I am about to say, it shall appear to some that my labour is unnecessary, and that I am like a man fighting a battle without enemies, such persons may be reminded, that, whatever be the language outwardly holden by men, a practical faith in the opinions which I am wishing to establish is almost unknown. If my conclusions are admitted, and carried as far as they must be carried if admitted at all, our judgments concerning the works of the greatest Poets both ancient and modern will be far different from what they are at present, both when we praise, and when we censure: and our moral feelings influencing and influenced by these judgments will, I believe, be corrected and purified.

Taking up the subject, then, upon general grounds, let me ask, what is meant by the word Poet? What is a Poet? To whom does he address himself? And what language is to be expected from him?—He is a man speaking to men: a man, it is true, endowed with more lively sensibility, more enthusiasm and tenderness, who has a greater knowledge of human nature, and a more comprehensive soul, than are supposed to be common among mankind; a man pleased with his own passions and volitions, and who rejoices more than other men in the spirit of life that is in him; delighting to contemplate similar volitions and passions as manifested in the goings-on of the Universe, and habitually impelled to create them where he does not find them. To these qualities he has added a disposition to be affected more than other men by absent things as if they were present; an ability of conjuring up in himself passions, which are indeed far from being the same as those produced by real events, yet (especially in those parts of the general sympathy which are pleasing and delightful) do more nearly resemble the passions produced by real events, than anything which, from the motions of their own minds merely, other men are accustomed to feel in themselves:—whence, and from practice, he has acquired a greater readiness and power in expressing what he thinks and feels, and especially those thoughts and feelings which, by his own choice, or from the structure of his own mind, arise in him without immediate external excitement.

But whatever portion of this faculty we may suppose even the greatest Poet to possess, there cannot be a doubt that the language which it will suggest to him, must often, in liveliness and truth, fall short of that which is uttered by men in real life, under the actual pressure of those passions, certain shadows of which the Poet thus produces, or feels to be produced, in himself.

However exalted a notion we would wish to cherish of the character of a Poet, it is obvious, that while he describes and imitates passions, his employment is in some degree mechanical, compared with the freedom and power of real and substantial action and suffering. So that it will be the wish of the Poet to bring his feelings near to those of the persons whose feelings he describes, nay, for short spaces of time, perhaps, to let himself slip into an entire delusion, and even confound and identify his own feelings with theirs; modifying only the language which is thus suggested to him by a consideration that he describes for a particular purpose, that of giving pleasure. Here, then, he will apply the principle of selection which has been already insisted upon. He will depend upon this for removing what would otherwise be painful or disgusting in the passion; he will feel that there is no necessity to trick out or to elevate nature: and, the more industriously he applies this principle, the deeper will be his faith that no words, which *his* fancy or imagination can suggest, will be to be compared with those which are the emanations of reality and truth.

But it may be said by those who do not object to the general spirit of these remarks, that, as it is impossible for the Poet to produce upon all occasions language as exquisitely fitted for the passion as that which the real passion itself suggests, it is proper that he should consider himself as in the situation of a translator, who does not scruple to substitute excellencies of another kind for those which are unattainable by him; and endeavours occasionally to surpass his original, in order to make some amends for the general inferiority to which he feels that he must submit. But this would be to encourage idleness and unmanly despair. Further, it is the language of men who speak of what they do not understand; who talk of Poetry as of a matter of amusement and idle pleasure; who will converse with us as gravely about a *taste* for Poetry, as they express it, as if it were a thing as indifferent as a taste for rope-dancing, or Frontiniac or Sherry. Aristotle, I have been told, has said, that Poetry is the most philosophic of all writing: it is so: its object is truth, not individual and local, but general, and operative; not standing upon external testimony, but carried alive into the heart by passion; truth which is its own testimony, which gives competence and confidence to the tribunal to which it appeals, and receives them from the same tribunal. Poetry is the image of man and nature. The obstacles which stand in the way of the fidelity of the Biographer and Historian, and of their consequent utility, are incalculably greater than those which are to be encountered by the Poet who comprehends the dignity of his art. The Poet writes under one restriction only, namely, the necessity of giving immediate pleasure to a human Being possessed of that information which may be expected from him, not as a lawyer, a physician, a mariner, an astronomer, or a natural philosopher, but as a Man. Except this one restriction, there is no object standing between the Poet and the image of things; between this, and the Biographer and Historian, there are a thousand.

Nor let this necessity of producing immediate pleasure be considered as a degradation of the Poet's art. It is far otherwise. It is an acknowledgment of the beauty of the universe, an acknowledgment the more sincere, because not formal, but indirect; it is a task light and easy to him who looks at the world in the spirit of love: further, it is a homage paid to the native and naked dignity of man, to the grand elementary principle of pleasure, by which he knows, and feels, and lives, and moves. We have no sympathy but what is propagated by pleasure: I would not be misunderstood; but wherever we sympathise with pain, it will be found that the sympathy is produced and carried on by subtle combinations with pleasure. We have no knowledge, that is, no general principles drawn from the contemplation of particular facts, but what has been built up by pleasure, and exists in us by pleasure alone. The Man of science, the Chemist and Mathematician, whatever difficulties and disgusts they may have had to struggle with, know and feel this. However painful may be the objects with which the Anatomist's knowledge is connected, he feels that his knowledge is pleasure; and where he has no pleasure he has no knowledge. What then does the Poet? He considers man and the objects that surround him as acting and re-acting upon each other, so as to produce an infinite complexity of pain and pleasure; he considers man in his own nature and in his ordinary life as contemplating this with a certain quantity of immediate knowledge, with certain convictions, intuitions, and deductions, which from habit acquire the quality of intuitions; he considers him as looking upon this complex scene of ideas and sensations, and finding everywhere objects that immediately excite in him sympathies which, from the necessities of his nature, are accompanied by an overbalance of enjoyment.

To this knowledge which all men carry about with them, and to these sympathies in which, without any other discipline than that of our daily life, we are fitted to take delight, the Poet principally directs his attention. He considers man and nature as essentially adapted to each other, and the mind of man as naturally the mirror of the fairest and most interesting properties of nature. And thus the Poet, prompted by this feeling of pleasure, which accompanies him through the whole course of his studies, converses with general nature, with affections akin to those studies. The knowledge both of the Poet and the Man of science has raised up in himself, by conversing with those particular parts of nature which are the objects of his studies. The knowledge both of the Poet and the Man of science is pleasure; but the knowledge of the one cleaves to us as a necessary part of our existence, our natural and unalienable inheritance; the other is a personal and individual acquisition, slow to come to us, and by no habitual and direct sympathy connecting us with our fellow-beings. The Man of science seeks truth as a remote and unknown benefactor; he cherishes and loves it in his solitude: the

Poet, singing a song in which all human beings join with him, rejoices in the presence of truth as our visible friend and hourly companion. Poetry is the breath and finer spirit of all knowledge; it is the impassioned expression which is in the countenance of all Science. Emphatically may it be said of the Poet, as Shakespeare hath said of man, "that he looks before and after." He is the rock of defence for human nature; an upholder and preserver, carrying everywhere with him relationship and love. In spite of difference of soil and climate, of language and manners, of laws and customs: in spite of things silently gone out of mind, and things violently destroyed; the Poet binds together by passion and knowledge the vast empire of human society, as it is spread over the whole earth, and over all time. The objects of the Poet's thoughts are everywhere; though the eyes and senses of man are, it is true, his favourite guides, yet he will follow wheresoever he can find an atmosphere of sensation in which to move his wings. Poetry is the first and last of all knowledge—it is as immortal as the heart of man. If the labours of Men of science should ever create any material revolution, direct or indirect, in our condition, and in the impressions which we habitually receive, the Poet will sleep then no more than at present; he will be ready to follow the steps of the Man of Science, not only in those general indirect effects, but he will be at his side, carrying sensation into the midst of the objects of the science itself. The remotest discoveries of the Chemist, the Botanist, or Mineralogist, will be as proper objects of the Poet's art as any upon which it can be employed, if the time should ever come when these things shall be familiar to us, and the relations under which they are contemplated by the followers of these respective sciences shall be manifestly and palpably material to us as enjoying and suffering beings. If the time should ever come when what is now called science, thus familiarised to men, shall be ready to put on, as it were, a form of flesh and blood, the Poet will lend his divine spirit to aid the transfiguration, and will welcome the Being thus produced, as a dear and genuine inmate of the household of man.—It is not, then, to be supposed that any one, who holds that sublime notion of Poetry which I have attempted to convey, will break in upon the sanctity and truth of his pictures by transitory and accidental ornaments and endeavour to excite admiration of himself by arts, the necessity of which must manifestly depend upon the assumed meanness of his subject.

What has been thus far said applies to Poetry in general; but especially to those parts of composition where the Poet speaks through the mouths of his characters; and upon this point it appears to authorise the conclusion that there are few persons of good sense, who would not allow that the dramatic parts of composition are defective, in proportion as they deviate from the real language of nature, and are coloured by a diction of the Poet's own, either peculiar to him as an individual Poet or belonging simply to Poets in general; to a body of men who, from the circumstance of their composition being in metre, it is expected will employ a particular language.

It is not, then, in the dramatic parts of composition that we look for this distinction of language; but still it may be proper and necessary where the Poet speaks to us in his own person and character. To this I answer by referring the Reader to the description before given of a Poet. Among the qualities there enumerated as principally conducing to form a Poet, is implied nothing differing in kind from other men, but only in degree. The sum of what was said is, that the Poet is chiefly distinguished from other men by a greater promptness to think and feel without immediate external excitement, and a greater power in expressing such thoughts and feelings as are produced in him in that manner. But these passions and thoughts and feelings are the general passions and thoughts and feelings of men. And with what are they connected? Undoubtedly with our moral sentiments and animal sensations, and with the causes which excite these; with the operations of the elements, and the appearances of the visible universe; with storm and sunshine, with the revolutions of the seasons, with cold and heat, with loss of friends and kindred, with injuries and resentments, gratitude and hope, with fear and sorrow. These, and the like, are the sensations and objects which the Poet describes, as they are the sensations of other men, and the objects which interest them. The Poet thinks and feels in the spirit of human passions. How, then, can his language differ in any material degree from that of all other men who feel vividly and see clearly? It might be *proved* that it is impossible. But supposing that this were not the case, the Poet might then be allowed to use a peculiar language when expressing his feelings for his own gratification, or that of men like himself. But Poets do not write for Poets alone, but for men. Unless therefore we are advocates for that admiration which subsists upon ignorance, and that pleasure which arises from hearing what we do not understand, the Poet must descend from this supposed height; and, in order to excite rational sympathy, he must express himself as other men express themselves. To this it may be added, that while he is only selecting from the real language of men, or, which amounts to the same thing, composing accurately in the spirit of such selection, he is treading upon safe ground, and we know what we are to expect from him. Our feelings are the same with respect to metre; for, as it may be proper to remind the Reader, the distinction of metre is regular and uniform, and, not, like that which is produced by what is usually called POETIC DICTION, arbitrary, and subject to infinite caprices upon which no calculation whatever can be made. In the one case, the Reader is utterly at the mercy of the Poet, respecting what imagery or diction he may choose to connect with the passion; whereas, in the other, the metre obeys certain laws, to which the Poet and Reader both willingly submit because they are certain, and because no interference is made by them with the passion, but such as the concurring testimony of ages has shown to heighten and improve the pleasure which co-exists with it.

It will now be proper to answer an obvious question, namely, Why, professing these opinions, have I written in verse? To this, in addition to such answer as is included in what has been already said, I reply, in the first place, Because, however I may have restricted myself, there is still left open to me what confessedly constitutes the most valuable object of all writing, whether in prose or verse; the great and universal passions of men, the most general and interesting of their occupations, and the entire world of nature before me—to supply endless combinations of forms and imagery. Now, supposing for a moment that whatever is interesting in these objects may be as vividly described in prose, why should I be condemned for attempting to superadd to such description the charm which, by the consent of all nations, is acknowledged to exist in metrical language? To this, by such as are yet unconvinced, it may be answered that a very small part of the pleasure given by Poetry depends upon the metre, and that it is injudicious to write in metre, unless it be accompanied with the other artificial distinctions of style with which metre is usually accompanied, and that, by such deviations, more will be lost from the shock which will thereby be given to the Reader's associations than will be counterbalanced by any pleasure which he can derive from the general power of numbers. In answer to those who still contend for the necessity of accompanying metre with certain appropriate colours of style in order to the accomplishment of its appropriate end, and who also, in my opinion, greatly underrate the power of metre in itself, it might, perhaps, as far as relates to these Volumes, have been almost sufficient to observe, that poems are extant, written upon more humble subjects, and in a still more naked and simple style, which have continued to give pleasure from generation to generation. Now, if nakedness and simplicity be a defect, the fact here mentioned affords a strong presumption that poems somewhat less naked and simple are capable of affording pleasure at the present day; and, what I wished *chiefly* to attempt, at present, was to justify myself for having written under the impression of this belief.

But various causes might be pointed out why, when the style is manly, and the subject of some importance, words metrically arranged will long continue to impart such a pleasure to mankind as he who proves the extent of that pleasure will be desirous to impart. The end of Poetry is to produce excitement in co-existence with an overbalance of pleasure; but, by the supposition, excitement is an unusual and irregular state of the mind; ideas and feelings do not, in that state, succeed each other in accustomed order. If the words, however, by which this excitement is produced be in themselves powerful, or the images and feelings have an undue proportion of pain connected with them, there is some danger that the excitement may be carried beyond its proper bounds. Now the co-presence of something regular, something to which the mind has been accustomed in various moods and in a less excited state, cannot but have great efficacy in tempering and restraining the passion by an intertexture of ordinary feeling, and of feeling not strictly and necessarily connected with the passion. This is unquestionably true; and hence, though the opinion will at first appear paradoxical, from the tendency of metre to divest language, in a certain degree, of its reality, and thus to throw a sort of half-consciousness of unsubstantial existence over the whole composition, there can be little doubt but that more pathetic situations and sentiments, that is, those which have a greater proportion of pain connected with them, may be endured in metrical composition, especially in rhyme, than in prose. The metre of the old ballads is very artless; yet they contain many passages which would illustrate this opinion; and, I hope, if the following Poems be attentively perused, similar instances will be found in them. This opinion may be further illustrated by appealing to the Reader's own experience of the reluctance with which he comes to the re-perusal of the distressful parts of "Clarissa Harlowe," or the "Gamester;" while Shakespeare's writings, in the most pathetic scenes, never act upon us, as pathetic, beyond the bounds of pleasure—an effect which, in a much greater degree than might at first be imagined, is to be ascribed to small, but continual and regular impulses of pleasurable surprise from the metrical arrangement.—On the other hand (what it must be allowed will much more frequently happen) if the Poet's words should be incommensurate with the passion, and inadequate to raise the Reader to a height of desirable excitement, then (unless the Poet's choice of his metre has been grossly injudicious) in the feelings of pleasure which the Reader has been accustomed to connect with metre in general, and in the feeling, whether cheerful or melancholy, which he has been accustomed to connect with that particular movement of metre, there will be found something which will greatly contribute to impart passion to the words, and to effect the complex end which the Poet proposes to himself.

If I had undertaken a SYSTEMATIC defence of the theory

here maintained, it would have been my duty to develope the various causes upon which the pleasure received from metrical language depends. Among the chief of these causes is to be reckoned a principle which must be well known to those who have made any of the Arts the object of accurate reflection; namely, the pleasure which the mind derives from the perception of similitude in dissimilitude. This principle is the great spring of the activity of our minds, and their chief feeder. From this principle the direction of the sexual appetite, and all the passions connected with it, take their origin: it is the life of our ordinary conversation; and upon the accuracy with which similitude in dissimilitude, and dissimilitude in similitude are perceived, depend our taste and our moral feelings. It would not be a useless employment to apply this principle to the consideration of metre, and to show that metre is hence enabled to afford much pleasure, and to point out in what manner that pleasure is produced. But my limits will not permit me to enter upon this subject, and I must content myself with a general summary.

I have said that poetry is the spontaneous overflow of powerful feelings: it takes its origin from emotion recollected in tranquillity: the emotion is contemplated till, by a species of reaction, the tranquillity gradually disappears, and an emotion, kindred to that which was before the subject of contemplation, is gradually produced, and does itself actually exist in the mind. In this mood successful composition generally begins, and in a mood similar to this it is carried on; but the emotion, of whatever kind, and in whatever degree, from various causes, is qualified by various pleasures, so that in describing any passions whatsoever, which are voluntarily described, the mind will, upon the whole, be in a state of enjoyment. If Nature be thus cautious to preserve in a state of enjoyment a being so employed, the Poet ought to profit by the lesson held forth to him, and ought especially to take care, that, whatever passions he communicates to his Reader, those passions, if his Reader's mind be sound and vigorous, should always be accompanied with an overbalance of pleasure. Now the music of harmonious metrical language, the sense of difficulty overcome, and the blind association of pleasure which has been previously received from works of rhyme or metre of the same or similar construction, an indistinct perception perpetually renewed of language closely resembling that of real life, and yet, in the circumstance of metre, differing from it so widely—all these imperceptibly make up a complex feeling of delight, which is of the most important use in tempering the painful feeling always found intermingled with powerful descriptions of the deeper passions. This effect is always produced in pathetic and impassioned poetry; while, in lighter compositions, the ease and gracefulness with which the Poet manages his numbers are themselves confessedly a principal source of the gratification of the Reader. All that it is *necessary* to say, however, upon this subject, may be effected by affirming, what few persons will deny, that, of two descriptions, either of passions, manners, or characters, each of them equally well executed, the one in prose and the other in verse, the verse will be read a hundred times where the prose is read once.

Having thus explained a few of my reasons for writing in verse, and why I have chosen subjects from common life, and endeavoured to bring my language near to the real language of men, if I have been too minute in pleading my own cause, I have at the same time been treating a subject of general interest; and for this reason a few words shall be added with reference solely to these particular poems, and to some defects which will probably be found in them. I am sensible that my associations must have sometimes been particular instead of general, and that, consequently, giving to things a false importance, I may have sometimes written upon unworthy subjects; but I am less apprehensive on this account, than that my language may frequently have suffered from those arbitrary connections of feelings and ideas with particular words and phrases, from which no man can altogether protect himself. Hence I have no doubt, that, in some instances, feelings even of the ludicrous may be given to my Readers by expressions which appeared to me tender and pathetic. Such faulty expressions, were I convinced they were faulty at present, and that they must necessarily continue to be so, I would willingly take all reasonable pains to correct. But it is dangerous to make these alterations on the simple authority of a few individuals, or even of certain classes of men; for where the understanding of an Author is not convinced, or his feelings altered, this cannot be done without great injury to himself: for his own feelings are his stay and support; and, if he set them aside in one instance, he may be induced to repeat this act till his mind shall lose all confidence in itself, and become utterly debilitated. To this it may be added, that the critic ought never to forget that he is himself exposed to the same errors as the Poet, and, perhaps, in a much greater degree: for there can be no presumption in saying of most readers, that it is not probable they will be so well acquainted with the various stages of meaning through which words have passed, or with the fickleness or stability of the relations of particular ideas to each other; and, above all, since they are so much less interested in the subject, they may decide lightly and carelessly.

Long as the Reader has been detained, I hope he will permit me to caution him against a mode of false criticism which has been applied to Poetry, in which the language closely resembles that of life and nature. Such verses have been triumphed over in parodies, of which Dr. Johnson's stanza is a fair specimen:—

> "I put my hat upon my head
> And walked into the Strand,
> And there I met another man
> Whose hat was in his hand."

Immediately under these lines let us place one of the most justly-admired stanzas of the "Babes in the Wood."

> "These pretty Babes with hand in hand
> Went wandering up and down:
> But never more they saw the Man
> Approaching from the Town."

In both these stanzas the words, and the order of the words, in no respect differ from the most unimpassioned conversation. There are words in both, for example, "the Strand," and "the Town," connected with none but the most familiar ideas; yet the one stanza we admit as admirable, and the other as a fair example of the superlatively contemptible. Whence arises this difference? Not from the metre, not from the language, not from the order of the words; but the *matter* expressed in Dr. Johnson's stanza is contemptible. The proper method of treating trivial and simple verses, to which Dr. Johnson's stanza would be a fair parallelism, is not to say, this is a bad kind of poetry, or, this is not poetry; but, this wants sense; it is neither interesting in itself, nor can *lead* to anything interesting; the images neither originate in that same state of feeling which arises out of thought, nor can excite thought or feeling in the Reader. This is the only sensible manner of dealing with such verses. Why trouble yourself about the species till you have previously decided upon the genus? Why take pains to prove that an ape is not a Newton, when it is self-evident that he is not a man?

One request I must make of my reader, which is, that in judging these Poems he would decide by his own feelings genuinely, and not by reflection upon what will probably be the judgment of others. How common is it to hear a person say, I myself do not object to this style of composition, or this or that expression, but, to such and such classes of people it will appear mean or ludicrous! This mode of criticism, so destructive of all sound unadulterated judgment, is almost universal: let the Reader then abide, independently, by his own feelings, and, if he finds himself affected, let him not suffer such conjectures to interfere with his pleasure.

If an Author, by any single composition, has impressed us with respect for his talents, it is useful to consider this as affording a presumption, that on other occasions where we have been displeased, he, nevertheless, may not have written ill or absurdly; and further, to give him so much credit for this one composition as may induce us to review what has displeased us, with more care than we should otherwise have bestowed upon it. This is not only an act of justice, but, in our decisions upon poetry especially, may conduce, in a high degree, to the improvement of our own taste; for an *accurate* taste in poetry, and in all the other arts, as Sir Joshua Reynolds has observed, is an *acquired* talent, which can only be produced by thought and a long-continued intercourse with the best models of composition. This is mentioned, not with so ridiculous a purpose as to prevent the most inexperienced Reader from judging for himself (I have already said that I wish him to judge for himself), but merely to temper the rashness of decision, and to suggest, that, if Poetry be a subject on which much time has not been bestowed, the judgment may be erroneous; and that, in many cases, it necessarily will be so.

Nothing would, I know, have so effectually contributed to further the end which I have in view, as to have shown of what kind the pleasure is, and how that pleasure is produced, which is confessedly produced by metrical composition essentially different from that which I have here endeavoured to recommend: for the Reader will say that he has been pleased by such composition; and what more can be done for him? The power of any art is limited; and he will suspect, that, if it be proposed to furnish him with new friends, that can be only upon condition of his abandoning his old friends. Besides, as I have said, the Reader is himself conscious of the pleasure which he has received from such composition, composition to which he has peculiarly attached the endearing name of Poetry; and all men feel an habitual gratitude, and something of an honourable bigotry, for the objects which have long continued to please them: we not only wish to be pleased, but to be pleased in that particular way in which we have been accustomed to be pleased. There is in these feelings enough to resist a host of arguments; and I should be the less able to combat them successfully, as I am willing to allow, that, in order entirely to enjoy the Poetry which I am recommending, it would be necessary to give up much of what is ordinarily enjoyed. But, would my limits have permitted me to point out how this pleasure is produced, many obstacles might have been removed, and the Reader assisted in perceiving that the powers of language are not so limited as he may suppose; and that it is possible for poetry to give other enjoyments, of a purer, more lasting, and more exquisite nature. This part of the subject has not been altogether neglected, but it has not been so much my present aim to prove, that the interest excited by some other kinds of poetry is less vivid, and less worthy of the nobler powers of the mind, as to offer reasons for presuming, that if my purpose were fulfilled, a species of poetry would be produced, which is genuine poetry; in its nature well adapted to interest mankind permanently, and likewise important in the multiplicity and quality of its moral relations.

From what has been said, and from a perusal of the Poems, the Reader will be able clearly to perceive the object which I had in view: he will determine how far it has been attained; and, what is a much more important question, whether it be worth attaining: and upon the decision of these two questions will rest my claim to the approbation of the Public.

INDEX OF FIRST LINES

INDEX OF FIRST LINES

THE MODERN
STUDENT'S LIBRARY

Each volume edited with an introduction by a leading
American authority

This series is composed of such works as are conspicuous in the
province of literature for their enduring influence. Every volume
is recognized as essential to a liberal education and will tend to infuse a love for true literature and an appreciation of the qualities
which cause it to endure.

A WEEK ON THE CONCORD AND
MERRIMAC RIVERS
By Henry David Thoreau

With an Introduction by
ODELL SHEPARD
Professor of English at Trinity College

". . . Here was a man who stood with his head in the clouds,
perhaps, but with his feet firmly planted on rubble and grit. He
was true to the kindred points of Heaven and Home. Thoreau's
eminently practical thought was really concerned in the last anal-
ysis with definite human problems. The major question how to live
was at the end of all his vistas."

EMERSON'S ESSAYS

Selected and edited, with an Introduction, by
ARTHUR HOBSON QUINN
Professor of English and Dean of the College University of
Pennsylvania

"Among the shifting values in our literary history, Emerson stands
secure. As a people we are rather prone to underestimate our native
writers in relation to English and continental authors, but even
among those who have been content to treat our literature as a by-
product of British letters, Emerson's significance has become only
more apparent with time."

ENGLISH POETS OF THE EIGHTEENTH CENTURY

Selected and Edited by

ERNEST BERNBAUM

Professor of English at the University of Illinois

The great age of the eighteenth century is, more than any other, perhaps, mirrored in its poetry, and this anthology reveals its manners and ideals.

While the text of the various poems is authentic, it is not burdened with scholastic editing and marginal comment. The collection and its form is one which satisfies in an unusual way the interest of the general reader as well as that of the specialist.

PILGRIM'S PROGRESS

By John Bunyan

With an Introduction and Notes by

DR. S. M. CROTHERS

This book is one of the most vivid and entertaining in the English language, one that has been read more than any other in our language, except the Bible.

PRIDE AND PREJUDICE

By Jane Austen

With an Introduction by

WILLIAM DEAN HOWELLS

To have this masterpiece of realistic literature introduced by so eminent a critic as William Dean Howells is, in itself, an event in the literary world. We cannot better comment upon the edition than by quoting from Mr. Howells's introduction:

He says: "When I came to read the book the tenth or fifteenth time for the purposes of this introduction, I found it as fresh as when I read it first in 1889, after long shying off from it."

THE ESSAYS OF
ADDISON AND STEELE

Selected and edited by

WILL D. HOWE
Professor of English at Indiana University

With the writings of these two remarkable essayists modern prose began. It is not merely that their style even to-day, after two centuries, commands attention, it is equally noteworthy that these men were among the first to show the possibilities of our language in developing a reading public.

BENJAMIN FRANKLIN AND
JONATHAN EDWARDS

With an Introduction by

CARL VAN DOREN

Franklin and Edwards often sharply contrasted in thought are, however, in the main, complementary to each other. In religion, Franklin was the utilitarian, Edwards the mystic. Franklin was more interested in practical morality than in revelation; Edwards sought a spiritual exaltation in religious ecstasy. In science Franklin was the practical experimenter, Edwards the detached observer, the theoretical investigator of causes.

THE
HEART OF MIDLOTHIAN

By Sir Walter Scott

With an Introduction by

WILLIAM P. TRENT
Professor of English at Columbia University

Universally admitted one of the world's greatest story-tellers, Scott himself considered "The Heart of Midlothian" his masterpiece, and it has been accepted as such by most of his admirers.

THE ORDEAL OF RICHARD FEVEREL

By George Meredith

With an Introduction by

FRANK W. CHANDLER

Professor of English at the University of Cincinnati

"The Ordeal of Richard Feverel," published in 1859, was Meredith's first modern novel and probably his best. Certainly it was, and has remained, the most generally popular of all this author's books and among the works of its type it stands pre-eminent. The story embodies in the most beautiful form the idea that in life the whole truth and nothing but the truth is best.

MEREDITH'S ESSAY ON COMEDY

With an Introduction, Notes, and Biographical Sketch by

LANE COOPER

Professor of English at Cornell University

"Good comedies," Meredith tells us, "are such rare productions that, notwithstanding the wealth of our literature in the comic element, it would not occupy us long to run over the English list." The "Essay on Comedy" is in a peculiarly intimate way the exposition of Meredith's attitude toward life and art. It helps us to understand more adequately the subtle delicacies of his novels.

CRITICAL ESSAYS OF THE NINETEENTH CENTURY

Selected and edited, with an Introduction, by

RAYMOND M. ALDEN

Professor of English at Leland Stanford University

The essays in this volume include those of Wordsworth, Copleston, Jeffrey, Scott, Coleridge, Lockhart, Lamb, Hazlitt, Byron, Shelley, Newman, DeQuincey, Macaulay, Wilson, and Hunt.

NINETEENTH CENTURY LETTERS

Selected and edited by

BYRON JOHNSON REES

Professor of English at Williams College

Contains letters from Blake, Wordsworth, Smith, Southey, Lamb, Irving, Keats, Emerson, Lincoln, Thackeray, Huxley, Meredith, "Lewis Carroll," Phillips Brooks, Sidney Lanier, and Stevenson.

PAST AND PRESENT

By Thomas Carlyle

With an Introduction by

EDWIN W. MIMS

Professor of English at Vanderbilt University

"Past and Present," written in 1843, when the industrial revolutions had just taken place in England and when democracy and freedom were the watchwords of liberals and progressives, reads like a contemporary volume on industrial and social problems.

BOSWELL'S LIFE OF JOHNSON

Abridged and edited, with an Introduction and Notes, by

CHARLES G. OSGOOD

Professor of English at Princeton University

Seldom has an abridgment been made with as great skill in omitting nothing vital and keeping proper proportions as this edition by Professor Osgood.

AMERICAN BALLADS AND SONGS

Collected and edited by

LOUISE POUND

Professor of English, University of Nebraska

An anthology intended to present to lovers of traditional songs such selections as illustrate the main classics and types having currency in English-speaking North America. It includes a number of imported ballads and songs, Western songs, dialogue and nursery songs, etc.

SELECTIONS FROM "THE FEDERALIST"

Edited with an Introduction by
JOHN SPENCER BASSETT
Professor of History in Smith College

A careful and discriminating selection of the "Essays written in favor of the new constitution, as agreed upon by the federal convention, September 17, 1787."

HISTORICAL ESSAYS
By Lord Macaulay

Selected with an Introduction by
CHARLES DOWNER HAZEN
Professor of History at Columbia University

A group of the better-known historical essays which includes "John Hampden," "William Pitt," "The Earl of Chatham," "Lord Clive," "Warren Hastings," "Machiavelli," and "Frederick the Great."

SARTOR RESARTUS
By Thomas Carlyle

Edited with an Introduction by
ASHLEY THORNDIKE
Professor of English at Columbia University

This "Nonsense on Clothes," as Carlyle referred to it in one entry of his journal, reaches into all the human realm and is perhaps the greatest philosophical expression of Carlyle's genius. Surely there is a power of pure thought which he has put into the mind of Professor Teufelsdröckh and a charm of words which he has given him to speak which he has nowhere surpassed.

A glossary in this edition will be of invaluable service to the student.

BACON'S ESSAYS

Selected, with an Introduction and Notes, by

MARY AUGUSTA SCOTT
Late Professor of English Literature at Smith College

These essays, the distilled wisdom of a great observer upon the affairs of common life, are of endless interest and profit. The more one reads them the more remarkable seem their compactness and their vitality.

ADAM BEDE
By George Eliot

With an Introduction by

LAURA J. WYLIE
Professor of English at Vassar College

With the publication of "Adam Bede" in 1859, it was evident both to England and America that a great novelist had appeared. "Adam Bede" is the most natural of George Eliot's books, simple in problem, direct in action, with the freshness and strength of the Derbyshire landscape and character and speech in its pages.

THE RING AND THE BOOK
By Robert Browning

With an Introduction by

FREDERICK MORGAN PADELFORD
Professor of English at Washington University

" 'The Ring and the Book,' " says Dr. Padelford in his introduction, "is Browning's supreme literary achievement. It was written after the poet had attained complete mastery of his very individual style; it absorbed his creative activity for a prolonged period; and it issued with the stamp of his characteristic genius on every page."

ROBERT LOUIS STEVENSON'S
ESSAYS

With an Introduction by
WILLIAM LYON PHELPS
Professor of English at Yale University

This volume includes not only essays in formal literary criticism, but also of personal monologue and gossip, as well as philosophical essays on the greatest themes that can occupy the mind of man. All reveal the complex, whimsical, humorous, romantic, imaginative, puritanical personality now known everywhere by the formula R. L. S.

PENDENNIS
By THACKERAY

With an Introduction by
ROBERT MORSS LOVETT
Professor of English at the University of Chicago

"Pendennis" stands as a great representative of biographical fiction and reflects more of the details of Thackeray's life than all his other writings. Of its kind there is probably no more interesting book in our literature.

THE
RETURN OF THE NATIVE
By THOMAS HARDY

With an Introduction and Notes by
JOHN W. CUNLIFFE
Professor of English at Columbia University

"The Return of the Native" is probably Thomas Hardy's great tragic masterpiece. It carries to the highest perfection the rare genius of the finished writer. It presents in the most remarkable way Hardy's interpretation of nature in which there is a perfect unison between the physical world and the human character.

EVAN HARRINGTON
By George Meredith

With an Introduction by
GEORGE G. REYNOLDS
Professor of English Literature, University of Colorado

Evan Harrington, one of the greatest demonstrations of George Meredith's genius, is an ironic comment on English society and manners in the latter part of the last century, done with amazing penetration and the best of his humor. In the large, it reflects the struggle between spiritual and moral ideals which was constantly going on in Meredith's mind and which ends in the triumph of the spirit of sacrifice.

THE MASTER OF BALLANTRAE
By Robert Louis Stevenson

With an Introduction by
H. S. CANBY
Formerly Professor of English Literature at Yale University, and present editor of the New York *Evening Post* Literary Review

Here is one of the most absorbing of Stevenson's romances, full of the spice of adventure and exciting incident, the thrill of danger and the chill of fear; it is, beside, a powerful and subtle study of Scotch character of different types, and brings into being one of the most amazing of all the dramatis personæ of romantic fiction.

POEMS AND PLAYS
By Robert Browning

Selected with an Introduction and Notes by
HEWLETTE ELWELL JOYCE
Assistant Professor of English in Dartmouth College

A volume intended for the student or less-advanced reader of Browning who does not require a complete edition. The introduction suggests an approach to Browning, points out such difficulties as often perplex one who reads Browning for the first time, and states simply a few of the poet's fundamental ideas.

THE AUTOBIOGRAPHY OF DAVID CROCKETT

With an Introduction by

HAMLIN GARLAND

The most characteristic figure of the New World for the first two centuries was the man of the "trace" or trail: the settler who, carrying a rifle and an axe, adventured into the wilderness and there hewed out a clearing, built a cabin, and planted corn; whose skill with the flint-lock provided meat for his family, skins for his clothing, and literally kept the wolf from the door. In Crockett's autobiography the reader will find the picture of such a man, a blunt, bold, prosaic account of a life, epic in its sweep, in a crude sort the direct progenitor of Lincoln and Mark Twain.

Included in this volume are: "A Narrative of the Life of David Crockett, of the State of Tennessee," "An Account of Colonel Crockett's Tour to the North and Down East," and "Colonel Crockett's Exploits and Adventures in Texas."

AMERICAN PROSE MASTERS

By W. C. BROWNELL

With an Introduction by

STUART P. SHERMAN

A book of vital and useful criticism, to produce which "it is necessary" (to use Mr. Brownell's own words) "to think, think, think, and then, when tired of thinking, to think more." Here one finds a critical estimate which leads him to a true appreciation of the work of Cooper, Hawthorne, Emerson, Poe, Lowell, and Henry James.

In his introduction, Mr. Sherman points out that "though the table of contents indicates that this book contains but six American prose masters, the reflective reader soon perceives that it contains a seventh, to whom the rest are indebted for no small part of the interest which they seem to possess in their own right."

CHARLES SCRIBNER'S SONS

PUBLISHERS   NEW YORK

Experience recollected
in tranquillity — or
Reading — to bring
back fond or sad
memories — of some one
or thing ——— E. Jawson

note [such as a
party or (?)
that certain party!

Jojo p.166